D1574670

Labor, Credit, and Goods Markets

Labor, Credit, and Goods Markets

The Macroeconomics of Search and Unemployment

Nicolas Petrosky-Nadeau and Etienne Wasmer

The MIT Press
Cambridge, Massachusetts
London, England

© 2017 Massachusetts Institute of Technology

All rights reserved. No part of this book may be reproduced in any form by any electronic or mechanical means (including photocopying, recording, or information storage and retrieval) without permission in writing from the publisher.

This book was set in Times Roman by diacriTech, Chennai. Printed and bound in the United States of America.

Library of Congress Cataloging-in-Publication Data

Names: Petrosky-Nadeau, Nicolas, 1980- author. | Wasmer, Etienne, author.
Title: Labor, credit, and goods markets : the macroeconomics of search and unemployment / Nicolas Petrosky-Nadeau and Etienne Wasmer.
Description: Cambridge, MA : MIT Press, [2017] | Includes bibliographical references and index.
Identifiers: LCCN 2016055268 | ISBN 9780262036450 (hardcover : alk. paper)
Subjects: LCSH: Markets. | Macroeconomics. | Frictional unemployment. | Capital market. | Credit.
Classification: LCC HF5470 .P49 2017 | DDC 339--dc23 LC record available at https://lccn.loc.gov/2016055268

10 9 8 7 6 5 4 3 2 1

Contents

Preface

In 2010, the Sveriges Riksbank Prize in Economic Sciences in Memory of Alfred Nobel was awarded to Peter A. Diamond, Dale T. Mortensen, and Christopher A. Pissarides for their "analysis of markets with frictions." The Nobel committee stated that, "on many markets, buyers and sellers do not always make contact with one another immediately," and that the three laureates had provided a fundamental theoretical framework for the analysis of search markets. This approach is well suited to the labor market and most of the seminal works were applied to labor issues, with a well-defined matching process between workers and firms.

The research perspective rewarded in 2010 is indeed radically different from that of competitive markets, in that it does not presuppose the existence of a centralized resource exchange and allocation mechanism leading to equilibrium. It is a marked departure from markets ruled by the Walrasian auctioneer, or built on bidding mechanisms. Convergence towards exchange is the outcome of an economic process that is precisely described, the process of search. Models with search frictions are therefore a well-founded alternative to the competitive model with market clearing. Search frictions imply that time and resources must be devoted to economic exchange, while competitive markets are only a specific cases of this more general view of economic activity with frictions. Competitive markets are a limit case in which economic agents pay no cost to trade, nor to acquire information. This limit case is based on a quite restrictive set of assumptions. The resulting optimal decentralized decisions by agents lead to a socially efficient equilibrium, in a first best sense. Away from these specific assumptions, various types of inefficiencies arise. First best efficiency cannot be reached. Instead, a constrained efficient equilibrium can be defined, where the constraint is the matching process. This constrained efficient outcome can be reached when agents internalize their actions on the search efficiency of other agents, but not always. In that case, policy interventions may be needed.

The concepts of search do not need to be restricted to labor markets only. The goal of our book is precisely to adopt this non-Walrasian paradigm to analyze simultaneously and systematically labor, financial, and goods markets with frictions. The overall result is an attempt to go beyond the traditional general equilibrium analysis of markets. That tradition sometimes considers a range of imperfections (such as moral hazard, asymmetries of information, or non-convexities) but when it does so, this is typically in isolation, without studying frictions in more than one market. This book offers in contrast an integrated, tractable framework to study frictions in credit, labor, and goods markets in general equilibrium.

Before studying frictional markets in interaction, we review, in the first part of the book, the main and most recent developments in the analysis of the labor market in the presence of search frictions, as they have emerged over the last decades. We offer here a systematic analysis of the main concepts, of normative issues and taxation, and dynamics in this environment. We discuss the notion of macroeconomic volatility and the response of the economy to shocks, as in the Real Business Cycle (RBC) literature. In the second part, taking stock of the generality and simplicity of the search analysis, we embed it into financial and goods markets.

Throughout, the analysis centers around a single equation, a job creation condition that summarizes the costs to meeting and trading in all three markets. Each market friction can be identified in this main equation, as well as the surplus sharing arrangements arrived at in each market. This equation can be compared to a similar equation defining the social planner's objectives. This clarifies the normative implications of frictions on multiple markets. It defines constrained efficiency conditions in multiple markets and their complementarity, linked to the existence of bottlenecks in some markets affecting the aggregate perfomance of the economy. The framework can finally be easily adapted to a stochastic environment for the analysis of the business cycle implications.

Along the way, we provide some results and insights that we believe are quite general and useful for macroeconomists. Equilibrium unemployment does not only depend on labor market frictions. Further, we establish the existence of a direct link between search frictions and the degree of volatility in the economy: the lower the transaction costs arising from these search frictions, the lower the volatility of the economy. An economy with higher transaction costs, conversely, is more sensitive to economic shocks and more volatile. This result is first established and studied in the analysis of financial frictions but it is actually more general. It applies when market frictions generate costs to entering the labor market that are independent of the tightness of the labor market. Further, volatility is amplified when the different sides of the market have an unequal sharing of the benefits of forming a match.

The existence of frictions in the goods market introduces many new features such as unused capacity by firms, demand shocks as a source of fluctuations, and a role for advertising by firms and consumer search effort. These are all important features of modern economies that are usually studied separately and mostly ignored in macroeconomic models. Goods market frictions also generate more volatility and in addition are unique in generating persistence in response to shocks.

An interesting feature of the analysis is also to offer a transparent decomposition of the size of frictions in each market. Each market is characterized by a quantifiable share in total entry costs paid by firms. It turns out that, despite the fact that firms face relatively low hiring costs (between 5 and 20% of total entry costs in quantitative exercises), their effect on unemployment is disproportionately large. The intuition is that some components of entry costs for firms have an effect on prices and wages that mitigate their adverse effect on firm's entry (this is the case of financial costs and goods market frictions), and thus do not affect unemployment much. Hiring frictions, in contrast, are not internalized into wages, thus magnifying their effect relative to other costs. A corollary of this result is that shocks on the cost of accessing credit might have a larger effect under wage rigidities. Hence, frictions in different markets can be highly complementary to each other when wages cannot absorb shocks, and less so when wages are more flexible.

Finally, our approach implies the existence of aggregate demand externalities, an element of propagation gaining recent popularity in macroeconomic research. Any supply shock on firms leads to fewer employed workers, imperfectly insured against these shocks, thus reducing the number of consumers or their intensity of search in the goods market. This leads to consumption multipliers, and fiscal multipliers arise from policy transfers, that can easily be quantified. These demand externality multipliers are not very large, ranging between 1.1 and 1.3, compared to the financial multipliers easily reaching values of 3 and above. However, they are sensitive to the specification of consumer preferences over consumption goods.

Our book unfortunately cannot cover all research questions. Many fascinating topics had to be left outside the scope of this book. We have little on geographic mobility and housing market fluctuations, nor do we address the recent developments in directed search. We do not focus on structural estimates of matching models and turnover, nor is heterogeneity in agents central, and we do not study equilibrium wage distributions. We do not explore the asset pricing implications, and we do not try a synthesis with the very innovative literature on search and money. Nonetheless, provide a suggested set of readings on these questions at the end of the relevant chapter, and discuss a few of the prominent questions and research approaches being developed by others. We also postpone the analysis of various policies to mitigate the effects of search frictions implied by the environments studied in this book. Our sense is that more work will be needed before the full lessons can be reached. Our framework can easily accommodate fundamental questions such as the optimal intervention in credit markets, the need or not of a fiscal stimulus, and more generally the optimal mix of policy interventions and timing of reforms in these markets.

The aim of this project is also to convince graduate students to enter the search and matching field and explore upon the issues we only touched in the book. It is a starting point toward more detailed analyses. Hence our title: *Labor, Credit, and Goods Markets: The Macroeconomics of Search and Unemployment.* Macroeconomic models have been heavily criticized after the financial crisis. We expect that the dynamic setup provided here, augmented with credit and goods market frictions, is a good compromise between simplicity and tractability on the one hand, and the necessary discipline in quantitative exercises that is a great virtue of dynamic general equilibrium models on the other.

We finally thank our families for their support and patience, and numerous colleagues and students for comments and suggestions on our various papers and versions of this book, most and foremost our advisors and coauthors Bob Hall, Chris Pissarides and Philippe Weil, and also, without exhaustivity, Emilio Bisetti, Thomas Brzustowski, Pierrick Clerc, Juan Dolado, Jan Eeckhout, Alexandre Janiak, André Kurmann, Etienne Lalé, Guido Menzio, Franck Malherbet, Espen Moen, Jean-Marc Robin, Guillaume Rocheteau, Ben Tengelsen, Shutian Zeng, and Lu Zhang. Patrick Kiernan and Jean-Benoît Eyméoud did an outstanding research assistance job on the intermediate versions of this book. We also thank the following institutions for visits in 2016–2017 to finalize the book: the Hoover Institution at Stanford University, University of Southern California, UC Santa Barbara, NYU Abu Dhabi, University of Lausanne, CREI, Pompeu Fabra, the European University Institute, the IIES at Stockholm University, the London School of Economics, and the Norwegian School of Business. Jessica Flakne should be thanked for her enthusiasm and help in the early editorial process. We also thank Christelle Hoteit for her great patience and help.

Guide to the book

Organization

This book follows a logical progress. We begin with the standard analysis of a single market, and then sequentially integrate more markets into the mainstream analysis, starting with financial markets and finally adding goods markets.

Part I: Frictions in the labor market

We first develop the standard labor-search model, and introduce the main concepts, the main notations, and the main tools. In particular in **chapter 1**, we develop the one worker–firm model, and show that it is very easy to switch from a continuous time representation to a discrete time representation. At the limit when the time period of the discrete time model goes to zero, the models deliver the same equations. In some instances the equations are identical even away from that limit when the model is at a steady state. This chapter also discusses various issues such as alternative bargaining games to determine wages. In **chapter 2**, we develop the tools for a global analysis of the model's dynamics, both the benchmark model and its extensions. We do not approximate the dynamics around a deterministic steady state, and instead solve the model with a global, precise, and nonlinear approximation method. New research has shown the quantitative errors from using local approximation methods are typically very large, especially in recessions. This stems from the congestion property, or concavity, of the matching function that results in matching becoming very sensitive to changes in job openings when unemployment is high. The nonlinear property is taken out of the model when it is solved with local approximation methods. Models with search frictions are sufficiently nonlinear for local approximations to be quantitatively very poor. **Chapter 3** develops the tools to analyze constrained-efficient allocations, that is, the solutions to a social planner's problem constrained by the matching technology. We also discuss how policy can affect the equilibrium and reach a constrained efficient outcome. In **chapter 4**, we extend the model to a large firm and to physical capital investments. We show how to solve the model with more sophisticated forms of bargaining, and in particular when firms can strategically use decreasing returns to scale in labor to bargain lower wages.

Part II: Frictions in financial and goods markets

We then extend the benchmark model to account for frictions in financial markets. We start in a steady-state economy and investigate its decentralized equilibrium and its efficiency properties in **chapter 5**. The equilibrium level of employment is, here, the outcome of frictions in these two markets. In each market, frictions lead to surplus and bargaining between different agents or entities in this economy. Creditors and the owners of investment projects first bargain over the terms of the financial contracts. Then firms— constituted of a block formed by a creditor and an investment project—bargain with workers. The environment is sufficiently tractable to obtain closed-form solutions and to allow for a clear discussion on the efficiency of this economy. The presence of multiple parties to bargaining raises additional strategic considerations which are studied in the books' on-line appendix available on the book's companion website. In **chapter 6**, we develop the dynamic properties of the credit–labor search economy. The new frictional block in credit markets introduces a term in the dynamics of job creation that reduces the pro-cyclicality of hiring costs, thereby increasing the responsiveness of job creation to temporary innovations in productivity.

We finally extend the setup to frictions in the goods market. In **chapter 7**, selling firms bargain over prices with the consumer after each side of the goods market has gone through a process of search. This new block is an important new development that is independent of the considerations raised by credit frictions. Goods market frictions lead to a whole set of new issues such as unused productive capacity, income pooling among consumers, and insurance against fluctuations. We study the properties of this model and in particular show how it can be solved by recursive blocks and that recursiveness remains true when finally integrating credit, labor, and goods markets, as well as its efficiency properties. In **chapter 8**, the dynamic extension of the full model is studied in detail. We show how the interaction of the three market imperfections solves puzzles concerning the volatility and persistence of the economy, as well as improves the cyclical properties of prices and quantities. Frictions in the goods market, by affecting the dynamics of the expected profits from hiring a worker, introduce both amplification and persistence to innovations in productivity.

Each topic is approached using the same substructure: we start from the main issues steady state, generally in continuous time; we then study the discrete-time dynamic properties extensively.

Structure of chapters

Throughout the book we try to organize each chapter around one main equilibrium condition: the job creation condition. The job creation condition states that the entry costs of a firm in the labor market have to be equal, in equilibrium, to its expected profits from hiring a worker. This equation summarizes well all new mechanisms and parameters introduced chapter after chapter, such as the cost of accessing external finance, the costs of prospecting in financial and goods markets, the consequences of alternative price and wage arrangements, and stochastic profits due to changing consumer tastes. This job creation condition is presented, depending on the context, at either a steady state or stochastic equilibrium. Other main equations are obtained for wages, prices, and internal rates of return of loans with wage bargaining, price bargaining, and bargaining over repayments to creditors. We sometimes extend the model to endogenous job destruction, but not systematically. We only do so when a job destruction margin leads to new insights with respect to the various new frictions introduced such as, for instance, credit market frictions in chapter 5, or the issue of financial fragility of firms explored in the online appendix. When they are still profitable but lack finance, firms may go bankrupt, leading to the inefficient destruction of social surplus. While many proofs are provided in the chapters, or their respective appendix, the online appendix studies more general specifications of the model, and explores additional results. This document is available on our homepages and the companion website, which also contains slides for each chapter (https://mitpress.mit.edu/lcgm).

Link with the literature

In each chapter, we only briefly review the main articles or books on which the analysis in the text is based, along with a more extensive review of the relevant literature in the last section of each chapter. Omissions are the inevitable consequence of the extremely large number of new papers each month on these topics, for which we hope to be forgiven, and we strive to be more comprehensive in each new iteration. Overall, chapter 1 mostly corresponds to Pissarides (2000) and Mortensen and Pissarides (1994), with in addition a detailed discussion on possible wage structures. Chapter 2 contains the dynamic extensions in Merz (1995) and Andolfatto

(1996), Cole and Rogerson (1999), Shimer (2005), and the discussion in Hall (2005) and Pissarides (2009). Chapter 3 is based on Hosios (1990) and Pissarides (2000). Chapter 4 discusses the size of the firm under alternative wage setups à la Stole and Zwiebel (1996a, 1996b) and Brügemann et al. (2015), as implemented in Cahuc et al. (2008). Part II extends the standard matching model to imperfect credit markets (chapters 5–6), based on Wasmer and Weil (2004) and Petrosky-Nadeau and Wasmer (2013), and to imperfect goods markets, (chapters 7–8), based on Petrosky-Nadeau and Wasmer (2015) and Brzustowski et al. (2017).

Notation and the environment

The book is centered around job creation conditions, and in some cases, job destruction conditions. The related equations are placed in shaded boxes throughout the book to help the reader to compare across chapters. Other endogenous variables (wages, financial repayment, price, shaded.) are in single-line boxes. Second-best efficiency conditions and modified Hosios rules are in double-line boxes. Finally, log-deviations around the steady state and dynamic multipliers are in shadowed boxes. It is also important to note that these log-deviations do not capture the dynamic quantitative properties of the model, which must be assessed with nonlinear solution algorithms. They only capture the linear impact of a small innovation near the steady state.

We keep consistent notation throughout the text, indexing the main matching and bargaining variables in each market with a subscript l, c, or g standing for, respectively, the labor, credit, or goods markets. Subscript π stands for profits and subscript v for vacancies. Since in part I we show the equivalence of the main equations in continuous and discrete time, we subsequently use the notion of time that is most adapted to the context of a chapter. In particular, the steady-state analyses of part II are in continuous time, while dynamics are dealt with in discrete time. Calligraphic letters such as $\mathcal{U}$, $\mathcal{V}$, or $\mathcal{N}_\pi$ are used for stocks and quantities of labor or masses of firms. Present discounted values (PDV) of income flows or profits are denoted by Latin capital letters such as J_g or W_{D_U}, and flows of income or consumption by Latin small letters such as w_g, z, or c_1. Tables 1 and 2 below summarize the timing of events and set of notations used in each chapter.

The time setup alternates between continuous time and discrete time, either in or out of steady state, as displayed in Table 3. In discrete time models, we ensure that transitions probabilities are between 0 and 1. In continuous time models, we follow the literature and assume a Poisson process rules the

Table 1
Timing of events

Model	Chapters 1–4 L	Chapters 5–6 CL	Chapters 7–8 CLG
Production requires	Labor	Creditor + Labor	Creditor + Labor + Consumer
Timing for firms	1: Search for labor	1: Search for creditor	1: Search for credit
	2: Produce, pay worker	2: Search for labor	2: Search for labor
		3: Produce, pay creditor and worker	3: Search for consumer
			4: Sell, pay creditor and worker
Timing for labor	1: Unemployed	1: Unemployed	1: Unemployed
	2: Employed	2: Employed	2: Employed
Timing for creditors		1: Search for project	1: Search for project
		2: Finance vacancy costs	2: Finance vacancy costs
		3: Repaid by firm	3: Finance wages and advertisement costs
			4: Repaid by firm
Timing for consumers			Unmatched: only consume Walrasian good
			Matched: consume both search goods and Walrasian good

transitions between states. The online appendix contains a short description of Poisson processes. In addition, some variables, such the rate at which profits end, are summarized by the same notation in both continuous and discrete time. For instance, in the continuous time chapter 5, $s^T = s^L + s^C$, and in the discrete time chapter 6, $s^T = s^C + (1 - s^C)s^L$ to account for the possibility of simultaneous shocks in discrete time that does not arise in continuous time. Similarly, in the continuous time chapter 7, $s^T = s^L + s^C + s^G$, but in the discrete time chapter 8, $s^T = s^C + (1 - s^C)\left[s^L + (1 - s^L)s^G\right]$. The transitions in the life-cycle of a firm are illustrated in figure 1. Figure 2 represents the overall environment once we have incorporated frictions in all three markets: credit, labor, and goods.

Table 2
Notations by chapter

	Labor Chapters 1–4 L	Credit Chapters 5–6 CL	Goods Chapters 7–8 CLG
Stocks in each market:			
"Vacant" firms in each market	$\mathcal{V}$	$\mathcal{N}_c$	$\mathcal{N}_g$
"Matched" firms in each market	$\mathcal{N}$	$\mathcal{V}$	$\mathcal{N}_\pi$
Workers (unemployed/employed)	$\mathcal{U}, 1-\mathcal{U}=\mathcal{N}$	$\mathcal{U}, 1-\mathcal{U}=\mathcal{N}$	$\mathcal{U}, 1-\mathcal{U}=\mathcal{N}_g+\mathcal{N}_\pi$
Creditors	$\mathcal{B}_l=\mathcal{V}$	$\mathcal{B}_c$	$\mathcal{B}_g, \mathcal{B}_\pi$
Consumers (unmatched/matched)			$\mathcal{D}_U, \mathcal{D}_M$
Matching functions:	$\mathcal{M}_L(\mathcal{V},\mathcal{U})$ $\left(=\chi_L\mathcal{U}^{\eta_L}\mathcal{V}^{1-\eta_L}\right)$	$\mathcal{M}_C(\mathcal{N}_c,\mathcal{B}_c)$ $\left(=\chi_C\mathcal{B}_c^{\eta_C}\mathcal{N}_c^{1-\eta_C}\right)$	$\mathcal{M}_G(\mathcal{D}_U,\mathcal{N}_g)$ $\left(=\chi_G\mathcal{D}_U^{\eta_G}\mathcal{N}_g^{1-\eta_G}\right)$
Level parameter	χ_L	χ_C	χ_G
Curvature parameter	η_L	η_C	η_G
Tightness of the market	$\theta=\mathcal{V}/\mathcal{U}$	$\phi=\mathcal{N}_c/\mathcal{B}_c$	$\xi=\mathcal{D}_U/\mathcal{N}_g$
Transition rates			
Matching rate of	vacancies	prospecting projects	firms selling goods
	$q(\theta)=\mathcal{M}_L/\mathcal{V}$	$p(\phi)=\mathcal{M}_C/\mathcal{N}_c$	$\lambda(\xi)=\mathcal{M}_G/\mathcal{N}_g$
	$q'(\theta)<0$	$p'(\phi)<0$	$\lambda'(\xi)>0$
	$\theta q'/q=-\eta_L$	$\phi p'/p=-\eta_C$	$\xi\lambda'/\lambda=\eta_G$
Matching rate of	unemployed workers	creditors, liquidity units	prospective consumers
	$f(\theta)=\mathcal{M}_L/\mathcal{U}$	$\check{p}(\phi)=\phi p(\phi)$	$\check{\lambda}(\xi)=\lambda(\xi)/\xi$
	$f'(\theta)>0$	$\check{p}'(\phi)>0$	$\check{\lambda}'(\xi)<0$
	$\theta f'/f=1-\eta_L$	$\phi\check{p}'/\check{p}(\phi)=1-\eta_C$	$\xi\check{\lambda}'/\check{\lambda}=-(1-\eta_G)$

Discount factor in discrete time	$\beta = 1/(1+r)$	$\beta^C = (1-s^C)\beta$	$\beta^{CLG} = \beta^C(1-s^G)(1-s^L)$
Separation rates	s^L (labor turnover)	s^C (bankruptcy)	s^G (consumer change)
Frictions measures:	$Q_v(\theta) = q(\theta)/[r+q(\theta)]$	$K(\phi) = \frac{\kappa_I}{p(\phi)} + \frac{\kappa_B}{\phi p(\phi)}$	$Q_\pi = \frac{s^G}{r+s^L(+s^C)+s^G}$
Compact notations		$k(\phi) = (r+s^C)K$ (c.t.)	$\mu_r^{CLG} = \frac{\lambda(\xi)}{r+s^L+s^C+\lambda(\xi)}$
		or $k(\phi) = (1-\beta^C)K$ (d.t.)	
Other parameters:			
Productivity	x (or $F(\mathbf{N})$ for large firms)	$x^{CL} = x - k(\phi)$	$x^{CLG} = \mu_r^{CLG} x - k(\phi)$
Entry costs	γ	$\gamma_k = \gamma + k(\phi)$	$\gamma_k = \gamma + k(\phi)$
Leisure and unemployment benefits	z	z	z
Barg. (workers, creditors, consumers)	α_L	α_C	α_G
Prices (wage, repayment, price)	w	ψ	$\mathcal{P}$
Large firm	Overemployment factor O_N		
Value functions:			
Workers	W_u, W_n	W_u, W_n	W_u, W_n or W_{D_U}, W_{D_M}
Firms	J_v, J_π	$J_i = E_i + B_i, i = c, v, \pi$	$J_i = E_i + B_i, i = c, v, g, \pi$
Projects		$E_i, i = c, v, \pi$	$E_i, i = c, v, g, \pi$
Creditors		$B_i, i = c, v, \pi$	$B_i, i = c, v, g, \pi$
Consumers			W_{D_U}, W_{D_M}
Surplus	$\Sigma_l^T = W_n - W_u + J_\pi - J_v$	$\Sigma_c^T = E_v - E_c + B_v - B_c = J_v$	$\Sigma_g^T = J_\pi - J_g + W_{D_M} - W_{D_U}$
Social planner	Ω^{SP}	Ω^{SP}	Ω^{SP}

Continues

Table 2(*Continued*)
Notations by chapter

	Labor Chapters 1–4 L	Credit Chapters 5–6 CL	Goods Chapters 7–8 CLG
Endogenous search margins:			
Worker's search effort, cost	$e_U, \bar{e}_U, \sigma_U(e_U)$		
Consumer's search effort, cost			$e_G, \bar{e}_G, \sigma_G(e_G)$
Firm's search effort, cost	$e_V, \bar{e}_V, \sigma_V(e_V)$	$e_I, \bar{e}_I, \sigma_I(e_I)$	$e_A, \bar{e}_A, \sigma_A(e_A)$
Creditor's search effort, cost		$e_B, \bar{e}_B, \sigma_B(e_B)$	
Matching rate of workers	$(e_L/\bar{e}_L) f(\theta)$		
Matching rate of firms	$(e_V/\bar{e}_V)\, q(\theta)$	$(e_I/\bar{e}_I)\, p(\phi)$	$(e_A/\bar{e}_A)\, \lambda(\xi)$
Matching rate of creditors		$(e_B/\bar{e}_B)\, \check{p}(\phi)$	
Matching rate of consumers			$(e_G/\bar{e}_G)\, \check{\lambda}(\xi)$

NB: c.t/d.t.: continuous/discrete time

Table 3
Time setup

		Continuous or discrete time	Steady state or dynamics
	Part I: Labor market frictions		
Benchmark	Chapter 1 (benchmark L model)	both	both
	Chapter 2 (business cycle)	discrete	dynamics
Topics	Chapter 3 (efficiency)	both	both
	Chapter 4 (large firms)	continuous	steady state
	Part II: Financial and goods market frictions		
Financial frictions	Chapter 5 (benchmark CL model)	continuous	steady state
	Chapter 6 (dynamics and financial multipliers)	discrete	dynamics
Goods market frictions	Chapter 7 (benchmark LG model and a variant)	continuous	steady state
	Chapter 8 (dynamic CLG model)	discrete	dynamics

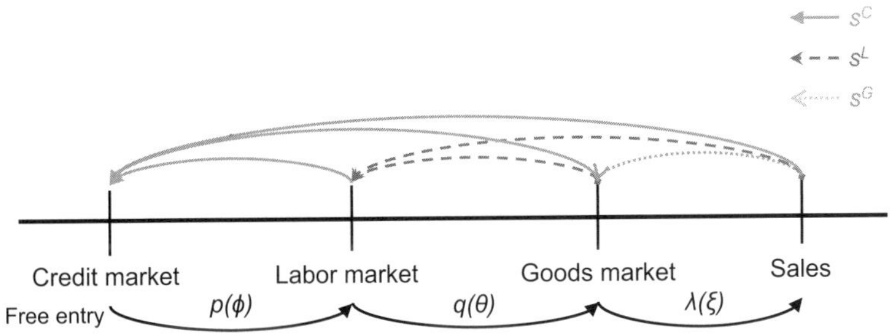

Figure 1
Markets and transition of the firm

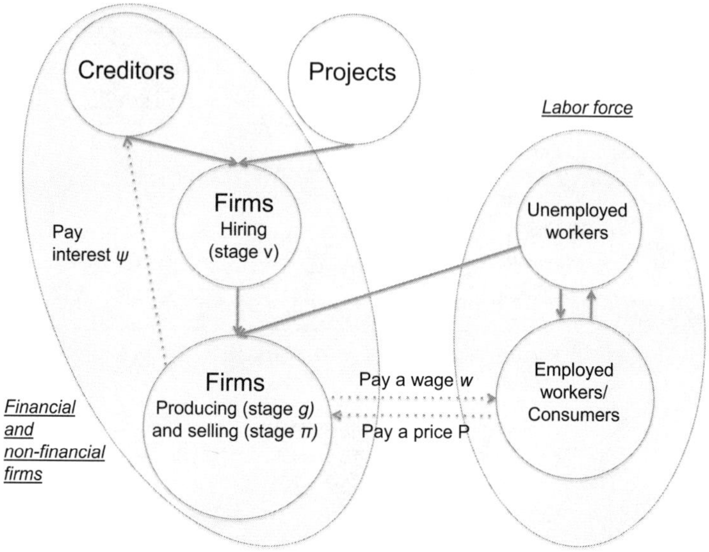

Figure 2

Markets, agents, and transactions

I FRICTIONS IN ONE MARKET: LABOR

1 The benchmark model: a single worker firm

This chapter begins by introducing the concept central to labor market frictions, the existence of a function matching two sides of the labor market. As we will argue, the simultaneous coexistence of job vacancies and unemployment implies that there must be a matching process leading to job creation that is a function of these two inputs. In this chapter we follow the assumption of basic matching models that a firm has either one worker or none. Later (in chapter 4), we present and discuss the assumptions under which a multi-worker firm environment leads to the same equilibrium conditions and the same allocations as the single worker firm. We then study the entry decisions of firms as well as different wage rules, and show how alternative assumptions about either discrete time or continuous time actually lead to identical equilibrium conditions in the steady state. Finally, we introduce a notion of endogenous job destruction. As in the rest of the book, details of the derivations for this chapter are presented in a chapter appendix containing a full treatment of both the continuous time and the discrete time models. Finally, we abstract from two important dimensions of the labor market: job search by currently employed workers, and labor force participation decisions. Job-to-job flows, as well as flows between employment, unemployment, and "not in the labor force" are features of the data and active areas of the research. These are briefly discussed at the end of the chapter.

1.1 Matching and separation in the labor market

1.1.1 Matching

At a given point in time t, a number of vacant positions $\mathcal{V}_t$ coexist with a number of unemployed job seekers $\mathcal{U}_t$ looking for jobs in the labor market. The labor force is normalized to $\mathcal{N}_t + \mathcal{U}_t = 1$, where $\mathcal{N}_t$ is the number of employed workers.

Consider a period of time, which may be a discrete time period or alternatively an infinitely small time interval in continuous time. Let f_t be the per-period rate at which unemployed workers find a job. Let also q_t be the per-period rate at which vacancies are filled. An identity in the labor market is that the total number of matches formed per unit of time $\mathcal{M}_{Lt}$ is both the total number of filled vacancies (first equality below) and the number of hired workers (second equality below):

$$\mathcal{M}_{Lt} = q_t \mathcal{V}_t \equiv f_t \mathcal{U}_t \tag{1.1}$$

In discrete time, since q_t and f_t are probabilities in the $(0, 1)$ interval, we necessarily have that

$$\mathcal{M}_{Lt} \leq \min(\mathcal{U}_t, \mathcal{V}_t) \tag{1.2}$$

and we will assume this to be the case throughout. In continuous time, the values of q_t and f_t are not bounded. However, in an arbitrarily small time interval dt, matching probabilities $f_t dt$ and $q_t dt$ are also below unity as dt approaches zero. We typically have in mind a time period of a week or a month, sometimes even a quarter.

We denote by

$$\theta_t = \frac{\mathcal{V}_t}{\mathcal{U}_t} \tag{1.3}$$

a measure of labor market conditions called *labor market tightness*. A tight labor market is one in which job seekers are scarce relative to the availability of jobs. It naturally follows from equation (1.1) that f_t and q_t are necessarily linked through θ_t, even in the absence of structural assumptions on the matching process. We indeed have from equation (1.1) that

$$f_t \equiv \theta_t q_t \tag{1.4}$$

Equation (1.4) implies that f_t and q_t cannot be simultaneously exogenous to labor market conditions summarized in θ_t. If q_t is an exogenous parameter, then f_t is linear in θ_t. If instead f_t is an exogenous parameter, then q_t is hyperbolic in θ_t. A more general specification is one in which both f_t and q_t depend, respectively, positively and negatively on θ_t.

Hereafter we follow the tradition of the search literature and assume a constant returns to scale matching function:

$$\mathcal{M}_{Lt} = \mathcal{M}_L(\mathcal{V}_t, \mathcal{U}_t) \tag{1.5}$$

with $\partial \log \mathcal{M}_L / \partial \log \mathcal{U}_t = \eta_L(\theta_t)$

and $\partial \log \mathcal{M}_L / \partial \log \mathcal{V}_t = 1 - \eta_L(\theta_t)$

where $\eta_L(\theta_t)$ is the elasticity of matching with respect to the amount of job seekers. In general, this elasticity may depend on the current tightness of the labor market.

Summarizing, vacant jobs and unemployed workers match at a rate determined through a constant returns to scale matching function $\mathcal{M}_L(\mathcal{V},\mathcal{U})$, and the transition rates for vacancies and for unemployed workers, respectively, are given by

$$\frac{\mathcal{M}_L(\mathcal{V}_t,\mathcal{U}_t)}{\mathcal{V}_t} = q(\theta_t) \quad \text{with } q'(\theta_t) \leq 0 \tag{1.6}$$

$$\frac{\mathcal{M}_L(\mathcal{V}_t,\mathcal{U}_t)}{\mathcal{U}_t} = \theta_t q(\theta_t) = f(\theta_t) \quad \text{with } f'(\theta_t) \geq 0 \tag{1.7}$$

Under iso-elastic functions f_t and q_t of θ_t, for instance, one would recover a Cobb–Douglas matching function, $\mathcal{M}_{Lt} = \chi_L \mathcal{U}_t^{\eta_L} \mathcal{V}_t^{1-\eta_L}$ with $\chi_L > 0$ and $\eta_L \in (0,1)$. In this instance the job filling and job finding rates are, respectively, $q(\theta_t) = \chi_L \theta_t^{-\eta_L}$ and $f(\theta_t) = \chi_L \theta_t^{1-\eta_L}$. A feature of this function is a constant elasticity of matching with respect to unemployment $\eta_L(\theta_t) = \eta_L$, with important implications for the efficiency of the decentralized allocation studied in chapter 3.

In discrete time settings, a common alternative is the functional form $\mathcal{M}_{Lt} = \mathcal{V}_t \mathcal{U}_t / \left(\mathcal{V}_t^{\nu_L} + \mathcal{U}_t^{\nu_L}\right)^{1/\nu_L}$, where $\nu_L > 0$. This function, proposed by den Haan et al. (2000), has the appealing feature of being bounded between 0 and 1. The job filling and job finding rates are, respectively, $q(\theta_t) = \left(1 + \theta_t^{\nu_L}\right)^{-1/\nu_L}$ and $f(\theta_t) = \left(1 + \theta_t^{-\nu_L}\right)^{-1/\nu_L}$. The elasticity of matching with respect to job seekers in this instance depends on the current level of labor market tightness, $\eta_L(\theta_t) = \theta_t^{\nu_L}\left(1 + \theta_t^{\nu_L}\right)^{-1}$.

1.1.2 Separation

Once formed, matches create profit streams. Before detailing the content of these profits, one needs to specify the separation process. We assume that profit streams end at exogenous rate s. This generic notation hides a number of possible events. Given the overall structure of the book, it is worth interpreting profit termination as the occurrence of three possible events: (i) as the firm's bankruptcy, whatever the reason, such as a financial or credit shock, arriving at rate s^C; (ii) as turnover of the worker leading to the job becoming vacant, an event occurring at rate s^L; or finally (iii) a lack of demand due to changes in consumer tastes, an event that would occur at rate s^G. We will see in Part II that, once financial and goods market frictions are introduced, the distinction will be meaningful and we need to separate these three different concepts of profit termination. Here they are confounded.

1.2 The job creation condition

Firms initially create vacancies by paying posting costs $\gamma > 0$ per unit of time the job is open and unfilled. Once matched with a worker, they produce a flow of output x and pay a wage w to the worker, resulting in flow profits $x - w$.

1.2.1 Continuous time

It is convenient to drop subscript t in continuous time, which we do in this subsection. Let W_n, W_u, J_π, and J_v be the value functions of the employed worker, the unemployed worker, the filled position, and the vacant position, respectively, and let r denote the rate of interest for discounting time. Denote by z the value of nonemployment for the worker. It is a composite of unemployment benefits and other income support programs for the unemployed, and the value of leisure and other nonmarket activities such as home production to the worker. We have

$$rW_n = w + s\,(W_u - W_n) + \partial W_n/\partial t \tag{1.8}$$

$$rW_u = z + \theta q(\theta)\,(W_n - W_u) + \partial W_u/\partial t \tag{1.9}$$

$$rJ_\pi = x - w + s\,(J_v - J_\pi) + \partial J_\pi/\partial t \tag{1.10}$$

$$rJ_v = -\gamma + q(\theta)\,(J_\pi - J_v) + \partial J_v/\partial t \tag{1.11}$$

A steady-state equilibrium implies that all partial time derivatives are equal to zero. It is assumed that firms may freely enter the labor market. This implies that the value of a vacancy is identically equal to zero in equilibrium, a result referred to as the free entry condition:

$$J_v \equiv 0 \text{ for all } t \tag{1.12}$$

From equation (1.12) and the value functions (1.10) and (1.11) above, we derive an equilibrium job creation condition that will be the central equation throughout the book:

Continuous time job creation condition:

$$\frac{\gamma}{q(\theta)} = \frac{x - w}{r + s} \tag{1.13}$$

This equation has a simple interpretation. It resembles an equality of costs and benefits. To discuss it, let $Q_v(\theta) \equiv q[\theta]/\,[r+q(\theta)]$ be a notation useful to account for discounting in the presence of frictional matching in the labor market. It represents the value of a particular asset that would bring one dollar of income after a random delay, with the event leading to that dollar occurring with probability q per unit of time. Under no discounting, that value is 1. Under a strictly positive discount rate, it has a value $q/(r+q) < 1$. When matching is infinitely fast, q goes to infinity and the ratio converges to 1. When matching is infinitely slow, the ratio goes to zero. Hence, when deciding to enter the market, tomorrow's profit flows considered by the firm have to be multiplied by a discounting coefficient $q/(r+q)$. This discounting reflects how much time it will take to match with a worker. The equilibrium job creation condition states that the present discounted cost of a vacancy at the time of entry in the market, $\gamma/\,[r+q(\theta)] = Q_v(\theta) \times \gamma/q$, has to be equal to the present discounted value of profits $Q_v(\theta) \times (x-w)/(r+s)$ evaluated from the same perspective of entry and vacancy creation. Simplifying the equality, we obtain the classic steady-state job creation condition in (1.13).

Existence and uniqueness

For a given wage, given the assumed monotonicity of q in θ, there is at most one value of labor market tightness satisfying equation (1.13). The same remains true for all wage functions if they are increasing in labor market tightness, which is the case of many wage determination processes, in particular the Nash bargaining solution derived later on in the chapter. Indeed, the right-hand side of (1.13) is either constant (if the wage is constant) or decreasing in θ (if the wage increases in θ), while search costs in the left-hand side are increasing in θ. Existence of a solution is then ensured by the condition

$$\frac{x-w(0)}{r+s} \geq \frac{\gamma}{q(0)} = 0$$

which states that at the lowest possible value of labor market tightness, $\theta = 0$, a firm can enter and make more profit than the expected costs of entering the market.

There is another intuitive way to understand the convergence toward the equilibrium, without mobilizing a formal dynamic system. Consider the out-of-equilibrium value of a vacancy at a given value of labor market tightness. To simplify the analysis, let us assume for the moment an exogenous wage. The value of a vacancy, after replacing the value of a filled position J_π from equation (1.10) into the value of a job vacancy, can be expressed as a function of θ, and is given by $rJ_v(\theta) = -\gamma + q(\theta)\left(\frac{x-w+sJ_v}{r+s} - J_v(\theta)\right)$. After some rearrangement, one has

$$rJ_v(\theta) = \frac{r+s}{r+s+q(\theta)}(-\gamma) + \frac{q(\theta)}{r+s+q(\theta)}(x-w) \tag{1.14}$$

Here, the value of a vacancy out of equilibrium appears as a weighted average of flow recruiting costs (negative term) and of future profit streams (strictly positive term under the assumption that $x > w$). Further, the weight $q(\theta)/(r+s+q(\theta))$ varies monotonically between 0 and 1 as θ describes the full range from 0 to infinity. In other words, the value of a vacancy varies from a positive value $(x-w)/r$ when tightness is zero (firms instantaneously fill a vacancy and enjoy a permanent income $x-w$, as job separation would be followed by immediate replacement of the worker) to a negative value $-\gamma/r$ when tightness goes to infinity (as firms would never fill a vacancy and would face perpetual losses γ). It follows that there is a unique value of θ for which $rJ_v(\theta)$ crosses the horizontal axis at zero. Further, any deviation implies a return to the equilibrium value: if θ is above the equilibrium value, the value of a vacancy is negative, leading vacancies to exit the labor market and reducing the number of vacancies $\mathcal{V}$. This leads to a decrease in labor market tightness at a fixed unemployment rate $\mathcal{U}$. Conversely, if θ is below the equilibrium value, the value of a vacancy is positive, leading to inflows of vacancies and increasing the value of labor market tightness.

Beveridge curve

A second important building block of the model is the steady-state condition for the stock of unemployment. Given the environment we have just described, unemployment evolves according to

$$\frac{d\mathcal{U}}{dt} = s(1-\mathcal{U}) - f(\theta)\mathcal{U} \tag{1.15}$$

where $s(1-\mathcal{U})$ are flows out of employment into unemployment, and $f(\theta)\mathcal{U}$ are flows out of unemployment into employment. A steady state $d\mathcal{U}/dt = 0$ requires the equality of the flows in and out of unemployment, leading to a steady-state rate of unemployment as a function of the transition rates:

$$\mathcal{U} = \frac{s}{s+f(\theta)} \tag{1.16}$$

Equation (1.16) delivers a downward sloping relation between vacancies and unemployment, which matches the empirical observation of a negative correlation between unemployment and vacancies discussed later on in chapter 2—the so-called Beveridge curve.

1.2.2 Discrete time

We present the derivation of the job creation condition in discrete time from the perspective of a firm choosing the number of job vacancies to post at unit cost γ, knowing and taking as given the probability of meeting a worker $q(\theta_t)$. The firm also takes as given the discrete time law of motion for employment, adapted from equation (1.15). Using the fact that at any time, $\mathcal{U}_t + \mathcal{N}_t = 1$, we have

$$\mathcal{N}_{t+1} = (1-s)\mathcal{N}_t + q(\theta_t)\mathcal{V}_t \tag{1.17}$$

Using the notation

$$\beta = \frac{1}{1+r}$$

for the discount factor, the optimality condition for vacancies to this firm's problem, detailed in appendix 1.8.2,

$$\gamma = q(\theta_t)\beta\mathbb{E}_t[J_{\pi t+1}] \tag{1.18}$$

equates the cost of posting γ to the expected discounted value of a hired worker $J_{\pi t+1}$, conditional on meeting a job seeker, through the probability $q(\theta_t)$, and on information at time t, through the expectations operator $\mathbb{E}_t$. The value of a hired worker to the firm, given by

$$J_{\pi t} = x_t - w_t + \beta(1-s)\mathbb{E}_t[J_{\pi t+1}] \tag{1.19}$$

is the sum of the per period profit flow $x_t - w_t$ and of the discounted value of an additional period of productive employment, conditional on survival to the next period, which occurs with probability $(1-s)$. By combining equation (1.19), iterated one period forward, with the optimality condition for job vacancies (1.18), we obtain the job creation condition in a discrete time setting:

Discrete time job creation condition:

$$\frac{\gamma}{q(\theta_t)} = \beta\mathbb{E}_t\left[x_{t+1} - w_{t+1} + (1-s)\frac{\gamma}{q(\theta_{t+1})}\right] \tag{1.20}$$

The left-hand side of (1.20) can be interpreted as the average cost of filling a job vacancy, inversely related to the meeting rate $q(\theta_t)$. The right-hand side is the discounted expected value to the firm of a filled job vacancy, conditional on the state of the economy at date t. This is comprised of a period profit flow $(x_{t+1} - w_{t+1})$ and a continuation value should the employment relationship survive to the next period.

At a steady state this job creation condition becomes

$$\frac{\gamma}{q(\theta)} = \frac{x - w}{r + s} \tag{1.21}$$

which is identical to the continuous time steady state condition in equation (1.13). There is thus an equivalence between the two assumptions on time, continuous or discrete, at a steady state. The discrete time law of motion for unemployment, $\mathcal{U}_{t+1} = s(1 - \mathcal{U}_t) + [1 - f(\theta_t)]\mathcal{U}_t$, also leads to a steady-state unemployment equation identical to (1.16), except that s and f are transition probabilities and not transition intensities.

1.3 Wages

Wages can be set according to several rules. In this section, we will go straight to the wage determination mechanism most frequently used in the literature (Nash bargaining), and show the equilibrium properties of the model in the next Section. However, the choice of this wage rule, as natural it may be, has several underlying assumptions and implications which are deepened in Section 1.5. These assumptions can be relaxed to provide alternative wage determination mechanisms, as we will do in the quantitative analysis of chapter 2.

1.3.1 Surplus and reservation wages

Matches create economic rents for workers and firms, which are measured as the private surplus of the relationship. In general, both firm and worker are willing to maintain a relationship as long as the private surplus is positive. Define the total surplus to a match by $\Sigma_l^T = \Sigma^f(w) + \Sigma^n(w)$, the sum of the labor surplus of the firm and of the worker, each being defined next.

The firm's surplus is the difference between the value of an employed worker paid a wage w, $J_\pi(w)$, and of searching in the labor market, J_v. That is, the surplus of a filled vacancy to a firm is $\Sigma^f(w) = J_\pi(w) - J_v$. The worker's surplus amounts to the difference between the value of working for a wage w, $W_n(w)$, and the value of unemployment, W_u. That is, the surplus from employment for a worker is $\Sigma^n(w) = W_n(w) - W_u$. We also define the reservation wages of both the worker and the firm. The lowest wage a worker would be willing to accept is denoted by $\underline{w}_n$, and the highest wage a firm would be willing to pay is denoted by $\underline{w}_f$. They are such that $\Sigma^f(\underline{w}_f) = 0$ and $\Sigma^n(\underline{w}_n) = 0$.

In continuous time, the asset values of unemployment and employment are defined by

$$rW_u = z + f(\theta)(W_n - W_u) + \partial W_u/\partial t \tag{1.22}$$

$$rW_n = w + s(W_u - W_n) + \partial W_n/\partial t \tag{1.23}$$

In discrete time, we have:

$$W_{ut} = z + \beta \mathbb{E}_t \left[f(\theta_t) W_{nt+1} + (1 - f(\theta_t)) W_{ut+1} \right] \tag{1.24}$$

$$W_{nt} = w_t + \beta \mathbb{E}_t \left[s W_{ut+1} + (1 - s) W_{nt+1} \right] \tag{1.25}$$

1.3.2 Surplus sharing and Nash bargaining over wages

The Nash solution has become the most popular in macroeconomics, following Mortensen's (1986) handbook survey. This wage allocates a share of the total surplus Σ_l^T to each party in the bargaining game. A corollary is that the joint surplus Σ_l^T needs to be strictly positive for a match to survive. This approach assumes that the wage is negotiated every period or, in continuous time, at any time if the outcome of negotiation leads to a different wage, as is the case if underlying parameters evolve over time. This convenient, yet strong, assumption can be relaxed as discussed later on.

The Nash wage solves the general maximization problem:

$$w_t = \text{argmax} \left[W_{nt}(w_t) - W_{ut} \right]^{\alpha_L} \left[J_{\pi t}(w_t) - J_{vt} \right]^{1-\alpha_L} \tag{1.26}$$

in which $\alpha_L \in (0, 1)$ denotes the relative bargaining weight of the worker in wage setting. From the Bellman equations for J_π and W_n above (either in continuous or in discrete time), the worker's surplus is linearly increasing in the wage while the firm's surplus is linearly decreasing in the wage, with opposite slopes. Thus the Nash problem's objective function of equation (1.26) is increasing and concave. It is equal to zero at the worker's reservation wage $\underline{w}_n$, reaches a maximum, and then decreases once again to zero at the firm's reservation wage $\underline{w}_f$.

The solution to this problem is a wage that results in a surplus-sharing rule:

$$(1 - \alpha_L)(W_{nt} - W_{ut}) = \alpha_L (J_{\pi t} - J_{vt}) \tag{1.27}$$

conveniently re-expressed as either $(W_{nt} - W_{ut}) = \alpha_L \Sigma_{lt}^T$ or $(J_{\pi t} - J_{vt}) = (1 - \alpha_L) \Sigma_{lt}^T$. The latter expressions focus on the Nash wage as dividing the total surplus of the match between worker and a firm into shares α_L and $(1 - \alpha_L)$, respectively.

In continuous time, using equations (1.22) and (1.23), the Nash wage can readily be expressed as the weighted average of the marginal product of labor and the value of the worker's outside option, here unemployment:

$$w = \alpha_L x + (1 - \alpha_L) r W_u \tag{1.28}$$

which illustrates the main forces affecting the Nash wage. It is increasing in the marginal product of labor, with the worker receiving a share α_L of the increase. It is also increasing in the value of being unemployed and searching in the labor market for another employer, itself a function of the rate at which workers find jobs, $f(\theta)$. Note that this expression is true both in the steady state and when the value function varies with time, to the extent that bargaining takes place in continuous time too. Indeed, in the latter case, the terms $\partial(W_n - W_u)/\partial t$ and $\partial(J_n - J_v)/\partial t$ cancel each other because the Nash sharing rule applies to both levels and their derivatives. Expanding this expression leads to the wage rule in equation (1.29) in continuous time, and (1.30) in discrete time.

Nash wage:

Continuous time: $w = \alpha_L (x + \gamma\theta) + (1 - \alpha_L) z$ (1.29)

Discrete time: $w_t = \alpha_L (x_t + \gamma\theta_t) + (1 - \alpha_L) z$ (1.30)

Two elements of this wage originate in the worker's outside option rW_u in equation (1.28). First, the wage is increasing in the flow value of unemployment, z. In addition, the wage is increasing in labor market tightness θ. This arises from another term from the worker's outside option, $f(\theta)(W_n - W_u)$, which affects the value to workers of searching in the labor market (by determining the frequency of meeting employers). This term is transformed, using the Nash bargaining equation, into $\frac{\alpha_L}{1-\alpha_L} f(\theta)(J_\pi - J_v)$. After inserting the free-entry equation, this term becomes $\frac{\alpha_L}{1-\alpha_L}\frac{f(\theta)}{q(\theta)}\gamma$. Finally, one obtains the term $\alpha_L \gamma\theta$ seen in the above wage equation. This captures the cost of recruiting for firms which pay a flow cost γ for open job vacancies as labor market tightness determines the frequency of meeting workers.

The Nash solution has become popular in part because of its simplicity and in part because it can be derived from first principles. In particular, it satisfies four axioms: Pareto-optimality, symmetry, invariance to equivalent utility representation, and the independence of irrelevant alternatives. It has also been rationalized as the outcome of a set of offers and counteroffers (see Osborne and Rubinstein, 1990).

The Nash solution is often the natural one when utility is linear. It can also be extended to concave utility functions as long as agents cannot smooth consumption. In this case, under concave utility $v(w)$, the Nash maximand leads to different effective shares $\tilde{\alpha}_L(v') = \alpha_L \frac{v'}{1-\alpha_L(1-v')}$ equal to α_L for linear utility, and increasing in marginal utility v'.

However, wage determination involves difficulties in specific contexts: (i) when the bargaining set is nonconvex; (ii) when taxes introduce a wedge between the worker and the firm slopes of the surplus; or (iii) when considering the possibility of renegotiation following a change in the environment.

In context (i), when the bargaining set is not convex, the Nash bargaining solution cannot be implemented. This is notably the case when there is on-the-job search, that is, when workers search for another job within the existing job. In this case, a higher wage reduces their search intensity. A higher wage may therefore increase the surplus of the firm over some range by reducing the probability a worker will quit the job. One will therefore either implement a sharing rule of the surplus, without referring to an underlying bargaining game à la Nash, or prefer alternative wage setting mechanisms, including some of those described below. Regarding context (ii), tax wedges introduce different slopes with respect to wages in the respective asset values of workers and firms. They therefore shift the bargaining strength of each bargaining party. Finally, regarding context (iii), the issue is whether the wage remains within the bargaining set after a change in the environment and if not, what rule is adopted to renegotiate. This is analyzed later on in this chapter.

1.4 Equilibrium

We consider first a steady-state equilibrium for a pair (θ, w). The discussion that follows is identical in either discrete or continuous time. As discussed earlier, for a given wage w, there is at most one value of labor market tightness satisfying the job creation condition (1.13). The same is true for all wage functions that depend positively on labor market tightness. Equilibrium labor market tightness θ^* and wage w^* are obtained through a wage setting rule.

In the case of Nash bargaining, we have an increasing function of labor market tightness $w = \alpha_L(x + \gamma\theta) + (1 - \alpha_L)z$. Both the wage rule and the job creation condition $w = x - (r+s)\gamma/q(\theta)$ are plotted in figure 1.1a in (θ, w) space. A crossing for an equilibrium with positive market tightness requires

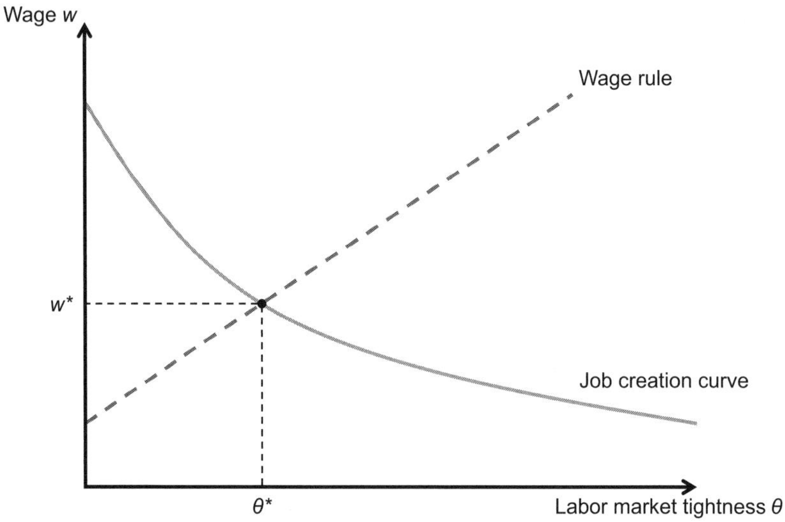

(a) Equilibrium labor market tightness and wage

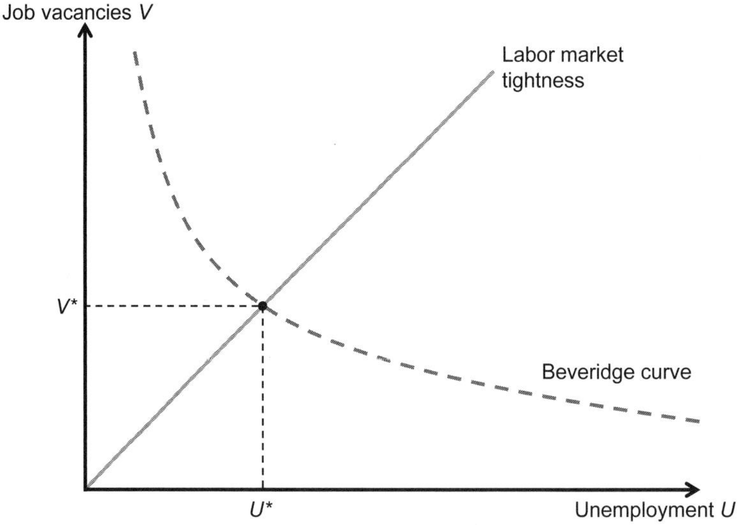

(b) Equilibrium unemployment and vacancies

Figure 1.1
Steady-state equilibrium θ^*, w^*, $\mathcal{U}^*$, and $\mathcal{V}^*$ in the benchmark model

that the marginal product of labor x be strictly greater than the flow value of unemployment z.

A steady-state equilibrium is a pair (θ^*, w^*) that satisfies the job creation condition in (1.13) and wage rule in (1.29) or (1.30). As long as $x > z$, a steady-state equilibrium exists and is unique. Combining the wage rule and job creation condition, equilibrium labor market tightness is determined by:

Equilibrium job creation condition:

$$\frac{\gamma}{q(\theta^*)} = \frac{(1-\alpha_L)(x-z) - \alpha_L \gamma \theta^*}{r+s} \tag{1.31}$$

Figure 1.1b plots the array of equilibrium labor market tightness θ^* in $(\mathcal{U}, \mathcal{V})$ space along with the Beveridge curve (1.16). The intersection of market tightness with the Beveridge curve gives the model's steady state unemployment rate, $\mathcal{U}^*$, and job vacancies, $\mathcal{V}^*$.

Some comparative statics can be easily derived, since many model parameters affect one curve but not the other. Consider the effect on the steady-state equilibrium of an increase in labor productivity x. The job creation curve shifts upward, tending toward higher labor market tightness and wage along the wage curve. The wage curve also shifts up, pushing up the wage but reducing labor market tightness along the job creation curve. The net result for the equilibrium wage is an unambiguous increase. Labor market tightness will also increase as long as $\alpha_L < 1$. The increase in labor market tightness, by the Beveridge relationship, results in a decrease in the unemployment rate. In chapter 2 we will consider the short run response of the labor market to changes in productivity and discuss the ability of the benchmark model to match the cyclical fluctuations of labor market variables in the data.

Table 1.1 summarizes the steady-state comparative statics for the main parameters of the model. An increase in vacancy posting cost γ tilts the job creation curve downwards and the wage curve upwards. As a result, equilibrium tightness decreases, as do vacancies, and unemployment increases. The effect on the wage is ambiguous. An increase in the share of the surplus accruing to the worker, α_L, shifts the equilibrium to a higher wage and lower labor

Table 1.1
Comparative statics—benchmark model

	x	γ	α_L	s	r
θ	+	−	−	−	−
w	+	?	+	−	−
$\mathcal{U}$	−	+	+	+	+
$\mathcal{V}$	+	−	−	?	−

market tightness along the job creation curve. Consequently, unemployment increases and vacancies decline. Changes in the job separation rate s and interest rate r act in a similar manner. By affecting the discounting of the profit flows from employing a worker, an increase in either s or r tilts the job creation curve downwards and moves the equilibrium to a lower wage and lower labor market tightness along the wage curve. This results in higher unemployment and lower job vacancies in the case of a change in the interest rate. A change in the job separation rate shifts the Beveridge curve outward such that the effect on job vacancies is ambiguous.

1.5 Further discussion of wages

In this section we deepen the analysis of wages and propose alternative wage setting mechanisms.

1.5.1 Acceptance set of wages

The fundamental block of wage determination is the acceptance set of wages. Wages must be above the minimal acceptable wage for workers and below the maximal acceptable wage of firms, respectively defined earlier as $\underline{w}_n$ and $\underline{w}_f$. A viability condition for a job is that $\underline{w}_n \leq \underline{w}_f$. When this is the case, any wage in the set $[\underline{w}_n, \underline{w}_f]$ could be a feasible wage. When the value of a worker's reservation wage is above the value of a firm's reservation wage, no wage can preserve the willingness of both parties to stay together. An efficient separation should arise. A representation of these two upper and lower values of wages can be seen in figure 1.2a.

The reservation wages are calculated, in continuous time, as

$$W_n(\underline{w}_n) = W_u \Leftrightarrow \underline{w}_n = z + [f(\theta) + s]\left(W_n' - W_u\right) - \partial(W_n - W_u)/\partial t \qquad (1.32)$$

$$J_\pi(\underline{w}_f) = 0 \Leftrightarrow \underline{w}_f = x - sJ_\pi' + \partial J_\pi/\partial t \qquad (1.33)$$

where W_n' and J_π' are the future value of employment for a worker and a firm after a transition shock. In the future, the wage paid will not necessarily be the reservation wage, in which case the match surplus would be positive. In a stationary equilibrium, the lowest wage acceptable to a worker in a match, defined in equation (1.32), is bounded below by the flow value of unemployment z. The second term captures the long-term nature of employment relationships. The worker is willing to accept a lower wage if it means remaining out of unemployment for a longer period of time, that is if the separation rate s is low. The worker is also willing to accept a lower wage if finding a new job is difficult that is, if $f(\theta)$ is low. Conversely, a higher job finding probability raises the

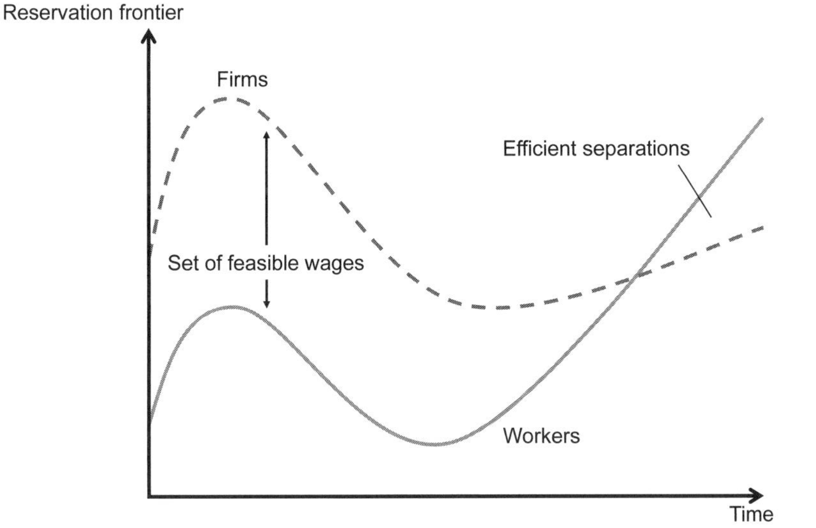

(a) Example of a feasible wage set over time and separations

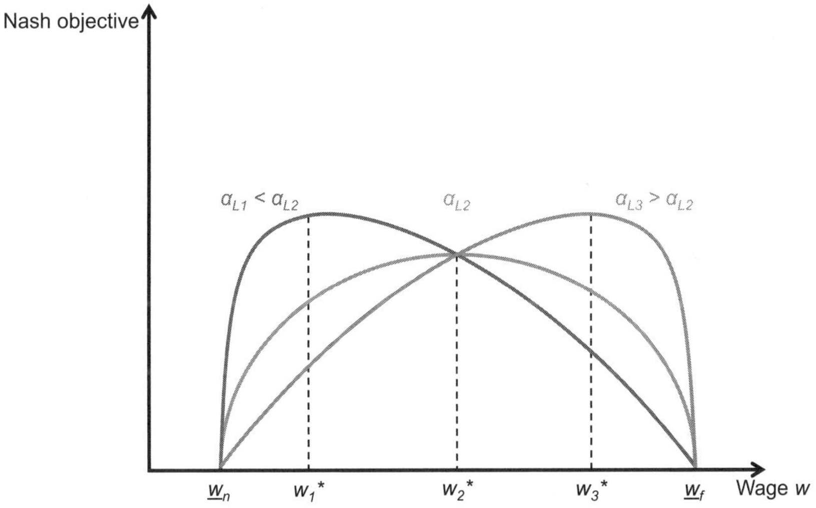

(b) Nash bargaining representation with Nash maximand

Figure 1.2

More on wage determination: (a) time-varying threat points, and (b) a view of the Nash maximand with $\alpha_{L1} < \alpha_{L2} = 0.5 < \alpha_{L3}$

reservation wage as this captures the value of forgoing the current match with a firm and possibly meeting another employer with whom the worker would generate an expected match surplus. Note that the reservation wage takes into account the possibility of future growth in asset values. In particular, workers are ready to accept lower wages if they expect that the future value of holding a job progresses faster than the current value of unemployment, that is, when $\partial(W_n - W_u)/\partial t$ is positive.

The reservation wage of the firm in equation (1.33) depends first on the current productivity x. It will exceed productivity if there is expected growth in the firm's surplus to the current match, that is, if $\partial J_\pi/\partial t > 0$. Finally, it is decreasing in the value of the job to the firm, J'_π. That value, by free entry, will be equal to the average cost of replacing a given worker after searching in the labor market.

In discrete time, we obtain similar expressions for reservation wages:

$$\underline{w}_{nt} = z - \frac{1 - s - f(\theta_t)}{1 + r} \mathbb{E}_t \left[W_{nt+1}(w) - W_{ut+1} \right] \tag{1.34}$$

$$\underline{w}_{ft} = x_t + \frac{1 - s}{1 + r} \mathbb{E}_t \left[J_{\pi t+1} \right] \tag{1.35}$$

A reinterpretation of the Nash program uses the reservation wages determined just above. For that, we can visually represent the Nash product as a function of the bargaining share α_L. Figure 1.2b plots the Nash maximand in (1.26) for three arbitrary values of bargaining weights $\alpha_{L1} < \alpha_{L2} = 0.5 < \alpha_{L3}$. A lower bargaining weight, α_{L1} in figure 1.2b, shifts the Nash wage towards the worker's reservation wage at w_1^*. A greater bargaining weight, α_{L3} in figure 1.2b, shifts the wage towards the firm's reservation wage at w_3^*. At the extremes, if the bargaining weight tends to 0, then the wage is such that the worker's surplus $(W_{nt} - W_{ut}) = 0$. The worker receives his or her reservation wage $\underline{w}_{nt}$. If the bargaining weight α_L tends to 1, the firm's surplus is pushed to $(J_{nt} - J_{vt}) = 0$. The firm receives its reservation wage $\underline{w}_{ft}$. The Nash bargained wage can, thus, be expressed as a weighted average of worker's and firm's reservation wages, with the bargaining parameter α_L as the weight:

$$w_t = \alpha_L \underline{w}_{ft} + (1 - \alpha_L) \underline{w}_{nt}$$

1.5.2 Credible bargaining

A number of other wage mechanisms are possible, as long as they fall in the feasible set $[\underline{w}_n, \underline{w}_f]$. An interesting alternative to Nash bargaining proposed by Hall and Milgrom (2008) builds on Binmore et al. (1986), and places a crucial distinction between a threat point and an outside option in the wage bargaining game. This approach recognizes that bargaining takes time, and that during this process, both parties make alternating offers which can be accepted, rejected to make a counteroffer, or rejected to abandon the bargaining altogether. In contrast, in standard Nash bargaining, disagreement leads immediately to the abandonment of the bargaining game altogether, meaning that the relevant threat point is the outside options for both parties. This may not necessarily be a credible strategy.

A possibly more credible set of strategies would instead consider as a threat point, when disagreeing with the wage offer, the possibility to make a counteroffer. In this bargaining game with alternating offers, disagreement makes the party disagreeing a little worse off, but not as much as under a full and permanent separation as in the Nash game. Here, disagreement simply leads to another round of alternating offers. The threat point is the payoff from another round of alternating offers, and outside options are taken only when abandoning bargaining altogether. In that sense, bargaining is a bit more credible, hence the name for this wage determination process: credible bargaining. Parties make just acceptable offers, offers that leave the other side indifferent between accepting and refusing in order to make a counteroffer. The wage that is the outcome of this more credible bargaining game will depend much less on the value of unemployment than the Nash wage (1.30). This feature, as we will see in chapter 2, improves the cyclical properties of the search model, although standard bargaining solutions offer easy closed-form solutions for wages.

The outside option for a worker—now different from the threat point—is the value of unemployment, and the value of an open job vacancy for the firm. During a period in which both parties engage in another round of alternating offers, the worker receives the flow value of unemployment activities, z, and the firm incurs a cost of delaying production, $\zeta > 0$. During this period, the negotiation can also break down with an exogenous probability of $\varphi \in (0, 1)$. We assume that the period during which an alternative offer is being made by the other bargaining party is in fact a subperiod. That is, each time period t is divided into M subperiods, and the discount factor across subperiods is, to a first approximation, therefore $r' = r/M$.

In this context, the indifference condition for a worker when considering a wage offer, w_t, from the firm is

$$W_{nt}^{w} = \varphi W_{ut} + (1-\varphi)z + \frac{1-\varphi}{1+r'}\mathbb{E}_t W_{nt+1/M}^{w'} \tag{1.36}$$

where W_{nt}^{w} is the value of being employed when accepting the wage offer from the employer, and $W_{nt+1/M}^{w'}$ is the value of employment when rejecting the firm's wage offer to make a counteroffer of $w'_{t+1/M}$ in the next subperiod, under the assumption that the firm will accept the counteroffer in the subperiod. The indifference condition in equation (1.36) says that the payoff to the worker when accepting the wage offer from the firm is just equal to the payoff from rejecting the offer. After rejecting the offer, with a probability of φ, the negotiation breaks down, and the worker returns to the labor market as a job seeker. With probability $1-\varphi$, the worker receives the flow value of unemployment, z, for the current period, and makes a counteroffer of $w'_{t+1/M}$ to the firm in the next subperiod.

The indifference condition for the firm when considering the worker's offer, w'_t, is

$$J^{w'}_{\pi t} = \varphi J_{vt} + (1-\varphi)\left(-\zeta + \mathbb{E}_t\left[\frac{1}{1+r'}J^{w}_{\pi t+1/M}\right]\right) \tag{1.37}$$

in which $J^{w'}_{\pi t}$ is the value of an employed worker to the firm when accepting the worker's offer, and $J^{w}_{\pi t+1/M}$ is the value of an employed worker to the firm when rejecting the worker's offer to make a counteroffer of $w_{t+1/M}$ in the next sub-period, under the assumption that the worker will accept the counteroffer. Equation (1.37) says that the firm is just indifferent between the payoff from accepting the worker's offer w'_t and the payoff from rejecting the offer to have an opportunity to make a counteroffer of $w_{t+1/M}$ in the next subperiod. When rejecting the offer, the firm pays the delaying cost of ζ if the bargaining does not break down. When the negotiation does break down, the firm's payoff is the value of a job vacancy.

When negotiations break down with certainty, that is, as φ tends to 1, the two indifference conditions (1.36) and (1.37) collapse to conditions that defined the reservation wages (1.34) and (1.35) in Nash bargaining. During the alternating bargaining, it is optimal for each party to make a just acceptable offer. Hall and Milgrom (2008) assume that the firm makes the first offer, which the worker accepts. As such, w_t is the equilibrium wage, and the delaying cost ζ is never paid in equilibrium.

In the special case of a steady state, one can offer a graphical representation of the equilibrium wage offers (w', w), which are characterized by two implicit equations. Indeed, one can show from (1.25) and (1.36) and from (1.19) and (1.37), respectively, that the two following equations hold:

$$\text{Firm offer curve: } w(w') \Rightarrow w = \bar{w}_0 + \frac{1-\varphi}{1+r'}w'$$

$$\text{Worker offer curve: } w'(w) \Rightarrow w = \bar{w}'_0 + \left(\frac{1-\varphi}{1+r'}\right)^{-1} w'$$

Further, assuming $r'=0$ and $J_v=0$, we calculate that $\bar{w}_0 = \frac{r+s}{1+r}\varphi W_u + \frac{r+s}{1+r}(1-\varphi)z > 0$, and $\bar{w}'_0 = -(r+s)\zeta - \frac{\varphi+r'}{1-\varphi}x < 0$. The solutions for the wages don't have simple explicit forms but since the relations between w and

w' are linear, they can easily be represented in (w', w), as in figure 1.3a. In this representation it is easy to see that an upward shift of $\bar{w}_0$ (obtained from an increase in the outside option W_u or in z) leads to a higher wage offer curve by firms $w(w')$ for workers. This, in turn, raises both w'^* and w^*. Furthermore, an increase in ζ or in x will shift $\bar{w}'_0$ downwards. Graphically, this shifts $w(w')$ rightwards and towards higher wages, as firms are more willing to conclude bargaining and workers will make higher counteroffers w'^*. Again, both wages w^* and w'^* increase.

1.5.3 Further wage alternatives

One alternative is to assume that wages are renegotiated only when the change in the environment moves the feasible set away from the current wage. This is indeed a quite natural alternative, equivalent to assuming that renegotiation costs are large enough to prevent constant renegotiation. The analytical tractability is, however, lost. Further, the cost of renegotiation should also have an impact on bargaining, because it introduces an interesting distinction between the threat point and the outside option of the bargaining parties. In terms of figure 1.2a, this implies an initial entry wage within the feasible set, a horizontal line until the reservation frontier of workers or firms is hit, and then a renegotiation either by firms or workers. This particular process is compatible with the Nash bargaining solution: each time the frontier is hit, a new wage bargaining solution applies. But is is also fully compatible with Hall and Milgrom (2008). For instance, one may assume that if the reservation frontier of the worker is hit, the new solution for wages is the offer w' that (s)he makes to the firm. If the reservation frontier of the firm is hit, the new solution for wages is the offer w that the firm makes to the worker. This is represented in figure 1.3b where, after setting an entry wage (left unspecified), the worker hits his or her reservation wage and renegotiates by proposing w'^*. Subsequently, it is the firm hitting its reservation frontier, in turn proposing w^*, etc.

Other approaches have recently been explored within matching models (see the last section of this chapter for references). As argued above, the Nash solution is based on four axioms (e.g., Osborne and Rubinstein, 1990, pp. 11–13). In particular, one can remove, among other axioms, the independence of irrelevant alternatives, under alternative wage determination mechanisms. For instance, the Kalai solution (Kalai, 1977) and the Kalai and Smorodinsky (1975) bargaining solution can be implemented in the small firm matching model of unemployment (l'Haridon et al., 2013) without this axiom. The Kalai wage simply solves a proportional sharing rule:

$$(1-\alpha_L)(W_n - W_u) = \alpha_L(J_\pi - J_v)$$

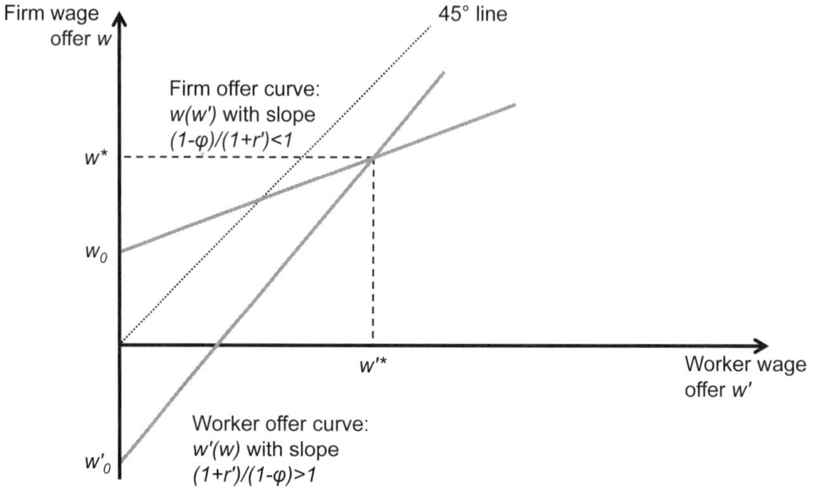

(a) Credible bargaining representation. Firm's offer curve has slope $b = \frac{1-\varphi}{1+r'} < 1$ and intercept w_0. Worker's offer curve has the inverse slope $b^{-1} > 1$, and intercept w_0'.

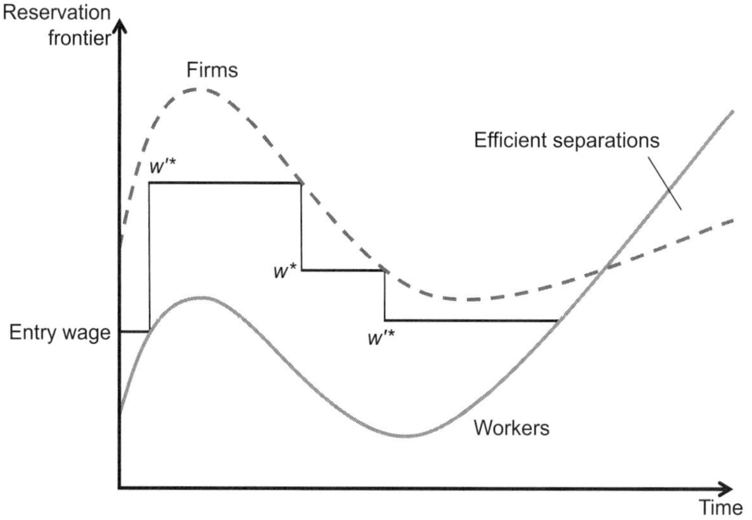

(b) Combining MacLeod–Malcomson and credible bargaining where the initiator of the wage offer is the one willing to initiate the separation

Figure 1.3

More on wage setting: (a) credible bargaining in a steady-state environment, and (b) in a time-varying environment

In practice, this solution only differs from Nash when the (absolute value of) the derivatives of the surplus with respect to wages is different between the bargaining parties. In the linear utility case, the solutions are the same. In other environments, in particular with concave utility and in the presence of taxes (see chapter 3), the two sets of solutions differ. These alternative solutions are simpler to derive and still satisfy the Pareto-Optimality and Symmetry axioms, and a strong monotonicity axiom which requires that both parties gain from an enlargement of the feasible set, even if the enlargement is biased with respect to one of the agents. The Kalai–Smorodinsky solution is the outcome of *"proportional concessions for both agents from their respective most favored bargaining points, called utopia points"* as defined in l'Haridon et al. (2013). It corresponds to the case where that agent captures all the surplus. Under different bargaining strength, it leads to

$$(1-\alpha_L)\frac{v(w)-rW_u}{v(x)-rW_u}=\alpha_L\frac{x-w}{x-v'^{-1}(rW_u)}$$

which again collapses to the conventional Nash solution when utility is linear. The denominator of each side captures the value of the surplus at a utopia point. On the left-hand side it is the worker being paid his marginal product x by the firm. On the right-hand side the compensation to the worker is the inverse of marginal utility evaluated at the worker's outside option, remaining unemployed.

Beyond bargaining, wage posting corresponds to the case where the firm announces a wage and commits to it. In this approach, the firm faces a trade-off between raising the arrival rate and acceptance probability of workers through higher wages, thereby minimizing search costs on the one hand, and reducing its profit flow from paying the higher wage. This solution may be relevant when workers are ex-ante heterogeneous in their reservation wage and when the firm cannot observe this reservation wage, or when it can observe it after the match but cannot change its initial offer.

1.6 Endogenous job destruction

So far, employment relationships have terminated at an exogenous and constant rate s assumed to be the combination of either labor turnover, changes in demand from consumers or exogenous profitability. In this section we select one of the underlying causes for profit termination, namely the changes in productivity at random times, and therefore endogenize job destruction. This is achieved by introducing a match-specific and time-varying stream of revenue

a, best interpreted as idiosyncratic productivity, but that can easily be assimilated to an idiosyncratic demand change for the good produced by the firm. Hereafter we call it productivity, but the demand interpretation remains valid and will be made more specific in part III of the book. This component a is random and enters multiplicatively in total production, so that the revenue of the firm is now ax. More specifically, we assume that upon meeting in the labor market, the match between a worker and a firm draws an idiosyncratic productivity a from a distribution $G(a)$. New idiosyncratic productivity draws from the same distribution arrive at the Poisson rate μ. The draw could be sufficiently low to, incite both worker and firm to dissolve the employment relationship. We present the main model in continuous time, and develop a discrete time variant in the chapter appendix.

This extension requires changes in the expression for profits of the firm over time, so that at some point the firm and the worker find it jointly profitable to separate. We represent this in figure 1.2a where the two reservation curves cross each other. When this occurs no renegotiation can lead to a positive surplus for both sides (we will return to this discussion in chapter 3 on efficiency). An implication of the time-varying profit structure is to have, in the cross-section, different types of firms coexisting.

We assume that, at the time of a meeting between a worker and a firm in the labor market, the entry level of a is also random. This introduces the possibility that, conditional on the value of a, a worker may prefer to remain a job seeker, and a firm may prefer to leave a job position open at the time of a meeting, or any point thereafter. So long as the wage reflects the idiosyncratic productivity, $w(a)$, the value of employment $W_n(a)$ is increasing in a, as is the value of an employed worker to the firm $J_\pi(a)$. Formally, the Bellman equations for worker and firm are now:

$$rW_u = z + \theta q(\theta)\left\{\int \max\left[W_n(a'), W_u\right] dG(a') - W_u\right\} \tag{1.38}$$

$$rW_n(a) = w(a) + s[W_u - W_n(a)] + \mu\left\{\int \max\left[W_n(a'), W_u\right] dG(a') - W_n(a)\right\} \tag{1.39}$$

$$rJ_v = -\gamma + q(\theta)\left\{\int \max\left[J_\pi(a'), J_v\right] dG(a') - J_v\right\} \tag{1.40}$$

$$rJ_\pi(a) = ax - w(a) + s(J_v - J_\pi(a)) + \mu\left\{\int \max\left[J_\pi(a'), J_v\right] dG(a') - J_\pi(a)\right\} \tag{1.41}$$

We study equilibria where the wage is always such that the surplus of workers and the surplus of firms have the same sign. This is discussed as an efficiency condition on separations in chapter 3. The economic surplus of a match with idiosyncratic productivity a, summing individual match surpluses from the above Bellman equations, is

$$(r+s+\mu)\,\Sigma_l^T(a) = ax + \mu \int \max\left[\Sigma_l^T(a'),0\right] \mathrm{d}G(a') - rW_u - rJ_v$$

Since $\Sigma_l^T(a)$ is strictly increasing in a, there exists a reservation strategy denoted by A such that if $a < A$, where A is such that $\Sigma_l^T(A) = 0$, the match is dissolved. That is to say, if the match draws $a' < A$, there is no value to the relationship to either party. Thus, A defines a job destruction threshold and the value for the match surplus $\Sigma_l^T(a)$ evaluated at this point defines a job destruction condition:

$$rW_u + rJ_v = Ax + \mu \int_A \Sigma_l^T(a')\mathrm{d}G(a')$$

For a match to remain viable, the sum of its current output and expected future value, conditional on drawing a productivity above A at arrival rate μ, must at least equal the worker's outside option rW_u (since free entry leads to $J_v = 0$). Inserting a solution $\Sigma_l^T(a) = \frac{(a-A)x}{r+s+\mu}$, along with the value of the worker's outside option when wages are set by Nash bargaining, leads to a job destruction condition in equation (1.42). There exists a unique equilibrium pair (θ, A) that satisfies the job destruction condition and a new job creation condition:

Continuous time job destruction condition:

$$z + \frac{\alpha_L}{1-\alpha_L}\gamma\theta = Ax + \frac{\mu x}{r+s+\mu}\int_A \left(a' - A\right)\mathrm{d}G(a') \tag{1.42}$$

Continuous time job creation condition:

$$\frac{\gamma}{q(\theta)} = \frac{(1-\alpha_L)\,x}{r+s+\mu}\int_A \left(a' - A\right)\mathrm{d}G(a') \tag{1.43}$$

These two expressions can be understood as follows. The job destruction condition says that the flow value of outside options—leisure plus future job prospects depending on θ—must equal the payoffs of the match at the destruction margin—the current value of marginal productivity plus the expected surplus from improvements of productivity. The job creation condition states that the discounted share of the expected surplus accruing to the firm—a share $(1-\alpha_L)$ of the surplus for idiosyncratic draws above A—must cover the expected cost of search in the labor market, $\gamma/q(\theta)$.

Employed workers now separate from the firm at an endogenous rate $G(A)$, and an exogenous rate s. The total separation rate is therefore the sum of two events:

$$s^T(A) = s + \mu G(A)$$

where the first component can be assimilated to the pure labor turnover shock (s^L in the notation of section 1.1.2), or other exogenous factors not modeled that can destroy a job. The unemployed exit the unemployment pool only if the match is successful. This occurs with probability $[1 - G(A)]$, such that $[1 - G(A)]f(\theta)$ is the job finding rate per unit of time. Thus unemployment now evolves according to:

$$\frac{d\mathcal{U}}{dt} = [s + \mu G(A)]\,(1 - \mathcal{U}) + [1 - G(A)]f(\theta)\mathcal{U}$$

As a result, steady-state unemployment is now given by

$$\mathcal{U} = \frac{s^T(A)}{s^T(A) + [1 - G(A)]f(\theta)}$$

1.7 Discussion of literature and remaining issues

The three main building blocks of this chapter are the matching function between vacancies and unemployed workers, Nash bargaining over wages between the firm and its worker and, finally, the steady-state equilibrium driven by a free entry of vacancies on the labor market. These blocks, introduced by Diamond and Maskin (1979), Pissarides (1979, 1985, 2000), Diamond (1982), and Mortensen (1982a, 1986), respectively, have become known as the DMP model. The foundations of the matching function and its empirical validity are surveyed in Petrongolo and Pissarides (2001).

These papers, as well as our analysis in this and subsequent chapters, focus solely on the nonexplosive solutions of the decentralized economy or of its social planner's solutions. Limit cycles and dynamics were studied in Mortensen (1999). Among the few recent examples of matching models with bubbles, one can refer to Cahuc and Challe (2012) in an OLG setup, or Kocherlakota (2011) and Vuillemey and Wasmer (2016) in infinite horizon models.

Endogenous job separation was developed and studied in Mortensen and Pissarides (1994, 1999a). The specification for endogenous job destruction we retained here slightly differs from their benchmark model in which the entry productivity is fixed at the upper value of the support. In our model, and as in chapter 6 in Pissarides (2000) on stochastic job matching, productivity is randomly drawn from the distribution and allows for meetings that are not necessarily followed by job creation. This gives a richer set of parameters affecting the job creation curve and the Beveridge curve, without introducing major differences in the analysis. In particular it leads to an identical separation productivity threshold in job creation and job destruction, and therefore the model remains tractable.

Discussions on wages, the existence of varying outside options, and efficiency frontiers can be found in MacLeod and Malcomson (1993) (see the survey in Malcomson, 1999). See also Hall (2005) and Galí and van Rens (2014) for an exposition that any wage in the set $[\underline{w}_n, \underline{w}_f]$ could be an equilibrium wage. Different bargaining solutions, such as the Kalai solution and the Kalai–Smorodinsky solution, were studied in search models in a recent paper by l'Haridon et al. (2013). See Aruoba et al. (2007) on Kalai (1977), adapted to the search-money framework. The credible wage approach was developed in Hall and Milgrom (2008).

Other modeling choices related to wages are not addressed in this chapter for the sake of brevity. For instance, the strong assumption that the wage is negotiated every period can be relaxed with either staggered bargaining, as in Gertler and Trigari (2009), or wage contracts, as in Rudanko (2009). The contracting approach followed by Rudanko (2009) is set in a competitive search environment (see chapter 3). Risk neutral firms post optimal long-term contracts to attract risk-averse workers. The wage is smoothed over the business cycle, depending on the ability of both parties, the employer and the worker, to commit to the contract. Another approach not considered here is to introduce an auction for the worker's labor services. Carrillo-Tudela et al. (2011) consider take-it-or-leave-it offers from firms when workers can recall past wage offers. When workers can recall previous offers and have firms enter a Bertrand competition, the firm will take this into account and offer the worker a sufficient share of match rents to avoid a bidding war in the future. Lastly, one can introduce asymmetries of information between workers and firms, for instance, over the productivity of the match. In Kennan (2010) firms have private information about match-specific productivity, and bargaining follows Myerson's (1984) neutral bargaining solution to accommodate the introduction of private information. The resulting wage is more rigid to changes in productivity.

This chapter does not address additioonal important issues regarding the turnover structure, namely on-the-job search, nor the issue of labor market participation. Both are empirically relevant topics and have nontrivial implications for theory. Shimer (2006) has shown that the bargaining set may not necessarily be convex in the case of on-the-job search, and this requires a different wage determination method with wages being determined once and for the rest of the employment relation. Different modeling strategies have been implemented to avoid this issue. In Burdett and Mortensen (1998), firms post permanent wages to retain workers. In Postel-Vinay and Robin (2002), entry workers receive their reservation wage and firms enter Bertrand competition later on in the case of an outside offer. There is an active strand of literature on the dynamics of on-the-job search, notably Menzio and Shi (2011) who model on-the-job search in a directed search environment. Their work can establish circumstances under which on-the-job search amplifies or mitigates the response of the economy to productivity shocks.

Garibaldi and Wasmer (2005), Pries and Rogerson (2009), and Krusell et al. (2011) have modeled endogenous participation with search frictions. In Garibaldi and Wasmer (2005), households face stochastic leisure shocks such that the household structure mimics that of the firm in Mortensen and Pissarides (1994). They first study a three-state economy (employment, unemployment, out of the labor force), and extend the model to a four-state economy by further dissociating those workers covered by unemployment insurance and those having exhausted their benefits. Pries and Rogerson (2009) and Krusell et al. (2011) develop an RBC-style three-state quantitative model replicating the corresponding six flows over the business cycle.

Estimates of the matching process have been summarized in Petrongolo and Pissarides (2001) and, generally speaking, support the random matching model with constant returns to scale. Burda and Profit (1996) also find constant returns when estimating a matching function in an environment in which workers are engaged in nonsequential search with endogenous search intensity and spatial spillovers. However, there is heterogeneity in the estimates of the elasticity of matching.

The matching framework is amenable to studying and measuring issues of geographic mismatch or to skill mismatch in the labor market, due to heterogenous skill requirements of jobs, in the pool of workers (Sahin et al., 2014).

The parameter summarizing efficiency of the matching function is χ_L, in our notation. More recent empirical work in this area include Hornstein and Kudlyak (2016) and Hall and Schulhofer-Wohl (2016). The latter show that vacancy filling rates in 19 different sectors, as well as the exit rate from unemployment for 18 categories of workers, comove almost perfectly with a single statistic: labor market tightness. Other forms of matching functions in which stocks enter as inputs on one side of the market, and the inflows into the market are an input on the other side, have been proposed in Taylor (1995) and Coles and Muthoo (1998). It was estimated with empirical success in Coles and Smith (1998) and Coles and Petrongolo (2009). Another interesting and more recent development is the concept of "phantom" vacancies, or obsolete vacancies, crowding out matching introduced in Cheron and Decreuse (2017) and Albrecht et al. (2015). Finally, the chapter does not address the size of the firm and its capital structure. These are left to chapter 4.

1.8 Chapter appendix

1.8.1 Wage bargaining: continuous time

Begin with the Nash sharing rule, in a steady state, and substitute W_n and J_π with their definitions:

$$(1-\alpha_L)(rW_n - rW_u) = \alpha_L r J_\pi$$

$$(1-\alpha_L)[w + s(W_u - W_n) - rW_u] = \alpha_L (x - w - sJ_\pi)$$

Noting that $s(1-\alpha_L)(W_n - W_u) = s\alpha_L J_\pi$, we obtain equation (1.28) in the text:

$$w = \alpha_L x + (1-\alpha_L) rW_u$$

Most wage equations involve the value of unemployment rW_u. We can solve it using the Nash bargaining condition (1.27) as well as the entry condition (1.13). First, apply the sharing rule in the value of unemployment:

$$rW_u = z + f(W_n - W_u) = z + f\frac{\alpha_L}{1-\alpha_L}J_\pi \tag{1.44}$$

Then use the implication of free entry, $J_\pi = \gamma/q$:

$$rW_u = z + \frac{\alpha_L}{1-\alpha_L}\gamma\theta$$

Hence, most wage equations can be expressed as a function of equilibrium market tightness.

1.8.2 Wage bargaining: discrete time

In order to derive the discrete time equivalent of the continuous time Bellman equations, it is useful to introduce the concept of representative household and firm. Following the contributions of Merz (1995) and Andolfatto (1996), this household is comprised of a continuum of members on the unit line, who may at any point in time be employed and earning a wage w_t, or unemployed and receiving unemployment benefits b and utility from leisure and other nonmarket activities. The household pools all l income members' and chooses a single consumption bundle c_t, over which it has linear preference, in order to maximize the following problem:

$$W_t = \max_{c_t}\left\{c_t + l\mathcal{U}_t + \beta\mathbb{E}_t\left[W_{t+1}\right]\right\} \tag{1.45}$$

$$\begin{aligned}\text{subject to}\quad c_t &= w_t\mathcal{N}_t + b\mathcal{U}_t + \pi_t\\ \mathcal{U}_{t+1} &= s\mathcal{N}_t + [1-f(\theta_t)]\mathcal{U}_t\\ \mathcal{N}_{t+1} &= (1-s)\mathcal{N}_t + f(\theta_t)\mathcal{U}_t\end{aligned}$$

Here π_t is firm profits, rebated lump sum to the household at the end of a time period. The choice is made subject to the discrete time laws of motion for unemployment and employment. Differentiating the household's value function with respect to unemployed and employee members yields the marginal values of both states in the labor market:

$$\begin{aligned} W_{ut} &= z + \beta \mathbb{E}_t \left[f(\theta_t) W_{nt+1} + (1 - f(\theta_t)) W_{ut+1} \right] \\ W_{nt} &= w_t + \beta \mathbb{E}_t \left[s W_{ut+1} + (1-s) W_{nt+1} \right] \end{aligned}$$

Under these assumptions, the marginal flow value to the household of an unemployed worker, $z = l + b$, is the sum of a leisure and benefits component. This distinction will matter in quantitative applications, informing an aspect of the calibration of the model important for its business cycle dynamics.

The representative firm, which operates with a linear production technology, maximizes the following problem by choice of job vacancies:

$$\begin{aligned} J_t &= \max_{\mathcal{V}_t} \left\{ x_t \mathcal{N}_t - w_t \mathcal{N}_t - \gamma \mathcal{V}_t + \beta \mathbb{E}_t [J_{t+1}] \right\} \\ &\quad \mathcal{N}_{t+1} = (1-s)\mathcal{N}_t + q_t \mathcal{V}_t \\ &\quad q_t \mathcal{V}_t \geq 0 \end{aligned}$$

subject to the law of motion for employment and a non-negativity constraint on job openings, equivalently expressed as nonnegative hiring $q_t \mathcal{V}_t \geq 0$. The latter can bind in some parameterizations of the model (see Petrosky-Nadeau and Zhang, forthcoming for a detailed treatment and discussion). We omit the constraint in the main text as it rarely binds in most applications of the search environment for the study of business cycle dynamics. Let Ψ_t be the Lagrange multiplier on the non-negativity constraint. The first-order condition for job openings is:

$$\begin{aligned} -\gamma + \Psi_t q_t + \beta \mathbb{E}_t \frac{\partial J_{t+1}}{\partial \mathcal{N}_{t+1}} \frac{\partial \mathcal{N}_{t+1}}{\partial \mathcal{V}_t} &= 0 \\ \frac{1}{1+r} \mathbb{E}_t \frac{\partial J_{t+1}}{\partial \mathcal{N}_{t+1}} &= \frac{\gamma}{q_t} - \Psi_t \end{aligned}$$

and the Kuhn–Tucker conditions are $q(\theta_t)\mathcal{V}_t \geq 0$, $\Psi_t \geq 0$, and $\Psi_t q(\theta_t)\mathcal{V}_t = 0$. Let $J_{\pi t} \equiv \partial J(\mathcal{N}_t)/\partial \mathcal{N}_t$. Then the firm's optimality condition for job vacancies can be written as:

$$\frac{\gamma}{q_t} - \Psi_t = \beta \mathbb{E}_t J_{\pi t+1}$$

Differentiating the firm's value function with respect to employment $\mathcal{N}_t$ and vacancies $\mathcal{V}_t$ we have:

$$\begin{aligned} J_{\pi t} &= x_t - w_t + (1-s)\beta \mathbb{E}_t J_{\pi t+1} \\ J_{vt} &= 0 \end{aligned}$$

yielding a discrete time job creation condition that coincides with equation (1.20) in the text when $\Psi_t = 0 \ \forall t$:

$$\frac{\gamma}{q_t} - \Psi_t = \beta \mathbb{E}_t \left[x_{t+1} - w_{t+1} + (1-s) \left(\frac{\gamma}{q_{t+1}} - \Psi_{t+1} \right) \right]$$

1.8.3 Credible wage bargaining in steady state

The worker offer in the steady state is obtained by combining (1.25) and (1.36) calculated at a steady state. We have

$$\begin{aligned} W_n^w &= \tfrac{1+r}{r+s} w + \tfrac{s}{r+s} W_u \\ W_n^w &= \varphi W_u + (1-\varphi)\Big(z + \tfrac{1}{1+r'} W_n^{w'} \Big) \end{aligned}$$

Combining them leads to

$$w = \bar{w}_0 + \frac{1-\varphi}{1+r'} w'$$

with

$$\bar{w}_0 = \frac{r+s}{1+r}\Big[\varphi W_u + (1-\varphi) z \Big] - \frac{s(\varphi + r')}{(1+r)(1+r')} W_u.$$

A sufficient condition for the coefficient to be positive is that $\varphi(1 - \frac{s}{M+r}) \geqslant \frac{s}{M+r}$ which turns out to be true for a sufficiently large number of sub-periods: when $M \longrightarrow +\infty$, the condition is $\varphi > 0$.

The firm's problem is similar. It combines (1.19) and (1.37) written in the steady state. This leads to:

$$\begin{aligned} J_\pi &= \tfrac{1+r}{r+s}(x - w) + \tfrac{s}{r+s} J_v \\ J_\pi^{w'} &= \varphi J_v + (1-\varphi)\Big(-\zeta + \tfrac{1}{1+r'} J_\pi^w \Big) \end{aligned}$$

Combining leads to

$$\frac{1-\varphi}{1+r'} w = \frac{r+s}{1+r}\Big[\varphi J_v - (1-\varphi)\zeta \Big] - \frac{s(\varphi + r')}{(1+r)(1+r')} J_v - \frac{\varphi + r'}{1+r'} x + w'$$

This can be written

$$w = \bar{w}_0' + \left(\frac{1-\varphi}{1+r'} \right)^{-1} w'$$

with

$$\bar{w}_0' = \frac{\varphi r(1+r') - sr'(1-\varphi)}{(1+r)(1-\varphi)} J_v - \frac{(1+r')(r+s)}{1+r} \zeta - \frac{\varphi + r'}{1-\varphi} x$$

or, using $J_v = 0$,

$$\bar{w}_0' = -\frac{(1+r')(r+s)}{1+r} \zeta - \frac{\varphi + r'}{1-\varphi} x < 0$$

Further, taking the limiting case $r' = 0$, we have

$$\bar{w}_0' = -\frac{(r+s)}{1+r} \zeta - \frac{\varphi}{1-\varphi} x$$

1.8.4 Endogenous job destruction: continuous time

$$rW_u = z + \theta q(\theta) \left\{ \int \max\left[W_n(a'), W_u\right] \mathrm{d}G(a') - W_u \right\} \tag{1.46}$$

$$rW_n(a) = w(a) + s(W_u - W_n(a)) + \mu \left\{ \int \max\left[W_n(a'), W_u\right] \mathrm{d}G(a') - W_n(a) \right\} \tag{1.47}$$

$$rJ_v = -\gamma + q(\theta) \left(\int \max\left[J_n(a'), J_v\right] \mathrm{d}G(a') - J_v \right) \tag{1.48}$$

$$rJ_\pi(a) = ax - w(a) + s(J_v - J_\pi(a)) + \mu \left\{ \int \max\left[J_\pi(a'), J_v\right] \mathrm{d}G(a') - J_\pi(a) \right\} \tag{1.49}$$

The match surplus, from the above Bellman equations, can be expressed as follows:

$$\begin{aligned}
r\Sigma_l^T(a) &= r\left[J_\pi(a) - J_v + W_n(a) - W_n\right] \\
r\Sigma_l^T(a) &= r\left[J_\pi(a) + W_n(a)\right] - rW_n - rJ_v \\
r\Sigma_l^T(a) &= ax - w(a) + (s+\mu)\left[J_v - J_\pi(a)\right] \\
&\quad + \mu \int \max\left[J_\pi(a') - J_v, 0\right] \mathrm{d}G(a') \\
&\quad + w(a) + (s+\mu)\left[W_u - W_n(a)\right] \\
&\quad + \mu \int \max\left[W_n(a') - W_u, 0\right] \mathrm{d}G(a') - rW_n - rJ_v \\
r\Sigma_l^T(a) &= ax - (s+\mu)\,\Sigma_l^T(a) + \mu \int \max\left[\Sigma_l^T(a'), 0\right] \mathrm{d}G(a') - rW_n - rJ_v \\
(r+s+\mu)\,\Sigma_l^T(a) &= ax + \mu \int \max\left[\Sigma_l^T(a'), 0\right] \mathrm{d}G(a') - rW_n - rJ_v
\end{aligned}$$

The surplus is strictly (linearly) increasing in the current idiosyncratic productivity draw a with slope $x/(r+s+\mu)$. Therefore there exists an a that we call A such that $\Sigma_l^T(A) = 0$, and a candidate solution for the surplus is $\Sigma_l^T(a) = x(a-A)/(r+s+\mu)$. Evaluating the surplus at the threshold A we have

$$\begin{aligned}
(r+s+\mu)\,\Sigma_l^T(A) = 0 &= Ax + \mu \int_A \Sigma_l^T(a') \mathrm{d}G(a') - rW_n - rJ_v \\
&= Ax + \frac{\mu x}{r+s+\mu} \int_A \left(a' - A\right) \mathrm{d}G(a') - rW_n - rJ_v
\end{aligned}$$

Free entry of firms in the labor market implies $J_v = 0$. Following similar steps as in the case with exogenous separation, the value of the outside option is $rW_u = z + \frac{\alpha_L}{1-\alpha_L}\gamma\theta$, such that we have the job destruction condition

$$z + \frac{\alpha_L}{1-\alpha_L}\gamma\theta = Ax + \frac{\mu x}{r+s+\mu} \int_A \left(a' - A\right) \mathrm{d}G(a') \tag{1.50}$$

Turning now to job creation, from the Bellman equation for J_v above and the free entry condition, we have

$$\begin{aligned}
\frac{\gamma}{q(\theta)} &= \int \max\left[J_\pi(a') - J_v, 0\right] \mathrm{d}G(a') \\
&= \int_A \left[J_\pi(a') - J_v\right] \mathrm{d}G(a') = (1-\alpha_L)\int_A \Sigma_l^T(a')\mathrm{d}G(a') \\
\frac{\gamma}{q(\theta)} &= \frac{(1-\alpha_L)x}{r+s+\mu}\int_A \left(a' - A\right)\mathrm{d}G(a')
\end{aligned}$$

1.8.5 Endogenous job destruction: discrete time

The discrete time model extends to endogenous job destruction as follows. New productivity is drawn each period. The Bellman equations are now, setting $s = 0$ is this extension,

$$\begin{aligned}
W_{ut} = z + \frac{1}{1+r}\mathbb{E}_t \Big\{ & f(\theta_t)\int \max\left[W_{nt+1}(a'), W_{ut+1}\right] dG(a') \\
& + (1 - f(\theta_t))\, W_{ut+1} \Big\}
\end{aligned} \tag{1.51}$$

$$W_{nt}(a) = w_t(a) + \frac{1}{1+r}\mathbb{E}_t\left\{\int \max\left[W_{nt+1}(a'), W_{ut+1}\right] dG(a')\right\} \tag{1.52}$$

$$J_{\pi t}(a_t) = ax_t - w_t(a) + \frac{1}{1+r}\mathbb{E}_t\left\{\int \max\left[J_{\pi t+1}(a'), J_{vt+1}\right] dG(a') + sJ_{vt+1}\right\} \tag{1.53}$$

$$\begin{aligned}
J_{vt} = -\gamma + q(\theta_t)\frac{1}{1+r}\mathbb{E}_t \Big\{ & q(\theta_t)\int \max\left[J_{\pi t+1}(a'), J_{vt+1}\right] dG(a') \\
& + (1 - q(\theta_t))\, J_{vt+1} \Big\}
\end{aligned} \tag{1.54}$$

It is easy to see that, as long as a_{t+1} is uncorrelated with a_t (that is, if the distribution from which a_{t+1} is drawn does not depend on a_t), then future values of W_{nt+1}, W_{ut+1}, $J_{\pi t+1}$, and J_{vt+1} are independent of a_t itself. Summing up $W_{nt}(a_t)$ and $J_{\pi t}(a_t)$ leads to a function independent of $w(a_t)$ and therefore, under the assumption of no serial correlation in a_t, this sum is linearly increasing in a_t. This implies the existence of a job destruction threshold A_t which is defined, as in the continuous time setup, as the productivity below which the joint surplus is negative. Using this job destruction cutoff and the free entry condition in the labor market, the previous Bellman equations become

$$\begin{aligned}
W_{ut} = z + \frac{1}{1+r}\mathbb{E}_t \Big\{ & f(\theta_t)\left[\int_{A_{t+1}} W_{nt+1}(a')dG(a') + \int^{A_{t+1}} W_{ut+1}dG(a')\right] \\
& + \left[1 - f(\theta_t)\right] W_{ut+1} \Big\}
\end{aligned} \tag{1.55}$$

$$W_{nt}(a) = w_t(a) + \frac{1}{1+r}\mathbb{E}_t\left[\int_{A_{t+1}} W_{nt+1}(a')dG(a') + \int^{A_{t+1}} W_{ut+1}dG(a')\right] \quad (1.56)$$

$$J_{\pi t}(a_t) = ax_t - w_t(a) + \frac{1}{1+r}\mathbb{E}_t\left[\int_{A_{t+1}} J_{\pi t+1}(a')dG(a')\right] \quad (1.57)$$

$$J_{vt} = 0 = -\gamma + q(\theta_t)\frac{1}{1+r}\mathbb{E}_t\left[\int_{A_{t+1}} J_{\pi t+1}(a')dG(a')\right] \quad (1.58)$$

Note that equation (1.58) can be expressed as

$$\frac{\gamma}{q(\theta_t)} = \frac{1}{1+r}\mathbb{E}_t\left[\int_{A_{t+1}} J_{\pi t+1}(a')dG(a')\right]$$

such that equation (1.57) becomes

$$J_{\pi t}(a_t) = ax_t - w_t(a) + \frac{\gamma}{q(\theta_t)}$$

which, combined with the previous expression, yields the following job creation condition:

$$\frac{\gamma}{q(\theta_t)} = \frac{1}{1+r}\mathbb{E}_t\left\{\int_{A_{t+1}} \left[a'x_{t+1} - w_{t+1}(a')\right]dG(a') + \left(1 - G(A_{t+1})\right)\frac{\gamma}{q(\theta_{t+1})}\right\} \quad (1.59)$$

To derive the job destruction condition we start with the surplus:

$$\begin{aligned}
\Sigma_{lt}^T(a) &= J_{\pi t}(a) - J_{vt} + W_{nt}(a) - W_{ut} \\
&= ax_t - w_t(a) + \frac{1}{1+r}\mathbb{E}_t\left[\int_{A_{t+1}} J_{\pi t+1}(a')dG(a')\right] - J_{vt} \\
&\quad + w_t(a) + \frac{1}{1+r}\mathbb{E}_t\left[\int_{A_{t+1}} W_{nt+1}(a')dG(a') + \int^{A_{t+1}} W_{ut+1}dG(a')\right] \\
&\quad - z - \frac{1}{1+r}\mathbb{E}_t\left\{f(\theta_t)\left[\int_{A_{t+1}} W_{nt+1}(a')dG(a') + \int^{A_{t+1}} W_{ut+1}dG(a')\right]\right. \\
&\quad \left. + (1 - f(\theta_t))\,W_{ut+1}\right\} \\
&= ax_t - z + \frac{1}{1+r}\mathbb{E}_t\left\{\int^{A_{t+1}} \left[J_{\pi t+1}(a') + W_{nt+1}(a') - W_{ut+1}\right]dG(a')\right\} \\
&\quad - \frac{f(\theta_t)}{1+r}\mathbb{E}_t\left\{\int_{A_{t+1}} \left[W_{nt+1}(a') - W_{ut+1}\right]dG(a')\right\} \\
\Sigma_{lt}^T(a) &= ax_t - z + \frac{1}{1+r}\mathbb{E}_t\left[\int^{A_{t+1}} \Sigma_{lt+1}^T(a')dG(a')\right] \\
&\quad - \alpha_L\frac{f(\theta_t)}{1+r}\mathbb{E}_t\left[\int_{A_{t+1}} \Sigma_{lt+1}^T(a')dG(a')\right]
\end{aligned}$$

in which the Nash sharing rule was used in the last step. With two additional steps we have

$$\Sigma_{lt}^{T}(a) = ax_t - z + \frac{1}{1+r}\mathbb{E}_t\left[\int^{A_{t+1}} \Sigma_{lt+1}^{T}(a')dG(a')\right] - \frac{\alpha_L}{1-\alpha_L}\gamma\theta_t$$

which is similar to the continuous time equation for the surplus. Evaluating the equation at $\Sigma_{lt}^{T}(A_t) = 0$:

$$0 = A_t x_t - z + \frac{1}{1+r}\mathbb{E}_t\left[\int^{A_{t+1}} \Sigma_{lt+1}^{T}(a')dG(a')\right] - \frac{\alpha_L}{1-\alpha_L}\gamma\theta_t$$

$$0 = A_t x_t + \frac{1}{1-\alpha_L}\frac{\gamma}{q(\theta_t)} - z - \frac{\alpha_L}{1-\alpha_L}\gamma\theta_t \tag{1.60}$$

which is the discrete time job destruction condition.

2 Business cycle properties

The previous chapter derived the new concepts central to the analysis of labor markets with search frictions, equilibrium job creation, and a locus of stationary combinations of unemployment and vacancies, or a Beveridge curve. We studied the properties of a steady-state equilibrium. In this chapter we develop a set of tools to study stochastic fluctuations driven by shocks to productivity. We are therefore going to study the transitional dynamics of the endogenous variables in the model of chapter 1, and assess the model's ability to fit the empirical data of the labor market over the business cycle. The original Real Business Cycle (RBC) paradigm has little to say with respect to fluctuations in unemployment over the business cycle. At its core is the neoclassical growth model with Walrasian labor markets in which supply always equals demand. Of course, improvements to these approaches can and have been undertaken. Nonetheless, it is more satisfactory to start from a framework where unemployment exists as a natural concept, as in the approach taken here. This is all the more important as movements in labor market variables are very volatile over the business cycle, even more so than most prominent macroeconomic variables such as aggregate output or consumption. "Fixing" unemployment in a model where it does not exist to start with cannot be the right solution. This is why a concerted effort to integrate search labor markets into business cycle analysis began in the late 1990s, and much has been learned about the great strengths, and relative weaknesses, of the model to fit the patterns in the data. This chapter reviews these developments by adapting the model developed in chapter 1.

Time will be discrete and labor productivity will follow a stationary stochastic process. Before analyzing the dynamics of the model we discuss a general approach to determining the value of model parameters. This calibration exercise matches a set of various empirical moments described in this chapter. We illustrate in section 2.1 that the dynamic properties of the benchmark model do not fit the data in terms of the volatility of unemployment, job vacancies, or labor market tightness. We then proceed to discuss different approaches to improve the fit of the model to the data. Section 2.3 explores two potential improvements. First, it explores the role of alternative wage setting mechanisms with more wage rigidity. Second, it introduces a fixed cost of job creation. Both aspects amplify the magnitude of cyclical fluctuations of labor market variables and get closer to the empirical volatility. We will also emphasize in Section 2.4 how the congestion effects in the matching process generate rich nonlinear dynamics that matter for approaching a calibration strategy and the choosing a numerical solution method.

2.1 Dynamics of the benchmark model

A useful starting point for understanding what features of the environment will amplify or attenuate the cyclical dynamics of the labor market in the search and matching environment is a local approximation of the job creation condition (1.20) around the deterministic steady state. This gives a local sense of the channels that can amplify or attenuate the effects of an exogenous shock to the model, a productivity shock for example. However, the quantitative properties of the model can only be properly assessed with a nonlinear solution algorithm, as will be shown below, as the dynamics of the model are highly nonlinear.

2.1.1 Loglinearization of the job creation condition

Let x_t be the time-varying stochastic value of productivity. It evolves around a stationary value x. Denote proportional deviations of x_t around its deterministic steady state as $\hat{x}_t \equiv (x_t - x)/x$. Similarly $\widehat{\theta_t}$ will denote proportional deviations of labor market tightness. We first assume for this exercise that the wage is fixed at some level $\bar{w}$ within the bargaining set. Second, over the range of observed fluctations in θ_t, the elasticity $\eta_L(\theta_t)$ fluctuates very little. We therefor assume for this exercise that the elasticity of the matching function $\eta_L(\theta)$ is a constant η_L.

Using equation (1.19), an approximation of the current deviation of labor market tightness from its steady state is the product of three terms, including expected future deviations of productivity from its steady state:

Log-linearization around the steady state of the job creation condition with a fixed wage:

$$\widehat{\theta_t} = \frac{1}{\eta_L} \times \frac{x}{x-\bar{w}} \times \frac{r+s}{1+r}\mathbb{E}_t\left[\sum_{i=0}\left(\frac{1-s}{1+r}\right)^i \widehat{x_{t+1+i}}\right] \tag{2.1}$$

See the steps in the chapter appendix. By the first element in (2.1), the response of equilibrium labor market tightness to changes in labor productivity is decreasing in the elasticity of the matching function with respect to unemployment. This captures changes in the congestion firms face in the labor market when trying to hire workers. Following an increase in productivity, firms enter the labor market thereby increasing market tightness and the average duration of search needed to fill a vacancy. The amount of entry of vacancies depends on the speed at which recruiting costs $\gamma/q(\theta)$ increase. This is inversely related to the elasticity of the matching function, η_L. Congestion is thus a natural dampening mechanism of fluctuations in the labor search model. By the second element, the response of market tightness is decreasing in the magnitude of the profit flow $x - \bar{w}$. Small profits are sensitive to changes in productivity, leading to greater variation in the incentives for firms to post job vacancies following a productivity shock. Allowing for the wage to adjust with changes in productivity, however, moderates fluctuations in profits and labor market tightness. The chapter appendix presents an expression similar to that of equation (2.1) under the assumption of Nash wages.

We can therefore quantify the amount of amplification in the response of labor market tightness to a deviation of productivity that arises from the congestion in the matching process in the labor market and the size of the labor surplus:

Amplification of labor market tightness due to labor market congestion and the size of profit flows:

$$\frac{1}{\eta_L}\frac{x}{x-\bar{w}} \tag{2.2}$$

2.1.2 Asymmetries in the cycle

Movements in labor market tightness affect the unemployment rate through the job finding rate $f(\theta_t)$. Large movements in unemployment over the business cycle require a volatile labor market tightness that induces large swings in the job finding rate. This is where the usefulness of the linear approximation for understanding the dynamics of the model comes to an end. The curvature of the matching function, and its concavity in particular, means that the increases in unemployment during recessions will be pronounced, while the declines during expansions will be modest. We illustrate this in figure 2.1 by plotting in the first panel the job finding rate as a function of labor market tightness. We compare stationary states of different productivity levels and, using the

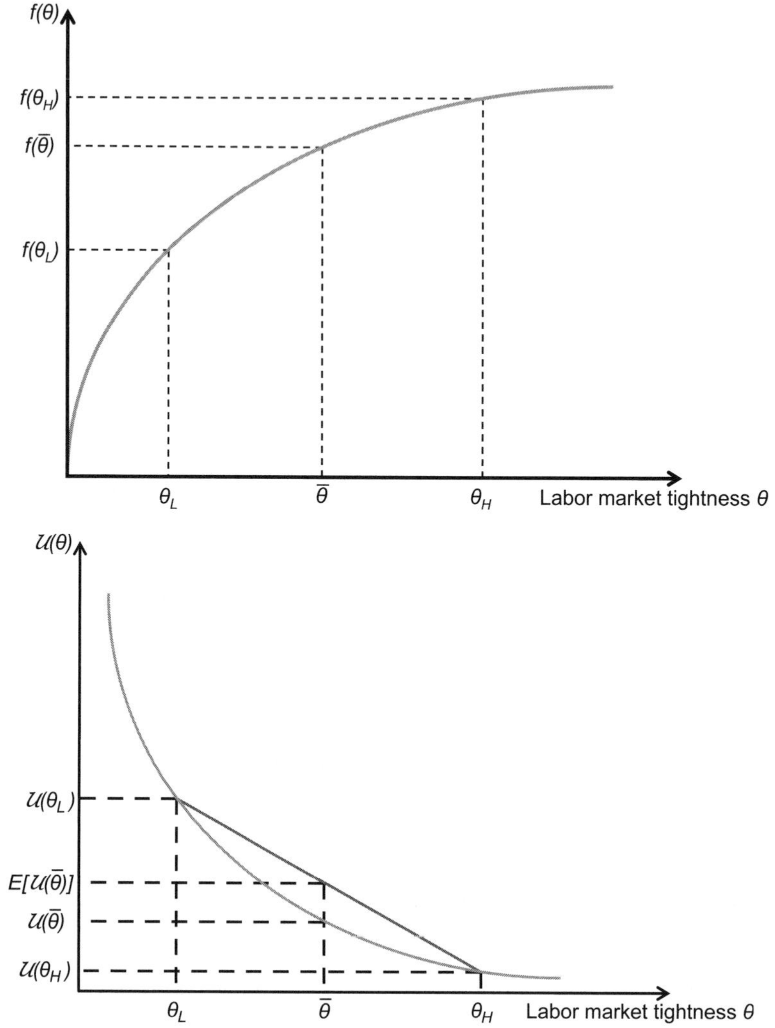

Figure 2.1

The hiring rate at the average value of $\theta = \bar{\theta}$ is below the average hiring rate over the cycle; the unemployment rate at the average value of θ is above the average value of unemployment over the cycle

steady-state expression $\mathcal{U}(\theta) = s/(s+f(\theta))$, we show the relation of market tightness to unemployment in the second panel. The figure focuses on three possible values for market tightness: low, denoted θ_L; steady state, denoted $\bar{\theta}$; and high, denoted θ_H. High and low market tightness are purposefully chosen as symmetric around steady-state market tightness. This is consistent with the fact that the model delivers symmetric fluctuations in labor market tightness in response to symmetric technology shocks around its long-term mean in the benchmark search model.

As the economy fluctuates between high and low unemployment, the average rate of unemployment $E[\mathcal{U}(\theta)]$ is strictly greater than steady-state unemployment $\mathcal{U}(\bar{\theta})$. The convexity of the unemployment–labor market tightness relationship is due to the congestion in the matching function, which implies a job finding rate $f(\theta)$ that is concave in labor market tightness (see the top panel of figure 2.1). The job finding rate decreases more as θ drops from its steady state to θ_L than it increases when θ rises to θ_H. The response of unemployment to a symmetric change in θ is asymmetric, the direction of the asymmetry going toward a larger increase in unemployment relative to the decline.

2.2 A calibration

This calibration starts with a few words of caution. It is common practice in macroeconomics to use steady-state relationships to calibrate model parameters to the data. This practice is innocuous in the RBC paradigm as the neoclassical growth model is approximately linear in a range around the point of approximation relevant for business cycles. However, in the search economies of this book, the practice has consequences. In particular, the stochastic mean unemployment, $E(\mathcal{U})$, differs significantly from its steady-state value. We therefore use the model's simulated moments, matching them to empirical moments in the calibration procedure.

2.2.1 Calibrated parameters

Table 2.1 lists the parameter values for a monthly calibration of the benchmark model to US data over the period from January 1951 to December 2012. The strategy for each parameter is as follows, with some references to agreements and disagreements in the literature regarding specific values.

Discounting and productivity The time discount rate r is set to 4% per annum, which is the average return on a 3-month US Treasury bill. Labor productivity x is assumed to follow an AR(1) process in logs: $\log x_t = \rho_x \log x_{t-1} + \sigma_x \epsilon_t$, where $\rho_x \in (0,1)$ is a persistence parameter, $\sigma_x > 0$ is the conditional volatility, and ϵ_t is a standard normal shock. To parameterize the log labor productivity process, we set its persistence, ρ_x, to a standard value of $0.95^{1/3}$. The conditional volatility, σ_x, is calibrated to match the standard deviation of labor productivity in the data. Labor productivity is measured as

Table 2.1
Parameter values in the monthly US calibration of the benchmark model

	Parameter	Value		Reference or Target
Technology:				
persistence parameter	ρ_x	$0.95^{1/3}$	$\rightarrow$	BLS labor productivity
standard deviation	σ_x	0.00625	$\rightarrow$	BLS labor productivity
Labor market:				
job separation rate	s	0.035	$\rightarrow$	JOLTS
matching curvature	ν_L	1.25	$\rightarrow$	den Haan et al. (2000)
vacancy cost	γ	0.26	$\rightarrow$	Unemployment rate
worker bargaining weight	α_L	0.50	$\rightarrow$	Equal surplus sharing
nonemployment value	z	0.71	$\rightarrow$	Hall and Milgrom (2008)

seasonally adjusted real average output per worker in the nonfarm business sector detrended with a Hodrick–Prescott (Hodrick and Prescott, 1997) filter. A value of 0.00625 for σ_x matches the standard deviation of 0.013 in the data.

Matching function parameters We adopt the matching function $\mathcal{M}_L = \mathcal{V}_t\mathcal{U}_t/\left(\mathcal{V}_t^{\nu_L} + \mathcal{U}_t^{\nu_L}\right)^{1/\nu_L}$, where $\nu_L > 0$, and set $\nu_L = 1.25$ as in den Haan et al. (2000). The appealing feature of this functional form is that the meeting rates $f(\theta_t)$ and $q(\theta_t)$ are bounded between 0 and 1. This is of practical concern in quantitative applications as the alternative Cobb–Douglas function leads to some numerical complications in that the bounds must be taken into account when solving and simulating the model. However, business cycle moments of the model using either functional form are similar. Given the calibration of the model, the elasticity of matching with respect to unemployment, $\eta_L(\theta_t)$, will average about 0.50 in simulations. This is within the range of the survey of empirical estimates of the matching function found in Petrongolo and Pissarides (2001).

Flow value of unemployment z The value of z involves two components: a value of leisure and nonmarket activities l, and the value of unemployment benefits b. On the one hand, Mulligan (2012) estimates a median replacement rate for nonemployment income compared to previous employment earnings of 63% in the US. This covers a variety of income support programs available to US workers. On the other hand, Chodorow-Reich and Karabarbounis (2015) conclude that, given the proportion of individuals eligible for unemployment and other benefit programs in the United States, the value of the benefits portion in a macroeconomic model is closer to 5% of average labor productivity. Allowing for a leisure component l in the flow value of unemployment z permits a calibration of z above the replacement value of unemployment benefits. Hagedorn and Manovskii (2008), for instance, argue that in a perfectly competitive labor market, z should be close to the value of employment. As such, z should be close to unity, which is the marginal product of labor in the model. Hall and Milgrom (2008) perform a calculation based on standard assumptions on preferences for the value of leisure, and conclude on a value for z of 0.71, which we adopt here.

Job separation rate s We set the job separation rate, s, to 3.5%, based on the Bureau of Labor Statistic's Job Openings and Labor Turnover Survey (JOLTS).

Vacancy costs γ In this calibration γ is set such that the mean rate of unemployment in the model corresponds to the empirical sample mean of 5.80 percent. This results in a value of $\gamma = 0.26$. Silva and Toledo (2009) report that recruiting costs are 14 percent of quarterly pay per hire, or 0.4 months of pay per hire, based on data collected by Price waterhouse Coopers. Merz and Yashiv (2007) estimate the marginal costs of hiring to be 1.48 times the average output per worker with a standard error of 0.57, indicating a wide range of empirically plausible values. The model average for $\gamma/(q_t \times w_t)$ of 0.35 is well below their estimates. If the matching function had been assumed to be Cobb–Douglas, then the additional level parameter in the matching function, χ_L, would be calibrated to a target mean unemployment rate, and the average cost of recruiting would be used as a target for γ.

Bargaining weight α_L The Nash bargaining weight affects the importance of the time-varying components x_t and θ_t in the wage. A low value of α_L places most weight on the time-invariant flow value of unemployment z. In this case, the equilibrium wage fluctuates little over the business cycle. A high value of α_L allows productivity x_t and labor market tightness θ_t to make the wage pro-cyclical, thereby dampening fluctuations in the profit flow $x_t - w_t$ from changes in labor productivity. Values in the literature are as dispersed as $\alpha_L = 0.72$ in Shimer (2005) and $\alpha_L = 0.052$ in Hagedorn and Manovskii (2008). We adopt a symmetric sharing parameterization in the benchmark model, setting $\alpha_L = 0.5$. In later chapters (6 and 8), we will use the empirical elasticity of wages to productivity to calibrate this parameter.

2.2.2 The business cycle in the calibrated model

The business cycle moments for labor market variables in the US time series in the postwar sample are presented in panel A of table 2.2. Volatility and

Table 2.2
Labor market moments—quarterly data and model

	Panel A: Data 1951:I–2012:IV					Panel B: Benchmark Model			
	$\mathcal{U}$	$\mathcal{V}$	θ	x		$\mathcal{U}$	$\mathcal{V}$	θ	x
Standard deviation	0.127	0.134	0.234	0.013		0.022	0.028	0.048	0.013
Autocorrelation	0.597	0.647	0.622	0.298		0.330	−0.110	0.182	0.183
Correlation matrix		−0.900	−0.898	−0.297	$\mathcal{U}$		−0.779	−0.928	−0.922
			0.938	0.394	$\mathcal{V}$			0.956	0.956
				0.302	θ				0.997

	Panel C: Nash Wage + Small Labor Surplus					Panel D: Credible Bargaining			
	$\mathcal{U}$	$\mathcal{V}$	θ	x		$\mathcal{U}$	$\mathcal{V}$	θ	x
Standard deviation	0.046	0.057	0.096	0.013		0.045	0.056	0.094	0.013
Autocorrelation	0.342	−0.108	0.184	0.184		0.332	−0.113	0.178	0.179
Correlation matrix		−0.745	−0.918	−0.885	$\mathcal{U}$		−0.752	−0.920	−0.894
			0.948	0.942	$\mathcal{V}$			0.949	0.947
				0.981	θ				0.986

	Panel E: Nash Wage + Fixed Hiring Costs					Panel F: Credible Bargaining + Fixed Hiring Costs			
	$\mathcal{U}$	$\mathcal{V}$	θ	x		$\mathcal{U}$	$\mathcal{V}$	θ	x
Standard deviation	0.127	0.165	0.238	0.013		0.127	0.143	0.251	0.013
Autocorrelation	0.341	−0.081	0.179	0.180		0.354	−0.104	0.177	0.180
Correlation matrix		−0.731	−0.905	−0.893	$\mathcal{U}$		−0.696	−0.906	−0.855
			0.950	0.954	$\mathcal{V}$			0.941	0.940
				0.997	θ				0.974

Panel A reports the moments for the US postwar data; see appendix 2.6.2 for details. Panel B takes the quarterly averages of simulated monthly $\mathcal{U}, \mathcal{V}$, and x to convert to quarterly series. We implement the same procedure as in panel A on the quarterly series, and report cross-simulation averages.

co-movement are measured from a variable's HP-filtered cyclical component. The standard deviations over the business cycle of the unemployment rate, job vacancies, and labor market tightness are 0.13, 0.13, and 0.23, respectively. Unemployment and vacancies have a contemporaneous correlation of -0.90, indicating a downward-sloping Beveridge curve over the business cycle. The second row of panel A reports the first-order autocorrelation for the growth rates of the variables in question. We emphasize the use of growth rates, rather than HP filtered data, for measuring autocorrelation in time series. The HP filter introduces a phase shift distorting the auto-covariance function which, as Cogley and Nason (1995) demonstrate, induces spurious autocorrelations. First differences do not suffer from this concern. The series are highly persistent at the first lag: the coefficients of autocorrelation for unemployment, vacancies, and labor market tightness are, respectively, 0.60, 0.65, and 0.62. Finally, the correlation between labor productivity and unemployment is -0.30, a moderate negative correlation.

Panel B reports the moments of simulated data for the benchmark model using the parameters values of table 2.1. The volatility of unemployment, 0.02, is well below the data. The same is true for the volatilities of job vacancies and labor market tightness, 0.03 and 0.05, respectively. The second row of panel B reports the first order autocorrelation for growth rates of the variables in question: 0.33, -0.11, and 0.18. Thus the model fails on a second dimension, that of persistence. Finally, the correlation between unemployment and productivity, -0.92, is much stronger in the benchmark model than in the data.

The reasons behind these results are easily understood by examining figure 2.2, a graphical representation of the equilibrium in the labor market. An increase in productivity shifts the job creation curve up, leading to more entry in the labor market by firms, and an upwards movement in the wage along the Nash wage curve from θ_0 to θ'. Simultaneously, there is an increase in the wage curve. This increase is in proportion α_L of the change in productivity, and there is a movement up the wage curve with the increase in labor market tightness. The rise in wages, dampening any increase in the profit flow from a filled job, limits the amount of entry by firms in the labor market. The new equilibrium tightness θ_1 is below θ'. If the movement in the wage curve is sufficiently large it may even neutralize all changes in the incentives for firms to post vacancies, leaving labor market tightness unchanged. This insight has led to extensive research into mechanisms that amplify the response of labor market tightness to productivity shocks. We begin to explore these next.

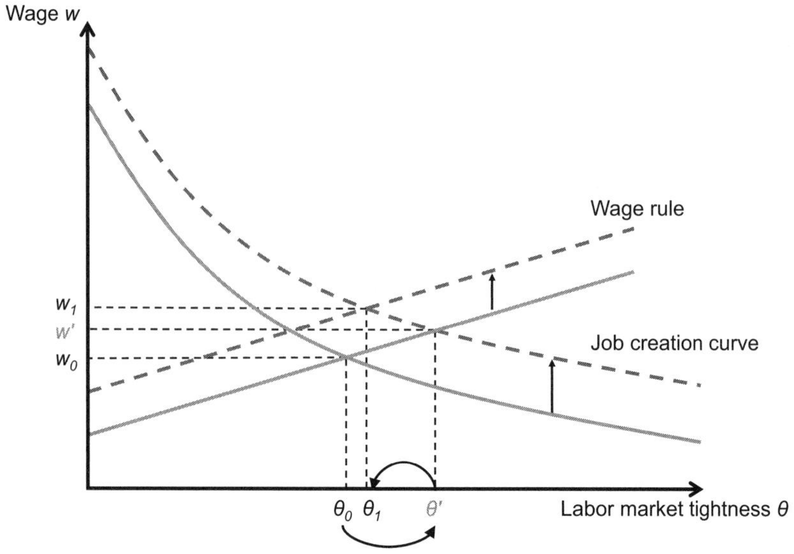

Figure 2.2
Shifts of the wage curve and the job creation curve in response to an increase in productivity

2.3 Volatility in alternative structures

As we outlined earlier in the discussion around equation (2.1), a large labor surplus, along with a pro-cyclical wage that absorbs much of the change in labor productivity, limits volatility in labor market tightness, job creation, and unemployment over the business cycle. We first present a calibration with a small labor surplus, achieved by assuming a larger flow value of nonemployment activities for the worker, z. Next, we draw on the discussion of alternative wage setting mechanisms at the end of chapter 1. In particular, the credible bargaining wage discussed in section 1.5 depends much less on the asset value of unemployment, the worker's outside option, than the Nash wage equation (1.30). This provides a mechanism to amplify the effects of productivity shocks. However, as we will see, this supplementary rigidity does not, on its own, generate enough amplification to match the volatility of labor market variables in the data.

We will then introduce another channel for amplification stemming from the cost side of job creation, rather than the profit flows from a filled vacancy. The inclusion of a fixed recruiting cost that does not depend on labor market tightness increases the response of the ratio of vacancies to unemployment to a given change in the benefit from hiring a worker as it introduces some rigidity in the average cost of job creation. This fixed component in the structure of job creation costs can be micro-founded by financial market imperfections, as will be studied in part II.

2.3.1 Small labor surplus

In section 2.1 we saw that the response of labor market tightness was decreasing in the size of the surplus in the labor market. In panel C of table 2.2 we increase the flow value of nonemployment z up to 0.85, close to the average value of labor market productivity, while keeping the bargaining strength of workers α_L constant at 0.5. All other parameters remain identical with the exception of the flow vacancy posting cost. This parameter is adjusted to match the same unemployment rate as in the benchmark model, which requires $\gamma = 0.13$.

Under this small labor surplus assumption, the volatility of labor market tightness is now 0.10, up from 0.05 in the baseline calibration. The intuition is simple: narrowing the gap between the flow value of nonmarket activities and market productivity causes even small changes in productivity to induce proportionally large changes in the surplus from hiring labor. This amplifies the effect of productivity shocks on θ_t over the business cycle by a factor of two. The volatility of unemployment increases from 0.02 to 0.05. Nonetheless, these moments still fall short of the data, and there is a limit in the ability of this approach to bridge the gap with the data. In fact, we cannot go beyond $z = 0.85$. Above this value the random draws of negative productivity frequently imply a negative value of job vacancies. The model hits the lower bound of job vacancies, $\mathcal{V} = 0$. If we went above $z = 0.85$, the volatility of unemployment would increase substantially as we continue to increase z, but given that vacancies are flat at zero over long periods of time, there is very little additional increase in the volatility of θ_t. In addition, episodes with no vacancy posting attenuate the correlation between unemployment and vacancies, pushing it further away from the empirical value of -0.90. We revisit this issue in greater detail in section 2.4.3.

2.3.2 Credible bargaining

This alternative to Nash bargaining, which depends less on labor market outcomes, leads to less volatile wages. The wage becomes less responsive to current labor market tightness, as long as bargaining is not very likely to breakdown. There are two additional parameters in this extension: the negotiation breakdown probability φ, and the cost of delaying to the firm ζ. We adapt the parameter values in Hall and Milgrom (2008) to a monthly frequency, applying a probability of breakdown in bargaining $\varphi = 0.1$, and setting the delaying cost parameter $\zeta = 0.25$. In addition, in order to make the results of both extensions more comparable, we reduce the flow value of unemployment to 0.60 such that $\zeta + z = 0.85$, the value of nonemployment in the small surplus calibration. As in the other calibrations, the value of γ is adjusted to 0.87 in order to match the mean rate of unemployment.

The resulting business cycle moments of labor market variables are presented in panel D of table 2.2. The volatility of unemployment increases from 0.02 to 0.05. This is an amplification factor, again, of about two. The volatilities of job vacancies and labor market tightness are now 0.06 and 0.09, compared to 0.03 and 0.05 in the benchmark calibration of panel B.

2.3.3 Entry costs and amplification

The costs of recruiting have been modeled as a per period vacancy posting cost γ, resulting in an average cost of recruiting a worker, $\gamma/q(\theta_t)$, that is very much tied to the tightness of the labor market. An increase in the congestion of the market—a decrease in the meeting probability q due to an increase in θ—reduces the incentive to recruit an unemployed worker by making it more costly to do so. This naturally dampens the response of labor market tightness and job creation to productivity shocks. However, certain costs involved in creating jobs do not depend on the state of the labor market. Creating a position may require securing finance from creditors as a first step in expanding productive capacity, or firms may need to find customers in goods markets before hiring workers. Either of these examples will introduce an element to job creation that is (quasi-)independent of the state of the labor market, as we will see in part II. For the moment we assume a job creation cost structure with a fixed post-match creation cost $C > 0$ to be payed upon hiring a worker—contrary to the cost of entering paid before the match γ. The resulting average cost of recruiting, $\gamma/q(\theta_t) + C$, is now augmented with C. The overall cost of recruiting, with the fixed cost, is less sensitive to changes in labor market tightness θ_t.

In equilibrium, the job creation condition (1.20) becomes:

Job creation condition with fixed entry costs:

$$\frac{\gamma}{q(\theta_t)} + C = \frac{1}{1+r}\mathbb{E}_t\left[x_{t+1} - w_{t+1} + (1-s)\left(\frac{\gamma}{q(\theta_{t+1})} + C\right)\right] \tag{2.3}$$

Under the assumption of a fixed wage, we take a log-linear approximation around the deterministic steady state and define an amplification factor that reveals that the response of labor market tightness to a productivity shock is increasing in C:

Log-linearization (around the steady state) of the job creation condition with additional entry costs:

$$\widehat{\theta}_t = \frac{1}{\eta_L} \times \frac{x}{x - \bar{w} - (r+s)C} \times \frac{r+s}{1+r}\mathbb{E}_t\left[\sum_{i=0}\left(\frac{1-s}{1+r}\right)^i \widehat{x}_{t+1+i}\right] \tag{2.4}$$

Amplification due to labor frictions with fixed wage and entry cost C:

$$\frac{1}{\eta_L}\frac{x}{x - \bar{w} - (r+s)C} \tag{2.5}$$

The expression for the multiplier shows that the amplifying effect of fixed job creation costs and a small labor surplus, that is, a small wedge between productivity and wage, have something in common. Both diminish the size of the surplus to firms entering the labor market. Therefore, this makes the entry decision more sensitive to productivity shocks. This small surplus principle is in fact quite general. It will arise again in part II, chapter 5 when firms must share the rents from a created job with creditors, and again in chapter 7, when firms are splitting the rents with consumers in the goods market.

Calibration and business cycles

We use this last amplifying element to match the volatility of unemployment of 0.127 in both the Nash wage and the credible bargaining wage settings. Each assumption on wage determination implies a different value of C to match the target empirical moments. This exercise serves to illustrate the amount of amplification that the fixed cost on job creation can achieve.

Under Nash bargaining, with business cycle moments presented in panel E of table 2.2, the required fixed cost's $C = 0.19$. The variable cost component γ equals 0.02. The volatilities of labor market tightness and job vacancies are both close to the data, which is what allows the model to match the volatility of unemployment in the data. In panel F, under credible wage bargaining and fixed costs, the fixed cost required to obtain a similar volatility of labor market tightness is $C = 0.77$, with $\gamma = 0.40$. The volatility of unemployment matches the data by design, and the volatilities of job vacancies and labor market tightness are close to the data as well.

In summary, different modeling elements affect the dynamics of job creation. Reducing the flow profits from hiring labor, as well as introducing rigidities in wages and job creation costs will bring the model closer to matching the volatilities of labor market variables observed in the data. However, even though each of these mechanisms achieves amplification of shocks, the model still falls short of generating endogenous persistence in labor market variables. Measured as the autocorrelations of their growth rate, these are typically between 0.5 and 0.6 in the data (see panel A for unemployment, vacancies, and labor market tightness), whereas they are instead always between -0.1 and 0.3 in any of panels B to F. Part II, in chapters 6 and 8, provides further foundations for propagation based on frictions in credit market and goods markets that will not only address the issue of volatility but also the challenge of persistence. For the moment we discuss the dynamics of the labor market further by looking at the impulse response functions of the model variables to a productivity shock.

2.4 Nonlinear dynamics in the labor market

Markets with search frictions have different deterministic steady state values and average variables with stochastic fluctuations, as compared to the standard RBC models. This has additional consequences and implications for the dynamics of the model that are examined in detail in this section. The rate at which workers find a job, $f(\theta_t)$, falls rapidly during recessions as market tightness declines. During an economic expansion with increasing labor market tightness, workers face intensifying congestion when searching for job vacancies, and a decelerating rise in the job finding rate. The curvature of the matching function thus generates asymmetric business cycle fluctuations in hiring and unemployment, and obtaining rich dynamics requires the right numerical methods for solving the model. In particular, approximate solutions such as log-linear approximations are highly inaccurate. We take this up in subsection 2.4.1. Second, a common tool for studying the dynamics of macroeconomic models, impulse response functions to exogenous shocks, depend in economically interesting ways on the state of the economy when a shock hits. We take this up in subsection 2.4.2. Third, the model can help with understanding higher moments of the data, such as spikes in unemployment during recessions or the skewness in the time series for unemployment.

2.4.1 Solving models with search frictions

The literature studying business cycles has, for the most part, relied on log-linearization around a deterministic steady state to quantify the dynamic properties of macroeconomic models. In order to illustrate the degree of inaccuracy from this approach for a search and matching model of the labor market, we first solve the same model in two different ways, with a global (projection) method and local (log-linearization), we then subject both solutions to a same path of labor productivity. Figure 2.3 plots the two resulting paths of unemployment with the solid line being the results from an accurate global method, and the dashed line the log-linear approximation. The accurate solution, which fully takes into account the curvature of the matching function for the evolution of unemployment as labor market tightness changes over time, has clear spikes in unemployment during recessions. This is just as in the data. These spikes are entirely absent in the path generated by the linear approximation of the model. One dramatic example of this inaccuracy occurs around period 400. While the log-linear approximation concludes that unemployment will peak at 8% during that particular contraction, the correct answer is an unemployment that peaks above 16%. These are two significantly different business cycle downturns. The approximation fails when it is most interesting and important: during recessions.

These large inaccuracies have important consequences for the dynamic properties of the model. A first-order approximation underestimates the volatility

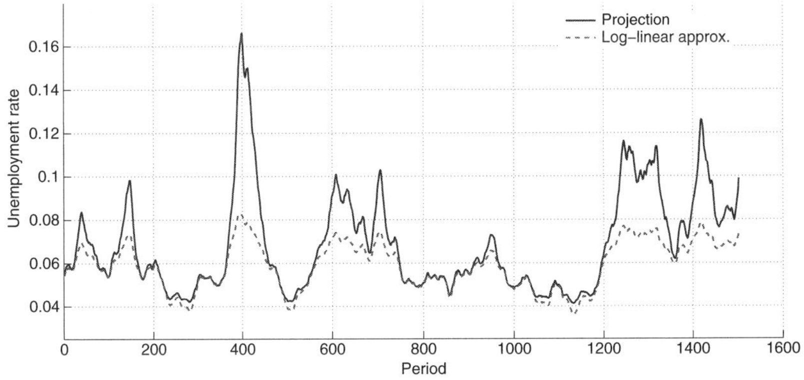

Figure 2.3

The difference between the global approximation (projection) and the log-linear approximation of the model: the example of the path of unemployment

of unemployment and overestimates the negative correlation between unemployment and vacancies, the slope of the Beveridge curve. This can be seen in table 2.3. The first set of columns follows a calibration in the spirit of the "small labor surplus" assumption, that is, increasing the value of nonemployment z close enough to the mean of productivity such that the model reaches a level of volatility in unemployment similar to the data. However, it is a log-linear approximation that is solved, and the dynamics are those of the approximation of the model with a search frictional labor market. The second set of columns uses a global method to solve the model with the same set of parameters. The volatility of unemployment is three times greater in panel B than in panel A, and the correlation between unemployment and vacancies is nearly halved.

2.4.2 Impulse response functions

Impulse responses to shocks are a useful tools and discuss to illustrate and examine the dynamics of a model. In this section we present the responses of labor market tightness, job vacancies, and unemployment to a positive one standard deviation shock to labor productivity. The impulse responses are plotted in figure 2.4. In addition, the panels of figure 2.4 plot the responses from three different initial points in the model's state space of unemployment: bad, median, and good economies. The bad economy is the 5th percentile of the model's stationary distribution of unemployment; the unemployment rate starts at $\mathcal{U}_t = 11.5\%$. The median economy is the median value of unemployment $\mathcal{U}_t = 5.41\%$. Finally, the good economy is the 95th percentile, when $\mathcal{U}_t = 4.75\%$.

Consider a shock during a midpoint of a business cycle, when unemployment is at its median. The strongest increase in labor market tightness θ_t is

Table 2.3
Labor market moments—the inaccuracy of local approximations

	Log-linear approximation					Global solution method			
	$\mathcal{U}$	$\mathcal{V}$	θ	x		$\mathcal{U}$	$\mathcal{V}$	θ	x
Standard deviation	0.108	0.115	0.291	0.013		0.291	0.158	0.216	0.013
Correlation matrix		−0.861	−0.818	−0.934	$\mathcal{U}$		−0.496	−0.542	−0.593
			0.817	0.986	$\mathcal{V}$			0.841	0.873
				0.842	θ				0.992

We take the quarterly averages of the monthly series for $\mathcal{U}, \mathcal{V}$, and x, and detrend the quarterly series using an HP-filter with a smoothing parameter of 1,600.

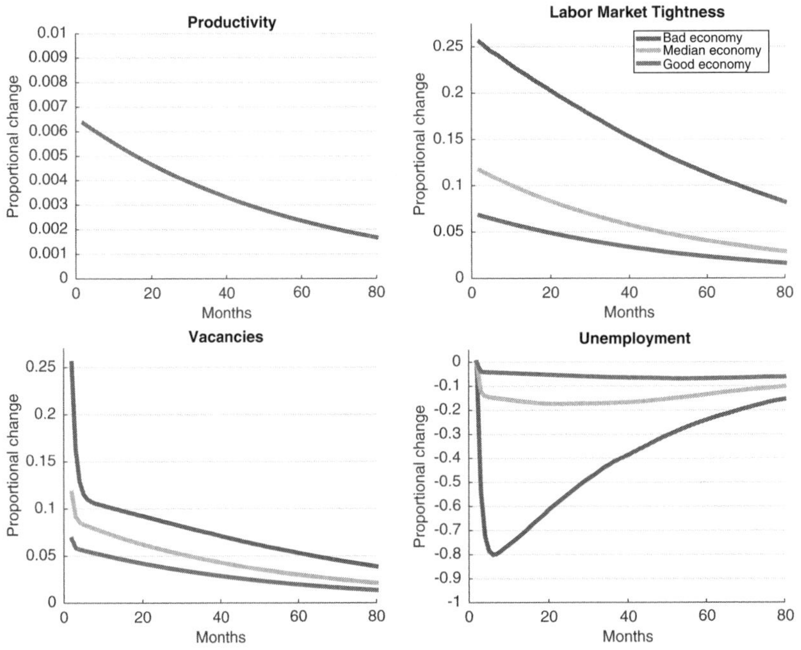

Figure 2.4

Asymmetries in the cycle: impulse responses to a positive one standard deviation productivity shock

contemporaneous to the shock, returning to trend at the same rate as labor productivity. Job vacancies exhibit a pronounced decline following the initial jump, then a progressive return to trend. This difference in the response relative to that of market tightness is explained by the response of the unemployment rate. The rise in market tightness pushes job creation above job destruction, and the unemployment rate declines. Job vacancies at a given level of labor productivity are increasing in unemployment: it is relatively easier to find a job seeker, and therefore more vacancies are posted. Thus during the first several months following the productivity shock, job vacancies are also responding to the sharp decline in unemployment. In the subsequent months, as job creation no longer exceeds than job destruction, unemployment and job vacancies follow a similar paths back towards their trends.

Consider now the responses to the same shock when it occurs in either the good or the bad state of the economy. In the good state of the economy, when the unemployment rate is 4.50%, there is very little response of labor market tightness following a productivity shock. In the bad state of the economy, when the unemployment rate is 11.5%, the same shock causes a significantly larger response of labor market tightness. The implications for the dynamics of unemployment are stark. The same innovation leads to a very strong response of unemployment when the economy is in a recession, and almost no response when the economy is in an expansion.

The asymmetry in the responses lies in the properties of the matching function. Job vacancies and unemployment are complementary in producing new meetings per unit of time. When unemployment is low, an additional job vacancy has a small effect on the number of matches and the unemployment rate. Conversely, when unemployment is high, an additional job vacancy has a large effect on the number of matches and the unemployment rate. This means that the dynamics of the labor market are more sensitive to shocks when the labor market is slack, in the sense of having a higher than usual unemployment rate, than when it is tight. The same is then true for the overall macroeconomy with a search frictional labor market.

2.4.3 Other nonlinearities: the small surplus assumption and the zero bound for vacancies

Firms enter the labor market, posting job vacancies, as long as the expected benefit from filling the job exceeds the cost of posting a vacancy. If the cost γ is greater than $\mathbb{E}_t[J_{\pi t+1}]$, then there is no surplus to entering and the result is a shutting down of hiring with $\mathcal{V}_t = 0$. This corner becomes quantitatively relevant when we push our small labor surplus calibration a little further, for example, in setting $z = 0.955$. The first panel of figure 2.5a plots the job vacancy policy function over the values of the current state variables of productivity and employment. As seen throughout the chapter, vacancies are increasing in the level of current productivity. In addition, fixing the level of current productivity, firms post more vacancies the lower the level of current employment, as the labor market is more slack, unemployed workers are abundant, and the jobs are filled rapidly. Finally, the focus of this section is on the appearance of a region in productivity space where hiring shuts down ($\mathcal{V}_t = 0$). Below a certain threshold for current productivity, the expected value of a filled vacancy is below its cost and $\mathcal{V}_t = 0$.

The implications for the model's dynamics are shown in figure 2.5b. The first 50 periods are the standard response of the model to stochastic changes in productivity, with a positive level of vacancies. Then, a series of negative shocks arrives and pushes productivity under its boundaries below which we reach the

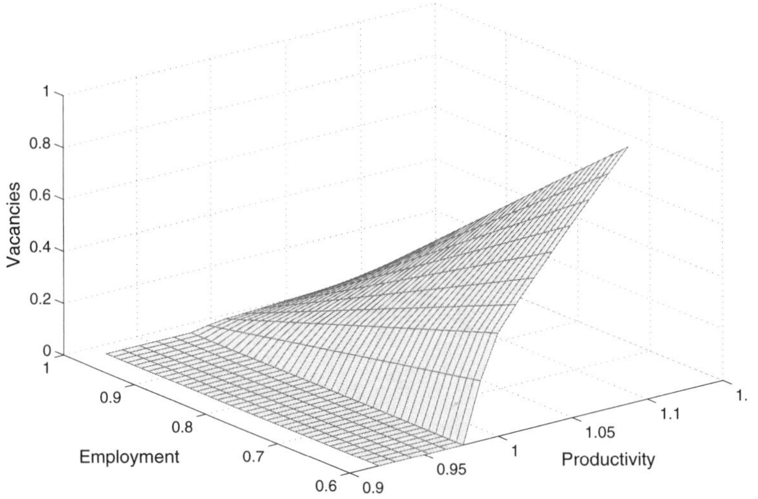

(a) Job vacancies in $(x, \mathcal{N})$ space

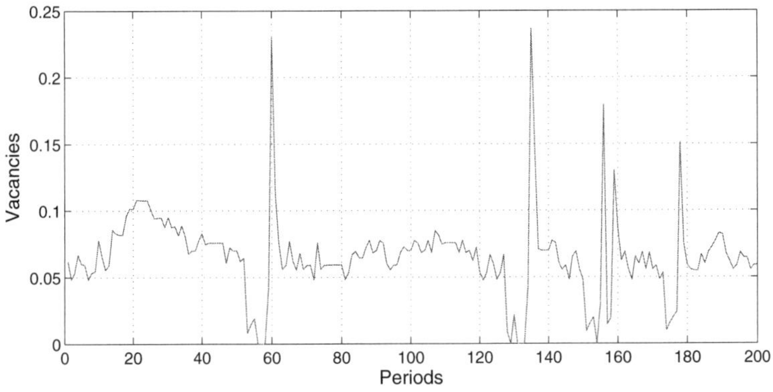

(b) Model job vacancies time series

Figure 2.5
The case of a zero lower bound for vacancies

corner solution $\mathcal{V}_t = 0$ for several periods. During that time, existing jobs continue to be destroyed at rate s and there is a sharp rise in unemployment. When productivity finally returns to a value such that firms enter the labor market once again, employment is very low and there is massive entry by firms into the market. Both the absence of job openings, and the following spikes, are not features of the data, but are generated by the model when the flow value of nonemployment z is close to the average value of labor productivity x.

2.5 Discussion of the literature and remaining issues

A growing body of research has looked into the ability of the conventional matching model to replicate US statistics regarding the volatilities of job vacancies, unemployment, and their ratio (labor market tightness) in response to productivity shocks. Burda and Wyplosz (1994) and Amaral and Tasci (2016) provide their business cycle properties. Cross-country evidence on labor market flows. The discussion on the ability of the matching model to fit stylized facts of the volatility of the US economy can be found in early work by Merz (1995) and Andolfatto (1996), as well as the less known but contemporaneous work of Langot (1995).

Cole and Rogerson (1999) and Shimer (2005) investigated the cyclical properties of search matching models following Pissarides (1985) and Mortensen and Pissarides (1994). Shimer (2005)'s main finding is that the elasticity of labor market tightness to productivity is around 20 in the data and around 1 in a calibration of the model. The issue, as emphasized in Hall (2005), is that, under Nash bargaining as a wage mechanism, wages absorb much of the change in the expected benefit to a new worker induced by fluctuations in labor productivity. Mortensen and Nagypal (2007) argue that a large part of fluctuations in the labor market tightness is not due to productivity shocks and Pissarides (2009) retains a target value for that elasticity of 7.56.

Subsequent research has focused on whether the lack of internal propagation, both in terms of amplification and persistence, stems from the structure of the model itself or whether it is a question of setting an appropriate calibration. Quite naturally, a first wave of research focused on the dynamics of wages as a means of generating amplification of exogenous innovations. This line of research has deepened the particulars of the wage determination mechanism (e.g., Shimer, 2005, Hall and Milgrom, 2008, Kennan, 2010, Gertler and Trigari, 2009). Another line of research using a different type of matching function, a stock-flow approach as in Ebrahimy and Shimer (2010), explains a third of the volatility in unemployment: Mortensen and Nagypal (2007) emphasize the importance of on-the-job search for this question. Clerc (2015) combines alternating offers and asymmetries of information to find improvements in elasticities to shocks in a calibrated model.

Along the alternative parameterization route the small labor surplus is assumption of Hagedorn and Manovskii (2008), in which firms make small profits that are more responsive to productivity shocks, leading the labor market to be more volatile overall. More precisely, Hagedorn and Manovskii impose a calibrated value of nonemployment utility that is close to market productivity, within only a few percentage points, and very low values for the bargaining power of workers. This result, however, is not without drawbacks: Costain and Reiter (2008) find the elasticity of unemployment to changes in unemployment benefits to be much too large, around 14.3, for the parameter values implied by Hagedorn and Manovskii (2008)'s calibration. This led to the criticism that it is difficult to match both the elasticity of labor market tightness to productivity and the elasticity of unemployment to policy parameters such as the replacement ratio. Moreover, recent empirical work by Chodorow-Reich and Karabarbounis (2015) finds evidence that the flow utility of nonemployment is pro-cyclical, imposing even greater challenges to amplification channels proposing to operate through the rigidity of a bargained wage.

Pissarides (2009) developed arguments for fixed matching costs, rather than wage rigidity as an avenue for generating amplification. Indeed, he argues that the wage relevant to job creation, the wage of new hires, is highly elastic to changes in productivity, as in Haefke et al. (2013) who find an almost one-to-one correspondence. This casts doubt on strategies that rely on rigid wages to obtain significant volatility in the labor market over the business cycle. The fixed cost approach proposed by Pissarides (2009) is promising, and will arise in part II as an equilibrium outcome of both credit and goods market frictions. A good summary of equations (2.2) and (2.5) can be found in Ljungqvist and Sargent (2015).

Another failure of the model is its difficulty replicating the autocorrelation of growth rates of the main variables (that is, the persistence of the response to exogenous shocks). This has received relatively less attention but was well emphasized in Fujita and Ramey (2007). In the benchmark model, the greatest responses of labor market tightness and job vacancies are contemporaneous to the shock. That is, the responses peaks immediately. This contrasts to the empirical VAR evidence uncovered in US time series by Fujita and Ramey (2007). Their work shows a peak response of labor market tightness to a productivity shock after 4 to 5 quarters. The empirical impulse responses have a pronounced hump-shaped pattern that the benchmark environment cannot replicate.

In order to address this second empirical shortcoming, an additional strand of research, has focused on the structure of vacancy costs. Fujita and Ramey (2007), for example, develop a story about sunk costs to vacancy creation such that the strongest change in market tightness occurs several periods after the original shock. Alternative approaches to modeling vacancy costs include the convexity of vacancy costs as in, for example, Rotemberg (2000) and Yashiv (2006). Petrosky-Nadeau and Wasmer (2013) argue that it is possible to match the observed volatilities with credit frictions. To match observed persistence, Petrosky-Nadeau and Wasmer (2015) show goods markets. Frictions must also be added to the model.

Another interesting attempt to take the search model of equilibrium unemployment to the data is Yashiv (2000). Cooper et al. (2007) bring the micro and macro data into a structural estimation of a model in which heterogeneous firms face a search frictional labor market for hiring workers, providing estimates of (nonconvex) costs of posting job vacancies. Merz and Yashiv (2007) deliver estimates of the cost of adjusting labor based on a firm's market value, an approach Hall (2017) brings to the labor search model.

The importance of asymmetries in cycles has been present in the business cycle literature for a long time (see, for instance, Neftci (1984)). Andolfatto (1997) is a first attempt to study the ability of the search model to replicate the steep nature of US business cycles where recoveries are slower than contractions. Petrosky-Nadeau and Zhang (2013) show how the deepness of cycles, with contractions more pronounced than the following peak expansion, arises naturally in the model of search and matching in the labor market, a subject also taken up in Jung and Kuester (2011) and Iliopulos et al. (2014). The recent research underscores the importance of solving the model with a nonlinear, global, numerical method. Log-linearization is inappropriate for assessing the quantitative properties of models with search frictional markets. See Petrosky-Nadeau and Zhang (forthcoming) for an assessment of numerical methods to solve models with search frictional labor markets. Lastly, this chapter did not address the dynamics of job destruction. One can refer to the comprehensive review by Fujita and Ramey (2009), who address the particular challenge of generating a negative correlation between unemployment and vacancies. This issue was already noted in the work of Krause and Lubik (2007). See also Abeille-Becker and Clerc (2013) for a recent calibrated example.

2.6 Chapter appendix

2.6.1 Log-linearization

Denote by $\widehat{Z}_t$ the log-deviation around the steady state of any variable Z_t. We begin with the job creation condition under the assumption of a wage fixed at $\bar{w}$:

$$\frac{\gamma}{q(\theta_t)} = \beta \mathbb{E}_t \left[x_{t+1} - \bar{w} + (1-s)\frac{\gamma}{q(\theta_{t+1})} \right]$$

approximated around a stationary steady state as

$$\eta_L \frac{\gamma}{q(\theta)} \widehat{\theta}_t = \beta \mathbb{E}_t \left[\widehat{x}_{t+1} + (1-s)\,\eta_L \frac{\gamma}{q(\theta)} \widehat{\theta}_{t+1} \right]$$

$$
\begin{aligned}
\eta_L \frac{\gamma}{q(\theta)}\left[1-(1-s)\,\beta\mathbb{E}_t L^{-1}\right]\widehat{\theta}_t &= \beta\mathbb{E}_t\widehat{x}_{t+1} \\
\widehat{\theta}_t &= \frac{q(\theta)}{\eta_L\gamma}\frac{\beta}{1-(1-s)\,\beta\mathbb{E}_t L^{-1}}\mathbb{E}_t\widehat{x}_{t+1} \\
\widehat{\theta}_t &= \frac{q(\theta)}{\eta_L\gamma}\beta\mathbb{E}_t\sum_{i=0}^{\infty}[(1-s)\,\beta]^i\widehat{x}_{t+1+i} \\
\widehat{\theta}_t &= \frac{q(\theta)}{\eta_L\gamma}\beta\mathbb{E}_t\sum_{i=0}^{\infty}[(1-s)\,\beta]^i\rho_x^{1+i}\epsilon_t \\
\widehat{\theta}_t &= \frac{q(\theta)}{\eta_L\gamma}\frac{\beta\rho_x}{1-(1-s)\,\beta\rho_x}
\end{aligned}
$$

The equations above can be simplified by introducing a forward operator, $X_{t+1} = L^{-1}X_t$, for any variable X_t using the fact that $(1-s)\,\beta < 1$, and assuming that productivity follows an AR(1) process.

In order to recover equation (2.1) of the text, we use the steady-state job creation condition $\frac{\gamma}{q(\theta)} = \frac{x-\bar{w}}{\frac{1}{\beta}-(1-s)}$:

$$
\begin{aligned}
\widehat{\theta}_t &= \frac{1}{\eta_L}\frac{x}{x-\bar{w}}\left[\frac{1}{\beta}-(1-s)\right]\beta\mathbb{E}_t\sum_{i=0}^{\infty}[(1-s)\,\beta]^i\widehat{x}_{t+1+i} \\
\widehat{\theta}_t &= \frac{1}{\eta_L}\frac{x}{x-\bar{w}}[1-\beta\,(1-s)]\,\mathbb{E}_t\sum_{i=0}^{\infty}[(1-s)\,\beta]^i\widehat{x}_{t+1+i} \\
\widehat{\theta}_t &= \frac{1}{\eta_L}\times\frac{x}{x-\bar{w}}\times\frac{r+s}{1+r}\mathbb{E}_t\sum_{i=0}^{\infty}\left(\frac{1-s}{1+r}\right)^i\widehat{x}_{t+1+i}
\end{aligned}
$$

Under the assumption of an endogenous wage, we begin with the job creation condition:

$$
\frac{\gamma}{q(\theta_t)} = \beta\mathbb{E}_t\left[(1-\alpha_L)\left(x_{t+1}-z\right)-\alpha_L\gamma\theta_{t+1}+(1-s)\,\frac{\gamma}{q(\theta_{t+1})}\right]
$$

approximated around a stationary steady state as

$$
\begin{aligned}
\eta_L\frac{\gamma}{q(\theta)}\widehat{\theta}_t &= \beta\mathbb{E}_t\Big[(1-\alpha_L)\widehat{x}_{t+1}-\alpha_L\gamma\theta\widehat{\theta}_{t+1} \\
&\quad +(1-s)\,\eta_L\frac{\gamma}{q(\theta)}\widehat{\theta}_{t+1}\Big]
\end{aligned}
$$

$$
\begin{aligned}
\left\{\eta_L\frac{\gamma}{q(\theta)}-\left[(1-s)\,\eta_L\frac{\gamma}{q(\theta)}-\alpha_L\gamma\theta\right]\beta\mathbb{E}_t L^{-1}\right\}\widehat{\theta}_t &= \beta\mathbb{E}_t\left[(1-\alpha_L)\widehat{x}_{t+1}\right] \\
\frac{\gamma}{q(\theta)}\left\{\eta_L-\left[(1-s)\,\eta_L-\alpha_L f(\theta)\right]\beta\mathbb{E}_t L^{-1}\right\}\widehat{\theta}_t &= \beta\mathbb{E}_t\left[(1-\alpha_L)\widehat{x}_{t+1}\right]
\end{aligned}
$$

$$\widehat{\theta}_t = \frac{(1-\alpha_L)\,q(\theta)\beta}{\eta_L\gamma\left\{1-\left[1-s-\frac{\alpha_L}{\eta_L}f(\theta)\right]\beta\mathbb{E}_tL^{-1}\right\}}\mathbb{E}_t\widehat{x}_{t+1}$$

$$\widehat{\theta}_t = \frac{(1-\alpha_L)\,q(\theta)\beta}{\eta_L\gamma}\mathbb{E}_t\sum_{i=0}^{\infty}\left\{\left[1-s-\frac{\alpha_L}{\eta_L}f(\theta)\right]\beta\right\}^i\rho_x^{1+i}\epsilon_t$$

$$\widehat{\theta}_t = \frac{(1-\alpha_L)\,q(\theta)\beta\rho_x\epsilon_t}{\eta_L\gamma\left\{1-\left[1-s-\frac{\alpha_L}{\eta_L}f(\theta)\right]\beta\rho_x\right\}}$$

The value of the elasticity in this case is:

Elasticity of labor market tightness under endogenous wage:

$$\varsigma_{L,w} = \frac{\partial\widehat{\theta}_t}{\partial x_t} = \frac{(1-\alpha_L)\,q(\theta)\beta\rho_x}{\eta_L\gamma\left\{1-\left[1-s-\frac{\alpha_L}{\eta_L}f(\theta)\right]\beta\rho_x\right\}} \tag{2.6}$$

2.6.2 Labor market data

We obtain a seasonally adjusted monthly unemployment rate (persons 16 years of age and older) from the Bureau of Labor Statistics (BLS), and a seasonally adjusted help wanted advertising index from the Conference Board. The sample is from January 1951 to June 2006. The Conference Board switched from the help wanted advertising index to the help wanted online index in June 2006. The two indexes are not directly comparable Barnichon (2010) provides a method for linking the two series. We take quarterly averages of the monthly series to obtain quarterly observations. The sample is quarterly from 1951 to 2012. It is detrended with a Hodrick–Prescott (Hodrick and Prescott, 1997) filter with a smoothing parameter of 1,600. The data and programs used in this chapter are available on the author's website.

3 Efficiency in the labor market

There are several aspects of markets with search and matching frictions that, relative to a frictionless competitive model, lead to particular efficiency properties of the equilibria that we study in this chapter. Understanding the differences relative to the first best allocation in Walrasian, competitive markets is a prerequisite before embarking on the policy implications and prescriptions in models with search and matching frictions.

A first important difference with the frictionless world is that search and matching frictions—sometimes called trading frictions—add the equivalent of a "technological constraint" which limits the number of possible matches per instant of time, even if these matches would, if created, produce positive social surplus. Contrary to the usual intuition that the marginal surplus of a transaction is zero in equilibrium, unexhausted transaction opportunities remain in a search equilibrium, and are only limited by this matching technology. Frictions thus reduce welfare in a first best sense: they lower the overall economic surplus of trading by making it more difficult and requiring resources. Social welfare is highest as the level of search frictions approaches zero, a limiting case in which the matching process is instantaneous.

An implication is that search frictions and their intensity cannot be controlled directly by a social planner. Hence, and this is the second important remark, a social planner can indirectly affect the allocative effects of both the production technology and the matching technology through institutions or taxes, but cannot act directly on them. We will refer to efficiency from the viewpoint of finding the best allocation given the constraints on trading imposed by search and matching frictions. This is actually a second-best allocation, deviating from the best allocation because of a technological constraint. The expression "second best" usually refers to situations analyzed in the optimal taxation literature where one tax instrument is missing. It also refers to situations where some agents exert a nonpecuniary externality on other agents, as it is the case here through these matching externalities. This second best is also sometimes called *constrained efficiency,* and we will prefer the term constrained efficiency to second best to avoid confusion with the optimal taxation literature.

A third related and important point is that search and matching frictions actually imply several trading externalities taken as given by agents. Some are positive and some are negative. Consider the two segments of the labor market, job vacancies and unemployed workers. A higher number of job vacancies creates a positive externality by raising the probability for a given unemployed worker of leaving unemployment and obtaining a job. At the same time, it creates a negative externality by increasing the congestion exerted by job vacancies on each other. It reduces the individual probability for a given vacancy to be filled. An increase in the other side of the market, unemployed workers, leads to similar negative and positive externalities. The negative externality on other unemployed workers arises from the crowding out of the individual probability of finding a job. The positive externality corresponds to an acceleration in the process of filling a job vacancy.

Finally, in variants of the model with endogenous job destruction, the model delivers an interesting distinction between efficient and inefficient separations. Efficient separation occurs when the total surplus of the match is negative. Inefficient separation occurs when the total surplus is positive but, due to a failure in splitting the surplus, one of the two sides decides unilaterally to leave the relationship. This occurs due to the inability to renegotiate, or when utility is not easily transferable.

Overall, for a given level of frictions, there must be a welfare-optimizing rate of unemployment and job vacancies that balances the effects of these externalities. In what follows, we discuss the optimal mix of vacancies and unemployment. In addition, we discuss how a decentralized economy can achieve this constrained efficient allocation under bargaining, and discuss how this allocation may also be reached in a decentralized economy with directed search.

3.1 Efficiency in continuous time

3.1.1 The Hosios condition with exogenous separations

As is standard in the literature, we assume that the flow of utility of the nonemployed workers z is not a transfer in the form of unemployment insurance, but instead a pure utility component. This allows us to neglect issues of taxation of wage earnings and transfers at this stage. A natural measure of social output is the present discounted value of output and leisure net of search costs:

$$\Omega^{SP} = \int_0^{\infty} e^{-rt} \left[x(1-\mathcal{U}) + z\mathcal{U} - \gamma\theta\mathcal{U}\right] dt$$

The social planner maximizes Ω^{SP} subject to the matching frictions imposed by the matching technology:

$$\max_{\mathcal{U},\mathcal{V}} \Omega^{SP} \quad \text{s.t. } \dot{\mathcal{U}} = s(1-\mathcal{U}) - \mathcal{M}_L(\mathcal{U},\mathcal{V})$$

Vacancies $\mathcal{V}$ are a control variable while $\mathcal{U}$ is a state variable whose law of motion was first presented in equation (1.15) of chapter 1. The Hamiltonian to the problem, denoting Ψ_U a co-state variable, is

$$H = e^{-rt}\left[x(1-\mathcal{U}) + z\mathcal{U} - \gamma\mathcal{V}\right] + \Psi_U\left[s(1-\mathcal{U}) - \mathcal{M}_L(\mathcal{U},\mathcal{V})\right]$$

The first-order conditions for labor market tightness and unemployment are (see appendix 3.6.1 for details related to this section):

$$\partial H/\partial\mathcal{V} = 0 \rightarrow -e^{-rt}\gamma - \Psi_U\left[1-\eta_L(\theta)\right]q(\theta) = 0$$

$$\dot{\Psi}_U = -\partial H/\partial\mathcal{U} \rightarrow \dot{\Psi}_U = e^{-rt}(x-z) + \Psi_U\left[s + \eta_L f(\theta)\right]$$

where $\eta_L(\theta)$ is the elasticity of the matching function with respect to unemployed workers, as used earlier, $\partial\mathcal{M}_L(\mathcal{U},\mathcal{V})/\partial\mathcal{U} = \eta_L f(\theta)$, and $\partial\mathcal{M}_L(\mathcal{U},\mathcal{V})/\partial\mathcal{V} = (1-\eta_L(\theta))q(\theta)$. The first optimality condition states that the social planner is equalizing the flow cost of job vacancies γ to the expected social gain from an additional employed worker, measured by the co-state Ψ_U.

The boundary condition requires that the co-state variable tends towards zero at the infinite time horizon. In this chapter as well as in all subsequent analysis of the book, we rule out explosive dynamics and will focus on stationary paths only.

Denote the allocation from the social planner's problem by the superscript *opt*, that is, the optimal level of tightness is denoted by θ^{opt}. Combining these conditions leads to the constrained efficient job creation condition:

Social planner's job creation condition:

$$\frac{\gamma}{q(\theta^{opt})} = \frac{(x-z)\left[1-\eta_L(\theta^{opt})\right] - \gamma\theta^{opt}\eta_L(\theta^{opt})}{r+s} \tag{3.1}$$

Decentralized job creation condition with Nash wage bargaining:

$$\frac{\gamma}{q(\theta)} = \frac{(x-z)(1-\alpha_L) - \gamma\theta\alpha_L}{r+s} \tag{3.2}$$

A comparison of equation (3.1) with the decentralized allocation with Nash wage bargaining of chapter 1, reproduced here in (3.2), reveals that the decentralized solution maximizes net social value if and only if:

> Hosios constrained efficiency condition in the labor market:
>
> $$\alpha_L = \eta_L(\theta^{opt}) \tag{3.3}$$

We will refer to this condition as the Hosios condition. It is sometimes called the Hosios–Pissarides condition. See the discussion at the end of the chapter for a detailed analysis of the earliest understanding of the relation in the seminal contributions of Peter Diamond, Christopher Pissarides, and Arthur Hosios. We will see throughout the book that this condition is fairly general. It holds in discrete time as well as in other search markets studied in chapters 5 and 7. Social welfare maximization, as stated by condition (3.3), implies that the share of the match surplus going to the worker should equal the elasticity of matching with respect to unemployment. The elasticity of the expected duration of a job search to a change in job seekers for unemployed workers is $1 - \eta_L(\theta)$. The elasticity of the expected duration of a job search for firms to fill a job opening to a change in job vacancies is $\eta_L(\theta)$. When $\eta_L(\theta)$ is high, vacancies create more congestion than unemployed workers in the labor market, and thus the social planner would like to reduce the share of the surplus to a match accruing to the firm by setting a higher α_L. That is, the social planner wants to give a higher share of the surplus to workers to limit job creation by firms and the associated costs.

Equation (3.3) is not likely to be satisfied in general. There may be too much unemployment if $\alpha_L > \eta_L(\theta)$, and too little unemployment if $\alpha_L < \eta_L(\theta)$. This latter case is a situation in which the congestion externality of an additional vacancy creates hiring costs that are too high for other firms. This is precisely why the bargaining power should be set to $\eta_L(\theta)$.

It is useful to use figure 3.1 to interpret the result, drawn under the assumption of an isoelastic matching function with elasticity η_L. It emphasizes the value of the wage bargaining parameters that ensures the constrained efficient amount of entry by firms in the labor market at the Hosios condition. The socially efficient level of labor market tightness determined by condition (3.1) is indicated by θ^{opt}. The figure represents the decentralized economy's job creation condition $\gamma/q(\theta) = (x - w)/(r + s)$ in labor market tightness and wage space, as in chapter 1, as a decreasing convex curve (solid line). The upper sloping solid and dashed lines represent the Nash wage rule

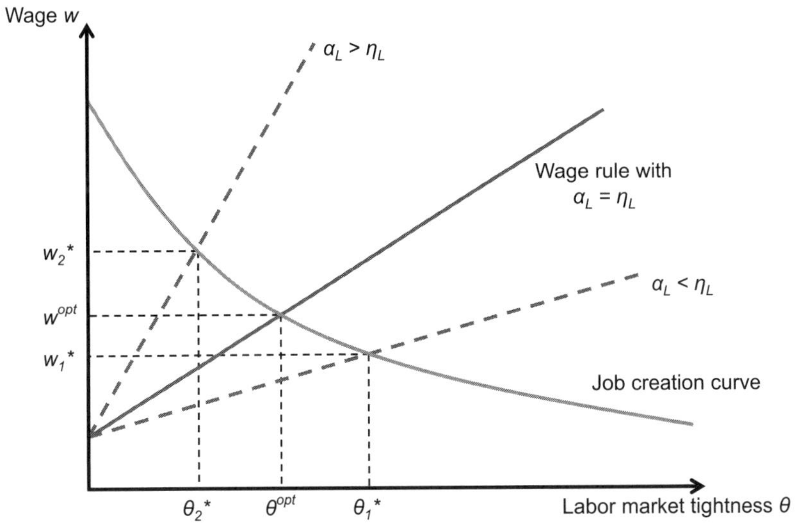

Figure 3.1
Illustrating the Hosios condition with different values of α_L relative to η_L

$w = \alpha_L (x + \gamma\theta) + (1 - \alpha_L) z$ for various values of α_L. When $\alpha_L > \eta_L$, wages are too high and tightness is too low and conversely, when $\alpha_L < \eta_L$, wages are too low and tightness is too high compared to the social optimum. In the first case, firms create too few vacancies and the unemployment congestion externality is too high. In the second case, the unemployed are too few, and thus vacancies create a too large congestion externality onto each other. When $\alpha_L = \eta_L$, the intersection of the wage setting curve and the job creation condition maps out a wage that results in the decentralized equilibrium labor market tightness coinciding with the social planner's allocation.

3.1.2 Hosios inefficient separations versus surplus-inefficient separations

In this subsection, we introduce and discuss two potential sources of inefficiencies related to job destruction. First, separations may be inefficient if the threshold for destroying jobs, which determines in turn the equilibrium level of labor market tightness, in the decentralized equilibrium is different from the optimum chosen by a social planner. Second, there could be excessive, inefficient, job separation destroying economic surplus. That is, it is possible for the match surplus as a whole to be positive, yet negative for one of the parties who decides to leave the match, thereby destroying some joint positive surplus. We therefore distinguish these two concepts, and label them, respectively, Hosios-inefficient separation versus surplus-inefficient separations. We start with the former (Hosios-inefficient separations) and then develop the latter (the concept of surplus-inefficient separations).

The Hosios constrained efficiency result also holds along the job destruction margin (Mortensen and Pissarides, 1999a). Using the same notation as in equation (1.42) of chapter 1, the socially efficient job creation and job destruction conditions can be shown to be:

Social planner's job creation and job destruction conditions:

$$\frac{\gamma}{q(\theta)} = \frac{[1-\eta_L(\theta)]x}{r+s+\mu}\int_A (a'-A)\,\mathrm{d}G(a') \tag{3.4}$$

$$z + \frac{\eta_L(\theta)}{1-\eta_L(\theta)}\gamma\theta = Ax + \frac{\mu x}{r+s+\mu}\int_A (a'-A)\,\mathrm{d}G(a') \tag{3.5}$$

The proof is in appendix 3.6.2 and is adapted from Mortensen and Pissarides (1999a) where the social planner maximizes social surplus in choosing optimally the reservation rule and job creation, taking into account their effect on total production and vacancy costs. It still turns out, from these optimality conditions, that job destruction in the decentralized economy is constrained efficient when the share of the match surplus in bargaining going to the worker is equal to the elasticity of matching with respect to unemployment. That is, the job destruction threshold is socially efficient if the Hosios condition holds. Moreover, a complete differentiation of the equilibrium conditions for job creation and job destruction establishes that the job destruction threshold A reaches a maximum when the Hosios condition is satisfied. The proof, unreported, can be found in Mortensen and Pissarides (1999a). The social planner maximizes the total surplus by maximizing the value of workers, which in turn reduces the total surplus of holding a job, there by maximizing the fragility of matches to shocks.

The expression "efficient separation" has another meaning which needs to be clarified. In the endogenous separation case studied earlier the surplus to each party is individually below zero when separation occurs. A truly inefficient outcome is when the total surplus $\Sigma_l^T = W_n - W_u + J_\pi$ is positive, but not for each of its subcomponents or parties. That is to say, it is a situation in which either the worker quits because his private surplus $W_n - W_u < 0$, or the firm lays off the worker unilaterally because $J_\pi < 0$, even though the total

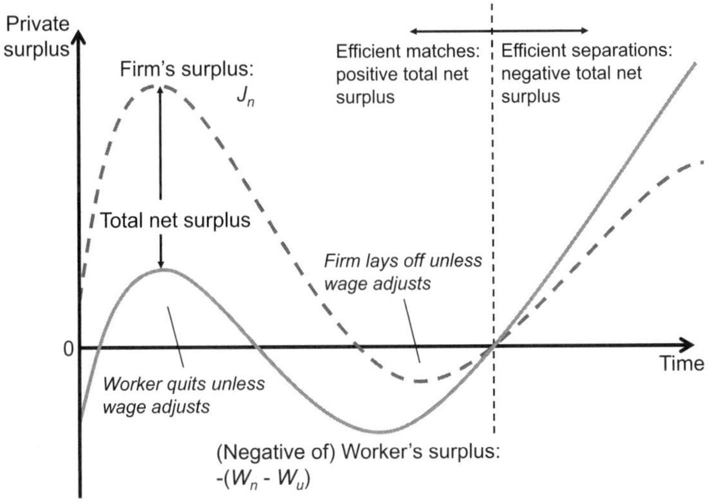

Figure 3.2
Efficient vs. inefficient separations

surplus Σ_l^T is positive. Separation occurs in these situations if the firm and the worker cannot agree on renegotiating a wage that would restore a positive private surplus to each party. This is in spite of such a renegotiation being a Pareto-improvement.

Figure 3.2 is a variant of figure 1.2a where the vertical axis has been replaced by firm's and worker's surplus instead of reservation wages. The vertical distance between the two curves is therefore the total labor surplus of the match. When either the worker's or the firm's surplus cross the zero-surplus line but when total surplus is still positive, an inefficient separation may occur since one of the parties would like to unilaterally quit the match while positive total surplus still exists. An efficient separation occurs only when two surplus curves cross the zero-surplus horizontal line together.

3.2 Competitive search equilibrium

Moen (1997) derives an interesting and important result in the context of directed search. In the context of random search, the private allocation may not be constrained efficient due to search externalities. In contrast with this conclusion, Moen shows that efficiency can be restored in a decentralized economy if firms post wages on segmented labor markets. In what follows we simplify the analysis to present his main results in a manner that is directly comparable to the model developed in the previous chapters.

We make the following four assumptions. First, the labor market is segmented, and each segment is characterized by a wage posted by firms willing to enter that segment. Hence, by definition, the same wage will be offered by all the firms in that segment. Denote by the subscript i a given segment, characterized by its wage w_i and a segment-specific labor market tightness θ_i. For simplicity we assume identical separation rates s across sectors, without loss of generality.

Second, unemployed workers can potentially search in all segments. This implies that, ex-ante, their utility is equalized across segments. After they have chosen a segment, the Bellman equation of the unemployed is

$$rW_{ui} = z + f(\theta_i)\frac{w_i - rW_{ui}}{r+s} = rW_u \text{ for all segments i}$$

using $rW_{ni} = w_i + s(W_{ui} - W_{ni})$. The second equality comes from the perfect ex-ante mobility across segments and is an arbitrage condition. As long as w_i is larger than rW_{ui}, this iso-utility condition for the unemployed workers implies a negative link between segment labor market tightness and wages in order to maintain rW_u constant:

$$f(\theta_i) = \frac{rW_u - z}{w_i - rW_u}(r+s) \tag{3.6}$$

Furthermore, this relation is convex in the space (w_i, θ_i), with a negative slope that tends towards zero as the wage increases. Workers trade off higher wages against lower chances of getting a job, or alternatively, lower wages against better chances of getting a job. This equation states that workers know that, in equilibrium, search in higher wage segments will be more difficult due to greater competition between workers and, as implied by the last two assumptions, possibly fewer vacancies on the segment.

Third, firms face entry costs in a new segment. This assumption prevents the value of vacancies in each segment, denoted J_{vi}, from being driven down to 0. Denote the costs to entering a new segment as a constant K assumed to be the same in all sectors.

Fourth, a decentralized equilibrium is defined as a free entry of firms subject to the entry costs, such that value of a vacancy in a segment will be $J_{vi} = K$ in equilibrium, along with wage posting by firms in segment i that takes into account the segment participation condition of workers in equation (3.6).

All firms have a productivity level x common to all segments. They also face identical costs of posting a vacancy, γ, and a job filling rate in segment i of $q(\theta_i)$.

Thus the value of a vacancy applied to segment i is

$$rJ_{vi} = -\gamma + q(\theta_i)(J_{\pi i} - J_{vi})$$

It is assumed that the destruction of a match is also a destruction of the firm, thereby leaving no value. As such, the value of an employed worker to the firm on segment i is

$$rJ_{\pi i} = x - w_i - sJ_{\pi i}$$

This implies that there is a relation between tightness θ_i and the segment wage w_i for a value of a vacancy J_{vi} given by

$$\frac{\gamma}{q(\theta_i)} + \left(1 + \frac{r}{q(\theta_i)}\right) J_{vi} = \frac{x - w_i}{r + s} \tag{3.7}$$

This equation is actually a job creation condition, an iso-profit curve at the vacancy stage. It implies, for a given value of J_{vi}, a negative link between θ_i and w_i. Firms trade off a lower profit flow, from offering a higher wage w_i, against attracting more workers to the segment and, hence, shorter search duration $1/q(\theta_i)$.

We can now define the optimization problem of a firm in segment i. It chooses to post a wage w_i to maximize the value of a job vacancy in segment i, defined by equation (3.7), subject to worker's arbitrage condition (3.6):

$$w_i = \text{argmax } J_{vi}(w_i, \theta_i) \quad \text{s.t.} \quad f(\theta_i) = \tfrac{rW_u - z}{w_i - rW_u}(r + s) \tag{3.8}$$

Hence, the wage is a function $w_i(\theta_i)$ of the local labor market tightness. The maximization of the value of a vacancy on a local market, after intermediate steps derived in appendix section 3.6.3, leads to:

Moen's job creation condition in a submarket:

$$\frac{\gamma}{q(\theta_i)} + \frac{rK}{q(\theta_i)} = \frac{1 - \eta_L(\theta_i)}{\eta_L(\theta_i)} \frac{w_i(\theta_i) - rW_u}{r + s} \tag{3.9}$$

The comparable random matching model, to which we will compare the equilibrium job creation condition in a given segment (3.9), is one in which firms must pay a cost $K > 0$ before entering the labor market. These costs are assumed sunk, are not recovered after job separation, and affect wage bargaining (by changing the value of the outside option of the firm in the bargaining process). In that model, the value of a job vacancy is no longer driven down to 0 in equilibrium, but rather to the cost of entry $J_v = K$. The asset value a job vacancy, $rJ_v = -\gamma + q(\theta)\,(J_\pi - J_v)$, in this environment is

$$rK = -\gamma + q(\theta)\,(J_\pi - K)$$

The fixed entry cost enters the total job match surplus, which is written as $W_n - W_u + J_\pi - K$. It thereby affects the Nash bargained wage. We have the firm's surplus in bargaining as being equal to $J_\pi - K = [(1-\alpha_L)/\alpha_L]\,(W_n - W_u)$, which in turn is equal to $[(1-\alpha_L)/\alpha_L]\,(w - rW_u)/(r+s)$. Hence the job creation condition in the random search and matching model with a fixed entry cost can be rewritten as:

Decentralized random matching job creation condition in a submarket:

$$\frac{\gamma}{q(\theta_i)} + \frac{rK}{q(\theta_i)} = \frac{1-\alpha_L}{\alpha_L}\frac{w_i - rW_u}{r+s} \tag{3.10}$$

The two equations (3.9) and (3.10) coincide under the Hosios condition (3.3) when the share of workers α_L equals the elasticity η_L. If the wages in each case were in addition identical, which turns out to be true (see appendix 3.6.4 for this point), then the decentralized equilibrium with bargaining would also be the efficient outcome under Moen's competitive equilibrium. Hence, Moen's result can be understood as follows: firms exploit the possibility of segmenting the labor market, but face the constraint that workers can freely move between segments. When they set the wage that maximizes the value of a vacancy in this segment, this corresponds to the constrained efficient allocation in the random search model. The combination of mobility across segments and of segmentation of the submarkets therefore restores efficiency. Firms are actually able to affect the tightness of the segment by choosing the wage. In that sense, they internalize the congestion externality of additional job vacancies and restore efficiency. A description of the equilibrium can be found in figure 3.3.

This suggests that it should be possible to remove all second-best inefficiencies by introducing new submarkets, at least up to a point where the economy behaves according to the efficient allocation rule described in (3.3). By extension, one can interpret Moen's result as indicating that, when market makers can create enough submarkets, the decentralized equilibrium is the social planner's allocation. In such a case, the analysis of the equilibrium in the decentralized economy should assume right away that the Hosios condition holds.

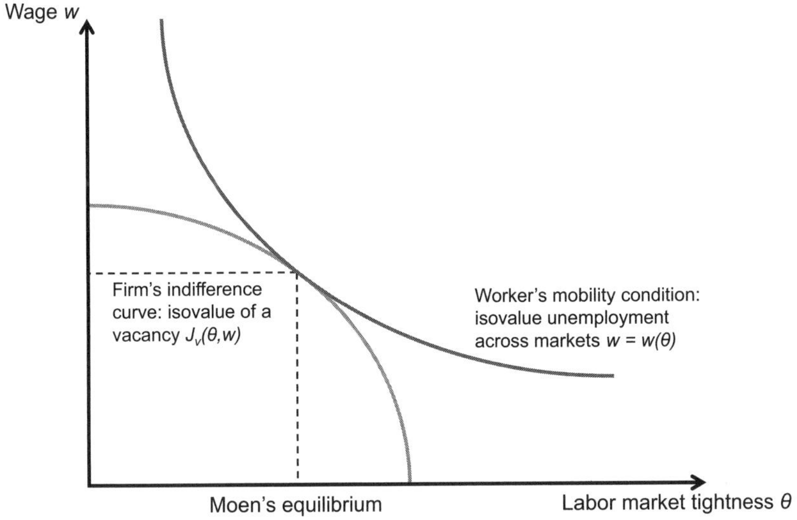

Figure 3.3
Moen's equilibrium

3.3 A discussion of policy instruments

In general, when this Hosios condition is not satisfied, there are ways to restore efficiency through either hiring subsidies, payroll, or layoff taxes. Each policy operates through either a positive or negative shift in the wage or job creation curves. Indeed, if a policy instrument is needed to correct for a situation of excessive unemployment, one expects it to induce job creation by reducing wages or creation costs. If instead it needs to reduce employment because of excessive competition between vacancies, and too much competition between firms trying to hire workers, then it must have some positive effect on wages to limit entry of firms.

Assume that for every successful meeting that results in an employed worker, the firm receives a subsidy from the government $\Upsilon > 0$. The subsidy is assumed to be paid out in the first period the job starts producing. As such, the Bellman equation for the value of the marginal job vacancy is now

$$rJ_v = -\gamma + q(\theta)\left(J_\pi + \Upsilon - J_v\right)$$
$$\implies \frac{\gamma}{q(\theta)} - \Upsilon = J_\pi$$

where the second line makes use of the free entry condition $J_v = 0$. The hiring subsidy shifts the entry curve towards more job creation. The marginal value of an employed worker in the presence of a payroll tax $\tau \in (0,1)$ and layoff tax $T > 0$ is now

$$\begin{aligned} rJ_\pi &= x - w(1+\tau) + s\,(J_v - T - J_\pi) \\ \Longrightarrow J_\pi &= \frac{x - w(1+\tau) - sT}{r+s} \end{aligned}$$

Payroll taxes reduce the period flow of profit generated from labor. Layoff taxes reduce the value of a filled vacancy as they will eventually be paid out, when a separation occurs, and have expected value sT.

Combining these two equations leads to a job creation condition in the presence of job creation subsidies and payroll and layoff taxes:

> Job creation condition in the presence of subsidies and taxes for a given wage:
>
> $$\frac{\gamma}{q(\theta)} - \Upsilon = \frac{x - w(1+\tau) - sT}{r+s} \tag{3.11}$$

It is easy to see that, in the plane (θ, w), the job creation curve is shifted upwards by higher subsidies and downwards by higher separation costs and higher payroll taxes. Each policy instrument will also affect the negotiated wage. Let us focus first on the effect of the payroll tax. The payroll tax affects the marginal cost of labor in the firm's surplus from employment. Its slope is now $-(1+\tau)$. However, the marginal value of the wage for the worker is still 1. This implies that the Nash maximand defined in equation (1.26) will deliver a different outcome. In particular, the total surplus will be shared with different weights, since firms now have a higher propensity to bargain for lower wages w:

$$(1+\tau)(1-\alpha_L)\,(W_n - W_u) = \alpha_L\,(J_\pi - J_v) \tag{3.12}$$

This rule states that the total surplus $\Sigma_l^T = W_n - W_u + J_\pi - J_v$ is shared among worker and firm as

$$W_n - W_u = \frac{\alpha_L}{1+\tau(1-\alpha_L)}\Sigma_l^T \text{ and } J_\pi - J_v = \frac{(1-\alpha_L)(1+\tau)}{1+\tau(1-\alpha_L)}\Sigma_l^T$$

The Nash wage now divides the surplus into shares $\alpha_L/\,[1+\tau(1-\alpha_L)]$ and $(1-\alpha_L)(1+\tau)/\,[1+\tau(1-\alpha_L)]$ that depend on the tax rate τ. When $\tau > 0$, the worker's share of the surplus is lower than in the absence of taxes, because a marginal increase in the wage costs more to the firm than it brings to the worker, thus shifting the bargaining equilibrium point to a lower wage.

The wage is

$$w = \frac{\alpha_L}{1+\tau}(x - sT) + (1-\alpha_L)z + \frac{\alpha_L}{1+\tau}[\gamma\theta - f(\theta)\Upsilon] \tag{3.13}$$

For a given level of labor market tightness θ, the job creation subsidy Υ lowers the bargained wage. The subsidy reduces the cost of searching in the labor market for the firm and improves its bargaining position. The layoff tax T also reduces the bargained wage by reducing the size of the match surplus. Increases in the payroll tax τ reduce the slope of the wage curve with respect to productivity and labor market tightness, while its net effect depends on the current tightness of the market and the level of the other policy parameters.

Combining the job creation curve (3.11) and the wage rule (3.13), we have our equilibrium job creation condition in the presence of three labor market policy instruments:

Job creation condition in the presence of subsidies and taxes, using equilibrium wage:

$$\frac{\gamma}{q(\theta)} - \Upsilon = \frac{(1-\alpha_L)[x-(1+\tau)z - sT] - \alpha_L[\gamma\theta - f(\theta)\Upsilon]}{r+s} \tag{3.14}$$

The combined effect of the instruments on labor demand and wages for the equilibrium is as follows. Subsidies raise labor market tightness, while payroll taxes and layoff taxes reduce it. Hence the effects are qualitatively the same as those discussed after equation (3.11), which in essence were the effects of policies on labor demand under the assumption of a fixed wage. However, quantitatively, the effect of subsidies is amplified when the wage is endogenous, comparing equations (3.11) and (3.14), while the effect of payroll taxes and layoff taxes is diminished. Indeed, all three policies reduce wages, which mitigates the negative demand effect of layoff taxes and payroll taxes, while amplifying the positive demand effect of subsidies.

Assuming the Hosios condition does not hold, that is, the elasticity of the matching function η_L and the worker's bargaining weight α_L are not equal, we can now consider how to bring the allocation in (3.14) closer to the constrained efficient allocation determined by the social planner's allocation:

$$\frac{\gamma}{q(\theta)} = \frac{(x-z)[1-\eta_L(\theta)] - \gamma\theta\eta_L(\theta)}{r+s}$$

An important conclusion we will arrive at is that the optimal policies each have a sign that depends on the comparison between the share of workers in wage bargaining and the elasticity of unemployment in the matching function.

Consider first the case with $\Upsilon > 0, T = \tau = 0$. Then equilibrium labor market tightness, following (3.14), is given by

$$\frac{\gamma}{q(\theta)} - \Upsilon = \frac{(1-\alpha_L)(x-z) - \alpha_L [\gamma\theta - f(\theta)\Upsilon]}{r+s}$$

A little algebra, detailed in the appendix, shows that the optimal subsidy should be set according to

$$\Upsilon^* = [\alpha_L - \eta_L(\theta)] \frac{x - z + \gamma\theta}{r + s + f(\theta)}$$

According to this rule, if the worker's share of the surplus is greater than the elasticity of the matching function, then a positive employment subsidy can move the economy towards the constrained efficient allocation. Recall that this case, with $\alpha_L > \eta_L$, corresponds to a decentralized equilibrium with too little employment. As a consequence, a positive employment subsidy reduces the inefficiency. On the other hand, if $\alpha_L < \eta_L$, then a tax on job creation would instead correct for excessive employment in the decentralized economy and reduce the excessive congestion on vacancy filling.

Consider now the case with $\tau > 0, \Upsilon = T = 0$. Then equilibrium labor market tightness, following (3.14), is given by

$$\frac{\gamma}{q(\theta)} = \frac{(1-\alpha_L)[x - (1+\tau)z] - \alpha_L\gamma\theta}{r+s}$$

For the two allocations to coincide we need $(1-\alpha_L)[x-(1+\tau)z] - \alpha_L\gamma\theta = (1-\eta_L)(x-z) - \eta_L\gamma\theta$, which is achieved with an optimal payroll tax rate:

$$\tau^* = [\eta_L(\theta) - \alpha_L] \frac{x - z + \gamma\theta}{(1-\alpha_L)z}$$

This rule has a rich interpretation. This condition states that at the Hosios condition, i.e., $\eta_L = \alpha_L$, the payroll tax rate should be 0 as the decentralized allocation is already constrained efficient. Away from Hosios, the payroll tax should be positive if the worker's bargaining weight α_L is less than the elasticity of the matching function η_L. When this is the case there is too much firm entry. Firms receive a larger share of the surplus than is socially optimal, and there are too many resources devoted to job creation. In line with this interpretation, the tax rate is increasing in the spread between the marginal product of labor, x, and the flow value of nonemployment z, as well as in the job posting cost γ.

The last policy instrument is the layoff tax. It will be shown to play exactly the same role as the payroll tax. Consider the case with $T > 0$, $\Upsilon = \tau = 0$. Layoff taxes reduce the payoff to hiring labor and will restrict job creation. The negotiated wage,

$$w = \alpha_L (x + \gamma\theta - sT) + (1 - \alpha_L) z$$

is lower in the presence of a layoff tax that reduces the size of the surplus over which worker and firm are bargaining. Equilibrium labor market tightness, following (3.14), is given by

$$\frac{\gamma}{q(\theta)} = \frac{(1 - \alpha_L)(x - sT) - \alpha_L \gamma\theta}{r + s}$$

and the optimal layoff tax should be set according to

$$T^* = [\eta_L(\theta) - \alpha_L] \frac{x - z + \gamma\theta}{s(1 - \alpha_L)}$$

The same logic as above applies here. Excessive employment can be compensated by a positive tax that will reduce job creation. Excessive unemployment can be compensated by a subsidy that raises job creations. Of course, this instrument should not be preferred to the payroll tax/subsidy instrument: if job destruction were not exogenous but endogenous, layoff taxes or subsidies would distort job separation decisions in the opposite way. See appendix 3.6.6 for some additional results with endogenous job destruction.

3.4 Efficiency in a discrete time dynamic setting

3.4.1 Hosios in a discrete setting

The efficiency results in section 3.1 are generally preserved in discrete time and out of the steady state. The main difference arises from possible variations in the elasticity of matching from one period to the next if the matching function is not isoelastic. This implies that the worker's share may need to be time varying, and introduces a new term in the efficiency condition reflecting changes in the matching elasticity across periods, a term that we call the stochastic matching elasticity factor. This new term disappears at the steady state, and the implications and interpretations remain the same. To see this, we now state the social planner's problem subject to a matching friction in the labor market in discrete time, with a time discounting factor $\beta = 1/(1 + r)$:

$$\Omega_t^{SP} = \max_{\mathcal{V}_t} \left\{ x_t \mathcal{N}_t + z(1 - \mathcal{N}_t) - \gamma \mathcal{V}_t + \beta \mathbb{E}_t \Omega_{t+1}^{SP} \right\} \tag{3.15}$$

$$\text{subject to } \mathcal{N}_{t+1} = (1 - s)\mathcal{N}_t + \mathcal{M}_L(\mathcal{V}_t, 1 - \mathcal{N}_t) \tag{3.16}$$

The social planner aims to maximize the value function Ω^{SP} by an adequate choice of job vacancies which affect aggregate production $x_t\mathcal{N}_t$ through the constraint that employment follows the law of motion (3.16). The constraint states that the social planner cannot get around the frictions in the labor market. The first order condition to this problem,

$$-\gamma + \beta\mathbb{E}_t \frac{\partial\Omega^{SP}_{t+1}}{\partial\mathcal{N}_{t+1}} \frac{\partial\mathcal{N}_{t+1}}{\partial\mathcal{V}_t} = 0 \tag{3.17}$$

equalizes the cost of the marginal vacancy, γ, to its marginal social benefit. This benefit stems from the marginal change in employment, $\partial\mathcal{N}_{t+1}/\partial\mathcal{V}_t$, times the social value for a marginal job. Differentiating the social planner's problem with respect to employment, this social value for a marginal job is

$$\frac{\partial\Omega^{SP}_t}{\partial\mathcal{N}_t} = x_t - z + (1-s)\beta\mathbb{E}_t \frac{\partial\Omega^{SP}_{t+1}}{\partial\mathcal{N}_{t+1}} - \frac{\partial\mathcal{M}_L(\mathcal{V}_t,\mathcal{U}_t)}{\partial\mathcal{U}_t}\beta\mathbb{E}_t \frac{\partial\Omega^{SP}_{t+1}}{\partial\mathcal{N}_{t+1}} \tag{3.18}$$

The first component, $x_t - z$ or the difference between a marginal contribution to aggregate output and the flow utility of nonemployment, is the net social flow surplus generated by a job. The second component states that a job is valued for its duration. It is expected to survive to the following period with probability $(1-s)$ and continue to contribute its marginal social value. Finally, the last component captures the negative externality of removing an additional worker from the pool of unemployed on the probability of a job vacancy being filled.

Recalling that $\partial\mathcal{M}_L(\mathcal{V}_t,\mathcal{U}_t)/\partial\mathcal{V}_t = (1-\eta_L(\theta_t))q_t$ is the marginal effect of an additional vacancy on matches, and the corresponding $\partial\mathcal{M}_L(\mathcal{V}_t,\mathcal{U}_t)/\partial\mathcal{U}_t = \eta_L(\theta_t)f_t$, the condition for the constrained efficient choice of vacancies, by combining (3.17) and (3.18),

$$\begin{aligned}\frac{\gamma}{[1-\eta_L(\theta_t)]\,q_t} = \beta\mathbb{E}_t \Bigg\{ & x_{t+1} - z + (1-s)\frac{\gamma}{\left[1-\eta_L(\theta_{t+1})\right]q_{t+1}} \\ & -\gamma\frac{\eta_L(\theta_{t+1})}{1-\eta_L(\theta_{t+1})}\theta_{t+1}\Bigg\}\end{aligned}$$

equates the marginal resource cost of creating a job, $\gamma/\left[(1-\eta_L(\theta_t))\,q_t\right]$, to the discounted marginal expected benefit of an employed worker. This benefit is comprised of the terms described in equation (3.18): a flow marginal social benefit, the continuation value of an existing job, and a cost capturing the effect of the change in vacancies and unemployment on the congestion of both sides of the market. After some algebra detailed in the appendix section 3.6.5, we can compare the social planner to the decentralized economy's job creation condition:

Social planner's job creation condition:

$$\frac{\gamma}{q_t} = \frac{1}{1+r}\mathbb{E}_t\left[\left[1-\eta_L(\theta_t^{opt})\right](x_{t+1}-z)+(1-s)\frac{\gamma}{q_{t+1}}\vartheta_{t,t+1}\right.$$
$$\left.-\gamma\eta_L(\theta_{t+1}^{opt})\theta_{t+1}^{opt}\vartheta_{t,t+1}\right] \quad (3.19)$$

Decentralized economy's job creation condition:

$$\frac{\gamma}{q_t} = \frac{1}{1+r}\mathbb{E}_t\left[(1-\alpha_L)(x_{t+1}-z)+(1-s)\frac{\gamma}{q_{t+1}}-\gamma\alpha_L\theta_{t+1}\right] \quad (3.20)$$

in which $\vartheta_{t,t+1} \equiv \frac{1-\eta_L(\theta_t^{opt})}{1-\eta_L(\theta_{t+1}^{opt})}$ is a term we call the stochastic matching elasticity factor, which would be equal to 1 in the steady state, or for a constant elasticity matching function.

These two conditions, and hence allocations, will coincide if two sufficient conditions are met:

1. $\vartheta_{t,t+1} = 1\ \forall t$, which arises either in the steady state or when the matching function is isoelastic, that is, η_L is a constant.
2. The worker's share of the surplus in bargaining, α_L, is equal to the elasticity of the matching function with respect to unemployment:

Hosios condition in the labor market:

$$\eta_L(\theta_t) = \alpha_L\ \forall\ t \quad (3.21)$$

The first of these conditions is satisfied under the assumption of a Cobb–Douglas matching function $\mathcal{M}_L(\mathcal{V}_t,\mathcal{U}_t) = \chi_L\mathcal{V}^{1-\eta_L}\mathcal{U}^{\eta_L}$. In this case, the decentralized allocation may be efficient both at, and out of, steady state if the second condition holds. However, if the matching function has a time-varying elasticity, as is the case with the den Haan et al. (2000) matching function, the decentralized allocation can be efficient at a steady state but not, in general, if there are fluctuations in market tightness. Indeed, in this instance the elasticity of the matching function is $\eta_L(\theta_t) = \theta_t^{\nu_L}\left(1+\theta_t^{\nu_L}\right)^{-1}$, and will be cyclical if there are fluctuations in market tightness.

Finally, note that at a steady state the efficient job creation condition (3.19) in discrete time is also the equation one would obtain from deriving the efficient job creation condition in continuous time:

Discrete time social planner's job creation condition at a steady state:

$$\frac{\gamma}{q} = \frac{[1-\eta_L(\theta)](x-z) - \gamma\eta_L(\theta)\theta}{r+s} \tag{3.22}$$

3.4.2 Constrained efficient fluctuations

In this section we compare the decentralized allocation of the dynamic model of chapter 2, which fits the cyclical dynamics of the unemployment rate in the US time series, to a corresponding constrained efficient allocation from solving problem (3.15) for the corresponding economy. That is, the social planner chooses allocations subject to the same matching and job creation cost constraints as private agents in the competitive economy.

We can now make a statement about the efficient rate of unemployment. The decentralized allocation, as calibrated in chapter 2, implied an average unemployment rate of 5.8%. The social planner's allocation implies an average unemployment rate of 6.5%. Firms create too many jobs in the decentralized allocation, that is, the parameter value from the calibration of the model resulted in $\alpha_L < \eta_L$. Relative to the Hosios condition, the wage is too low, too much of the surplus is accruing to firms. This causes excess entry, because job creation costs are too small compared to what is socially efficient.

In addition to a higher rate of unemployment, the constrained efficient allocation implies fluctuations in job creation and unemployment, that are much more moderate. This is illustrated in figure 3.4. In this example both allocations are generated by the same realizations for productivity, x_t. The solid line corresponds to the decentralized allocation that mimics the business cycle of unemployment in the US time series. The dotted line plots the unemployment rate in the constraint efficient allocation, that chosen by the social planner. This unemployment rate never strays far from its mean of 6.5%. For instance, there is a recession around period 325 in which the decentralized economy's unemployment rate nears 9%, whereas the social planner's unemployment rate barely reaches 6.7%. This leads to a more complex view of the efficiency aspects of observed changes in the rate of unemployment, along with the appropriate stance of policy over the business cycle. Excess volatility (in normative terms) of the decentralized equilibrium is clearly inefficient.

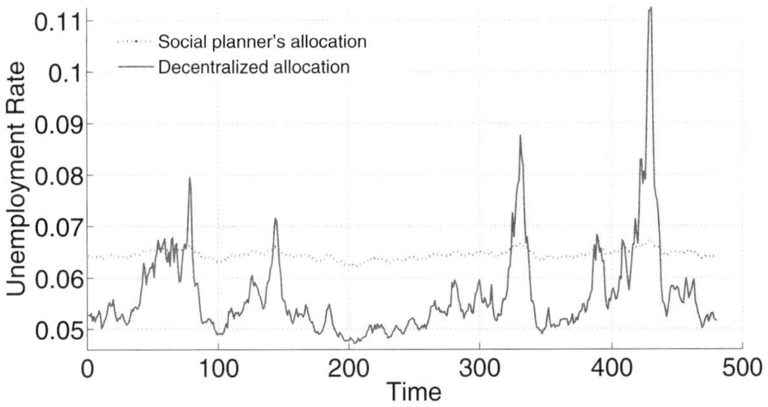

Figure 3.4
Sample unemployment paths, social planner, and decentralized allocations

3.5 Discussion of the literature and remaining issues

The efficiency condition in (3.1) was derived in Hosios (1990) and in Pissarides (2000) in the steady state and generalized in a more dynamic environment in Mortensen and Pissarides (1999a). Earlier papers had already recognized the close connection between worker's bargaining share and matching elasticity parameters. As put in Mortensen and Pissarides (2011), "*Diamond (1982b) had already hinted that there might be an internalized Nash wage rule and Pissarides (1984) derived explicitly the share of labor in the wage bargain that internalizes the externalities, what became later known as the 'Hosios rule' (Hosios, 1990).*"

Moen (1997) linked this condition to the existence of an endogenous number of subsegments and developed the competitive search equilibrium. Directed search models are another active branch of the literature. Introducing workers' moral hazard in competitive search efficiency, Moen and Rosén (2011) find a modified Hosios condition for efficiency. Menzio and Moen (2010) introduce limited commitment to show that wage of entry workers and insiders cannot be easily differentiated, with implications on the volatility puzzle emphasized in the previous chapter. Recent attempts to disentangle random versus directed search such as Engelhardt and Rupert (2009) lead to mixed conclusions about their respective relevance, and find that it depends on the sector of activity. Faberman and Menzio (2010) find that jobs with higher starting wages do not necessarily lead to more applicants and faster matching, although this might not invalidate directed search given other mechanisms such as training, heterogeneity of skills, and selection that could mask directed search mechanisms. A survey of US workers by Hall and Krueger (2012) found a quite large share of workers bargaining over their wage, and argue that this is as large as the share of posted wages. However, Marinescu and Wolthoff (2015) show that on a website such as CareerBuilder.com, 80% of vacancies do not contain information about wage, a key ingredient of directed search models.

This discussion on efficiency of search and matching models can be extended to several other environments. For instance, in the presence of ex-ante investments in capital, Acemoglu and Shimer (1999b) show that the classical investment hold-up problem and the associated underinvestment can be solved. In their environment, efficiency can be restored if workers observe, ex-ante, capital investments by firms and can direct their search accordingly. They argue that the underlying reason for efficiency being restored is not wage posting per se, but the ability of workers to direct their search toward more capital-intensive jobs. This is the same idea as that underlying the trade-off between tightness and wages in equation (3.6). Interesting insights on the congestion of the matching process under "phantom" vacancies have been discussed in a random search context by Cheron and Decreuse (2017), and in a directed search context by Albrecht et al. (2015). Under the existence of already matched vacancies still on the market but dead (so-called phantom vacancies), there is excess congestion from the vacancy side of the market leading to a new source of inefficiency of the search equilibrium.

The discussion on efficient versus inefficient separation arises naturally from the endogenous job destruction extension of the matching model offered in Mortensen and Pissarides (1994). The key concepts of surplus and inefficient separations can be found in Malcomson (1999). Some interesting inefficiencies from separation arise in the context of asymmetric information, when agents do not have the ability to credibly signal their utility on the job or outside the job. See Delacroix and Wasmer (2009) for such a discussion in a random search world. Under directed search, it is however possible to restore efficiency. For instance, Menzio and Shi (2011) show that the social planner solution is also the decentralized one in a model of directed search where agents agree on bilaterally efficient contracts. The efficiency result remains true even in the presence of match-specific private information and limited commitment on the worker's side, at least in a steady state. In a dynamic setting, a worker's outside option changes over time with the severity of the informational friction (Guerrieri, 2008). When firms offer a wage contract at a given point in time, they do not take into account the effect on the outside option of workers hired in previous periods. This creates an externality rendering the allocation dynamically inefficient. Guerrieri et al. (2010) tackle the problem of adverse selection in competitive search equilibrium.

Inefficiencies of the decentralized economy naturally lead to introducing policy instruments, which we did along the lines of the discussion on hiring subsidies and firing costs and the associated Hosios conditions introduced in Pissarides (2000) (chapter 9.8). Progressive payroll taxes have been shown to raise employment by reducing bargained wages in Pissarides (1998). Shi and Wen (1999) study the dynamic effects of labor and capital income taxes, investment tax credits, and unemployment and job vacancy subsidies. Of the schemes studied, a vacancy subsidy is most desirable as it is efficient and self-financed. Optimal tax dynamics results are discussed in Arseneau and Chugh (2012) who argue that optimal tax smoothing, and the absence of a wedge and intertemporal distortions, depends on wage setting. Another important topic is the analysis of the efficiency of unemployment insurance. In a search equilibrium, Acemoglu and Shimer (1999a) find a sharp result with risk-averse workers: unemployment insurance raises output and efficiency. Without the insurance, workers accept lower wages and firms create too many jobs relative to the social optimum. Moreover, unemployment insurance can lead to productivity gains as workers can seek the best jobs (e.g., Acemoglu and Shimer, 2000). When there is two-sided heterogeneity, of workers and firms, unemployment insurance can allow workers to find the right job. Marimon and Zilibotti (1999) show that, in a period of skill-biased technical change, cross-country difference in unemployment insurance can result in differences in productivity growth, wage inequality, and the rate of unemployment itself (see also Mortensen and Pissarides (1999b) for work on the interaction of unemployment benefits and skill-biased technical change). In a recent investigation into the effects of reforms to the generosity and duration of unemployment benefits, Launov and Walde (2013) use German micro data and a structural search model with endogenous worker search effort, and find that the effect on unemployment of Hartz IV reforms was very small. Employment protection has been introduced in search models by Mortensen and Pissarides (1999a), and its effect on employment discussed in Burda (1992) and Ljunqvist (2002). An interesting model with a limited ability for consumption smoothing by Lale (2016) gives rise to nontrivial trade-offs between employment protection and wage determination, with a limited role for employment protection on welfare. See also Wasmer (2006) for mechanisms leading to positive effects of employment protection under the possibility of investments in specific skills by workers. See also the related paper with heterogeneous quality by Pries and Rogerson (2005) where quality is either an experience good or an inspection good.

Due to nonlinearities in the dynamics of the labor market, which also give rise to the existence of extreme values in unemployment during deep recessions (or "crises" as studied in Petrosky-Nadeau and Zhang, 2013), the welfare costs of business cycles is much larger than claimed in Lucas (1987, 2003). Lucas argues that the welfare cost of business cycles is negligible. Assuming log utility for the representative consumer and a log-normal distribution for the consumption growth, calculations indicate that the consumer would only sacrifice a mere 0.008% of consumption in perpetuity to get rid of all its aggregate fluctuations. However, Lucas's analysis underestimates the welfare cost by overlooking crisis states, in which the agent's marginal utility is high, by assuming that fluctuations have no effect on the mean of variables. Arguments along these lines can also be found in Hairault et al. (2010) and Jung and Kuester (2011).

3.6 Chapter appendix

3.6.1 Continuous time constrained efficiency: baseline

The social planner maximizes Ω^{SP} subject to the matching frictions imposed by the matching technology:

$$\Omega^{SP} = \max_{\mathcal{U},\mathcal{V}} \int_0^{\infty} e^{-rt}[x(1-\mathcal{U}) + z\mathcal{U} - \gamma\theta\mathcal{U}]dt \ \text{ s.t. } \ \dot{\mathcal{U}} = s(1-\mathcal{U}) - \theta q(\theta)\mathcal{U}$$

Although the social planner program is derived with respect to vacancies as a control and unemployment as a state variable, it has often been derived in the literature with respect to labor market tightness θ as a control variable. Since the social planner can choose freely vacancies, it may also choose freely the ratio of vacancies to unemployment. Here we derive the social planner's program as a function of quantities (vacancies and unemployment), as in the rest of the book except in a few instances (notably in parts where we simultaneously introduce endogenous destruction). The Hamiltonian of the problem, denoting Ψ_U as a co-state variable, is therefore

$$H = e^{-rt}[x(1-\mathcal{U}) + z\mathcal{U} - \gamma\mathcal{V}] + \Psi_U[s(1-\mathcal{U}) - \mathcal{M}(\mathcal{U},\mathcal{V})]$$

and the first order conditions are

$$\frac{\partial H}{\partial \mathcal{V}} = 0 \ \text{ and } \ \dot{\Psi}_U = -\frac{\partial H}{\partial \mathcal{U}}$$

which imply

$$-e^{-rt}\gamma - \Psi_U(1-\eta_L(\theta))q(\theta) = 0$$
$$e^{-rt}(x-z) + \Psi_U[s + \eta_L(\theta)f(\theta)] = \dot{\Psi}_U$$

using $\partial\mathcal{M}(\mathcal{U},\mathcal{V})/\partial\mathcal{V} = (1-\eta_L(\theta))q(\theta)$ and $\partial\mathcal{M}(\mathcal{U},\mathcal{V})/\partial\mathcal{U} = \eta_L(\theta)f(\theta)$ where $\eta_L(\theta)$ is the elasticity of the matching function with respect to θ. From the first equation we obtain

$$\Psi_U = \frac{-\gamma e^{-rt}}{q(\theta)(1-\eta_L)} \text{ and } \dot{\Psi}_U = \frac{r\gamma e^{-rt}}{q(\theta)(1-\eta_L)}$$

which can be substituted into the second equation at a steady state to obtain

$$\begin{aligned} e^{-rt}(x-z) - \frac{\gamma e^{-rt}}{q(\theta)(1-\eta_L)}[s+\eta_L(\theta)f(\theta)] &= \frac{r\gamma e^{-rt}}{q(\theta)(1-\eta_L)} \\ (1-\eta_L)(x-z) - \frac{\gamma s}{q(\theta)} - \gamma\theta\eta_L(\theta) &= \frac{r\gamma}{q(\theta)} \end{aligned}$$

and finally

$$\frac{\gamma}{q(\theta)} = \frac{(1-\eta_L)(x-z) - \eta_L\gamma\theta}{r+s}$$

as in the text.

3.6.2 Continuous time constrained efficiency: endogenous job destruction

The social planner maximizes Ω^{SP} subject to the matching frictions imposed by the matching technology and endogenous job destruction. The social planner thus has one additional instrument, the reservation cutoff rule denoted by A, which now affects both the average flow output that we denote $\bar{x}$ and the entry and exit into unemployment. Following Mortensen and Pissarides, we treat the two constraints on hiring flows and output changes symmetrically, and the program can be written as

$$\begin{aligned} \Omega^{SP} &= \max_{A,\theta,\mathcal{U},\bar{x}} \int_0^\infty e^{-rt}(\bar{x} + z\mathcal{U} - \gamma\theta\mathcal{U})\,dt \\ \text{subject to}\quad & \dot{\mathcal{U}} = [s+\mu G(A)](1-\mathcal{U}) - \theta q(\theta)[1-G(A)]\mathcal{U} \\ & \partial\bar{x}/\partial t = \theta q(\theta)\int_A a'\mathrm{d}G(a')x\mathcal{U} + \mu\int_A a'\mathrm{d}G(a')x(1-\mathcal{U}) - (s+\mu)\bar{x} \end{aligned}$$

The Hamiltonian to this problem is

$$\begin{aligned} H = {} & e^{-rt}[\bar{x} + z\mathcal{U} - \gamma\theta\mathcal{U}] + \Psi_U[-\theta q(\theta)(1-G(A))\mathcal{U} + (s+\mu G(A))(1-\mathcal{U})] \\ & + \Psi_A\left[-(s+\mu)\bar{x} + \theta q(\theta)\int_A a'\mathrm{d}G(a')x\mathcal{U} - \mu\int_A a'G(a')x(1-\mathcal{U})\right] \end{aligned}$$

with optimality conditions

$$\begin{aligned} \frac{\partial H}{\partial A} = 0 \to 0 = {} & \Psi_U[\theta q(\theta)g(A)\mathcal{U} + \mu g(A)(1-\mathcal{U})] - \Psi_A[\theta q(\theta)x\mathcal{U}Ag(A) \\ & + \mu Ag(A)x(1-\mathcal{U})] \end{aligned}$$

$$\text{which leads to}\quad \Psi_U = Ax\Psi_A \tag{3.23}$$

$$\text{and}\quad \dot{\Psi}_U = Ax\dot{\Psi}_A \tag{3.24}$$

$$
\begin{aligned}
\frac{\partial H}{\partial \theta} = 0 \to 0 \quad &= \quad -e^{-rt}\gamma\mathcal{U} - \Psi_U (1-\eta_L)\, q(\theta)\,(1-G(A))\,\mathcal{U} \\
&\quad + \Psi_A (1-\eta_L)\, q(\theta) x \mathcal{U} \int_A a' \mathrm{d}G(a') \\
e^{-rt}\gamma &= (1-\eta_L)\, q(\theta) \left[-\Psi_U \int_A \mathrm{d}G(a')x + \Psi_A \int_A a' \mathrm{d}G(a')x \right] \\
e^{-rt}\gamma &= (1-\eta_L)\, q(\theta) \left[A\Psi_A \int_A \mathrm{d}G(a')x + \Psi_A \int_R a' \mathrm{d}G(a')x \right]
\end{aligned}
$$

which leads to
$$e^{-rt}\gamma = -(1-\eta_L)\, q(\theta)\Psi_A \int_A \left(A - a'\right) \mathrm{d}G(a')x \tag{3.25}$$

and
$$re^{-rt}\gamma = -(1-\eta_L)\, q(\theta)\dot{\Psi}_A \int_A \left(a' - A\right) \mathrm{d}G(a')x \tag{3.26}$$

$$
\begin{aligned}
\frac{\partial H}{\partial \mathcal{U}} &= -\dot{\Psi}_U \to e^{-rt}(z - \gamma\theta) - \Psi_U \left[\theta q(\theta)(1-G(A)) + s + \mu G(A)\right] \\
&\quad -\Psi_A \left[\mu - \theta q(\theta)\right] \int_A a' \mathrm{d}G(a')x = -\dot{\Psi}_U
\end{aligned} \tag{3.27}
$$

$$\frac{\partial H}{\partial \bar{x}} = -\dot{\Psi}_A \to e^{-rt} - (s+\mu)\Psi_A = -\dot{\Psi}_A \tag{3.28}$$

The steps to deriving the job creation condition are as follows. Begin with the optimality condition for $\bar{x}$ in equation (3.28) in which we substitute Ψ_A and $\dot{\Psi}_A$ using equations (3.23) and (3.24):

$$
\begin{aligned}
\dot{\Psi}_A &= -e^{-rt} + (s+\mu)\Psi_A \\
\frac{re^{-rt}\gamma}{(1-\eta_L)\, q(\theta) \int_A \left(a' - A\right) \mathrm{d}G(a')x} &= e^{-rt} + \frac{(s+\mu)\, e^{-rt}\gamma}{(1-\eta_L)\, q(\theta) \int_A \left(A - a'\right) \mathrm{d}G(a')x} \\
(r+s+\mu)\,\gamma &= (1-\eta_L)\, q(\theta) \int_A \left(a' - A\right) \mathrm{d}G(a')x \\
\frac{\gamma}{q(\theta)} &= \frac{(1-\eta_L)\,x}{r+s+\mu} \int_A \left(a' - A\right) \mathrm{d}G(a')
\end{aligned} \tag{3.29}
$$

The steps to deriving the job destruction condition are as follows. Start with combining conditions (3.28) and (3.23):

$$
\begin{aligned}
e^{-rt} + (s+\mu)\frac{-\Psi_U}{Ax} &= \frac{-\dot{\Psi}_U}{Ax} \\
Axe^{-rt} - (s+\mu)\Psi_U &= -\dot{\Psi}_U
\end{aligned}
$$

Then work from the optimality condition for $\mathcal{U}$ in equation (3.25):

$$
\begin{aligned}
&e^{-rt}(z - \gamma\theta) - \Psi_U \left[\theta q(\theta)(1-G(A)) + s + \mu G(A)\right] \\
&\quad - \Psi_A \left[\mu - \theta q(\theta)\right] \int_A a' \mathrm{d}G(a')x = Axe^{-rt} - (s+\mu)\Psi_U
\end{aligned}
$$

$$
\begin{aligned}
&e^{-rt}(z-\gamma\theta-Ax)-\Psi_U[\theta q(\theta)-\mu](1-G(A))\\
&\quad -\Psi_A[\mu-\theta q(\theta)]\int_A a'\mathrm{d}G(a')x=0\\
&e^{-rt}(z-\gamma\theta-Ax)-\Psi_A Ax[\theta q(\theta)-\mu]\int_A \mathrm{d}G(a')\\
&\quad -\Psi_A[\mu-\theta q(\theta)]\int_A a'\mathrm{d}G(a')x=0\\
&e^{-rt}(z-\gamma\theta-Ax)-\Psi_A[\mu-\theta q(\theta)]\int_A \left(a'-A\right)\mathrm{d}G(a')x=0\\
&e^{-rt}(z-\gamma\theta-Ax)-\mu\Psi_A\int_A \left(a'-A\right)\mathrm{d}G(a')x=-\theta\Psi_A q(\theta)\int_A \left(a'-A\right)\mathrm{d}G(a')x
\end{aligned}
$$

Now use the fact, from equation (3.23), that $-e^{-rt}\gamma/(1-\eta_L)=-\Psi_A q(\theta)$ $\int_A \left(a'-A\right)\mathrm{d}G(a')x$, and also $-\Psi_A\int_A \left(a'-A\right)\mathrm{d}G(a')x=-e^{-rt}\gamma/[q(\theta)(1-\eta_L)]$, to obtain

$$
\begin{aligned}
e^{-rt}(z-\gamma\theta-Ax)-\mu\frac{e^{-rt}\gamma}{q(\theta)(1-\eta_L)} &= -\frac{e^{-rt}\gamma}{(1-\eta_L)}\theta\\
z-\gamma\theta+\frac{\gamma}{(1-\eta_L)}\theta &= Ax+\mu\frac{\gamma}{q(\theta)(1-\eta_L)}\\
z+\frac{\eta_L}{1-\eta_L}\gamma\theta &= Ax+\frac{\mu x}{r+s+\mu}\int_A \left(a'-A\right)\mathrm{d}G(a')
\end{aligned}
$$

3.6.3 Moen's efficiency result

Start from the maximization of $J_v(w_i,\theta_i)$ defined in equation (3.7) under the constraint (3.6) for a given level of W_u. Differentiation of (3.7) with respect to w_i leads to

$$
\frac{-1}{q^2(\theta_i)}(\gamma+rJ_{vi})\frac{\partial q(\theta_i)}{\partial w_i}+\left(1+\frac{r}{q(\theta_i)}\right)\frac{\partial J_{vi}}{\partial w_i}=\frac{-1}{r+s} \tag{3.30}
$$

The value of $\partial q(\theta_i)/\partial w_i$ is obtained as follows, using (3.6):

$$
\begin{aligned}
\frac{\partial q(\theta_i)}{\partial w_i} &= \frac{\partial q_i}{\partial f_i}\times\frac{\partial f_i}{\partial w_i}=\frac{\partial q_i}{\partial f_i}\times\frac{\partial\left(\frac{rW_u-z}{w_i-rW_u}(r+s)\right)}{\partial w_i}\\
&=\frac{\partial q_i}{\partial f_i}\times\frac{-f_i}{w_i-rW_{ui}}
\end{aligned} \tag{3.31}
$$

We have that

$$
\begin{aligned}
&q_i=f_i/\theta_i\\
&\Rightarrow\frac{\partial q_i}{\partial f_i}=\frac{1}{\theta_i}-\frac{f_i}{\theta_i^2}\frac{\partial\theta_i}{\partial f_i}=\frac{1}{\theta_i}\left(1-\frac{1}{1-\eta_L(\theta_i)}\right)=\frac{-1}{\theta_i}\frac{\eta_L(\theta_i)}{1-\eta_L(\theta_i)}
\end{aligned} \tag{3.32}
$$

using $\frac{\theta_i}{f_i}\frac{\partial f}{\partial \theta_i} = 1 - \eta_L(\theta_i)$. Then, at the optimum value of the wage, $\frac{\partial J_{vi}}{\partial w_i} = 0$. Combining (3.31) and (3.32) and plugging into (3.30), we have at an optimum of J_{Vi} that

$$\frac{1}{q^2(\theta_i)}(\gamma + rJ_{vi})\frac{f_i}{\theta_i}\frac{\eta_L(\theta_i)}{1-\eta_L(\theta_i)} = \frac{w_i - rW_{ui}}{r+s}$$

$$\Leftrightarrow \frac{\gamma}{q(\theta_i)} + \frac{rJ_{vi}}{q(\theta_i)} = \frac{1-\eta_L(\theta_i)}{\eta_L(\theta_i)}\frac{w_i - rW_{ui}}{r+s}$$

leading to (3.9) with $J_{vi} = K$ in a free-entry equilibrium.

3.6.4 Coincidence of the wage in the decentralized equilibrium with entry costs and Moen's Efficient wage

Start from Moen's equilibrium. One has

$$\frac{\gamma}{q(\theta_i)} + \frac{rK}{q(\theta_i)} = \frac{1-\eta_L(\theta_i)}{\eta_L(\theta_i)}\frac{w_i(\theta_i) - rW_u}{r+s}$$

Now, from the value of $rW_u = z + f(\theta_i)(W_n - W_u) = z + f(\theta)\frac{w_i - rW_u}{r+s}$, one can rewrite this equation as

$$\frac{\gamma}{q(\theta_i)} + \frac{rK}{q(\theta_i)} = \frac{1-\eta_L(\theta_i)}{\eta_L(\theta_i)}\frac{w_i - z}{r+s+f}$$

or, after multiplication by $r+s+f(\theta)$,

$$\left[\frac{\gamma}{q(\theta_i)} + \frac{rK}{q(\theta_i)}\right](r+s) + \theta(\gamma + rK) = \frac{1-\eta_L(\theta_i)}{\eta_L(\theta_i)}(w_i - z)$$

Add up $K(r+s)$ to the left and to the right to obtain a term $\left[\frac{\gamma}{q(\theta_i)} + \frac{(r+q(\theta_i)K}{q(\theta_i)}\right] = J$ in the left-hand side, and using $J = \frac{x - w_i + sK}{r+s}$, one obtains Moen's efficient wage:

$$\eta\left[x - w_i + sK + \theta(\gamma + rK)\right] = \left[1 - \eta_L\right](w_i - z) + (r+s)K\eta$$

or, after re-arrangement,

$$w_i = (1-\eta_L)z + \eta_L\left[x + \theta\gamma + (\theta - 1)rK\right]$$

The Nash bargaining wage in the case where firms face a fixed entry cost is exactly identical: one has

$$\alpha_L\left(\frac{x - w_i + sK}{r+s} - K\right) = (1-\alpha_L)\left(\frac{w_i - rW_u}{r+s}\right)$$

or

$$w = (1-\alpha_L)rW_u + \alpha_L(x - rK)$$

Using as usual $rW_u = z + f(\theta)(W_n - W_u) = z + f(\theta)(J_n - K)\alpha_L/(1-\alpha_L) = z + \theta(\gamma + rK)\alpha_L/(1-\alpha_L)$, one finally obtains:

$$w_i = (1-\alpha_L)z + \theta(\gamma + rK)\alpha_L + \alpha_L(x - rK)$$
$$w_i = (1-\alpha_L)z + \alpha_L\left[x + \theta\gamma + rK(\theta - 1)\right] \tag{3.33}$$

Hence the two wages do coincide if tightness coincides and $\alpha_L = \eta_L$.

3.6.5 Hosios in discrete time

For the purposes of comparison with the decentralized job creation condition, we multiply and divide the last term in the bracketed expression of the RHS by labor market tightness θ_{t+1}, and by the number of matches in $t+1$, which yields

$$\frac{\gamma}{(1-\eta_L(\theta_t))\,q_t} = \beta \mathbb{E}_t\left[x_{t+1} - z + (1-s)\frac{\gamma}{\left(1-\eta_L(\theta_{t+1})\right)q_{t+1}} - \gamma\frac{\eta_L(\theta_{t+1})}{1-\eta_L(\theta_{t+1})}\theta_{t+1}\right] \tag{3.34}$$

where $\eta_L(\theta_t) \equiv \frac{\partial \mathcal{M}_L}{\partial \mathcal{U}_t}\frac{\mathcal{U}_t}{\mathcal{M}_L(\mathcal{V}_t,\mathcal{U}_t)}$ is the elasticity of matching with respect to the unemployed, and where we have made use of the fact that $\frac{\partial \mathcal{M}_L}{\partial \mathcal{V}_t} = (1-\eta_L(\theta_t))\,q_t$. Next, recall the job creation condition for the decentralized equilibrium when wages are determined by Nash bargaining from chapter 1:

$$\frac{\gamma}{(1-\alpha_L)\,q_t} = \frac{1}{1+r}\mathbb{E}_t\left[x_{t+1} - z + (1-s)\frac{\gamma}{(1-\alpha_L)\,q_{t+1}} - \gamma\frac{\alpha_L}{1-\alpha_L}\theta_{t+1}\right] \tag{3.35}$$

3.6.6 Efficient layoff taxes with endogenous separations

We now introduce a layoff tax $T > 0$ to the model of endogenous job destruction developed in section 1.6. The layoff tax is paid only when an endogenous separation occurs, as opposed to exogenous separation which arrives at Poisson rate s. When a new idiosyncratic productivity draw occurs, with arrival rate μ, the firm chooses between a surplus at the new level of productivity, and destroying the job. Thus only the Bellman equation for a filled position is affected by the introduction of the layoff tax:

$$rJ_\pi(a) = ax - w(a) + (s+\mu)\left[J_v - J_\pi(a)\right] + \mu\int \max\left[J_\pi(a') - J_v, -T\right]\mathrm{d}G(a') \tag{3.36}$$

The total surplus of the employment relationship is still defined as $\Sigma_l^T(a) = W_n(a) - W_u + J_\pi(a) - J_v$, and is equal to

$$(r+s+\mu)\,\Sigma_l^T(a) = ax + \mu\int \max\left[\Sigma_l^T(a'), -T\right]\mathrm{d}G(a') - rW_u$$

This surplus is strictly increasing in idiosyncratic productivity a with slope $x/(r+s+\mu)$. Thus there exists an idiosyncratic productivity A such that $\Sigma_l^T(A) = -T$ which defines a reservation strategy for continuing or destroying the match. That is, the match is destroyed if the draw $a < A$, and continues otherwise. Using this result, a solution for the surplus is $S(a) = (a - A)\,x/\,(r+s+\mu) - T$, and the surplus evaluated at the job destruction threshold yields

$$Ax + \frac{\mu x}{r+s+\mu}\int_A (a' - A)\,\mathrm{d}G(a') = rW_u - (r+s)\,T$$

Under Nash wage bargaining, the equilibrium is a pair (A, θ) that satisfies the modified job creation and job destruction conditions:

Job creation with layoff tax:

$$\frac{\gamma}{q(\theta)} = \frac{x(1-\alpha_L)}{r+s+\mu}\int_A (a' - A)\,\mathrm{d}G(a') - (1-\alpha_L)T \tag{3.37}$$

Job destruction with layoff tax:

$$Ax + \frac{\mu x}{r+s+\mu}\int_A (a' - A)\,\mathrm{d}G(a') = z + \gamma\theta\frac{\alpha_L}{1-\alpha_L} - (r+s)\,T \tag{3.38}$$

The tax reduces the total surplus and thus the job creation curve shifts inwards. This tends to lead to a reduction of labor market tightness and the cutoff productivity by equation (3.37). The layoff tax also tends to reduce the job destruction threshold by equation (3.38) by shifting the job destruction curve downwards. The effect on job creation can appear ambiguous, as we shift along the job creation curve. It can be shown, however, that the effect is unambiguous and that layoff taxes reduce equilibrium labor market tightness.

4 Firm size and strategic bargaining

In practice, the one-worker/one-firm assumption made so far is too restrictive, and the size of firms may matter, at least if the model is not scale-invariant. For instance, strategic interactions that do not occur in the one worker firm may arise in a large firm. In this chapter, we relax the assumption that the firm has only one worker. We instead introduce a model of a large representative firm with a continuum of labor inputs on several labor markets, such as skilled and unskilled workers, or differentiated by occupation, age, or experience. The model provided here introduces new wage bargaining solutions compared to the previous chapter (chapter 1), because of the possibility for the firm to bargain simultaneously with several workers of different types. We discuss the micro-foundations of the bargaining solutions that we will emphasize later at the end of this chapter. They lead to what has been called intrafirm bargaining or strategic bargaining, that is the ability of the firm to set individual wages taking into account the effect on other wages.

Strategic bargaining over wages has a large set of implications, and leads in the generic case to "over-employment" as compared to situations when the strategic motive is absent. Firms exploit decreasing returns to scale in labor, finding it profitable to marginally raise employment so as to decrease the marginal product of labor, thereby strategically affecting the wage bargaining process through the size of the firm.

However, to solve for this more complex bargaining problem, we need to solve for a set of partial equilibrium differential equations. The general solution found by Cahuc et al. (2008), that we follow closely here, uses spherical coordinates, and is developed in this chapter's appendix. The chapter further shows that, with several types of workers, overemployment is not a general result. The converse—underemployment—may actually hold under strategic bargaining, in particular when different groups have different bargaining power. In this case the firm actually overemploys groups with high bargaining power, and reduces employment of groups with low bargaining power.

The large firm model leads to a rich set of predictions, permits a discussion of the determinants of the size of the firm and the role of aggregate returns to scale, and allows us to discuss the demand for different factors of production in the presence of labor frictions, a topic widely studied empirically. Finally, we discuss the role of the complementarity-substitutability between types of labor, and introduce and study the determinants and efficiency of investment in physical capital.

4.1 Strategic bargaining with discrete labor

The intuition for why and how the wage will depend on the size of the firm can be understood with a simple example. Assume that employment is discrete and there is a single type of worker in order to simplify the analysis. Consider the problem faced by a firm with three workers with whom it bargains *individually, bilaterally,* and *symmetrically.* By the latter term, we mean that within a category of labor, all workers are marginal in discussions with the firm. Alternative assumptions have recently been introduced in the literature (see section 4.6) but they do not deliver *asymmetric* solutions in the benchmark case. In addition, assume equal sharing. The wage is such that the surplus of the marginal worker is equal to the firm's marginal surplus. Each worker's individual surplus is defined as $w(3) - \underline{w}$, where $w(3)$ is the wage of a three-worker firm, and $\underline{w}$ is a worker's outside option.

The firm's marginal surplus from any of the three marginal workers is the revenue net of their wages generated by these three workers, $F(3) - 3 \times w(3)$, net of the firm's outside option. In the one-worker firm, that outside option in bargaining would simply be the value of a vacancy, driven down to zero in a free-entry equilibrium. However, in the bargaining game between the firm and one of its marginal workers this is no longer the case. The outside option is simply the revenue of *two* workers, $F(2)$, minus their wages, $2 \times w(2)$. Wage bargaining with the third worker thus leads to a wage $w(3)$ that satisfies the following condition:

$$[F(3) - 3w(3)] - [F(2) - 2w(2)] = w(3) - \underline{w}$$

The wage of the three-worker firm thus depends on the wage paid to the two-worker firm, $w(2)$, which is itself the outcome of a bargaining process that needs to be calculated. Taking one step back, the wage and the surplus of the firm with two workers has to be computed and, under similar reasoning, is

$$[F(2) - 2w(2)] - [F(1) - w(1)] = w(2) - \underline{w}$$

Finally, the outcome of bargaining with the first worker for a one-worker firm is

$$[F(1) - w(1)] - F(0) = w(1) - \underline{w}$$

Working forward, it can be shown that for any $\mathcal{N}$, the wage of a worker in a firm with $\mathcal{N}$ workers is a recursive function of differences $[F(i) - F(i-1)]$ for $i = 1$ to $\mathcal{N}$. These are the infra-marginal products of labor, the difference between production at employment i and production at employment $(i-1)$. To be precise, the wage in a firm with $\mathcal{N}$ workers is (Stole and Zwiebel, 1996b, p. 199)

$$w(\mathcal{N}) = \frac{\underline{w}}{2} + \frac{1}{\mathcal{N}(\mathcal{N}+1)} \sum_{i=1}^{\mathcal{N}} i[F(i) - F(i-1)]$$

In this expression, the wage is a weighted average of all infra-marginal products of labor. At any given size, the firm has to consider the outcome of the negotiation with one fewer worker, and the wage with one fewer worker will itself depend on the wage with two fewer workers, etc., until the point of zero employment in the firm.

4.2 The large firm matching model with one type of worker

Before going further, we can switch to continuous employment and consider a large representative firm with only one type of worker in total supply of a unit mass. The firm produces $F(\mathcal{N})$, where $\mathcal{N}$ is the mass of employed workers. The process of hires and separations remains stochastic, and governed by Poisson processes. Through the law of large numbers, the firm knows its size across periods, at least in the steady state, yet it takes labor market tightness and the associated job filling hazard q as given in the market.

The value of the surplus for the worker is the same as previously, denoted by $W_n - W_u$, while the firm's program is different. It includes the optimization over one control variable, the firm's number of vacancies $\mathcal{V}$, and a wage that may depend on the size of the firm since firms are not necessarily wage takers. For the moment the wage is a function of employment $\mathcal{N}$.

4.2.1 Firm's program and wage bargaining

The program of the firm is therefore to maximize the value $\Pi(\mathcal{N})$:

$$\Pi(\mathcal{N}) = \max_{\mathcal{N},\mathcal{V}} \int_0^\infty e^{-rt}[F(\mathcal{N}) - w(\mathcal{N})\mathcal{N} - \gamma\mathcal{V}]dt \text{ s.t. } \dot{\mathcal{N}} = q\mathcal{V} - s\mathcal{N}$$

where q is taken as given by the firm (contrary to the social planner's program studied in the previous chapter where the social planner precisely aimed at internalizing matching externalities). The Hamiltonian of the problem is therefore given by

$$H = e^{-rt}[F(\mathcal{N}) - w(\mathcal{N})\mathcal{N} - \gamma\mathcal{V}] + \Psi_N [q\mathcal{V} - s\mathcal{N}]$$

and the optimality conditions are

$$\frac{\partial H}{\partial \mathcal{V}} = 0 = -\gamma e^{-rt} + q\Psi_N$$

and

$$\dot{\Psi}_N = -\frac{\partial H}{\partial \mathcal{N}} \rightarrow \left[F'(\mathcal{N}) - w'(\mathcal{N})\mathcal{N} - w(\mathcal{N})\right] e^{-rt} - s\Psi_N = -\dot{\Psi}_N$$

Eliminate the multiplier $\Psi_N = \gamma/q(\theta)e^{-rt}$, and one obtains the first-order condition in the steady state:

Large-firm (marginal) job creation condition, single type of worker case:

$$\frac{\gamma}{q} = \frac{F'(\mathcal{N}) - w(\mathcal{N}) - \mathcal{N}w'(\mathcal{N})}{r+s} = J_\pi(\mathcal{N}) \tag{4.1}$$

where $J_\pi(\mathcal{N})$ is the derivative of $\pi(\mathcal{N})$ with respect to $\mathcal{N}$.

Using the usual Nash sharing rule, adapted to the marginal value of employment, we have

$$\alpha_L J_\pi(\mathcal{N}) = (1-\alpha_L)(W_n - W_u) \tag{4.2}$$

which leads to a differential equation:

$$w(\mathcal{N}) = (1-\alpha_L)rW_u + \alpha_L\left[F'(\mathcal{N}) - \mathcal{N}w'(\mathcal{N})\right] \tag{4.3}$$

The proof is in the appendix. The solution to that equation is determined through standard techniques. First one solves the differential equation without the constant term $(1-\alpha_L)rW_u$, called the homogenous associated differential equation. The solution contains a constant of integration that is next assumed to be a function of employment. We then solve for the full differential equation (with the constant term) in deriving the "variation of the constant," as the solution of a simpler differential equation derived from equation (4.2). In the end, we obtain

$$w(\mathcal{N}) = (1-\alpha_L)rW_u + \int_0^1 \nu^{\frac{1-\alpha_L}{\alpha_L}} F'(\mathcal{N}\nu)d\nu \tag{4.4}$$

4.2.2 Large-firm/small-firm equivalence result under constant returns to scale

Equation (4.4) converges to the classic wage equation of chapter 1 under constant returns to scale in labor. Indeed, if $F'(\mathcal{N}) = x$, the wage equation above becomes independent of the level, of employment,

$$w(\mathcal{N}) = (1-\alpha_L)rW_u + \alpha_L x \tag{4.5}$$

while the equilibrium value of unemployment is, as in chapter 1,

$$rW_u = z + f(\theta)(W_n - W_u) = z + \frac{\alpha_L}{1-\alpha_L}\gamma\theta^* \tag{4.6}$$

Hence combining (4.5) and (4.6), the fact that $w' = 0$ in equation (4.1) leads to the standard job creation condition seen in previous chapters, i.e., equation (1.31).

Further, as employment and labor market tightness are linked through the steady-state employment condition,

$$1 - \mathcal{N} = \mathcal{U} = \frac{s}{s + f(\theta)}$$

the large firm model is perfectly equivalent to the one-worker model under constant returns to scale. This result was used in the first edition of Pissarides (1990).

4.2.3 An overemployment result under decreasing returns to scale

Under decreasing returns to scale the model is no longer equivalent to our benchmark of chapter 1. In particular, as can be seen from equation (4.4), the wage is now a weighted function of infra-marginal products of labor. A nice interpretation of this result is as follows. When the firm bargains individually with an additional unit of labor, it considers as a threat point the value of profits at current employment less one (marginal) unit of labor, which involves production and wages at this lower employment level. In turn, that value of wages at this lower employment level would be negotiated with each worker individually, with as a new outside option that level of employment minus one unit of labor. The reasoning carries through until $\mathcal{N}$ reaches 0, and the overall wage equation involves all infra-marginal profits, just as exposed in section 4.1.

We introduce a convenient and compact notation for the ratio of weighted infra-marginal products of labor over the range $(0, \mathcal{N})$ to the marginal product evaluated at $\mathcal{N}$. Denoted by O_N, standing for overemployment for reasons that will be apparent in a few lines, this is defined as

$$O_N = \frac{\int_0^1 \frac{1}{\alpha_L} v^{\frac{1-\alpha_L}{\alpha_L}} F'(\mathcal{N}v)dv}{F'(\mathcal{N})} \tag{4.7}$$

With a Cobb–Douglas production $F(\mathcal{N}) = x\mathcal{N}^{1-\bar{\epsilon}}$, one obtains $O_N = (1 - \alpha_L\bar{\epsilon})^{-1} > 1$ under strict decreasing returns to scale ($0 < \bar{\epsilon} < 1$), and equal to 1 under constant returns to scale ($\bar{\epsilon} = 0$).

We can now rewrite the model's equilibrium conditions as:

Wage and job creation conditions, large firm with single worker type and intrafirm bargaining:

$$\frac{\gamma}{q(\theta^*)} = \frac{O_N F'(\mathcal{N}^*) - w(\mathcal{N}^*)}{r+s} \tag{4.8}$$

$$w(\mathcal{N}) = (1-\alpha_L)rW_u + \alpha_L O_N F'(\mathcal{N}) \text{ for all } \mathcal{N} \tag{4.9}$$

where the superscript * refers to the optimal value of employment and the equilibrium value of labor market tightness. These conditions are identical to the one-worker model when $O_N = 1$ (under constant returns to scale). Under decreasing returns to scale, as O_N is larger than 1, this multiple on the marginal product leads in equilibrium to more employment than under constant returns and $O_N = 1$. Substituting the wage in equation (4.8) with its definition in equation (4.9), we obtain a new job creation condition:

Intrafirm bargaining job creation condition, single worker type:

$$\frac{\gamma}{q(\theta)} = \frac{(1-\alpha_L)\left[O_N F'(\mathcal{N}) - z\right] - \gamma\theta\alpha_L}{r+s} \tag{4.10}$$

The interpretation of this equation is as follows: the firm will need to hire more labor than it would have otherwise done under $O_N = 1$, because hiring more workers, which decreases the marginal product of labor, is profitable as it reduces the wage bill. To see the extent to this overemployment result, one may calculate the equilibrium wage. Instead of eliminating the wage from equations (4.9) and (4.8), one can eliminate $O_N F'(\mathcal{N})$ and then obtain the equilibrium value of the wage:

$$w(\mathcal{N}^*) = rW_u + (r+s)\frac{\alpha_L}{1-\alpha_L}\frac{\gamma}{q(\theta^*)}$$

The wage at optimal employment is a markup over the reservation wage rW_u, plus the replacement cost of labor accruing to firms, reflected by the term proportional to γ/q. This result generalizes the earlier result of Stole and Zwiebel (1996a,b) that, in the absence of turnover costs but under bargaining, firms hire above the competitive level, and up to a point where the wage reaches the reservation wage of workers. We show that the overemployment result remains valid with search frictions, but the wage remains above the reservation wage.

4.2.4 Second-best efficiency

Adapting the social planner's problem described in chapter 3 to a production technology with decreasing returns to scale, we have

$$\max_{\mathcal{U},\theta} \int_0^\infty e^{-rt}\left[F(1-\mathcal{U})+z\mathcal{U}-\gamma\theta\mathcal{U}\right]dt \text{ s.t. } \dot{\mathcal{U}} = s(1-\mathcal{U})-\theta q(\theta)\mathcal{U}$$

and the resulting social planner's job creation condition is:

Social planner job creation condition:

$$\frac{\gamma}{q(\theta^{opt})} = \frac{(1-\eta_L)\left[F'(\mathcal{N}^{opt})-z\right]-\eta_L(\theta^{opt})\theta^{opt}\gamma}{r+s} \tag{4.11}$$

The optimization by the social planner would be a standard efficient job creation condition with no overemployment factor $O_N = 1$. In the general case with $OE \neq 1$, for labor market tightness and employment to be equal, from both (4.11) and (4.10), we need that

$$(1-\alpha_L)\left[O_N F'(\mathcal{N})-z\right]-\alpha_L\gamma\theta = (1-\eta_L)[F'(\mathcal{N})-z]-\eta_L\theta\gamma$$

The Hosios condition $\alpha_L = \eta_L$ is not sufficient here. There is no simple rule for α_L independent of the equilibrium value θ that restores constrained efficiency to the decentralized equilibrium. There may, however, exist an efficiency rule specific to the equilibrium value of θ. Given that O_N is larger than 1 under decreasing returns to scale, α_L must now be larger than η_L in order to push the decentralized economy towards the constrained efficient allocation. Given the propensity of employers to overemploy in the presence of strategic wage bargaining, one needs to give more bargaining power to workers in order to reduce employment and the associated job creation costs.

4.3 The large firm with several worker types

The multi-factor economy is not a simple extension of the one work type model. However, it leads to interesting results that warrant the effort. For example, the overemployment result may not always hold and, for specific groups of workers, it may even turn into a underemployment result. This will be the case for groups of workers with the lowest bargaining power who, in a sense, bare the cost of the overemployment of workers with larger bargaining power.

4.3.1 Environment

Assume now n distinct types of workers, such as skilled and unskilled, or young and experienced workers, or even different occupations. We use notations $\mathbf{N} = (\mathcal{N}_1, ..., \mathcal{N}_n)$, $\mathbf{V} = (\mathcal{V}_1, ..., \mathcal{V}_n)$, and $\Theta = (\theta_1, \theta_2, ...\theta_n)$ for, respectively, the vector of employment, the supply of job vacancies, and labor market tightness on each submarket index by $i = 1, 2, ...n$. All other labor market parameters – search costs, matching functions, unemployment benefits—are also specific to each labor submarket (e.g. the turnover rate is s_i, where $i = 1, ...n.$), with the exception of the wage bargaining weight α_L, common to all submarket (until subsection 4.3.3). The discount rate remains common and denoted by $r > 0$.

The aim is to derive optimal employment and wage determination when firms can hire or fire each worker, and freely negotiate their wages, individually.

Firms take into account the effect of a marginal hire of a given labor type on all wages of all labor types when making their employment decisions. Each marginal worker of type i has value to the firm:

$$J_{\pi i} = \frac{\frac{\partial F(\mathbf{N})}{\partial \mathcal{N}_i} - w_i(\mathbf{N}) - \sum_{j=1}^{n} \mathcal{N}_j \frac{\partial w_j(\mathbf{N})}{\partial \mathcal{N}_i}}{r+s}$$

that is, the marginal worker brings to the firm his marginal product net of his wage, as well as his potential effect on the total wage bill of the firm, reflected by the last term in the equation above.

The wage of labor input i, for $i = 1, .., n$, is the solution of a Nash sharing rule

$$\alpha_L J_{\pi i} = (1 - \alpha_L)(W_{ni} - W_{ui})$$

and must therefore satisfy

$$w_i(\mathbf{N}) = (1 - \alpha_L) r W_{ui} + \alpha_L \left(\frac{\partial F(\mathbf{N})}{\partial \mathcal{N}_i} - \sum_{j=1}^{n} N_j \frac{\partial w_j(\mathbf{N})}{\partial \mathcal{N}_i} \right), \text{ for } i = 1, .., n \tag{4.12}$$

4.3.2 Wage solutions and equilibrium

Equation (4.12) is a set of partial differential equations where the wage in a given group i depends not only on its marginal product, but also on the partial derivatives of wages in other groups with respect to group i's employment. The strategy for a solution is based on differentiating this equation with respect to N_j, and then exploiting the symmetry of the second-order partial derivatives. This allows us to obtain a simpler set of equations that is then transformed into spherical coordinates. The strategy is detailed in appendix 4.7.3. These steps lead to the following expression for the wage $w_i(\mathbf{N})$:

Nash bargained wage in the large firm with n types of workers:

$$w_i(\mathbf{N}) = (1-\alpha_L)rW_{ui} + \int_0^1 \nu^{\frac{1-\alpha_L}{\alpha_L}} F_i'(\mathbf{N}\nu)d\nu \tag{4.13}$$

In the wage equation above, F_i' is the partial derivative of the production function F with respect to the argument i, and applied to vector $\mathbf{N}\nu$ where ν varies between 0 and 1 so that the firm takes into account as before all infra-marginal products of labor between 0 and its current size $\mathbf{N}$. It contains the usual term representing the reservation wage rW_{ui} of individuals in group i. It also contains a new term replacing the product of the marginal product of labor and the bargaining weight α_L in our previous Nash wage equations. This new term is an integral representing a weighted sum of infra-marginal products generated by workers of all types.

The O_{Ni} factor depends on the type i of the worker and, significantly, it is no longer always greater than 1:

Overemployment term in the large firm with n types of workers:

$$O_{Ni} = \frac{\int_0^1 \frac{1}{\alpha_L}\nu^{\frac{1-\alpha_L}{\alpha_L}} F_i'(\mathbf{N}\nu)d\nu}{F_i'(\mathbf{N})} > 0 \text{ and } \lesseqgtr 1 \tag{4.14}$$

Consider for instance the case of a homogenous production function, $F(\mathbf{N}) = x\mathcal{N}_1{}^{\epsilon_1}\mathcal{N}_2^{\epsilon_2}...\mathcal{N}_n{}^{\epsilon_n}$ where $\epsilon_1+\epsilon_2+...+\epsilon_n = 1-\bar{\epsilon}$ and $0 \leq \epsilon_i, \bar{\epsilon} \leq 1$. The parameter $\bar{\epsilon}$ reflects the distance from constant returns to scale. In this case the overemployment term O_{Ni} is a simple function of parameters, independent of i if workers have identical bargaining power, and is greater than 1:

$$O_{Ni} = \frac{1}{1-\alpha_L\bar{\epsilon}} \geq 1 \tag{4.15}$$

If the worker's bargaining power is strictly positive and the production function displays decreasing returns to scale ($\bar{\epsilon} > 0$), than equation (4.15) holds with strict inequality. The term $O_{Ni} = 1$ if either workers have no bargaining power ($\alpha_L = 0$), or the production function has constant returns to scale ($\bar{\epsilon} = 0$). In the former case, workers are paid their reservation wage such that the firm, even under decreasing returns, does not need to expand employment in order to drive down wages. In the latter case, constant returns to scale in production, there is no scope for the firm to expand beyond the level of employment it would reach without intrafirm bargaining and the model is isomorphic to several small firms employing one unit of labor in n submarkets, each with with labor market tightness θ_i.

One can then rewrite the wage and job creation conditions that determine the model's equilibrium as:

Intrafirm bargaining equilibrium with several labor inputs:

$$w_i(\mathbf{N}) = (1 - \alpha_L) r W_{ui} + \alpha_L O_{Ni} F_i'(\mathbf{N}), \text{ for } i = 1, .., n, \tag{4.16}$$

$$\frac{\gamma_i}{q_i} = \frac{O_{Ni} F_i'(\mathbf{N}) - w_i(\mathbf{N})}{r + s_i} \tag{4.17}$$

The two equations (4.16) and (4.17) finally combine into a new job creation condition:

$$\frac{\gamma_i}{q_i} = \frac{(1 - \alpha_L)\left[O_{Ni} F_i'(\mathbf{N}) - r W_{ui}\right]}{r + s_i} \tag{4.18}$$

Finally, the model is closed by linking the vectors of labor inputs $\mathbf{N}$, and the vector of labor market tightness Θ, through n steady-state equations:

$$\mathcal{N}_i(1 - s_i) = (1 - \mathcal{N}_i)\theta_i q(\theta_i)$$

It is easy to prove uniqueness of the solution of the 2n-tuple $(\mathbf{N}, \Theta)$ under homogenous production functions; the proof is unreported but can be found in Cahuc et al. (2008). Conditions for existence are simple equivalents of the viability conditions, discussed in chapter 1, that the value of leisure must be lower than the marginal product of labor at zero employment.

A value of O_{Ni} greater than one implies too much creation as compared to that standard solution when $O_{Ni} = 1$ for labor group i. The intuition is the same as for the single labor case. Under decreasing returns to scale in factor i, the marginal product is larger than its infra-marginal products. Hence the firm has the ability to reduce the marginal product of labor by expanding employment. In doing so, it reduces the surplus of a marginal hire, and then has the ability to reduce the wage of each marginal worker. The optimal level of employment for each input is therefore above the level of employment reached in the absence of intrafirm bargaining. A higher $\mathcal{N}_i$ is required to keep the value of the product $O_{Ni}F_i(\mathbf{N})$ at the same level, for a given labor market tightness.

4.3.3 Generalization: different bargaining weights and the "underemployment" result

It remains possible to derive a Nash wage equation of a general form when the bargaining weights α_{Li} differ across groups:

$$w_i(\mathbf{N}) = (1-\alpha_{Li})rW_{ui} + \int_0^1 z^{\frac{1-\alpha_{Li}}{\alpha_{Li}}} F_i'(\widetilde{\mathbf{N}}_\mathbf{i}(z))dz \tag{4.19}$$

where F_i' is the partial derivative of F with respect to the argument i applied to vector $\widetilde{\mathbf{N}}_\mathbf{i}$, which turns out to be a simple linear transformation of vector $\mathbf{N}$, multiplying the vector of employment by a diagonal matrix that weights the distortion of labor inputs in the outcome of wage bargaining. The vector $\widetilde{\mathbf{N}}_\mathbf{i}(z)$ reads

$$\widetilde{\mathbf{N}}_\mathbf{i}(z) = (\mathcal{N}_1 z^{\varpi_{i1}}, \mathcal{N}_2 z^{\varpi_{i2}}, ..., \mathcal{N}_n z^{\varpi_{ni}}) \tag{4.20}$$

where ϖ_{ij} is a distortion factor due to differences in bargaining power, defined as $\varpi_{ij} = \frac{1-\alpha_{Li}}{\alpha_{Li}}\frac{\alpha_{Lj}}{1-\alpha_{Lj}}$ with $\varpi_{ii} = 1$ and $\varpi_{ij} = \varpi_{ji}^{-1}$. For a geometrical interpretation of the ϖ_{ij} factors and the distortion they induce in firm's hiring choices, see the chapter appendix. In short, groups with higher bargaining power than group i are given higher weights. In the Cobb–Douglas case, with a production technology $F(\mathbf{N}) = \prod_i N_i^{\epsilon_i}$, where $\bar{\epsilon} = 1 - \Sigma_j \epsilon_j$, it turns out that the overemployment factor O_{Ni} becomes:

$$O_{Ni} = [1 - \alpha_{Li}\bar{\epsilon} + \alpha_{Li}\Sigma_{j\neq i}\epsilon_j(\varpi_{ij} - 1)]^{-1} \tag{4.21}$$

A higher bargaining weight α_{Lj} for group j, implies a higher level of ϖ_{ij}, which in turn lowers O_{Ni} for group i. This may even lead to a situation of underemployment, in which the marginal productivity of type-i workers is higher than their marginal cost. This arises when parameters are such that they lead to $O_{Ni} < 1$. The intuition is that decreasing the employment of type-i workers allows the firm to decrease the marginal productivity of type-j workers when they have higher bargaining power to reduce their wages. It is easy to provide an example of such a situation. With two labor factors, constant returns to scale, and sufficiently different bargaining powers, the large bargaining power group will be overemployed and the low bargaining power will be underemployed, in the sense that their respective O_N factors weighting the marginal product of labor in the job creation condition will be respectively larger and lower than one.

4.4 Predetermined capital and labor with intrafirm bargaining

We now return to the case of a common wage bargaining weight α_L across the different types of workers derived in section 4.3.2. Incorporating physical capital is a simple extension once we write the wage function as $w(\mathbf{N}, K)$. The wage partial differential equations are solved according to the same strategy, and the wage solution is therefore

$$w_i(\mathbf{N}, K) = (1-\alpha_L)rW_{ui} + \int_0^1 \nu^{\frac{1-\alpha_L}{\alpha_L}} F'_{Ni}(\mathbf{N}\nu, K)d\nu, \quad \text{for } i = 1, .., n, \tag{4.22}$$

where $F'_{Ni}(\mathbf{N}\nu, K)$ denotes the partial derivative of F with respect to the ith labor input evaluated at $\mathbf{N}\nu$. Capital is predetermined and chosen simultaneously with the number of optimal vacancies. The capital equation is given by

$$F'_K(\mathbf{N}, K) = r + \delta + \sum_{i=1}^{n} \mathcal{N}_i \frac{\partial w_i(\mathbf{N}, K)}{\partial K} \tag{4.23}$$

where F'_K is the marginal product of capital, and $\delta > 0$ the rate of capital depreciation. With one type of worker only, the system is a variant of the traditional job creation condition under intrafirm bargaining and a capital demand equation:

Intrafirm bargaining equilibrium condition with capital and labor and capital demand with intrafirm bargaining:

$$\frac{\gamma}{q} = \frac{O_N F'_N(\mathcal{N}, K) - w(\mathcal{N}, K)}{r+s} \tag{4.24}$$

$$r + \delta = (1-\alpha_L) O_N F'_K(\mathcal{N}, K) \tag{4.25}$$

The labor demand equation (4.24) is identical to that already discussed in equation (4.8), and the overemployment result with one type of worker continues to hold. The capital demand equation has two distinct terms, and resembles the neoclassical demand for capital in that it equates the marginal revenue of capital to the firm with the sum of the rates of depreciation and interest. In the right-hand side of equation (4.25), the term $(1-\alpha_L)$ reflects a well-known hold-up problem. Since workers obtain a share of the returns to physical capital investments, firms underinvest in proportion to this share $(1-\alpha_L)$. The novelty here is that this effect is partly undone by the overemployment result.

The fact that O_N may be greater than 1 mitigates this effect since overemployment raises the marginal productivity of capital. This provides incentives towards more capital accumulation. However, in the specific case of a Cobb–Douglas production function $F(\mathcal{N},K) = \mathcal{N}^b K^{1-b}$, $O_N = \frac{1}{1-\alpha_L b}$ and the product $(1-\alpha_L)O_N$ remains smaller than 1. There is still underinvestment in physical capital. Nonetheless, the product $(1-\alpha_L)O_N$ may be larger than 1 under more general production functions. This shows the potential insights of combining intrafirm bargaining features with physical investment in a generalized matching model.

Finally, note that equation (4.25) would simplify in the absence of intrafirm bargaining to the classical demand for capital under the presence of hold-up, namely $(1-\alpha_L)F'_K(\mathcal{N},K) = r+\delta$.

4.5 Dynamic implications of intrafirm bargaining

The dynamic implications of Stole and Zwiebel's bargaining analysis are twofold. First, there is the issue of the dynamics of an existing, large firm in a stochastic environment. Second, there is the issue of the dynamics of a newborn firm, which by definition starts with zero employees and has first to reach its stationary steady state, even in the absence of stochastic changes in aggregate conditions. In what follows, we focus on the first type of dynamic issues, more relevant in a macroeconomic setup. We refer to the literature studying the other case at the end of the chapter. The latter was studied by Wolinsky (2000), under a slightly different set of assumptions as in the above chapters (under instantaneous adjustment, but with convex hiring costs).

Let us start from an existing firm, in discrete time, with no destruction of firms, and no idiosyncratic shocks. We also assume that the firm has already converged to its desired employment value at time t. In discrete time, we have

$$\max_{\mathcal{V}_t} \Pi_t(\mathcal{N}_t) = F_t(\mathcal{N}_t) - w_t(\mathcal{N}_t)\mathcal{N}_t - \gamma\mathcal{V}_t + \frac{1}{1+r}\mathbb{E}\Pi_{t+1}(\mathcal{N}_{t+1})$$

subject to

$$\mathcal{N}_{t+1} = (1-s)\mathcal{N}_t + q_t\mathcal{V}_t$$

This leads to

$$\frac{\gamma}{q_t} = \frac{1}{1+r}\mathbb{E}\left[F'_{t+1}(\mathcal{N}_{t+1}) - w_{t+1}(\mathcal{N}_{t+1}) - w'(\mathcal{N}_{t+1})\mathcal{N}_{t+1} + (1-s)\frac{\gamma}{q_{t+1}}\right]$$

Intrafirm bargaining must follow at any time t

$$(1-\alpha_L)J_{\pi t} = \alpha_L\left(W_{nt} - W_{ut}\right)$$

where

$$J_{\pi t} = \frac{\partial \Pi_t}{\partial \mathcal{N}_t} = F'_{t+1}(\mathcal{N}_{t+1}) - w_{t+1}(\mathcal{N}_{t+1}) - w'(\mathcal{N}_{t+1})\mathcal{N}_{t+1} + (1-s)\frac{\gamma}{q_{t+1}}$$

and

$$W_{nt} - W_{ut} = w_t(\mathcal{N}_t) - W_{ut} + \frac{1-s}{1+r}\mathbb{E}(W_{nt+1}) + \frac{s}{1+r}\mathbb{E}(W_{ut+1})$$

leading to, after a few steps that eliminate all future values in the Nash program,

$$\alpha_L\left[F'_t(\mathcal{N}_t) - w_t(\mathcal{N}_t) - w'(\mathcal{N}_t)\mathcal{N}_t + \gamma\theta_t\right] = (1-\alpha_L)\left[w_t(\mathcal{N}_t) - z\right]$$

The bargaining within the firm takes place at time t and does not have any intertemporal consequences, since the sequence of employment at time $t+1$ and afterwards only depends on the hiring decisions today. The wage solution at time t is therefore

$$w(\mathcal{N}_t) = (1-\alpha_L)z + \alpha_L\left[O_{Nt}F'(\mathcal{N}_t) + \gamma\theta_t\right].$$

where, as before,

$$O_{Nt} = \left(\int_0^1 \frac{1}{\alpha_L}\nu^{\frac{1-\alpha_L}{\alpha_L}}F'(\mathcal{N}_t\nu)d\nu\right)/F'(\mathcal{N}_t)$$

where the overemployment factor may potentially depend on t. In a Cobb-Douglas case, O_{Nt} is however a constant of time: for example, if $F(N) = N^{1-\bar{\epsilon}}$ then $O_{Nt} \equiv \frac{1}{1-\alpha_L\bar{\epsilon}} \geq 1$. Finally

$$\frac{\gamma}{q_t} = \frac{1}{1+r}\mathbb{E}\left[F'_{t+1}(\mathcal{N}_{t+1})O_{Nt+1} - w_{t+1}(\mathcal{N}_{t+1}) + (1-s)\frac{\gamma}{q_{t+1}}\right]$$

and thus we obtain similar equations with, as usual, an additional overemployment factor that is now dynamic.

4.6 Discussion of the literature and remaining issues

The conclusion of the analysis of the present chapter is that the main job creation conditions, and dynamic extensions equations in a discrete time setting can accommodate the intra-bargaining setup of Stole and Zwiebel (1996a,b) by incorporating the conveniently defined overemployment factor.

The large firm matching model was introduced under constant returns to scale by Pissarides (2000), as well as Pissarides (1990). Augmented with endogenous capital, he showed the equivalence of the equations of the model between the large firm model and the one-worker model, under a set of assumptions discussed and relaxed in Cahuc and Wasmer (2001), who discuss the role of predetermined capital versus rented capital. With predetermined capital and constant aggregate returns to scale, the large firm matching model leads to different wage equations, with overemployment weighting factors exhibited in this chapter. In contrast, under the assumption of a perfect secondhand capital market as assumed in Pissarides (1990), endogenous capital is always at its optimum value. This implies that the large representative firm behaves like a firm with constant returns to scale in labor, once capital is replaced by its optimal value. This is how the large firm matching model can safely ignore the dimension of intrafirm wage bargaining.

Smith (1999) was the first to explore the effect of decreasing returns to scale in labor in a matching model. Intrafirm bargaining features were also present in an early work by Rotemberg (2000) in the presence of convex hiring costs. More recently, Kaas and Kircher (2015) have pleaded in favor of convex hiring costs as a substitute to intrafirm bargaining frictions in the large-firm context. Instead, Cahuc et al. (2008) provided a complete characterization of the job creation equations and wage equations with several types of labor, and show that underemployment may actually be the result of intrafirm bargaining—the overemployment result is not generic and proves the uniqueness of a solution with n labor inputs. Incidentally, the conditions for existence and uniqueness of the equilibrium also apply to a large firm matching model with no strategic wage interactions (that is where overemployment factors O_{Ni} are equal to unity). To our knowledge this had not been done in the large firm matching model. Janiak and Wasmer (2014) and Elsby and Michaels (2013) have developed the large firm matching model with intrafirm bargaining to incorporate endogenous job destruction. Janiak and Wasmer (2014) have also introduced layoff costs and capital investments. Their analysis is focused on the effect of employment protection on the capital-labor ratio.

The intrafirm bargaining framework has then been widely used in various contexts. Without exhaustivity, Mortensen (2009) and Helpman and Itskhoki (2010) study heterogeneous firms under intrafirm bargaining. Mortensen (2009) shows the existence of a unique equilibrium wage distribution under costly worker's search.

On the policy side, a welfare analysis with one labor factor is present in Cahuc and Wasmer (2001) and in Brugemann (2014). Bauducco and Janiak (2015) introduce minimum wage under strategic overhiring and obtain multiple equilibria. The analysis was introduced in the context of international trade in Felbermayr et al. (2012), while Ebell and Haefke (2006, 2009) have studied the role of product market regulations and labor unions in a large firm matching model. Janiak (2013) introduces a life cycle of firms and studies the impact of layoff restrictions. Carbonnier (2014) has extended the result of Pissarides

(1998) and studied payroll taxes in the intrafirm bargaining context with heterogeneous agents. Tripier (2011) introduced intrafirm bargaining in a model of ex-ante training: intrafirm bargaining totally alleviates the hold-up problem of ex-ante investments leading to underinvestment. He shows that firms therefore train their workers efficiently both with general and specific skills.

Out-of-the-steady-state dynamics were studied in Wolinsky (2000), which focuses on the convergence of a newborn firm to its steady state under strategic bargaining. Acemoglu and Hawkins (2014) also study ex-ante heterogeneous firms and derive some out-of-the-steady-state dynamics. Business cycle implications have been studied by Krause and Lubik (2013), Hertweck (2013), and Hawkins (2011), with generally no strong differences in the volatility pattern of the calibrated model with intrafirm bargaining, although a recent attempt by Kim (2015) suggests instead some gains in amplification of hours volatility. More work is needed here to reach a stable and definitive conclusion on the quantitative importance of intrafirm strategic interactions. Another example of interesting dynamics, with a focus on the firm size distribution, is Elsby and Michaels (2013). Kurmann (2014) introduced the logic of intrafirm bargaining to bargaining over the interest rate between the owners of the firm and the additional capital units.

A thorough discussion of the micro-foundations of the intrafirm bargaining game have been proposed in an asymmetric extensive form game by Brügemann et al. (2015). Originally, Stole and Zwiebel (1996a) had described their game theoretic paper with assumptions suggesting symmetry in the setup. In particular, on pages 376-377, they emphasized the at-will nature of the firm: "*We take labour contracts as non-binding in nature. (...) At any time before production, an employee may approach the firm and enter into wage negotiations. Likewise, the firm may choose at any moment before production to call the employee in for wage negotiation.*" Under these assumptions, the order of workers in the firm should be irrelevant, and thus any extended form game should be symmetrical. However, even in the case where the order matters, it is possible to get the same outcome, as shown in Brügemann et al. (2015). They assume instead that wages *a priori* depend on the order of negotiation but that disagreement does not imply separation: the worker is only put at the end of the sequence of negotiation (hence the term "*Rolodex*" used to name the game). It turns out that the solutions of this game are still symmetric ex-post and equal to those from the ex-ante symmetrical negotiation case analyzed in Stole and Zwiebel. Hence, both bargaining structures lead to the same, stable equilibrium wage profile emphasized in this chapter. One should finally note that de Fontenay and Gans (2003) have reassessed the result of Stole and Zwiebel. They argue that, when there is a finite pool of replacement workers available to the firm to replace workers they bargain with at no cost, the overemployment result may disappear entirely and underemployment may actually be an outcome. They have also extended their setup to two types of workers in de Fontenay and Gans (2004). Overall, however, the symmetrical solutions exhibited in this chapter are simple and intuitive and have sound micro-foundations from even an underlying asymmetric bargaining structure as shown in Brügemann et al. (2015). They can thus be used safely and should always be used in quantitative macroeconomic approaches where a large firm, endogenous wages, and capital investment are important ingredients of the analysis.

4.7 Chapter appendix

4.7.1 Value function of the firms

The profit function $\Pi(\mathbf{N})$ maximizes

$$\Pi(\mathbf{N}) = \max_{\mathbf{N},\mathbf{V}} \int_0^\infty e^{-rt}[F(\mathbf{N}) - \sum_{j=1}^{n} \left(w_j(\mathbf{N})\mathcal{N}_j - \gamma_j \mathcal{V}_j\right)]dt$$

subject to $\partial \mathcal{N}_i/\partial t = \mathcal{N}_i(1-s_i) + \mathcal{V}_i q_i$

The stationary optimal policy of the firm, using the standard optimality condition as exposed in the chapter for each labor type i, is a vector $\mathbf{N}^*$ that satisfies

$$J_{\pi i}(\mathbf{N}^*) = \frac{\gamma_i}{q_i} \tag{4.26}$$

with $J_{\pi i}(\mathbf{N}) = \frac{\partial \Pi(\mathbf{N})}{\partial \mathcal{N}_i}$.

The marginal profit of employment N_i obtained as

$$J_{\pi i}(\mathbf{N}) = \frac{F_i(\mathbf{N}) - w_i(\mathbf{N}) - \sum_{j=1}^{n} N_j \frac{\partial w_j(\mathbf{N})}{\partial \mathcal{N}_i}}{r+s_i} \tag{4.27}$$

If we combine the two equations, one finally gets the job creation condition reexpressed as the equality between the marginal product of labor and a sum of three terms: wages, turnover costs, and the employment effect on total wages:

$$F_i(\mathbf{N}) = \underbrace{w_i(\mathbf{N})}_{\text{Wage}} + \underbrace{\frac{\gamma_i(r+s_i)}{q_i}}_{\text{Turnover costs}} + \underbrace{\sum_{j=1}^{n} N_j \frac{\partial w_j(\mathbf{N})}{\partial \mathcal{N}_i}}_{\text{Employment effect on wages}} \tag{4.28}$$

4.7.2 Value function of workers and Nash bargaining

One first calculates the worker's surplus from

$$rW_{ni} = w_i(\mathbf{N}) + s_i(W_{ui} - W_{ni}) \tag{4.29}$$

leading to

$$W_{ni} - W_{ui} = \frac{w_i(\mathbf{N}) - rW_{ui}}{r + s_i}$$

The Nash sharing rule implies that

$$\alpha_L J_{\pi i}(\mathbf{N}) = (1 - \alpha_L)(W_{ni} - W_{ui}) \tag{4.30}$$

which leads to a differential equation in labor input i:

$$w_i(\mathbf{N}) = (1 - \alpha_L) rW_{ui} + \alpha_L \left(\frac{\partial F(\mathbf{N})}{\partial \mathcal{N}_i} - \sum_{j=1}^{n} \mathcal{N}_j \frac{\partial w_j(\mathbf{N})}{\partial \mathcal{N}_i} \right), \text{ for } i = 1, .., n \tag{4.31}$$

Finally,

$$\begin{aligned} rW_{ui} &= z_i + f_i(W_{ni} - W_{ui}) = z_i + \frac{\alpha_L}{1 - \alpha_L} J_{\pi i} f_i \\ &= z_i + \frac{\alpha_L}{1 - \alpha_L} \gamma_i \theta_i^* \end{aligned}$$

in using respectively (4.30) and (4.26).

4.7.3 Sketch of solution with identical bargaining power

We focus on the proof's strategy in the case of identical bargaining power. The strategy follows Cahuc et al. (2008) who solve the n differential equations for wages with respect to n labor types by first transforming the problem to obtain a single differential equation and then adopt spherical coordinates to bring back the model to only a one-dimensional differential equation. For that, the trick is to do a new iteration of partial derivatives on equation (4.31) for a given i with respect to a labor input l, $i \neq l$. We obtain

$$\frac{\partial w_i}{\partial \mathcal{N}_l} + \alpha_L \frac{\partial w_l}{\partial \mathcal{N}_i} = \alpha_L \left(\frac{\partial^2 F(\mathbf{N})}{\partial \mathcal{N}_i \partial \mathcal{N}_l} - \sum_{j=1}^{n} \mathcal{N}_j \frac{\partial^2 w_j}{\partial \mathcal{N}_i \partial \mathcal{N}_l} \right)$$

which, denoting by $(E_i)'_l$ the second-order differential equation, can be rewritten as:

$$\frac{\partial w_i}{\partial \mathcal{N}_l}(1 - \alpha_L) = \alpha_L \frac{\partial^2}{\partial \mathcal{N}_i \partial \mathcal{N}_l} \left(F(\mathbf{N}) - \sum_{j=1}^{n} \mathcal{N}_j w_j \right) \tag{$(E_i)'_l$}$$

for all $i, l = 1, ...n$. The difference between $(E_i)'_l$ and $(E_v)'_i$ eliminates the symmetric terms, which, given that $0 < \alpha_L < 1$, leads to

$$\frac{\partial w_l}{\partial \mathcal{N}_i} = \frac{\partial w_i}{\partial \mathcal{N}_l} \tag{4.32}$$

for all $i, l = 1, ...n$. It implies that

$$\sum_{j=1}^{n} N_j \frac{\partial w_j(\mathbf{N})}{\partial \mathcal{N}_i} = \sum_{j=1}^{n} \mathcal{N}_j \frac{\partial w_i(\mathbf{N})}{\partial \mathcal{N}_j} \tag{4.33}$$

which allows us to conveniently rewrite (4.31) as

$$w_i(\mathbf{N}) = (1-\alpha_L) r W_{ui} + \alpha_L \left(\frac{\partial F(\mathbf{N})}{\partial \mathcal{N}_i} - \sum_{j=1}^{n} \mathcal{N}_j \frac{\partial w_i(\mathbf{N})}{\partial \mathcal{N}_j} \right) \tag{4.34}$$

The term $\sum_{j=1}^{n} N_j \frac{\partial w_i(\mathbf{N})}{\partial \mathcal{N}_j}$ actually has a simple expression in spherical coordinates, $\psi, \phi_1,...,\phi_{n-1}$, where ψ is the distance from the origin such that $\sum_{j=1}^{n} \mathcal{N}_j^2 = \psi^2$ and ϕ_i are the angles of projection in different subplanes. With

$$\begin{aligned}
\mathcal{N}_1 &= \psi \cos\phi_1 ... \cos\phi_{n-2} \cos\phi_{n-1} \\
\mathcal{N}_2 &= \psi \cos\phi_1 ... \cos\phi_{n-3} \sin\phi_{n-2} \\
&\vdots \\
\mathcal{N}_{n-1} &= \psi \cos\phi_1 \sin\phi_2 \\
\mathcal{N}_n &= \psi \sin\phi_1
\end{aligned}$$

and with notation $\phi = (\phi_1, ..., \phi_{n-1})$ one indeed has that

$$\sum_{j=1}^{k} \mathcal{N}_j \frac{\partial w_i(\mathbf{N})}{\partial \mathcal{N}_j} = \psi \frac{\partial w_i(\psi, \phi)}{\partial \psi}$$

Then, (4.34) in this system of coordinates is simplified to

$$\alpha_L \frac{\partial w_i(\psi, \phi)}{\partial \psi} + w(\psi, \phi) = (1-\alpha_L) r W_{ui} + \alpha_L \frac{\partial F(\psi, \phi)}{\partial \mathcal{N}_i} \tag{4.35}$$

which is a one-dimensional differential equation in distance ψ. One then gets

$$w_i(\psi, \phi) = (1-\alpha_L) r W_{ui} + \psi^{-1/\alpha_L} \left(\kappa_i(\phi) + \int_0^{\psi} v^{\frac{1-\alpha_L}{\alpha_L}} \frac{\partial F(v, \phi)}{\partial \mathcal{N}_i} dv \right) \tag{4.36}$$

where $\kappa_i(\phi)$ is a constant which is function of ψ and then, switching back to standard notations for employment vector $\mathbf{N}$,

$$w_i(\mathbf{N}) = (1-\alpha_L) r W_{ui} + \int_0^1 v^{\frac{1-\alpha_L}{\alpha_L}} F_i(v\mathbf{N}) dv \tag{4.37}$$

where F_i stands for the derivative of the function F with respect to its argument $i = 1, .., n$.

4.7.4 Extension to capital

Denote by I the investment, and by δ the depreciation rate of capital. The value function of the firm, $\Pi(\mathbf{N}, K)$, maximizes

$$\Pi(\mathcal{N}, K) = \max_{\mathcal{N},K,\mathcal{V},I} \int_0^{\infty} e^{-rt} \left[F(\mathbf{N}, K) - \sum_{j=1}^{n} \left(w_j(\mathbf{N})\mathcal{N}_j - \gamma_j \mathcal{V}_j \right) - I \right] dt$$

$$\text{s.t. } \dot{\mathcal{N}}_i = -s_i\mathcal{N}_i + q_i\mathcal{V}_i$$

$$\text{s.t. } \dot{K} = -\delta K + I$$

where q_i is still taken as given by the firm, δ is a depreciation rate of capital, and I is the firm's investment policy. The Hamiltonian of the problem is therefore given by

$$H = e^{-rt} \left[F(\mathbf{N}, K) - \sum_{j=1}^{n} \left(w_j(\mathbf{N})\mathcal{N}_j - \gamma_j \mathcal{V}_j \right) - I \right] + \Psi_N \left[-s\mathcal{N} + q\mathcal{V} \right] + \Psi_K \left[-\delta K + I \right]$$

and the optimality conditions are

$$\frac{\partial H}{\partial \mathcal{V}_i} = 0 = -\gamma_i e^{-rt} + q_i \Psi_{Ni}$$

$$\frac{\partial H}{\partial I} = 0 = -\, e^{-rt} + \Psi_K$$

and, now denoting by F'_{Ni} the derivative of the production function by labor factor $\mathcal{N}_i$ and by F'_K the derivative of the production function by capital K:

$$\frac{\partial H}{\partial \mathcal{N}_i} = -\dot{\Psi}_{Ni} = \left[F'_{Ni}(\mathbf{N}, K) - w_i(\mathbf{N}, K) - \sum_{j=1}^{n} N_j \frac{\partial w_j(\mathbf{N}, K)}{\partial \mathcal{N}_i} \right] e^{-rt} - s\Psi_{Ni}$$

$$\frac{\partial H}{\partial K} = -\dot{\Psi}_K = \left[F'_K(\mathbf{N}, K) - \sum_{j=1}^{n} N_j \frac{\partial w_j(\mathbf{N}, K)}{\partial K} \right] e^{-rt} - \delta \Psi_K$$

Eliminating the multipliers $\Psi_{Ni} = \gamma_i / q(\theta_i) e^{-rt}$ and $\Psi_K = e^{-rt}$, one obtains the first-order conditions in the steady state,

$$\frac{F'_{Ni}(\mathbf{N}, K) - w_i(\mathbf{N}, K) - \sum_{j=1}^{n} N_j \frac{\partial w_j(\mathbf{N}, K)}{\partial \mathcal{N}_i}}{r+s} = \frac{\gamma}{q_i(\theta_i)} = J_{\pi i}(N) = \frac{\partial \Pi}{\partial \mathcal{N}_i}(\mathbf{N}, K)$$

$$F'_K - w_K(\mathbf{N}, K)\mathcal{N} = r + \delta$$

Wage can be calculated as

$$w_i(\mathbf{N}, K) = (1-\alpha_L) r W_{ui} + \int_0^1 \nu^{\frac{1-\alpha_L}{\alpha_L}} F_{Ni}(\mathbf{N}\nu, K) d\nu, \; i = 1, .., n \tag{4.38}$$

Using the wage equation (4.38) to substitute into first-order conditions, one obtains the demand for labor and demand for capital as

$$F'_{Ni}(\mathbf{N},K) = \underbrace{w_i(\mathbf{N},K) + \frac{\gamma_i(r+s_i)}{q_i(\theta_i)}}_{\text{Labor costs}} + \underbrace{\sum_{j=1}^{n} N_j \int_0^1 \nu^{\frac{1}{\alpha_L}} F\text{''}_{NjNi}(\mathbf{N}\nu,K)dz}_{\text{Empl. effect on wages}} \tag{4.39}$$

$$F'_K(\mathbf{N},K) = r + \delta + \underbrace{\int_0^1 \sum_{i=1}^{k} N_i \nu^{\frac{1-\alpha_L}{\alpha_L}} F\text{''}_{NiK}(\mathbf{N}\nu,K)d\nu}_{\text{Cap. effect on wages}} \tag{4.40}$$

where we now denote by $F\text{''}_{NiNj}$ the second-order, cross-derivative of the production function by labor factors $\mathcal{N}_i$ and $\mathcal{N}_j$ and by $F\text{''}_{NiK}$ the second-order, cross-derivative of the production function by labor factor $\mathcal{N}_i$ and capital K.

II FRICTIONS IN FINANCIAL AND GOODS MARKETS

In this second part, we introduce frictions in both goods and financial markets. Following the search approach to financial frictions of Wasmer and Weil (2004), we start in chapters 5 and 6 with the introduction of a cost of external finance in the corporate sector. Firms need a creditor to finance job creation. We will adopt the tools studied in the first part of the book to the creation of matches between an agent requiring liquidity and an agent ready to supply this liquidity. Entry in financial markets is free but subject to financial frictions, for both the demand and supply side, will lead to closed form solutions through a property of block recursiveness of solutions in each market. The financial block can be solved first, and the equilibrium in the labor market is then a function of the credit market block. We call this model the CL model for credit and labor market frictions.

We introduce goods market frictions in chapters 7 and 8, first with perfect credit market, in what we call the LG model. In each chapter we also add financial frictions to get the full, CLG model. New insights appear in models with goods market frictions: a fraction of firms can produce but cannot sell, so that profits are ex ante discounted by their probability of selling. The latter discount factor is also, in the steady-state, a rate of capacity utilization, below one and depending on the magnitude of goods market frictions. In the steady-state, goods market tightness, defined as the ratio of consumers willing to buy new good to firms willing to sell, is independent of profits and of other parameters. Out of the steady-state, goods market tightness evolves in response to consumer demand and the response of the economy to shocks is more sluggish, slowed down by this additional step incurred by firms. Overall, the steady-state CLG model delivers a convenient way to measure and decompose the entry costs into frictions in the three markets. The dynamic CLG model is a good basis to study the response of the economy to technology, credit, and demand shocks, which can take the form of either preference shocks or fiscal shocks.

5 Credit and labor market frictions: the CL model

In an economy with frictions in the credit and labor markets, that we will refer to as the CL economy, there are three types of agents to consider: the owner of a new business project, creditors, and workers. As a matter of notation, we will use subscripts c, v, and π to indicate the different stages of activity for an investment project in the environment: search in the credit market (c), search in the labor market (v), and the production/profit stage (π). In what follows we will use interchangeably the words credit and financial markets. It is important to note that a business project here is a marginal investment project of a potentially large firm. Similarly, the creditor here represents the marginal supply of liquidity of a potentially large financial institution.

The wage bargaining assumptions in this chapter lead to a particular equilibrium with important efficiency properties, namely, there exists Hosios conditions in the labor and credit markets that ensure the decentralized equilibrium is constrained efficient. Moreover, the resulting equations of the model, developed after subsection 5.2.4, are extremely close to those of chapter 1, and make for an easy interpretation of the implications of introducing credit market frictions. It becomes apparent how credit market frictions affect both streams of profits and the costs of hiring.

Time is continuous in this chapter. The discrete time equivalent is developed for the business cycle implications of financial market frictions in chapter 6. The analysis here is restricted to frictions in the corporate sector. However, we discuss research modeling financial frictions affecting for consumers or workers that has emerged following the financial crisis at the end of this chapter, and discuss the implications of alternative time and bargaining assumptions in credit and labor markets.

5.1 Random matching in financial markets

Projects are run by cashless firms, and the liquidity needed for the project until it begins producing is supplied by creditors. Moreover, creditors have a monopoly over the storage of wealth and the ability to provide liquidity. At any point in time there coexists a number of creditors ready to finance a project, denoted by $\mathcal{B}_c$, and a number of projects looking for liquidity, denoted by $\mathcal{N}_c$. The subscript c stands for the search in the credit market by both the owner of the project and a creditor. Denote by p the rate at which the project meets the creditor, and by $\check{p}$ the rate at which the creditor meets—and implicitly both screens and accepts—the project. As in the labor market of chapter 1, there is an identity in the financial market between the total number of matches, $\mathcal{M}_C$, the number of matched projects, and the number of matched creditors in a unit of time:

$$\mathcal{M}_C = p\mathcal{N}_c = \check{p}\mathcal{B}_c \tag{5.1}$$

We denote the ratio of projects to creditors searching in the credit market by

$$\phi = \frac{\mathcal{N}_c}{\mathcal{B}_c} \tag{5.2}$$

This is a measure of conditions in the financial market called *financial market tightness*. The financial market is *tight* when there are many projects looking for financing relative to the number of available creditors. Financial market tightness is considered from the perspective of the firm.

Just as with the concept of labor market tightness, it follows from equation (5.1) that p and $\check{p}$ are necessarily linked through ϕ:

$$\check{p} = \phi p$$

The transition rates p and $\check{p}$ cannot be considered as exogenous simultaneously. At least one of them must depend on ϕ. A general matching function in the financial market encompasses all special cases of exogeneity of these two rates. We assume a constant returns to scale matching function with the mass of investment projects and creditors searching in the financial market as arguments:

$$\mathcal{M}_C(\mathcal{N}_c, \mathcal{B}_c) \text{ with } \partial \log \mathcal{M}_C / \partial \log \mathcal{B}_c = \eta_C(\phi) \tag{5.3}$$
$$\text{and } \partial \log \mathcal{M}_C / \partial \log \mathcal{N}_c = 1 - \eta_C(\phi)$$

where $\eta_C(\phi)$ is the elasticity of matching in the financial market with respect to searching creditors. The transition rates for investment projects and creditors are given by

$$\frac{\mathcal{M}_C(\mathcal{N}_c,\mathcal{B}_c)}{\mathcal{N}_c} = \quad p(\phi) \qquad \text{with } p'(\phi) < 0$$

$$\frac{\mathcal{M}_C(\mathcal{N}_c,\mathcal{B}_c)}{\mathcal{B}_c} = \check{p}(\phi) = \phi p(\phi) \quad \text{with } \check{p}'(\phi) > 0$$

The rate at which investment projects are matched with a creditor, $p(\phi)$, is decreasing in financial market tightness ϕ. It is relatively difficult for an investment project to meet a creditor when there is abundant demand from other projects in the market relative to the amount of creditors. Just as in the labor market, the entry of an additional investment project generates a congestion externality on those projects already in the financial market and searching for a creditor. The entry of the project, at the same time, increases the meeting rate for creditors. That is, the meeting rate $\check{p}(\phi)$ is increasing in financial market tightness. However, entry of additional creditors causes a bottleneck for existing creditors, increasing their duration of search.

5.2 Integrating labor and financial market frictions

The financial and labor market blocks of the model integrate quite naturally. The timing of events is represented in figure 5.1. As before, the match between a vacancy and a worker is not instantaneous. It requires time and resources. In contrast with chapter 1 however, the posting of a vacancy needs to be externally financed, because the firm has only imperfect access to liquidity. To pay for the cash outflow γ, the investment project requires liquidity from a creditor for as

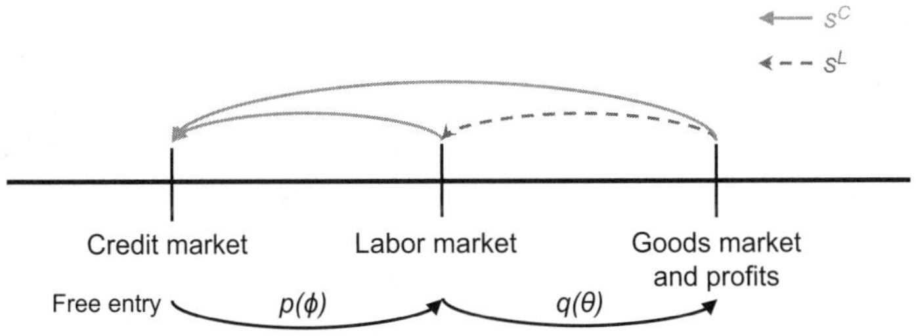

Figure 5.1
Markets and transitions of the firm

long as the worker has not been found. We assume that the financial contract will specify that the creditor commits to paying this cost γ until the project has found the worker, and in return, the project will provide a flow return ψ to the creditor once (and as long as) the firm produces. This begins after the hiring of a worker. The value of ψ is determined endogenously as the outcome of a bargaining process at the time of the formation of a match in the financial market.

This match in the labor market, which will generate profits, is subject to destructive shocks which need to be defined with care. Different shocks may now occur at either of the two stages where the firm is active: the vacancy stage (v) and the profit stage (π). Further, in the profit stage, the shock may also be of two types. A shock may lead to a separation from the worker only, that is, a destruction of the labor match after which the firm reverts to the vacancy stage. This is a pure labor turnover shock that arrives with Poisson rate s^L. It does not destroy the firm, which keeps its match with its creditor. There is also a fully disruptive shock which destroys the match with the creditor (and also leads to separation with the worker). Such a shock arrives with Poisson rate s^C. When this occurs, both the labor match and the financial match dissolve. In this event the employed worker returns to unemployment, and the filled vacancy and matched creditor both return to the credit stage (c) (see figure 5.1). In this sense, the superscript C associated with the Poisson rate reflects the final value of the firm after the shock has occurred, not the nature of the underlying shock. Indeed, the fundamental source of the destructive shock may be either from technology, credit, or changes in demand. It is left here exogenous and unspecified. This issue was already touched on in chapter 1, subsection 1.1.2. In what follows, the sum of s^L and s^C is a *total* turnover rate. By analogy with the first part, we denote it by $s^T = s^L + s^C$.

Given the environment described so far, we have the following equivalence for masses of agents in different stages. First, $1 - \mathcal{U} = \mathcal{N}_\pi = \mathcal{B}_\pi$. The rate of employment $1 - \mathcal{U}$ is equal to the stock of firms and creditors in the profit stage, $\mathcal{N}_\pi$ and $\mathcal{B}_\pi$, respectively. Second, the number of job vacancies is amount of firms in the labor market search stage, which is also the number of creditors in stage v. That is, we have $\mathcal{V} = \mathcal{N}_v = \mathcal{B}_v$. The stock-flow equations (by which we mean the dynamics of stocks in the labor market and the credit market) in the CL model are:

Creditors funding projects: $$\dot{\mathcal{B}}_v = \phi p(\phi)\mathcal{B}_c - q(\theta)\mathcal{V} \tag{5.4}$$

Vacant jobs: $$\dot{\mathcal{V}} = p(\phi)\mathcal{N}_c + s^L\mathcal{N}_\pi - \left[q(\theta) + s^C\right]\mathcal{V} \tag{5.5}$$

$$\text{Profit-generating jobs:} \quad \dot{\mathcal{N}_\pi} = q(\theta)\mathcal{V} - \left(s^C + s^L\right)\mathcal{N}_\pi \tag{5.6}$$

$$\text{Unemployed workers:} \quad \dot{\mathcal{U}} = \left(s^C + s^L\right)\mathcal{N}_\pi - q(\theta)\mathcal{V} \tag{5.7}$$

5.2.1 Projects, creditors, and "the firm"

Let E_c, E_v, and E_π be the respective steady-state asset values of a project run by a firm in each stage (credit search, labor search, and profit). The Bellman equations for each stage are

$$rE_c = -\kappa_I + p(\phi)\left(E_v - E_c\right) \tag{5.8}$$

$$rE_v = -\gamma + \gamma + q(\theta)\left(E_\pi - E_v\right) + s^C\left(E_c - E_v\right) \tag{5.9}$$

$$rE_\pi = x - w - \psi + s^C\left(E_c - E_\pi\right) + s^L\left(E_v - E_\pi\right) \tag{5.10}$$

The manager of the investment project makes an effort $\kappa_I > 0$ to locate a creditor in the financial market and moves to the labor market stage at rate $p(\phi)$, leading to the capital gain $E_v - E_c$ in equation (5.8). Recruiting a worker has a flow cost γ which, as stated in equation (5.9), is not born by the project as it receives a transfer in the same amount from the creditor. Lastly, the project generates flow profits in the third stage, described in equation (5.10). These profits are the difference between the revenue x, wage payments to labor w, and the flow repayment to the creditor ψ. The profit stage terminates at the sum of rates s^C and s^L. At rate s^C there is a return to the financial market search stage and asset value E_c, and at rate s^L the firm reverts to the vacancy stage.

Let B_c, B_v, and B_π be the respective steady-state asset values of a creditor in each stage. Searching in the financial market and evaluating potential projects has a flow cost $\kappa_B > 0$. In the labor market stage there is an outflow cost $\gamma > 0$ while the firm searches for a worker. In the profit stage the creditor receives the flow payment ψ from the firm. The Bellman equations for creditors in each stage, with similar interpretation as in the case of investment the project, are

$$rB_c = -\kappa_B + \phi p(\phi)\left(B_v - B_c\right) \tag{5.11}$$

$$rB_v = -\gamma + q(\theta)\left(B_\pi - B_v\right) + s^C\left(B_c - B_v\right) \tag{5.12}$$

$$rB_\pi = \psi + s^C\left(B_c - B_\pi\right) + s^L\left(E_v - E_\pi\right) \tag{5.13}$$

5.2.2 Entry in credit and labor markets

The natural assumption is to allow creditors and projects to freely enter the market until exhaustion of expected economic rents occurs. Under free entry of both projects looking for creditors and creditors searching for projects, we have in equilibrium that the value of the credit search stage for each side of the market is driven to zero. That is, free entry implies that $E_c = 0$ and $B_c = 0$. Projects will want to enter the financial market as long as the value of a project waiting to start production once a worker has been hired, E_v, is greater than the expected costs of search in the credit market $\kappa_I/p(\phi)$. Likewise, creditors enter the market until the value of being matched, B_v, is equal to the expected cost of searching $\kappa_B/\check{p}(\phi)$. Each agent's respective search costs in the financial market is the flow cost, κ_B and κ_I, multiplied by the expected length of search, $1/p(\phi)$ and $1/(\phi p(\phi))$, respectively.

Applying the free entry condition to the values of searching the financial market (5.8) and (5.11) leads to

$$E_v = \frac{\kappa_I}{p(\phi)} \quad \text{and} \quad B_v = \frac{\kappa_B}{\check{p}(\phi)}$$

Both creditors and project enter the financial market until their respective average search costs in the financial market equal their respective value of being in the labor search stage.

We can now define the concept of a "firm" as the management of an investment project in the joint interest of the creditor and of the manager of the investment project. Let $J_c = E_c + B_c$, $J_v = E_v + B_v$, and $J_\pi = E_\pi + B_\pi$ be the respective steady-state asset values of such a creditor–project pair in each of the three stages. The notation J_c is a slight abuse in that it applies to a match that has formally not yet been formed. However, the notation will prove useful in making future value equations more compact with no loss of precision. This entity is indeed a firm owned jointly by its creditor and the owner of the investment project for the purposes of producing output. In each of the labor search and profit stages we thus have

$$\left(r + s^C\right) J_v = -\gamma + q(\theta)\left(J_\pi - J_v\right) \tag{5.14}$$

$$\left(r + s^C\right) J_\pi = x - w + s^L \left(J_v - J_\pi\right) \tag{5.15}$$

The Bellman equations are identical to the corresponding expression for the benchmark model of chapter 1 in equations (1.11) and (1.10). In this very important sense the baseline model is a special case of the current model with financial frictions as the meeting rate in the financial market becomes instantaneous. In particular, as matching in financial markets goes to infinity, the value of a job vacancy J_v tends to zero, and we are back to the model of chapter 1. This will be made clear below.

The value of an open job vacancy J_v from the perspective of the "firm" is equal to the sum of E_v and B_v. Free entry in the financial market leads to an equilibrium value of a vacancy to the firm:

$$J_v = \frac{\kappa_B}{\phi p(\phi)} + \frac{\kappa_I}{p(\phi)} \equiv K(\phi) \tag{5.16}$$

$K(\phi)$ is a convenient notation for the sum of all frictional costs in the financial market. The notation K will play a very important role in all subsequent chapters, as a summary indicator of credit market imperfections. The equation above says that the value of a vacancy for the creditor–project block is equal to the value of expected entry costs in the financial market. The latter is the sum of each party to the firm's search costs in the financial market. Frictions in the financial market are thus an entry cost to the labor market stage that is absent in the baseline model of chapter 1, and the total costs of search in the financial market to create a new vacant job position are summarized by the variable $K(\phi)$. In a free entry equilibrium in the model with credit frictions, the value of an open job vacancy is no longer driven down to 0 but to $K(\phi)$.

The value of the profit stage to the firm, using the result that $J_v = K$, can now be expressed as

$$J_\pi = \frac{x - w + s^L K}{r + s^C + s^L} \tag{5.17}$$

This value is comprised, first, of the discounted profit flow from a job $(x - w) / \left(r + s^C + s^L\right)$, as in the benchmark model, and second, of a term that takes into account the residual value of the firm upon labor turnover, $s^L K$. Combining equations (5.16) and (5.17) leads to a new job creation condition in the presence of financial market frictions.

$$K(\phi)\left(1 + \frac{r + s^C}{q(\theta)}\right) + \frac{\gamma}{q(\theta)} = \frac{x - w + s^L K}{r + s^C + s^L} \tag{5.18}$$

Equation (5.18) is an equilibrium condition requiring the equality between the costs of job creation, which are now the sum of labor turnover costs and total transaction costs in financial markets, and discounted profits generated by the job. The costs of frictions in the financial market increase the cost of job creation. As a result, for a given discounted stream of profits from hiring labor, financial market frictions will lead to lower labor market tightness, less job creation, and higher unemployment. Again, all the relevant information about the financial market for the equilibrium in the labor market is contained in $K(\phi)$. Finally, we recover the job creation condition of the baseline model of chapter 1, or equation (1.13) when $K(\phi)$ tends to zero.

Introducing the notation

$$k(\phi) = (r + s^C)K(\phi) \tag{5.19}$$

for the annuitized value of financial costs, one has a more compact expression for the entry equation:

Job creation condition in the presence of financial market frictions for a given wage:

$$\frac{\gamma_k}{q(\theta)} = \frac{x^{CL} - w}{r + s^C + s^L} \tag{5.20}$$

$$\text{with} \quad \gamma_k = \gamma + k(\phi)$$

$$\text{and} \quad x^{CL} = x - k(\phi)$$

We encountered a similar job creation condition in previous chapters, such as in section 2.3 of chapter 2 or section 3.2 of chapter 3. In both instances K (C in that chapter) was an exogenous entry cost that changed the average cost of job creation, with important implications for both the steady-state equilibrium and the dynamics out of steady state. Here, such costs arise endogenously from frictions in the financial market. These costs have to be paid before the match in the labor market is actually created.

Another interesting way of writing this equation is to express it at the time of the payment of job creation costs, that is multiply everything by $Q_v = q(\theta)/\left(r + s^C + q(\theta)\right)$. Remember that Q_v is both a summary measure of labor market frictions (equal to zero when labor frictions are infinite and to 1 when the labor market becomes more efficient), and the market value of a contract delivering one dollar that would be paid upon the realization of a random event of Poisson intensity $q(\theta)$. This simple reformulation places the emphasis on an entrants' view point. In a free entry equilibrium, the sum of the costs in financial markets, $K(\phi)$, and search in the labor market must equal the present discounted value of profits:

$$K(\phi) + \frac{\gamma}{r + s^C + q(\theta)} = Q_v \left(\frac{x + s^L K - w}{r + s^C + s^L} \right) \tag{5.21}$$

5.2.3 Bargaining over credit

The presence of frictions in financial markets implies the existence of a positive surplus to a match between a creditor and a project. The two partners in the financial market match engage in bargaining over the terms of the repayment ψ at the time of the first contact in the financial market. The repayment ψ is the solution to the following, conventional, Nash bargaining game:

$$\psi = \text{argmax}(B_v - B_c)^{\alpha_C}(E_v - E_c)^{1-\alpha_C}$$

where $\alpha_C \in (0,1)$ is the relative bargaining strength of the creditor. The solution to this problem depends on the assumed effect of the repayment ψ on the wage to labor w. Under the assumption that, from the perspective of bargaining in the financial market, the future wage w paid to the worker does not depend on the repayment ψ, the slopes of the value of the profit stage for both the creditor and the project are equal in absolute value. That is, $\partial B_\pi/\partial\psi = -\partial E_\pi/\partial\psi = 1/(r + s^L + s^C)$. It then follows that the absolute value of slopes for the asset values of the labor search stage are also equal: $\partial B_v/\partial\psi = -\partial E_v/\partial\psi = Q_v \times 1/(r + s^L + s^C)$. The Nash sharing rule for ψ can thus be written as

$$(1 - \alpha_C)(B_v - B_c) = \alpha_C(E_v - E_c) \tag{5.22}$$

The sharing rule (5.22) rearranged as

$$B_v = \alpha_C J_v \text{ and } E_v = (1 - \alpha_C)J_v \tag{5.23}$$

states that the creditor receives a share α_C of the match surplus J_v, while a share $(1 - \alpha_C)$ accrues to the project.

Recall that free entry in the financial market implies $B_v = \kappa_B/(\phi p(\phi))$ and $E_v = \kappa_I/p(\phi)$. Combining these equations with the equation for Nash bargaining over the repayment (5.23) leads to a unique solution for financial market tightness, ϕ^*, that is a simple function of parameters. Equilibrium financial market tightness, represented in equation (5.24), is increasing in the ratio of search costs for creditor κ_B to flow search costs for investment project κ_I. An increase in κ_B leads to fewer creditors searching in the market and hence a longer duration of search for projects. In contrast, if the creditor receives a larger share of the credit match surplus, and thus a larger share of the value of a job opening and the profit flows during production, the free entry equilibrium will have a lower tightness of the financial market.

Equilibrium financial market tightness and repayment:

$$\phi^* = \frac{\kappa_B}{\kappa_I}\frac{1-\alpha_C}{\alpha_C} \tag{5.24}$$

$$\psi = \alpha_C(x-w) + (1-\alpha_C)\frac{\gamma(r+s^C+s^L)}{q(\theta)} \tag{5.25}$$

This last argument is clear once we have solved for the repayment ψ in equation (5.25) (see appendix 5.5.1 for the derivation) and is better understood in dividing both sides by $r+s^C+s^L$. This equation states that the present discounted value of the repayment to the creditor during the profit stage, $\psi/(r+s^C+s^L)$, is a weighted average of future profits, $(x-w)\,/\,\left(r+s^C+s^L\right)$ with weight α_C, and their past search costs in the labor market $\gamma/q(\theta)$ with weight $(1-\alpha_C)$.

The model is now partially solved since the first block, financial market tightness, is fully determined. We now need to establish the setting of wages in order to determine equilibrium labor market tightness.

5.2.4 Block bargaining over wages

Recall that there are three agents: the manager of the investment project, the creditor, and the worker. There are several possibilities as to how wages are negotiated, each with different implications. Bargaining over wages and over credit repayment can occur independently, or the outcome of bargaining in one market may be allowed to strategically affect bargaining in the other market. This chapter adopts a setup that we call *block bargaining* in which the firm, the joint value of the creditor–project pair, bargains with a worker. This assumption, in which the wage will be independent of the bargained repayment ψ, is adopted because it brings us closer to the conventional equations of the benchmark matching model of chapter 1. Moreover, it delivers the important efficiency results studied in section 5.3. In appendix 5.5.4, we will show the precise role of the different assumptions on the consequence of disagreement during wage bargaining.

Our definition of the firm as the joint values to the creditor and the owner of the investment project makes this assumption natural. This firm, managed for the interest of both member parties, bargains as a single entity with the worker over the wage to split the match surplus in the labor market. Since the wage is negotiated over the total surplus of the creditor and the investment project, it does not depend on the repayment ψ negotiated in the credit market. ψ is a transfer with no incidence on either the value of a filled job, J_π, or an open vacancy, J_v, in equations (5.15) and (5.14), respectively. As a result of this set of assumptions, the negotiated wage is the solution to

$$w = \text{argmax}(J_\pi - J_v)^{1-\alpha_L}(W_n - W_u)^{\alpha_L}$$

where W_n and W_u are the standard present-discounted values of being employed or unemployed, exactly as in chapter 1, and α_L is the worker's wage bargaining weight.

The wage rule from Nash bargaining has an intermediate step similar to the benchmark environment:

$$w = \alpha_L x + (1 - \alpha_L) r W_u - \alpha_L k(\phi)$$

This intermediate wage equation differs from the equivalent one in chapter 1 by the presence of the annuitized value of the total cost to search in credit markets $k(\phi)$ defined in equation (5.19). This term reflects the outside option for the firm of returning to the labor market stage. This reduces the total surplus to a match in the labor market, leading to a lower wage in proportion α_L of the value of this option.

The Nash-bargained wage rule in equation (5.26) is obtained by replacing rW_u by its equilibrium value, which itself makes use of the Nash sharing rule to substitute out the worker's labor surplus. We thus have, still using notations $\gamma_k = \gamma + k(\phi)$, and $x^{CL} = x - k(\phi)$:

Block bargained Nash wage in the presence of financial market frictions:

$$w = (1 - \alpha_L) z + \alpha_L \left(x^{CL} + \gamma_k \theta\right) \tag{5.26}$$

or

$$w = (1 - \alpha_L) z + \alpha_L (x + \gamma\theta) + (\theta - 1)\alpha_L k(\phi) \tag{5.27}$$

The first line shows the proximity of the wage equation in CL with the conventional solution of chapter 1, provided that hiring costs and productivity include $k(\phi)$. The second line illustrates that, beyond the traditional wage equation $(1 - \alpha_L) z + \alpha_L (x + \gamma\theta)$, the effect on wages of financial market imperfections is summarized by $k(\phi)$ multiplied by both a positive and a negative term. The latter is due to the fact that financial market frictions reduce the size of the surplus in the labor market. This negative surplus effect, captured by $-\alpha_L k(\phi)$, lowers the wage curve for any given level of labor market tightness. On the other hand, these same financial market frictions improve the relative threat point of the worker vis à vis the firm, which increases the slope of the wage curve with respect to labor market tightness by a factor $\theta\alpha_L k(\phi)$.

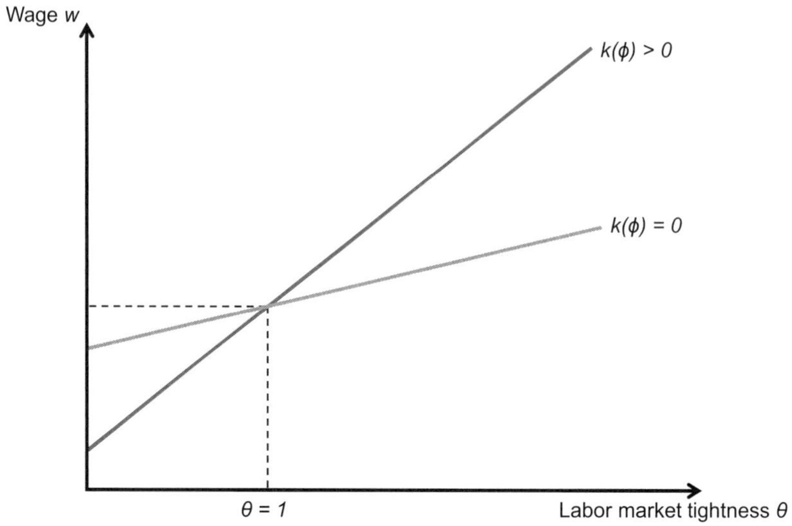

Figure 5.2
Nash-bargained wage curve in the CL model

Of these two forces, the positive slope effect dominates if and only if $\theta > 1$. This is illustrated in figure 5.2. This comes from the fact that when the labor market is tight, the workers' threat point is high and they can take advantage of financial frictions to raise wages. In the model calibrated to US data, which is developed in chapter 6, labor market tightness will be below this value of $\theta = 1$. This does not mean that due to lower wages, entry is higher with credit market frictions, because the equilibrium value of θ will depend on the position of the job creation curve. This curve is itself impacted by $k(\phi)$. This is what we explore in the next section. Finally, note that this wage equation is very close to that obtained in the fixed entry cost model developed in chapter 3 when comparing Moen's competitive equilibrium and the decentralized bargaining model. In particular, appendix equation (3.33) corresponded exactly to this wage rule, with the exception that $k(\phi) = (r + s^C)K$ above is replaced by rK given that $s^C = 0$ in chapter 3.

5.2.5 Equilibrium

After substituting the wage equation (5.26) into the job creation condition (5.20), we can now define the equilibrium in the model with frictions in financial and labor markets as the pair (θ^*, ϕ^*) that satisfies both a free entry condition in the financial market and a job creation condition:

Summary of the equilibrium (ϕ, θ) in the model with both financial and labor market frictions:

$$\text{Credit market tightness: } \phi^* = \frac{\kappa_B}{\kappa_I}\frac{1-\alpha_C}{\alpha_C} \tag{5.28}$$

$$\text{Labor market tightness: } \frac{\gamma_k}{q(\theta^*)} = \frac{(1-\alpha_L)(x^{CL}-z) - \alpha_L\theta^*\gamma_k}{r+s^C+s^L} \tag{5.29}$$

with

$$\text{Wage: } w = (1-\alpha_L)\,z + \alpha_L\left(x^{CL} + \gamma_k\theta\right)$$

$$\text{Repayment: } \Psi = \alpha_C(x-w) + (1-\alpha_C)\frac{\gamma(r+s^C+s^L)}{q(\theta)}$$

$$\text{Adjusted productivity: } x^{CL} = x - k(\phi) = x - (r+s^C)K(\phi)\ ;$$

$$K(\phi) = \frac{\kappa_B}{\phi p(\phi)} + \frac{\kappa_I}{p(\phi)}$$

$$\text{Ajusted labor entry costs: } \gamma_k = \gamma + k(\phi)$$

The left-hand side of (5.29) represents a measure of the costs of entering the labor market. Using its alternative formulation derived in equation (5.18), one can rewrite it as

$$K(\phi^*)\left[1-\alpha_L+\frac{r+s^C}{q(\theta^*)}\right]+\frac{\gamma}{q(\theta^*)}$$
$$= \frac{(1-\alpha_L)\left[x+s^LK(\phi^*)-z\right]-\alpha_L\theta^*\left[\gamma+k(\phi^*)\right]}{r+s^C+s^L}$$

The presence of α_L in the left-hand side reflects the costs in the financial sector which are paid indirectly by lower wages, as indicated in the wage equation where wages decreased by $-\alpha_L k(\phi)$. This quasi-cost function is represented by the increasing concave curve in figure 5.3. As labor market tightness tends towards zero, job filling becomes infinitely fast so that only the costs in the financial market $K(\phi)(1-\alpha_L)$ remain. As the labor market tightness goes up, the rate of job filling slows down. As $K=0$, the increasing concave cost curve starts at zero and has a lower slope. It is represented by the lowest of the two increasing concave curves.

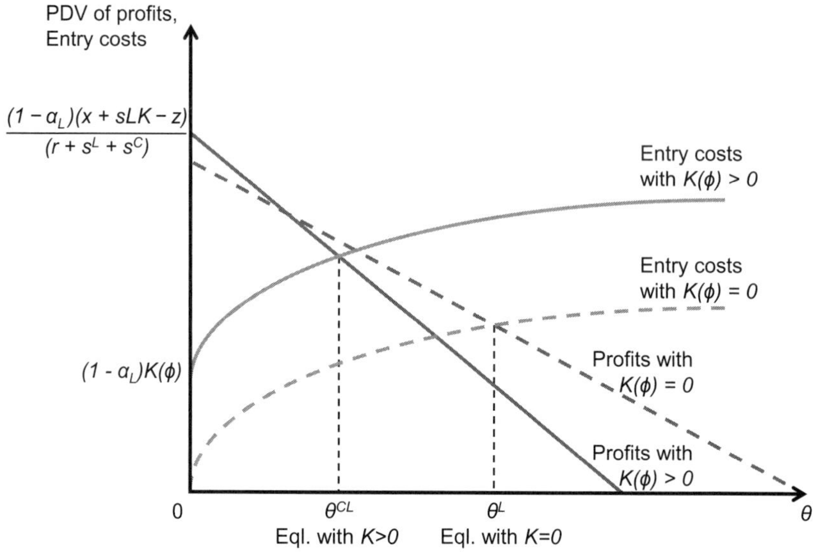

Figure 5.3

Entry costs and ex-post profits: the impact of financial market search costs $K(\phi)$ on equilibrium labor market tightness

The profit side, or the right-hand side of equation (5.29), is a linearly decreasing function of θ. As θ tends towards zero, the profits tend towards $(1-\alpha_L)(x+s^LK-z)/(r+s^C+s^L)$, and the slope with respect to θ is $-\alpha_L(\gamma+rK)/(r+s^C+s^L)$. The profit line with positive K is represented by the solid line in figure 5.3, and by the dashed lines when $K=0$. The crossing of cost and profit curves pins down equilibrium labor market tightness in the CL model, denoted by θ^{CL}, which is lower than in the absence of financial frictions $K=0$ at the point θ^L.

Labor market tightness in the CL model is decreasing in $K(\phi)$, and a condition for the existence of positive labor market tightness is that these total costs must satisfy the inequality

$$K(\phi^*) < \frac{x+s^LK(\phi^*)-z}{r+s^C+s^L} \quad \text{or simply} \quad K(\phi^*) < \frac{x-z}{r+s^C} \tag{5.30}$$

An equilibrium with positive labor market tightness exists if the total search costs in the financial market are not too large relative to the present value of economic rents generated in the labor market. These rents are the present value of flow difference between productivity x and nonmarket value z, $(x-z)/(r+s^C)$. The labor market is not viable if the condition is not satisfied. In that case, the entry costs would be too large to allow for an *ex ante* positive surplus of investment projects and their return to creditors. If the condition is satisfied, then the value of labor market tightness is uniquely determined from equation (5.29). There is at most one solution that is increasing in $x-z$ and decreasing in $K(\phi^*)$.

Finally, absent the financial costs, or when $K \to 0$, the model converges to the conventional equation (1.31) of chapter 1, which defines a level of labor market highness θ^L. This level of labor market tightness is always higher than in the presence of frictions in the financial market. It follows that the equilibrium rate of unemployment in the presence of frictions in the credit market is always greater than in the benchmark model.

5.3 Efficiency and Hosios in the financial market

As in chapter 3, we assume that the flow of utility of the nonemployed workers z is pure utility and not a transfer in the form of unemployment insurance. Frictions in the financial market, just as in the labor market, generate inefficiencies due to the presence of congestion externalities. This leads to a second best efficiency condition similar to that in Hosios (1990) and Pissarides (1990), as studied in chapter 3.

5.3.1 Social planner's problem with frictional labor and credit markets

Social output is the present discounted value of output and leisure net of search costs in all markets. The social planner's problem is

$$\begin{aligned} \Omega^{SP} &= \max_{\mathcal{B}_c,\mathcal{N}_c,\mathcal{U},\mathcal{V}} \int_0^{\infty} e^{-rt}[x(1-\mathcal{U}) + z\mathcal{U} - \gamma\mathcal{V} - \kappa_B\mathcal{B}_c - \kappa_I\mathcal{N}_c]dt \\ \text{s.t.} \quad & \dot{\mathcal{U}} = \left(s^C + s^L\right)(1-\mathcal{U}) - \mathcal{M}_L(\mathcal{U},\mathcal{V}) \\ & \dot{\mathcal{V}} = \mathcal{M}_C(\mathcal{N}_c,\mathcal{B}_c) + s^L(1-\mathcal{U}) - \mathcal{M}_L(\mathcal{U},\mathcal{V}) - s^C\mathcal{V} \end{aligned}$$

The control variables in the planner's problem are the masses on each side of the financial market, $\mathcal{N}_c$ and $\mathcal{B}_c$, while unemployment and vacancies, $\mathcal{U}$ and $\mathcal{V}$, are state variables. The first constraint on the planner is the well-known law of motion for unemployment. The second constraint is the law of motion for job vacancies, the difference between vacancy creation, the flow of matches in the credit market $\mathcal{M}_C(\mathcal{N}_c,\mathcal{B}_c)$, to which are added jobs hit by a labor turnover shock $s^L(1-\mathcal{U})$, and the flow of job vacancies either filled or destroyed due to a credit match destruction shock, $\mathcal{M}_L(\mathcal{U},\mathcal{V})$ and $s^C\mathcal{V}$, respectively.

Denoting Ψ_i for $i = U, V$ the co-state variables, the Hamiltonian to the problem is

$$
\begin{aligned}
H &= e^{-rt}\left[x(1-\mathcal{U}) + z\mathcal{U} - \gamma\mathcal{V} - \kappa_B\mathcal{B}_c - \kappa_I\mathcal{N}_c\right] \\
&\quad + \Psi_U\left[\left(s^C + s^L\right)(1-\mathcal{U}) - \mathcal{M}_L(\mathcal{U},\mathcal{V})\right] \\
&\quad + \Psi_V\left[\mathcal{M}_C(\mathcal{N}_c,\mathcal{B}_c) + s^L(1-\mathcal{U}) - \mathcal{M}_L(\mathcal{U},\mathcal{V}) - s^C\mathcal{V}\right]
\end{aligned}
$$

The first-order conditions for financial market, followed by labor market, variables, dropping for convenience the parenthesis and tightness after the elasticities $\eta_L(\theta)$ and $\eta_C(\phi)$, are

$$\partial H/\partial \mathcal{B}_c = 0 \rightarrow e^{-rt}(-\kappa_B) + \Psi_V\phi p(\phi)\eta_C = 0 \tag{5.31}$$

$$\partial H/\partial \mathcal{N}_c = 0 \rightarrow e^{-rt}(-\kappa_I) + \Psi_V p(\phi)(1-\eta_C) = 0 \tag{5.32}$$

$$
\begin{aligned}
\dot{\Psi}_U = -\partial H/\partial \mathcal{U} = \rightarrow \dot{\Psi}_U &= e^{-rt}(x-z) + \Psi_U\left[s^C + s^L + \eta_L\theta q(\theta)\right] \\
&\quad + \Psi_V[\eta_L\theta q(\theta)]
\end{aligned} \tag{5.33}
$$

$$
\begin{aligned}
\dot{\Psi}_V = -\partial H/\partial \mathcal{V} = \rightarrow \dot{\Psi}_V &= e^{-rt}\gamma + \Psi_U(1-\eta_L)q(\theta) \\
&\quad + \Psi_V(1-\eta_L)q(\theta) + s^C\Psi_V
\end{aligned} \tag{5.34}
$$

5.3.2 Socially optimal credit and labor market tightness

The solution to this optimization problem turns out to be dichotomic. The first two optimality conditions for control variables, equations (5.31) and (5.32), deliver the value of the multiplier Ψ_V and the optimal level of tightness in the credit market. The last two equations, combined with optimal credit market tightness, then deliver a social planner's job creation equation that leads to the optimality condition in the labor market.

The steps are as follows. First, summing cquations (5.31) and (5.32) provides the value of the multiplier Ψ_V, the shadow value of a newly created vacancy: $\Psi_V = e^{-rt}K(\phi)$. The planner is trying to minimize the social costs of search in the financial market, seeking a shadow value as close as possible to what can be achieved absent financial market frictions (a shadow value of a vacancy of zero). The resulting multiplier Ψ_V is proportional to the credit market creation costs $K(\phi)$, which are minimized as we will show at the optimal ϕ^{opt}. Eliminating Ψ_V from either (5.31) or (5.32) implies that the optimal, cost-minimizing tightness of the credit market is:

Socially optimal level of credit market tightness:

$$\phi^{opt} = \frac{1-\eta_C}{\eta_C}\frac{\kappa_B}{\kappa_I} \tag{5.35}$$

The second step is to solve for the multiplier Ψ_U, the shadow value of a new hire given labor and financial market frictions:

$$\Psi_U = -e^{-rt}\left[\frac{\gamma + (r+s^C)K(\phi^{opt})}{(1-\eta_L)q(\theta^{opt})} + K(\phi^{opt})\right]$$

The social planner's desired labor market tightness θ^{opt} solves a social planner's job creation condition $K(\phi^{opt})\left(1-\eta_L+\frac{r+s^C}{q(\theta^{opt})}\right)+\frac{\gamma}{q(\theta^{opt})} = \frac{(1-\eta_L)[x+s^L K(\phi^{opt})-z]-\eta_L\theta^{opt}\left[\gamma+(r+s^C)K(\phi^{opt})\right]}{r+s^C+s^L}$, which can conveniently be summarized as follows:

Socially optimal level of labor market tightness:

$$\frac{\gamma_k^{opt}}{q(\theta^{opt})} = \frac{(1-\eta_L)(x^{CL,opt}-z)-\eta_L\theta^{opt}\gamma_k^{opt}}{r+s^C+s^L} \tag{5.36}$$

with $\gamma_k^{opt} = \gamma + k(\phi^{opt})$

and $x^{CL,opt} = x + k(\phi^{opt})$

5.3.3 Hosios in credit and labor markets

To summarize, the following equations need to be compared to verify whether the decentralized allocation corresponds to the constrained efficient allocation:

Social planner and decentralized job creation conditions with financial market frictions:

Social planner:
$$\frac{\gamma_k^{opt}}{q(\theta^{opt})} = \frac{(1-\eta_L)\left(x^{CL,opt}-z\right)-\eta_L\theta^{opt}\gamma_k^{opt}}{r+s^C+s^L} \tag{5.37}$$

$$\phi^{opt} = \frac{1-\eta_C}{\eta_C}\frac{\kappa_B}{\kappa_I} \tag{5.38}$$

Decentralized:
$$\frac{\gamma_k}{q(\theta^*)} = \frac{(1-\alpha_L)\left(x^{CL}-z\right)-\alpha_L\theta^*\gamma_k}{r+s^C+s^L} \tag{5.39}$$

$$\phi^* = \frac{1-\alpha_C}{\alpha_C}\frac{\kappa_B}{\kappa_I} \tag{5.40}$$

A comparison of equations (5.37) and (5.38) determining the constrained efficient labor and credit market tightness with equations (5.39) and (5.40) for the decentralized allocation reveals that the decentralized solution maximizes social net output if and only if the Hosios conditions in the credit *and* the labor market are met. That is, ϕ^* is constrained efficient if $\alpha_C = \eta_C$, and θ^* is constrained efficient if $\alpha_L = \eta_L$ and $\phi^* = \phi^{opt}$. In this case, $\gamma_k = \gamma_k^{opt}$ and $x^{CL} = x^{CL,opt}$. Overall, we have the following constrained efficiency result:

Hosios constrained efficiency conditions in the CL model:

$$\phi^* = \phi^{opt} \quad \text{if and only if} \quad \alpha_C = \eta_C(\phi^{opt}) \tag{5.41}$$

$$\theta^* = \theta^{opt} \quad \text{if and only if} \quad \alpha_L = \eta_L(\theta^{opt}) \text{ and } \phi^* = \phi^{opt} \tag{5.42}$$

5.3.4 Properties of the constrained efficient allocation

The socially optimal value of credit market tightness has an important property with respect to $K(\phi)$. It corresponds to the value of ϕ minimizing K. Indeed, in the limit when credit market tightness tends to zero, $K(0) \to +\infty$, and as $\phi \to \infty$, $K(\phi)$ also tends toward infinity. The total costs of search in the financial market are highest when either side faces difficulties locating a trading partner. An abundance of creditors relative to projects, that is a low ϕ, leads to high search costs for creditors. An abundance of projects relative to creditors, a high ϕ, leads to high search costs for projects. Given the properties of the matching function emphasized above, total search costs $K(\phi)$ have a minimum for a positive value of ϕ. It turns out that this minimum is reached at ϕ^{opt} and one can show that $K'(\phi^{opt}) = 0$, illustrated in figure 5.4a.

The constraint efficient credit market tightness is achieved if and only if the creditor's share of the surplus α_C is equal to the elasticity of the credit matching function $\eta_C(\phi^{opt})$. In the solution to the Hamiltonian, the planner first chooses the ratio $\mathcal{N}_c/\mathcal{B}_c$ to minimize the financial cost of a marginal vacancy creation. This determines the optimal credit market tightness. If $\alpha_C > \eta_C$ then there is too much entry on the creditor side of the market relative to the congestion externality each creditor generates by entering the market. Equilibrium ϕ^* is below ϕ^{opt}, and the total transaction costs in the financial market are inefficiently high. That is, $K(\phi^*) > K(\phi^{opt})$. If $\alpha_C < \eta_C$, the decentralized credit market tightness is too high, there is excess entry of projects, and again the total transaction costs in the financial market are inefficiently high. That is, $K(\phi^*) > K(\phi^{opt})$. This is a classic Hosios condition in markets with congestion externalities and bargaining.

Inspection of ϕ^* determined in equation (5.28) and ϕ^{opt} shows that a Hosios-condition $\alpha_C = \eta_C$ in the financial market is necessary and sufficient to reach the efficient credit market tightness. This rule states that there is a value

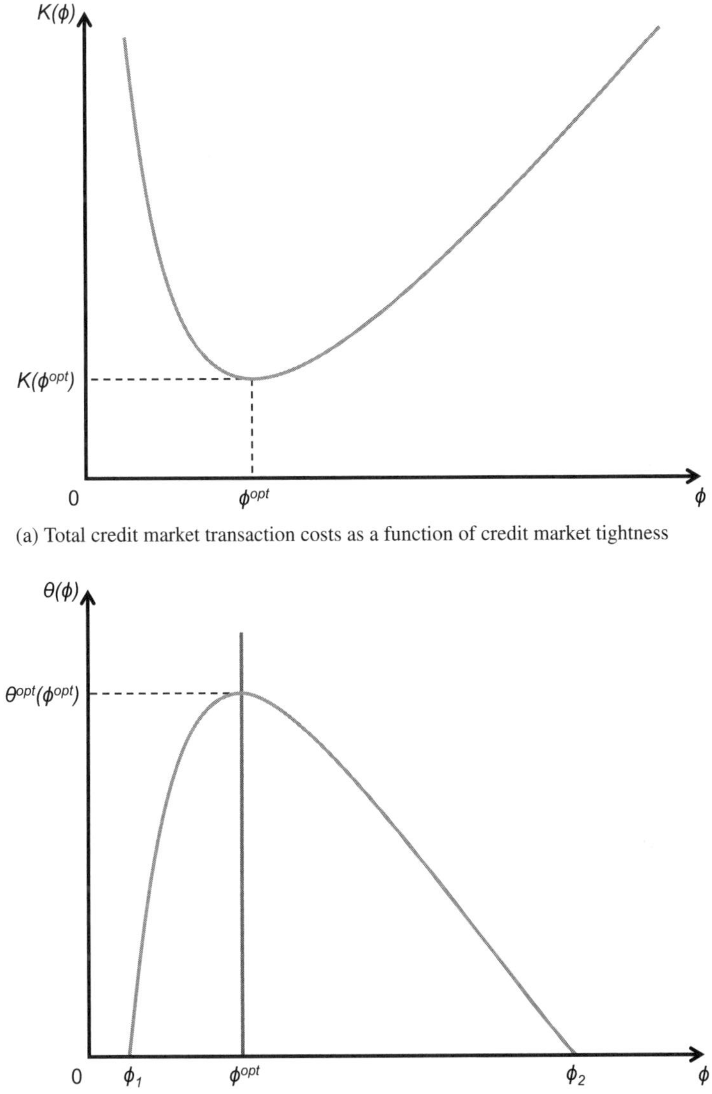

(a) Total credit market transaction costs as a function of credit market tightness

(b) Labor market tightness as a function of credit market tightness

Figure 5.4

Total credit market transaction costs $K(\phi)$ and labor market tightness $\theta(\phi)$ as functions of credit market tightness

of the bargaining parameter over ψ that internalizes the matching externalities due to frictions in the financial market, and again, it turns out that this is the value that *minimizes* $K(\phi)$. To check this formally, consider $K(\phi)$ at the value of the decentralized equilibrium by replacing ϕ by its equilibrium value. Hence $K(\phi^*)$ is now a function K^* of α_C: $K^*(\alpha_C) = \frac{\kappa_B}{p\left(\frac{\kappa_B}{\kappa_I}\frac{1-\alpha_C}{\alpha_C}\right)} + \frac{\kappa_I}{\left(\frac{\kappa_B}{\kappa_I}\frac{1-\alpha_C}{\alpha_C}\right)p\left(\frac{\kappa_B}{\kappa_I}\frac{1-\alpha_C}{\alpha_C}\right)}$. Straightforward calculation leads to

$$\frac{dK^*}{d\alpha_C} = 0 \Leftrightarrow \alpha_C = \eta_C \tag{5.43}$$

The second step in the credit–labor market Hosios condition is to determine the scale of the economy, or to achieve the optimal labor market tightness θ^{opt}. Here there is an interdependence between the equilibrium in the credit and labor markets. The social planner's choice for labor market tightness is defined in equation (5.36). It determines labor market tightness as a function $\theta(\phi)$ of credit market tightness. This concave function is plotted in (ϕ, θ) space in figure 5.4b. Existence of an equilibrium with positive labor market tightness defines an upper bound for the total cost in the financial market that we denote $\bar{K} = \frac{x-z}{r+s^C}$. Above this value, the market is not viable and there is no entry in the market. Given the properties of the function $K(\phi)$ just discussed, there will exist two values of credit market tightness, ϕ_1 and ϕ_2 with $\phi_1 < \phi_2$, for which $K(\phi) = \bar{K}$. Either the credit market is too slack, ϕ_1, and the cost of search for creditors pushes the total search cost in the credit market over $\bar{K}$, or the credit market is too tight, $\phi_2 > \phi_1$, in which case the search costs of investment projects push the total costs above the threshold. In both cases there cannot be an equilibrium with positive labor market tightness. In the range $[\phi_1, \phi_2]$, where $K(\phi) < \bar{K}$, the job creation condition defines an increasing and concave function $\theta(\phi)$ that crosses the horizontal axis of $\theta = 0$ at the two points ϕ_1 and ϕ_2 (see again figure 5.4b). As we move away from ϕ_1 towards ϕ_2, the total financial market search costs $K(\phi)$ decline, and labor market tightness θ increases, until a level of credit market tightness for which $K(\phi)$ reaches a minimum. This level, as we have just seen, is the socially efficient level of credit market tightness ϕ^{opt}, represented by the vertical line in figure 5.4b. Above ϕ^{opt}, the entry costs in the labor market begin to increase, reducing equilibrium labor market tightness.

The decentralized allocation is constrained efficient if, first, the usual labor market condition $\alpha_L = \eta_L$ holds and, second, the credit market Hosios condition holds at the same time. If only the first condition is satisfied, $\alpha_L = \eta_L$, there is still insufficient job creation as the credit market creation costs are inefficiently high.

Likewise, if $\alpha_L > \eta_L$, the share of the labor surplus to the worker is inefficiently large, restricting entry into the labor market by firms. Thus for any given level of credit market tightness, the equilibrium labor market tightness will be below the value that would be achieved when $\alpha_L = \eta_L$, as in figure 5.5a. Figure 5.5b illustrates deviations from Hosios in the credit market, with $\alpha_C < \eta_C$. In this case the vertical line shifts to the right as there is too much

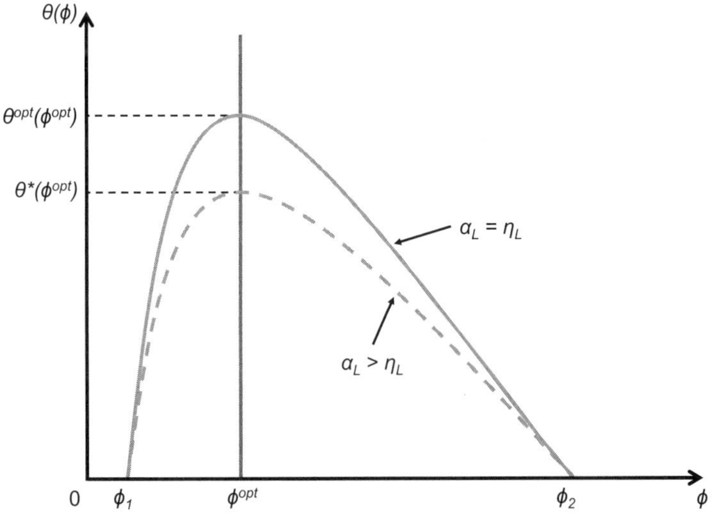

(a) Deviations from Hosios in the labor market

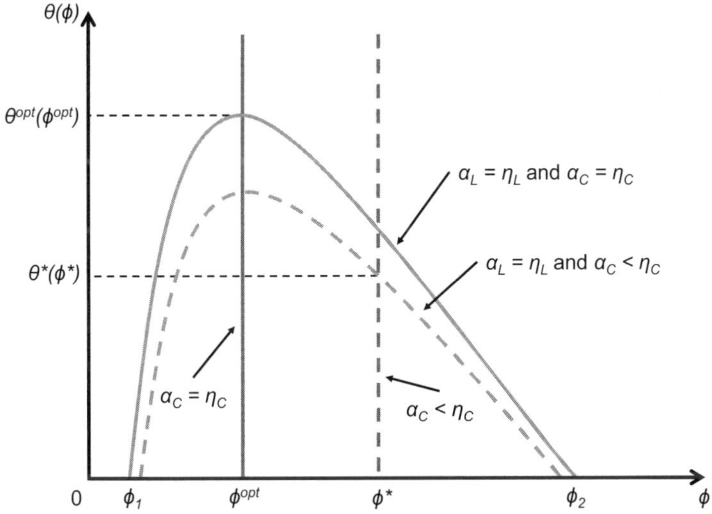

(b) Deviations from Hosios in the credit market

Figure 5.5
Constrained efficiency in the CL model. The inverted U-curve is the relation between θ and ϕ defined in equation (5.37)

entry by projects relative to entry by creditors. The increase in credit market costs resulting from $\phi^* > \phi^{opt}$ causes the equilibrium to set at lower level of labor market tightness $\theta^*(\phi^*)$.

5.4 Discussion of the literature and remaining issues

Search frictions in financial markets for production firms were introduced by Wasmer and Weil (2000), Wasmer and Weil (2004), and den Haan et al. (2003), following arguments in Jaffee and Stiglitz (1990) that the market for credit is better conceived as a customer market in which borrowers form a single relationship with a lender. It is also based on empirical evidence. Firms tend to concentrate their lending from one source (Petersen and Rajan, 1994) and the benefits to borrowers increase with the length of the relationship with banks (Petersen and Rajan, 1994, Berger and Udell, 1995). Relationship lending appears to even be present in private equity (Fenn et al., 1995). Surveys of potential entrepreneurs reveal that failing to "locate" credit is a major reason for failing to start a business (Blanchflower and Oswald 1998). Further, lenders tend to specialize in particular sectors or regions, bringing specificity to the relationships that are formed. Recent attempts to estimate matching frictions in the credit market include Cipollone and Giordani (2015, 2016) on venture capitalists/business angels data. In the Cobb–Douglas case, entrepreneurs have a share in matching between 1/3 and 2/3, and venture capitalists have the opposite proportions.

This chapter follows closely the structure of Wasmer and Weil (2004), extended to a richer structure of shocks, and differs more substantially after wages are introduced in subsection 5.2.4. Regarding to the small versus large firm assumption, Petrosky-Nadeau et al. (2015) show the Bellman equations and allocations are identical in a multi-project firm and financial institutions environment under the set of assumptions of the decentralization equilibrium that is followed here. The special case with $s^L = 0$ was originally studied in Wasmer and Weil (2004). It is slightly simpler and ignores the recovery value of the firm after labor turnover. It also assumes away s^C shocks in the vacancy stage. The online appendix provides a model with the fully differentiated notations for shocks in various stages.

Many recent papers have studied how financial frictions affect job creation, job destruction, and equilibrium unemployment. To cite only a few among a growing line of research, especially since the financial crisis: Monacelli et al. (2011a), Boeri et al. (2015), Bentolila et al. (2013).

Our treatment of liquidity in financial markets is simple and leads to tractable solutions. More sophisticated models of markets trading assets were pioneered by Kiyotaki and Wright (1989) and Lagos and Wright (2005), followed by Duffie et al. (2005) and Lagos and Rocheteau (2009), and synthesized in Nosal and Rocheteau (2011). For a discussion of constrained efficiency in a money-search environment with credit, see for instance one of the early papers by Shi (1996).

A treatment of the endogenous destruction case in the CL model is discussed in appendix 5.5.4, and in Petrosky-Nadeau (2013). Further discussions related to the possible extensions of the CL model are in the online appendix, such as the inefficiency of endogenous destruction due to liquidity constraints, and the strategic interactions arising from the time sequence of bargaining. These are important questions that deserve a specific treatment but are left aside in this and subsequent chapters, which focus solely on the benchmark model. In Michelacci and Quadrini (2009) financial constraints on firms affect the wage offered to workers in an environment of firms with a life cycle. Growing, financially constrained firms can somewhat relax this constraint by writing wage contracts that promise higher wages in the future.

5.5 Chapter appendix

5.5.1 Detail of the calculations of repayment ψ

The forward value of E_v and B_v are, respectively,

$$\left(r+s^C\right)E_v = q\left(E_\pi - E_v\right) = q\left(\frac{x+s^L E_v - w - \psi}{r+s^C+s^L} - E_v\right)$$

and

$$\left(r+s^C\right)B_v = -\gamma + q\left(B_\pi - B_v\right) = -\gamma + q\left(\frac{\psi + s^L B_v}{r+s^C+s^L} - B_v\right)$$

Combining with the Nash sharing rule (5.22), $E_v/(1-\alpha_C) = B_v/\alpha_C = J_v$, we obtain

$$\begin{aligned}
\frac{q}{r+s^C+q}\frac{1}{1-\alpha_C}\frac{x-w-\psi}{r+s^C+s^L} &= \frac{1}{\alpha_C}\left(-\frac{\gamma}{r+s^C+q} + \frac{q}{r+s^C+q}\frac{\psi}{r+s^C+s^L}\right)\\
\alpha_C\frac{x-w-\psi}{r+s^C+s^L} &= (1-\alpha_C)\left(-\frac{\gamma}{q} + \frac{\psi}{r+s^C+s^L}\right)\\
\frac{\psi}{r+s^C+s^L} &= (1-\alpha_C)\frac{\gamma}{q} + \alpha_C\frac{x-w}{r+s^C+s^L}
\end{aligned}$$

which corresponds to equation (5.25).

5.5.2 Wage setting: block bargaining

We have: $w = \text{argmax}(J_\pi - J_v)^{1-\alpha_L}(W_n - W_u)^{\alpha_L}$. The first-order condition results in the sharing rule:

$$(1-\alpha_L)(rW_n - rW_u) = \alpha_L (rJ_\pi - rJ_v)$$

The value of employment is now

$$rW_n = w + (s^L + s^C)(W_u - W_n)$$
$$rJ_\pi = x - w + s^L(J_v - J_\pi) + s^C(0 - J_\pi)$$

so that

$$r(W_n - W_u) = \frac{w - rW_u}{r + s^L + s^C}$$

$$r(J\pi - \iota J_v) = \frac{x - w - \left(r + s^C + s^L\right) J_v}{r + s^L + s^C}$$

leading to

$$w = \alpha_L x + (1-\alpha_L) rW_u - \alpha_L \left(r + s^C\right) J_v$$

Next, we work from $rW_u = z + \theta q(\theta)[W_n - W_u]$ to obtain after a few steps that

$$rW_u = z + \gamma\theta \frac{\alpha_L}{1-\alpha_L} + \theta q(\theta)\frac{\alpha_L}{1-\alpha_L} K(\phi)\left(\frac{r+s^C}{q(\theta)}\right)$$

and thus that

$$w = \alpha_L(x + \gamma\theta) + (1-\alpha_L) z + \alpha_L K(\phi)\left[\theta\left(q(\theta) + r + s^C\right) - \left(\theta q(\theta) + r + s^C\right)\right]$$

or eventually

$$w = \alpha_L(x+\gamma\theta) + (1-\alpha_L)z + \alpha_L K(\phi)(\theta - 1)\left(r + s^C\right) \tag{5.44}$$
$$= \omega(\theta) + \alpha_L k(\phi)(\theta - 1)$$

The labor market tightness equilibrium condition replaces the value of wages in

$$K(\phi)\left(1 + \frac{r+s^C}{q(\theta)}\right) + \frac{\gamma}{q(\theta)} = \frac{x + s^L K - w}{r + s^C + s^L}$$

or, using the notation $k(\phi)$,

$$\frac{\gamma + k(\phi)}{q(\theta)} = \frac{x - w - k(\phi)}{r + s^C + s^L}$$

5.5.3 Social planner's problem

Social output is the present discounted value of output and leisure net of all search costs:

$$\Omega^{SP} = \int_0^{\infty} e^{-rt}[x(1-\mathcal{U}) + z\mathcal{U} - \gamma\mathcal{V} - \kappa_B\mathcal{B}_c - \kappa_I\mathcal{N}_c]dt$$

The control variables are now $\mathcal{N}_c$ and $\mathcal{B}_c$ while $\mathcal{U}$ and $\mathcal{V}$ are state variables. The first is associated with a law of motion for unemployment:

$$\dot{\mathcal{U}} = (s^C + s^L)(1-\mathcal{U}) - \mathcal{M}_L(\mathcal{U},\mathcal{V}) = (s^C + s^L)(1-\mathcal{U}) - \theta q(\theta)\mathcal{U}$$

The second is a law of motion for job vacancies, the difference between vacancy creation and the number of vacancies filled:

$$\dot{\mathcal{V}} = \mathcal{M}_C(\mathcal{N}_c,\mathcal{B}_c) - \mathcal{M}_L(\mathcal{U},\mathcal{V}) - s^C\mathcal{V} + s^L(1-\mathcal{U})$$

Note that $\mathcal{M}_C(\mathcal{N}_c,\mathcal{B}_c)$ is equal to both the flows of matched creditors and matched investment projects in the financial market, $\mathcal{B}_c\phi p(\phi)$ and $\mathcal{N}_c p(\phi)$, respectively. The Hamiltonian to the problem, denoting Ψ_i the co-states variables, is

$$\begin{aligned} H = {} & e^{-rt}[x(1-\mathcal{U}) + z\mathcal{U} - \gamma\mathcal{V} - \kappa_B\mathcal{B}_c - \kappa_I\mathcal{N}_c] + \Psi_U[-\mathcal{M}_L(\mathcal{U},\mathcal{V}) + (s^C+s^L)(1-\mathcal{U})] \\ & + \Psi_V[-\mathcal{M}_L(\mathcal{U},\mathcal{V}) + \mathcal{M}_C(\mathcal{N}_c,\mathcal{B}_c) - s^C\mathcal{V} + s^L(1-\mathcal{U})] \end{aligned}$$

Using $\partial\mathcal{M}_C/\partial\mathcal{B}_c = \phi p(\phi)\eta_C(\phi)$ and $\partial\mathcal{M}_C/\partial\mathcal{N}_c = p(\phi)(1-\eta_C(\phi))$, and similarly, $\partial\mathcal{M}_L/\partial\mathcal{U} = \theta q(\theta)\eta_L(\theta)$ and $\partial\mathcal{M}_L/\partial\mathcal{V} = q(\theta)(1-\eta_L(\theta))$, the first-order conditions for labor market tightness, unemployment, and financial market variables, are, respectively, with $\mathcal{V}$, $\mathcal{U}$, and replacing $\mathcal{N}_c$ by $\phi\mathcal{B}_c$ and dropping by convenience the parenthesis and tightness after the elasticities $\eta_L(\theta)$ and $\eta_C(\phi)$

$$\partial H/\partial\mathcal{B}_c = e^{-rt}[-\kappa_B] + \Psi_V\phi p(\phi)\eta_C = 0 \tag{5.45}$$

$$\partial H/\partial\mathcal{N}_c = e^{-rt}[-\kappa_I] + \Psi_V p(\phi)(1-\eta_C) = 0 \tag{5.46}$$

$$\dot{\Psi}_U = -\partial H/\partial\mathcal{U} = e^{-rt}(x-z) + \Psi_U\left[s^C + s^L + \eta_L\theta q(\theta)\right] + \Psi_V\left(\eta_L\theta q(\theta) + s^L\right) \tag{5.47}$$

$$\dot{\Psi}_V = -\partial H/\partial\mathcal{V} = e^{-rt}\gamma + \Psi_U(1-\eta_L)q(\theta) + \Psi_V\left[(1-\eta_L)q(\theta) + s^C\right] \tag{5.48}$$

where $\eta_L(\theta)$ is the elasticity of the matching function with respect to unemployed workers, as earlier. It follows from the first two expressions (5.45) and (5.46) that the optimal tightness of the credit market must be such that

$$K'(\phi) = 0 \Leftrightarrow \phi^{opt} = \frac{1-\eta_C}{\eta_C}\frac{\kappa_B}{\kappa_I} \tag{5.49}$$

To be precise, $K'(\phi) = 0$ admits two solutions, the value of ϕ^{opt} defined in (5.35), and a second irrelevant solution in $+\infty$. Moreover, K is convex over the range $[0,\bar{\phi}]$, which includes ϕ^{opt}, and has an inflection point at $\bar{\phi}$. The second multiplier is proportional to $K(\phi)$: it is the shadow value of a newly created vacancy:

$$\Psi_V = e^{-rt}K(\phi)$$

$$\dot{\Psi}_V = -re^{-rt}K(\phi)$$

which can be reinjected in the last two equations (5.47) and (5.48):

$$\dot{\Psi}_U = e^{-rt}(x-z) + \Psi_U\left[s^C + s^L + \eta_L\theta q(\theta)\right] + e^{-rt}K(\phi)[\eta_L\theta q(\theta) + s^L] \tag{5.50}$$

$$\gamma e^{-rt} + \Psi_U(1-\eta_L)q(\theta) + e^{-rt}K(\phi)(1-\eta_L)q(\theta) = -(r+s^C)e^{-rt}K(\phi) \tag{5.51}$$

The second line (5.51) provides, posing $k(\phi) = (r+s^C)K(\phi)$, the annualized value of $K(\phi)$:

$$\Psi_U = -e^{-rt}\left(\frac{\gamma + k(\phi)}{(1-\eta_L)q(\theta)} + K(\phi)\right)$$

$$\dot{\Psi}_U = re^{-rt}\left(\frac{\gamma + k(\phi)}{(1-\eta_L)q(\theta)} + K(\phi)\right)$$

The first multiplier is the shadow cost of a new recruitment given labor frictions. Equation (5.50) can therefore be rewritten as, posing $\gamma_k = \gamma + k(\phi)$ and $x^{CL} = x - k(\phi)$,

$$(x-z) - \left[\frac{\gamma_k}{(1-\eta_L)q(\theta)} + K(\phi)\right]\left[s^C + s^L + \eta_L\theta q(\theta)\right]$$
$$+ K(\phi)[\eta_L\theta q(\theta) + s^L] = r\left(\frac{\gamma_k}{(1-\eta_L)q(\theta)} + K(\phi)\right)$$

$$\left[\frac{\gamma_k}{(1-\eta_L)q(\theta)} + K(\phi)\right]\left[r + s^C + s^L + \eta_L\theta q(\theta)\right] - K(\phi)[\eta_L\theta q(\theta) + s^L] = x - z$$

$$\left[\frac{\gamma_k}{(1-\eta_L)q(\theta)}\right]\left(r + s^C + s^L\right) + \left[\frac{\eta_L\gamma_k\theta}{(1-\eta_L)}\right]$$
$$+ K(\phi)\left[r + s^C + s^L + \eta_L\theta q(\theta)\right] - K(\phi)[\eta_L\theta q(\theta) + s^L] = (x-z)$$

$$\frac{\gamma_k}{q(\theta)}\left(r + s^C + s^L\right) = [x - k(\phi) - z](1-\eta_L) - \eta_L\gamma_k\theta$$

or eventually the expression of the text at $\phi = \phi^{opt}$:

$$\frac{\gamma_k}{q(\theta^{opt})} = \frac{(1-\eta_L)(x^{CL} - z) - \eta_L\theta^{opt}\gamma_k}{r + s^C + s^L}$$

5.5.4 Alternative bargaining arrangements: varying the specificity in labor relationships

We simplify the exposition here in assuming that $s^L = 0$, as this does not yield any additional qualitative result. We first generalize the model in allowing for varying degrees of specificity in labor relationships and in particular in allowing for the firm's outside option in bargaining to be $(1-\iota)J_c + \iota J_v$ where ι takes any value between 0 and 1 and $J_k = E_k + B_k, k = c, v$. If we assume that disagreement leads to the dissolution of the credit match and a return to the financial market stage, then $\iota = 0$ and the firm's outside option when negotiating with the worker is $J_c = 0$. If instead we assume that disagreement leads to a maintained credit match that must return to the labor market to search for another worker, then $\iota = 1$ and the firm's outside option in bargaining with the worker is $J_v = K(\phi)$ in equilibrium. Either assumption may be relevant, depending on the context. In the specific context of block bargaining (investment project–creditor block) it could be argued that $\iota = 1$ is a better assumption on two grounds: first it delivers an important Hosios condition while $\iota = 1$ does not; and second it is empirically more plausible that labor turnover does not destroy the credit market relationship. As we will show in the next section, away from $\iota = 1$, the standard Hosios condition in the labor market does not apply.

The negotiated wage is the solution to this more general problem:

$$w = \text{argmax}(J_\pi - \iota J_v)^{1-\alpha_L}(W_n - W_u)^{\alpha_L}$$

where W_n and W_u are the standard present-discounted values of being employed or unemployed, exactly as in chapter 1, and α_L is the worker's wage bargaining weight. The wage rule from Nash bargaining has an intermediate step similar to the benchmark environment, $w = \alpha_L x + (1-\alpha_L) rW_u - \alpha_L(r+s^C)\iota K(\phi)$, with the exception that the total cost to search in financial markets appears in the case when the outside option to the firm in wage bargaining is to return to the labor market stage to search for another worker. The Nash-bargained wage rule in equation (5.52) is then obtained by replacing rW_u by its equilibrium value, which itself makes use of the Nash sharing rule to substitute out the worker's labor surplus. We thus have:

Block-bargained Nash wage:

$$w = \alpha_L [x + \gamma\theta] + (1-\alpha_L) z + \alpha_L K(\phi) \left[\theta\,(q(\theta) + r) - \iota\left(\theta q(\theta) + r + s^C\right)\right] \tag{5.52}$$

with $w = \alpha_L [x + \gamma\theta] + (1-\alpha_L) z + \alpha_L \theta\,(r + q(\theta))\, K(\phi)$ if $\iota = 0$

with $w = \alpha_L [x + (\gamma + rK(\phi))\theta] + (1-\alpha_L) z - \left(r + s^C\right) \alpha_L K(\phi)$ if $\iota = 1$ (5.53)

The top line highlights the incidence of the assumption regarding the firm's outside option on the bargained wage. In the first case with $\iota = 1$, that is to say, when the termination of bargaining does not dissolve the firm, the effect of financial market imperfections on the wage was ambiguous. Here, with $\iota = 0$, the effect is an unambiguous increase the wage. The presence of financial market friction increases the slope of the wage curve in (θ, w) space. Not agreeing is more costly to the firm which must return to search in financial markets before resuming its search for another worker in the labor market. As a result the worker is in a relatively stronger bargaining position and can obtain a higher wage. In equilibrium, the job creation condition becomes:

Job creation condition with credit and labor market frictions:

$$K(\phi^*)\left[1+\frac{r+s^C}{q(\theta^*)}\right]+\frac{\gamma}{q(\theta^*)} = \frac{(1-\alpha_L)(x-z)-\alpha_L\theta^*\left\{\gamma+\left[r+q(\theta^*)\,(1-\iota)\right]K(\phi^*)\right\}}{r+s}+\alpha_L\iota K(\phi^*) \tag{5.54}$$

$$\text{with } K(\phi^*)\left[1+\frac{r+s^C}{q(\theta^*)}\right]+\frac{\gamma}{q(\theta^*)} = \frac{(1-\alpha_L)(x-z)-\alpha_L\theta^*\left\{\gamma+\left[r+q(\theta^*)\right]K(\phi^*)\right\}}{r+s} \quad \text{if} \quad \iota=0 \tag{5.55}$$

$$K(\phi^*)\left[1+\frac{r}{q(\theta^*)}\right]+\frac{\gamma}{q(\theta^*)} = \frac{(1-\alpha_L)(x-z)-\alpha_L\theta^*\left[\gamma+rK(\phi^*)\right]}{r+s}+\alpha_L K(\phi^*) \quad \text{if} \quad \iota=1 \tag{5.56}$$

The condition for existence is that there is a positive value of equilibrium market tightness insuring equality (5.54) which is the case if:

$$K(\phi^*)(1-\alpha_L\iota)\leq\frac{(1-\alpha_L)(x-z)}{r+s^C}$$

This value is different from the viability condition in the text of this chapter by the addition of the proportionality factor $(1-\alpha_L\iota)$: with $\iota>0$, firms can raise their threat point during bargaining, the overall viability condition is easier to satisfy.

Finally, note that in the case $\iota=0$, the right-hand side of the decentralized allocation is, for a given θ, and at a Hosios condition, always lower than the RHS of the social planner JC condition, leading to a too low θ^* in the decentralized equilibrium. The decentralized equation in which agents do not recover the search capital costs in the financial market leads to entry that is too low compared to what is socially optimal.

To summarize, the assumption $\iota=1$, that is the firm's threat point in bargaining over wage is positive and equal to $K(\phi)$, has two desirable properties: it leads to a similar Hosios efficiency condition as in the model without credit frictions, and the main equations of the model (wage curve and entry curve) are very similar to those in part I of the book, both in the discrete time case and the continuous time case.

Endogenous job destruction

The environment of chapter 5 can also be extended to allow for the endogenous destruction of a job along the lines followed in chapter 1 of part I. This will lead to endogenous bankruptcies, that is giving an expression for s^C, which has been treated as a parameter so far. Productivity of the firm has an idiosyncratic component which evolves randomly over time. We drop any exogenous shock to have only endogenous destructions due to changes in productivity.

Assume that a new firm draws an idiosyncratic productivity a, where a is drawn from cdf $G(a)$, when meeting a worker in the labor market. Subsequently, new productivities are drawn at the Poisson rate μ. Once their match is formed, they jointly operate as a firm on the labor and goods markets. The equilibrium condition in the financial market remains unchanged, and the asset values of being on either market for a firms are:

$$J_v = K(\phi) = \kappa_B/\check{p}(\phi) + \kappa_B/p(\phi) \tag{5.57}$$

$$rJ_v = -\gamma + q(\theta)\int \max\left[J_\pi(a') - J_v, 0\right] \mathrm{d}G(a') \tag{5.58}$$

$$rJ_\pi(a) = ax - w(a) + \mu \int \max\left[J_\pi(a'), J_v, 0\right] \mathrm{d}G(a') - \mu J_\pi(x). \tag{5.59}$$

Similarly, we can obtain a Bellman equation for the surplus of a worker–firm pair $\Sigma_l^T(a) = J_\pi(a) - J_v + W_n(a) - W_u$ as

$$(r+\mu)\Sigma_l^T(a) = xa + \mu \int \max\left[\Sigma_l^T(a'), 0\right] \mathrm{d}G(a') - rJ_v - rW_u.$$

Since $d\Sigma_l^T(a)/da = \frac{x}{r+\mu} > 0$, there exists a reservation strategy such that if $a < A$, where A is such that $\Sigma_l^T(A) = 0$, the match is dissolved. That is to say, if the job draws $a < A$, there is no value to the relationship for either party. Thus, A defines a job destruction threshold.

There exists a unique equilibrium for this economy defined by a pair (A, θ) that solve the job creation and job destruction conditions:

Job creation and job destruction conditions in the presence of financial market frictions:

$$\text{JC:} \frac{r}{q(\theta)} K(\phi) + \frac{\gamma}{q(\theta)} = \frac{(1-\alpha_L)x}{r+\mu} \int_A (a' - A)\mathrm{d}G(a') \tag{5.60}$$

$$\text{JD:} rK(\phi) + rW_u = Ax + \mu \int_A \Sigma_l^T(a')\mathrm{d}G(a') \tag{5.61}$$

The job creation condition (5.60) has the usual shape, with one difference: expected value of a job in future states is conditional on drawing a productivity above the threshold A. For a job to remain viable, defined by the job destruction condition (5.61), its expected future value must at least equal the values of the firm's and worker's outside options net of the match's current production A. Increases in $K(\phi)$ render all existing matches less profitable, and some no longer viable. In the benchmark environment, as treated in Mortensen and Pissarides (1994), $K(\phi) = 0$. As such, financial costs raise the lowest viable job productivity relative to that benchmark.

The Beveridge curve and "matching efficiency" can be discussed via

$$\mathcal{U} = \frac{\mu G(A)}{\theta q(\theta)\,[1 - G(A)] + \mu G(A)} \tag{5.62}$$

Only firms with productivity greater than the threshold A, determined by frictions on labor and financial markets, are producing goods. That implies that the average productivity of firms actually producing is given by the expected productivity conditional on surviving: $\frac{\int_A a' \mathrm{d}G(a')}{1-G(A)}$. Before going further, it is useful to express the cross-sectional dispersion in the productivity of producing firms with the distribution $H(a) = \frac{G(a)-G(A)}{1-G(A)}$ and density $h(a) = \frac{g(a)}{1-G(A)}$, where the threshold A is the lower bound of the support. The cross-section of firms depends on the marginal job, and the latter has the property $\int_A a' \mathrm{d}H(a') = \frac{\int_A a' \mathrm{d}G(a')}{1-G(A)}$ which we use to express aggregate output:

$$Y = (1 - \mathcal{U}) \int_A a' \mathrm{d}H(a') \Rightarrow Y = Y_0 \mathcal{N} \tag{5.63}$$

where $Y_0 \equiv \int_A a' \mathrm{d}H(a')$.

6 Financial multipliers and business cycles

The financial market frictions introduced in chapter 5 lead to an equilibrium with higher unemployment due to the additional costs involved in creating a job. These costs from searching in the credit market are independent of the tightness of the labor market, which has important implications for the dynamics of job creation and unemployment over the business cycle. In this chapter we apply the techniques developed in chapter 2 to a discrete time version of the CL model of chapter 5. That version of the model is well suited to illustrate the effects of financial market shocks on hiring and unemployment, an active area of empirical research since the financial crises and the Great Recession.

A financial multiplier that is increasing in credit market frictions is easily characterized. Moreover, the multiplier is tightly linked to efficiency for the following reason: at the credit market Hosios condition, the decentralized equilibrium minimizes the distortions, thereby minimizing the size of the financial multiplier. This arises from the monotonicity of the size of the financial multiplier in the size of the surplus. The smaller the remaining surplus, the larger the fluctuations in the economy and the financial multiplier.

In addition, economies with search frictions in both credit and labor markets exhibit strong asymmetries. Credit market shocks can have mild effects when the economy is doing well, and may have significantly larger consequences when the economy has already begun to slow down. In recessions, surpluses are smaller brought about by negative financial shocks, and economies are more fragile to other shocks. Asymmetry and state dependence in responses to shocks are a new and fertile area of research.

6.1 The equilibrium dynamics of the CL model

The environment is an adaptation of the model in chapter 5.

6.1.1 Projects and creditors: asset values

A new project requires a creditor. The creditor must be searched for in the financial market at a flow cost κ_I, and search is successful with a probability $p(\phi_t)$ that is decreasing in the ratio of projects searching in the market, $\mathcal{N}_{ct}$, to the amount of creditors $\mathcal{B}_{ct}$. This ratio is still denoted $\phi_t = \mathcal{N}_{ct}/\mathcal{B}_{ct}$, now with a time subscript. This tightness of the credit market affects the probability of a successful search for a creditor, $\check{p}(\phi_t)$, who expends κ_B in resources searching for investment projects. We assume a constant returns to scale matching function in the credit market $\mathcal{M}_C(\mathcal{N}_{ct}, \mathcal{B}_{ct})$. The project–creditor pair can dissolve in either the labor market search or profit stage with probability s^C, while the worker–firm pair dissolves with probability s^L during the profit stage. In the event of labor turnover the firm retains the job as a vacant position and returns to the labor market. Denoting by β^C the effective discount factor, defined as

$$\beta^C = \frac{1 - s^C}{1 + r}$$

the asset values of the project are

$$E_{ct} = -\kappa_I + p(\phi_t)E_{vt} + \frac{1 - p(\phi_t)}{1 + r}\mathbb{E}_t E_{ct+1} \tag{6.1}$$

$$E_{vt} = \beta^C \mathbb{E}_t \left[q(\theta_t)E_{\pi t+1} + (1 - q(\theta_t))\, E_{vt+1} \right] + \frac{s^C}{1 + r}\mathbb{E}_t E_{ct+1} \tag{6.2}$$

$$E_{\pi t} = x_t - w_t - \psi_t + \beta^C \mathbb{E}_t \left[\left(1 - s^L\right) E_{\pi t+1} + s^L E_{vt+1} \right] + \frac{s^C}{1 + r}\mathbb{E}_t E_{ct+1} \tag{6.3}$$

The asset values of the creditor in each stage are

$$B_{ct} = -\kappa_B + \check{p}(\phi_t)B_{vt} + \frac{1 - \check{p}(\phi_t)}{1 + r}\mathbb{E}_t B_{ct+1} \tag{6.4}$$

$$B_{vt} = -\gamma + \beta^C \mathbb{E}_t \left[q(\theta_t)B_{\pi t+1} + (1 - q(\theta_t))\, B_{vt+1} \right] + \frac{s^C}{1 + r}\mathbb{E}_t B_{ct+1} \tag{6.5}$$

$$B_{\pi t} = \psi_t + \beta^C \mathbb{E}_t \left[\left(1 - s^L\right) B_{\pi t+1} + s^L B_{vt+1} \right] + \frac{s^C}{1 + r}\mathbb{E}_t B_{ct+1} \tag{6.6}$$

The interpretation of the asset values equations are similar to their continuous time equivalent in chapter 5 with one distinction. We made one additional assumption for convenience. In the sequence of events—search in the credit market followed by search in the labor market—a new project meeting a creditor begins the recruiting process within the period, while a match in the labor market begins production the following period (as was assumed in part I). Hence the term $p(\phi_t)E_{vt}$ in the right-hand side of equation (6.1) and the term $\check{p}(\phi_t)B_{vt}$ in the right-hand side of equation (6.4). If a match forms in the labor market, the project moves to the next stage, production, the following period. Hence the terms $q(\theta_t)E_{\pi t+1}$, and $q(\theta_t)B_{\pi t+1}$, in equations (6.2), and (6.5).

6.1.2 Bargaining and equilibrium in the financial market

There is free entry in the financial market at all dates t such that projects and creditors enter until exhaustion of profit opportunities. This implies $E_{ct} = 0$, and $B_{ct} = 0$ at all dates, and the value of being in the labor market stage v for the creditor and project are

$$B_{vt} = \frac{\kappa_B}{\phi_t p(\phi_t)} \quad \text{and} \quad E_{vt} = \frac{\kappa_I}{p(\phi_t)} \tag{6.7}$$

As in chapter 5, creditor and project bargain over the division of the surplus from their match following a Nash protocol. They determine at the time of contact a repayment rule in expectation that solves the Nash problem:

$$\mathbb{E}_t \psi_{t+1} = argmax \left(E_{vt} - E_{ct}\right)^{1-\alpha_C} \left(B_{vt} - B_{ct}\right)^{\alpha_C}$$

It is important to note that with this Nash-rule, the expected the value of the repayment is contingent on the realization of productivity in a linear way. Hence the solution to the negotiation problem is to find the parameters of the linear function $\psi_t(x_t)$ that imply that the above equation is satisfied. The solution is an expected repayment that ensures a sharing of the current match surplus in which a proportion α_C goes to the creditor:

$$\alpha_C \left(E_{vt} - E_{ct}\right) = (1 - \alpha_C)\left(B_{vt} - B_{ct}\right) \tag{6.8}$$

Combining the credit market bargaining condition (6.8) with the free entry conditions for both sides of the financial market in (6.7) leads to an equilibrium tightness of the financial market that is time invariant:

Time-invariant equilibrium credit market tightness:

$$\phi_t^* \equiv \phi^* = \frac{\kappa_B}{\kappa_I} \frac{1 - \alpha_C}{\alpha_C} \quad \forall t \tag{6.9}$$

This result states the ratio of projects to creditors is constant over time, or over the business cycle. It is important to note, however, that both the number of projects and creditors searching in the financial market will fluctuate over the business cycle. Only their ratio remains constant. This is a direct consequence of allowing free entry on both sides of the credit market. Entrants respond to the same changes in the surplus of creating a credit market match, a surplus which under Nash bargaining they share in constant proportions. Thus changes in their masses always vary in equal proportion over time, maintaining a constant ratio.

The expected repayment rule that solves the Nash bargaining problem is:

Repayment rule in the credit market:

$$\mathbb{E}_t \psi_{t+1} = \alpha_C \mathbb{E}_t\left[x_{t+1} - w_{t+1}\right] + (1-\alpha_C)\left[\frac{1}{\beta^C}\frac{\gamma}{q(\theta_t)} - \left(1-s^L\right)\mathbb{E}_t\frac{\gamma}{q(\theta_{t+1})}\right]$$

The above expression for the negotiated repayment states that the creditor will receive a fraction α_C of the expected profit flow from labor at date $t+1$ and, by the second term, will receive more if the current costs to fill a vacancy γ/q_t—which are being paid by the creditor in the period of price setting—are large relative to what they are expected to be in the future. A higher bargaining share of the creditor α_C raises the expected repayment. Consider the extreme case in which the creditor receives no surplus, which is closest to the case of a competitive pricing in the credit market ($\alpha_C = 0$). In this case the creditor expects a flow repayment that corresponds exactly to the opportunity cost of the resources extended to fill a job vacancy. Giving the creditor some bargaining power diverts a share of the net profit from hiring and producing with labor away from the firm.

6.1.3 Job creation

The asset values of the joint project–creditor pair are the sum of the value to the creditor and the project of the labor search (v) and profit (π) stages:

$$J_{vt} = -\gamma + \beta^C \mathbb{E}_t\left[q(\theta_t) J_{\pi t+1} + (1-q(\theta_t))\, J_{vt+1}\right]$$
$$J_{\pi t} = x_t - w_t + \beta^C \mathbb{E}_t\left[\left(1-s^L\right) J_{\pi t+1} + s^L J_{vt+1}\right]$$

As in the previous chapter the value of a job vacancy to the firm (the project–creditor pair) is equal to the search costs in the credit market, $K(\phi)$:

$$J_{vt} = E_{vt} + B_{vt} = \frac{\kappa_I}{p(\phi)} + \frac{\kappa_B}{\phi p(\phi)} = K(\phi)$$

The first equation for J_{vt} can thus be re-expressed as

$$\underbrace{K(\phi^*)(1+o_t)}_{\text{Cost of credit frictions}} \quad \underbrace{+\frac{\gamma}{q(\theta_t)}}_{\text{Cost of labor frictions}} \quad \underbrace{= \beta^C \mathbb{E}_t J_{\pi t+1}}_{\text{Expected profits}} \qquad (6.10)$$

where $o_t \equiv \frac{(1-q_t)(r+s^C)}{q_t(1+r)} = \frac{1-q_t}{q_t}\left(1-\beta^C\right)$ is a number close to zero as β^C approaches 1. The above expression equates the total cost of entering the labor market with a vacancy—the sum of search costs in the financial market and the labor market—to the properly discounted expected benefit from filling the job vacancy.

With a reasoning similar to that in the previous chapter, one can define the discrete time annuity value of $K(\phi)$ as

$$k(\phi) = (1 - \beta^C)K(\phi)$$

Using the notations $\gamma_k = \gamma + k(\phi)$, and $x_t^{CL} = x_t - k(\phi)$, one can easily obtain a job creation condition very similar to the model with search frictional credit and labor markets in continuous time:

Discrete time job creation condition in the CL model:

$$\frac{\gamma_k}{q_t} = \beta^C \mathbb{E}_t \left[x_{t+1}^{CL} - w_{t+1} + \left(1 - s^L\right) \frac{\gamma_k}{q_{t+1}} \right] \tag{6.11}$$

The average cost of creating a job, γ_k/q_t, includes the costs associated with the financial market $K(\phi^*)$, just as was the case in job creation condition (5.20) of Chapter 5.

6.1.4 Wage bargaining

The value of unemployment, W_{ut}, is the same as in earlier chapters, while the value of employment, W_{nt}, for a worker differs only in the distinction between types of labor match termination events. As a reminder, z is the value of nonemployment activities, and $f(\theta)$ the job-finding rate. The wage is the solution to a the Nash bargaining problem between the worker and the project–creditor block. It is the solution to the following problem:

$$Argmax\ (W_{nt} - W_{ut})^{\alpha_L} (J_{\pi t} - J_{vt})^{1-\alpha_L}$$

The worker–firm negotiated wage must satisfy the usual sharing rule $\alpha_L (J_{\pi t} - K) = (1 - \alpha_L)(W_{nt} - W_{ut})$, and the resulting wage is:

Block-bargained wage in the discrete time CL model:

$$w_t = (1 - \alpha_L) z + \alpha_L \left[x_t + \theta_t \left(\frac{\gamma + k(\phi)}{1 - s^C} \right) \right] - \alpha_L k(\phi)$$

or

$$w_t = (1 - \alpha_L) z + \alpha_L \left[x_t^{CL} + \theta_t \left(\frac{\gamma_k}{1 - s^C} \right) \right]$$

The wage rule is very similar to the bargained wage in equation (5.26) of chapter 5.

6.2 A financial multiplier and the amplification of business cycles

In this section we study how the existence of a search frictional financial market leads to greater volatility in the labor market and overall economy. We start by illustrating the channel of amplification with the assumption of an exogenous fixed wage. This gets to the core of the mechanism. Amplification is related to the magnitude of search costs in the financial market, greater financial market frictions causing more volatility. As a result, volatility is intimately related to efficiency in the sense that it is minimized when the Hosios condition in the financial market is satisfied. The quantitative properties are evaluated in a calibration of the model, solved with a global method as we did for the baseline model in chapter 2, in the next section. Finally, the model is used to illustrate the effects of a shock to the financial market, modeled as a shock to the cost of searching for and screening investment projects. The main text works through a financial multiplier under the assumption of a fixed wage, and we present the derivations and results under a Nash-bargained wage in the chapter appendix.

6.2.1 Understanding amplification

Assuming that wages are exogenously fixed at $w_t = \bar{w}$, a log-linear approximation of equation (6.11) around a steady state allows us to express deviations in labor market tightness as follows:

Log-linearization around the steady state in the CL model:

$$\widehat{\theta}_t = \frac{1}{\eta_L} \times \frac{x}{x - \bar{w} - k(\phi)} \times \left(1 - \beta^{CL}\right) \mathbb{E}_t \sum_{i=0} \left(\beta^{CL}\right)^i \widehat{x}_{t+1+i} \tag{6.12}$$

where $\beta^{CL} = \left(1 - s^L\right) \beta^C$, "hatted" variables denote proportional deviations from the steady state, and η_L is the absolute value of the elasticity of $q(\theta_t)$ to θ_t. The first component is identical to the approximation (2.1) in the benchmark model. The second component $\frac{x}{x-\bar{w}-k(\phi)}$ relates to the financial multiplier. The multiplier, as we will discuss, is related to the size of the joint creditor–project surplus to hiring a worker, which is now reduced by the annuitized financial market search costs $k(\phi)$. A smaller surplus, due to a larger $k(\phi)$, leads to greater responses of labor market tightness to changes in productivity. There is a strong general result that was discussed in chapter 2 and will appear again in chapter 8: a small economic surplus to a labor match, be it due to financial market frictions, goods market frictions, or a particular calibration of the baseline model, will render hiring and unemployment sensitive to shocks.

Let us proceed further in deriving the elasticity of labor market tightness to productivity shocks both in the absence and presence of financial imperfections. In the absence of financial market frictions, the job creation condition in equation (1.20) in chapter 1 means that deviations in labor market tightness appear as the discounted sum of deviations in future expected labor productivity.

Denoting by ρ_x the auto-correlation of productivity, the elasticity of labor market tightness to a productivity innovations ϵ_t in the discrete time CL model, after a log-linear approximation and with a fixed wage, is given by

$$\varsigma^{CL} = \frac{\partial \widehat{\theta_t^{CL}}}{\partial \epsilon_t} = \frac{1}{\eta_L} \times \frac{q(\theta^{CL})}{\gamma_k} \times \frac{\beta^C \rho_x}{1 - \beta^{CL} \rho_x} \tag{6.13}$$

Remember that in the standard matching model, one would have instead

$$\varsigma^{L} = \frac{\partial \widehat{\theta_t^{L}}}{\partial \epsilon_t} = \frac{1}{\eta_L} \times \frac{q(\theta^{L})}{\gamma} \times \frac{\beta \rho_x}{1 - \left(1 - s^L\right) \beta \rho_x} \tag{6.14}$$

In what follows, assume, without significant quantitative consequence, that $s^C = 0$. The financial market multiplier can be written as the increment in the responsiveness of labor market tightness to a productivity shock from the introduction of frictional financial markets:

Financial frictions multiplier in the CL model:

$$\Lambda_C \equiv \frac{\varsigma^{CL}}{\varsigma^{L}} = \frac{q(\theta^{CL})}{q(\theta^{L})} \frac{\gamma}{\gamma_k} = \frac{x - \bar{w}}{x - \bar{w} - k(\phi)} \tag{6.15}$$

This multiplier, always greater than one, is increasing in the gap between equilibrium labor market tightness with frictional financial markets θ^{CL} and equilibrium labor market tightness in the baseline model θ^L with perfect financial markets. The expression for Λ_C makes clear that the financial multiplier is a function of the distortions induced by frictional financial markets. The multiplier is greater than 1 as current financial costs reduce the surplus, the $-k(\phi)$ term in the denominator. This holds in the case of endogenous wages.

6.2.2 Volatility and efficiency in financial markets

The costs of financial frictions are a function of not only the flow costs κ_I and κ_B, but also of equilibrium financial market tightness ϕ^*. We have already shown that the Hosios condition in the financial market minimizes the economy-wide costs of financial market frictions (section 5.3 in chapter 5). This occurs when the creditor's share of the surplus α_C is equal to the elasticity of matching in the credit market with respect to projects, η_C. Therefore, the Hosios condition also minimizes the business cycle volatility of the macroeconomy induced by financial frictions. Away from this condition the financial multiplier can be arbitrarily large. This result is a variant of the "small surplus" assumption. When one side receives an arbitrarily small surplus, the economy becomes infinitely reactive to small shocks given the complementarity between creditors and projects in the matching function.

Figure 6.1 provides a graphic illustration of this result in which the elasticity of labor market tightness to productivity shocks increases symmetrically as the bargaining weight α_C deviates from the elasticity of the matching function $\eta_C(\phi^{opt})$, set here to a constant value of 0.5. Note that this figure is provided for a set of parameters discussed below but with the assumption of a fixed wage. The general shape of the elasticity of the v–u ratio to productivity shocks as

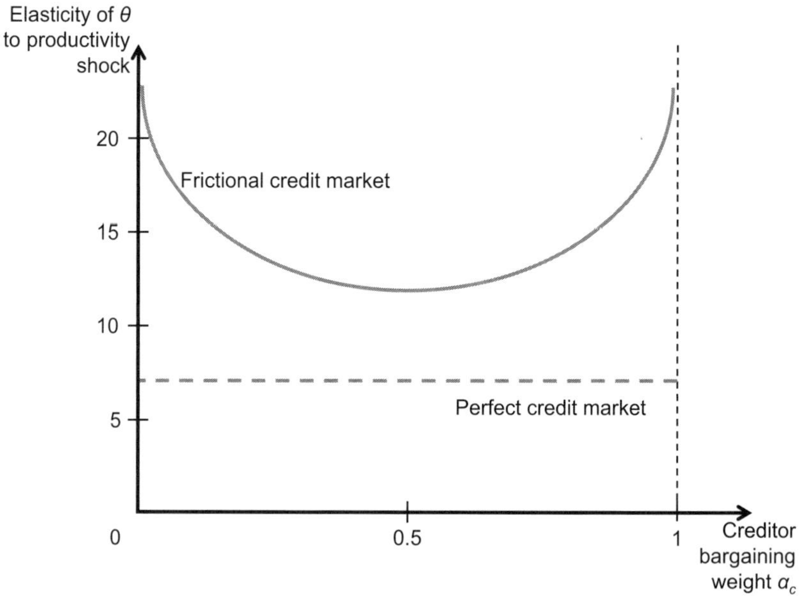

Figure 6.1
Hosios in the financial market and the financial multiplier for an elasticity of the credit matching function η_C of 0.5.

the financial market parameters α_C and η_C deviate from the Hosios condition does not depend on the specific parameterization.

6.3 Quantitative properties

As in the analysis of the business cycle properties of the benchmark model with a search labor market of chapter 2, the basic unit of time is a month. We first review the calibration strategy for labor market parameters which is adapted to take into account the equilibrium interactions with the search credit market. Next we describe the calibration strategy for credit market parameters.

6.3.1 Calibration strategy

The basic unit of time is a month. The process for productivity is assumed to be an AR(1) in logs with persistence of $\rho_x = 0.95^{1/3}$, and conditional volatility, σ_x, of 0.00625. The matching functions in the labor and credit markets take the functional form proposed in den Haan et al. (2000). All parameter values are reported in Table 6.1.

Labor market parameters s^L, ν_L, γ, z, and α_L
The calibration strategy for labor market parameters follows that developed in chapter 2, to which we refer for further details. It is described briefly here.

Table 6.1
A calibration of labor and credit markets: Parameter values

	Parameter	Value		Reference or Target
Technology:				
persistence parameter	ρ_x	$0.95^{1/3}$	→	BLS labor productivity
standard deviation	σ_x	0.00625	→	BLS labor productivity
Labor market:				
job separation rate	s^L	0.032	→	JOLTS
matching curvature	ν_L	1.25	→	den Haan et al. (2000)
vacancy cost	γ	0.15	→	Unemployment rate
worker bargaining weight	α_L	0.15	→	Wage elasticity
nonemployment value	z	0.71	→	Chapter 2
Credit market:				
separation rate	s^C	0.01/3	→	Bernanke et al. (1996)
creditor bargaining weight	α_C	0.12	→	Spread on returns
project search costs	κ_I	0.33	→	Volatility of unemployment
creditor search costs	κ_B	0.47	→	Financial sector's share of GDP
matching curvature	ν_C	1.35	→	Credit market transition rate
risk-free rate	r	0.01/3	→	3-month US T-bill

The five parameters related to the labor market, s^L, ν_L, γ, α_L, and z, are set as follows. The rate of labor separation s^L is set such that the total rate of job separation, $s^T = s^C + (1 - s^C)s^L$, equals 0.035 per month, consistent with the estimate based on JOLTS data. Given a value of $s^C = 0.01/3$ explained below, we set $s^L = \left(0.035 - s^C\right)/(1 - s^C) = 0.032$. The curvature parameter in the matching function $\mathcal{V}_l\mathcal{U}/\left(\mathcal{V}_l^{\nu_L} + \mathcal{U}^{\nu_L}\right)^{1/\nu_L}$ is set to 1.25, as in chapter 2. The unit vacancy costs are set to $\gamma = 0.15$ to be consistent and bring the model's unemployment rate in line with the empirical rate. The two remaining parameters z and α_L entering the Nash-bargained wages are set as follows. The flow value of nonemployment z is set to 0.71 following the arguments presented in chapter 2. The worker's share in wage bargaining α_L is set to 0.15 such that the model's elasticity of wages to productivity is 0.70.

Credit market parameters r, s^C, α_C, ν_C, κ_I, and κ_B

The discount factor β is set such that the risk-free rate r averages an annualized 4%. The separation rate s^C is set for a 1% quarterly firm exit rate. The curvature of the credit matching function $\mathcal{N}_c\mathcal{B}_c/\left(\mathcal{N}_c^{\nu_C} + \mathcal{B}_c^{\nu_C}\right)^{1/\nu_C}$ is set such that the average duration of search in the credit market by creditors is four months, resulting in $\nu_C = 1.35$. The search flow costs for the project, κ_I, are obtained by targeting the volatility of the unemployment rate. The return to loans in the credit market, R_t, is the rate which sets the expected discounted value of a loan, $\gamma/[R_t + q_t]$, to the expected discounted repayment $[q_t/(R_t + q_t)] \times \mathbb{E}_t\left[\psi_{t+1}\right]/\left[R_t + s^C + \left(1 - s^C\right)s^L\right]$. These returns, presented below in equation (6.16), are an increasing function of the creditor's bargaining weight α_C. The particular case of competitive pricing in the financial market, with no surplus to the creditor, arises when $\alpha_C = 0$. The returns on loans in this competitive pricing are denoted R_t^*. The model's credit spread is the difference between the bargained R_t and the competitive R_t^*. The creditor's bargaining weight α_C is chosen to target an average in an excess of a competitively priced return R_t^* of 3.5%, resulting in $\alpha_C = 0.12$.

Calibration targets:

- Returns to loans in the credit market

$$R_t = \frac{\mathbb{E}_t\left(\psi_{t+1}\right)}{\gamma/q_t} - s^T \tag{6.16}$$

- Share of the financial sector in aggregate value added

$$\Sigma_B = \frac{\psi(1 - \mathcal{U}) - \gamma\mathcal{V} - \kappa_B\mathcal{B}_c}{x(1 - \mathcal{U})} \tag{6.17}$$

Our final moment in the credit market is the share of the financial sector in aggregate value added, presented for the model in equation (6.17). This allows us to determine the value of κ_B. The first term in the numerator represents total gross profits made by creditors. It is the amount of repayment ψ times the number of creditors in the profit state, which is the number of producing firms $1-\mathcal{U}$. The second term represents the negative cash flows of creditors financing vacancies. The last term represents the costs of financial intermediation paid by creditors. Note that we assumed the costs κ_I paid by firms are effort costs and don't enter GDP. The denominator is total production. Calculating the empirical counterpart to Σ_B is not straightforward. The model captures the entire cycle of a new—marginal—production project and the costs of external finance. The costs of financial frictions therefore encompass both a firm's creation and the development in existing firms of new projects and the associated new hires. The value added to the corporate financial sector should therefore be used as our target. This represents approximately 7.4% of GDP based on industry value added tables for the US over the period 1985-2002. We then subtract the share in GDP of household financial services and insurance from the National Income and Product Accounts tables, which averaged to 4.9% of GDP over the period in question. Therefore, the value of Σ_B we match in our numerical exercise is 2.5%.

6.3.2 Quantitative moments and dynamics

The business cycle moments of the model's labor market variables are presented in Table 6.2. Panel A reports the moments for the model with credit market frictions calibrated in the previous section. Panel B presents the moments after removing the frictions in the credit market, that is, when the value of search costs in financial markets $K(\phi^*)$ is set to zero, and when we adjust the flow cost of vacancy posting such that the average unemployment rate in simulations is the same across models.

The financial multiplier increases the volatility of labor market tightness by a factor just over 3. The standard deviation of labor market tightness is 0.27 in the CL model, while it is merely 0.09 in the model with labor market frictions alone. This amplification translates into a similar increment in the volatility of unemployment. The standard deviation of unemployment generated by the model with a frictional financial market is 0.13, compared to 0.04 in the model with labor market frictions alone.

Another way to observe the amplification from the financial multiplier is to look at the impulse response function to a one-time, positive innovation to productivity. Figure 6.2 plots the impulse responses of labor market tightness to a

Table 6.2
Labor market moments: Model with credit and labor market frictions

	$\mathcal{U}$	$\mathcal{V}$	θ		$\mathcal{U}$	$\mathcal{V}$	θ
	Panel A: Credit and Labor Frictions				Panel B: Removing Credit Frictions		
Standard deviation	0.127	0.147	0.272		0.042	0.061	0.098
Autocorrelation	0.336	−0.090	0.165		0.341	−0.098	0.174
Correlation matrix		−0.721	−0.896	$\mathcal{U}$		−0.772	−0.912
			0.950	$\mathcal{V}$			0.946
				θ			

In Panel A, we take the quarterly averages of monthly $\mathcal{U}$, $\mathcal{V}$, and x to convert to quarterly series, and all variables are in HP-filtered proportional deviations from the mean with a smoothing parameter of 1,600. We then report cross-simulation averages.

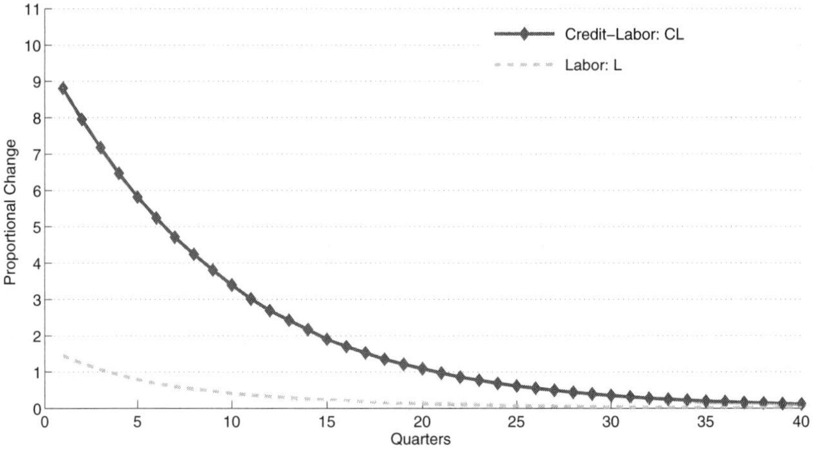

Figure 6.2
IRF of labor market tightness to a positive productivity shock, CL and L models

one-time positive productivity shock. The response in the model with financial frictions has greater amplitude, generating much stronger changes in hires and job creation flows. This leads to the greater volatility of unemployment seen in table 6.2. However, the peak response is contemporaneous to the shock. Financial market frictions amplify the economy's response to shocks, but do not add persistence in the response. The peak response of labor market tightness occurs in the same period as the shock to productivity.

6.4 Introducing shocks in financial markets

At this stage, it is interesting to introduce a new type of innovation affecting the firm, namely a tightening of credit market conditions. This requires a small change to the model by including time-varying shock to the search cost in the credit market. This is empirically relevant as credit market conditions vary over time in a way that is correlated with unemployment. Indeed, measures of credit market tightness such as the spread between BAA corporate bonds and 10-year treasury notes, or the composite measure constructed by Gilchrist and Zakrajšek (2012) are highly correlated with unemployment. In particular, a dynamic regression of unemployment on lagged values of the credit spread series give positive and significant coefficients not only at a one-quarter lag but also at two- and four-quarter lags (Petrosky-Nadeau et al., 2015).

6.4.1 Parameterization and calibration

We maintain the parameter values of table 6.1, and now must specify the parameter values of the shock process for the search costs to the creditor. Specifically, the search costs in the financial market κ_B are assumed to follow an AR(1) in logs: $\log \kappa_{Bt} = \left(1 - \rho_{\kappa_B}\right) \log \kappa_B + \rho_{\kappa_B} \log \kappa_{B_{t-1}} + \sigma_{\kappa B} \epsilon_t^{\kappa B}$. The persistence parameter, ρ_{κ_B}, is set to the same value as for productivity shocks. The conditional volatility, σ_{κ_B}, is such that the model credit spread, defined in the description of the calibration of the credit market parameters above, matches the volatility of the credit spread in the data. This results in $\sigma_{\kappa_B} = 0.018$.

6.4.2 Stationary and business cycle moments

A sample simulation of the unemployment rate and credit market spread is presented in figure 6.3. The figure clearly illustrates the nonlinearities in the model. The unemployment rate and credit spread spike during recessions. In addition, the correlation is not perfect, as in the data. For example, there is a recession around period 100 with a spike in unemployment but no noticeable increase in the credit spread, while during the recession of period 200 both series move hand in hand.

An interesting interaction of credit and labor markets is the asymmetric effect of credit market shocks over the business cycle. That is, the effects of a negative credit market shock are much more severe when the economy is already in a slowdown and the labor market is slack. This is illustrated in figure 6.4. In this experiment the economy is hit with a shock increasing the creditor's search cost κ_B at two different states of the world. In the first the economy is at its long run mean and the unemployment rate is 5.9 percent. In

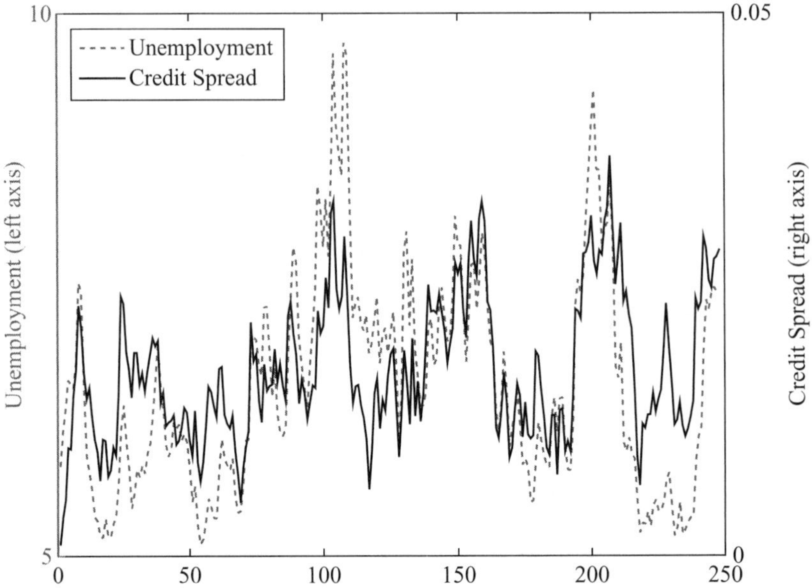

Figure 6.3
Model simulated paths for unemployment rate and credit market spread

the second the economy is in a recession and the rate of unemployment has increased to just over 9 percent. The response of labor market tightness to the credit market shock is nearly twice as large in the recession, and the effect on unemployment is dramatic. In the model, credit market shocks matter a lot to the economy when they occur during bad times.

6.5 Discussion of the literature and remaining issues

Early papers such as Bernanke and Gertler (1989) and Kiyotaki and Moore (1997), and subsequent papers (such as Bernanke and Gertler (1995) and Bernanke et al. (1996), among others), have emphasized the amplification role of financial markets and the existence of a *financial accelerator*. Although part of this literature is centered on the credit channel of monetary policy, the elements that give rise to amplification may be relevant for the study of cyclical fluctuations in labor markets.

The credit channel, developed in a search setting in Wasmer and Weil (2004), has been extended in a dynamic setup as here in Petrosky-Nadeau and Wasmer (2013), reinterpreting the firm as an entity managing several "marginal"

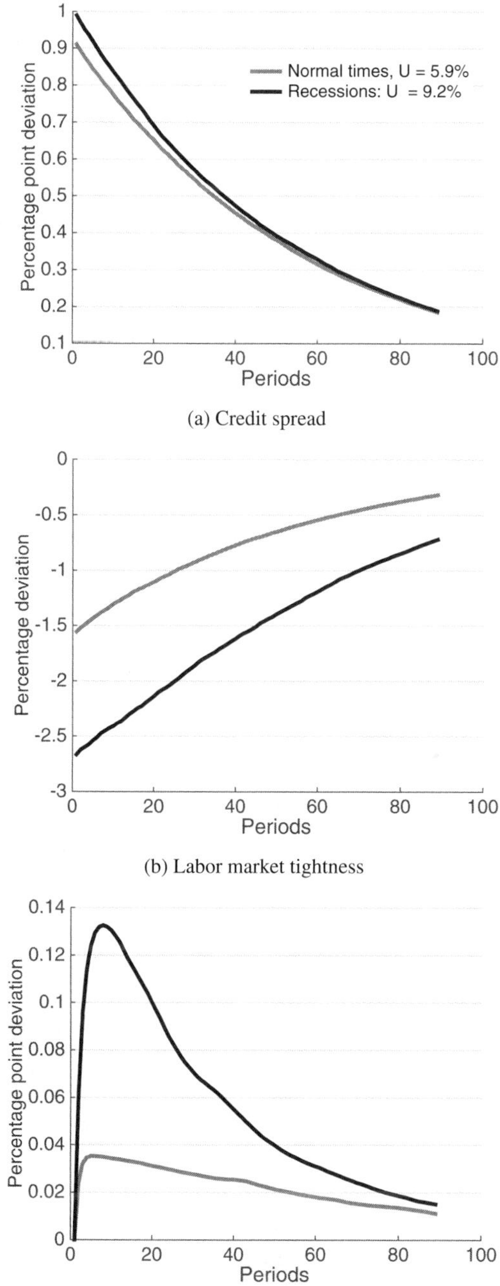

(a) Credit spread

(b) Labor market tightness

(c) Unemployment rate

Figure 6.4

Impulse response to a negative credit shock causes a 1 percentage-point increase in the spread

investment projects, each requiring labor and financing from a creditor on a frictional financial market. In this interpretation, the relevant financial costs affect all firms, not only new firms.

The notion of financial multipliers has been put forward by Ljungqvist and Sargent (2015) in a generalization of the surplus in the economy. As they point out, this multiplier exists in a variety of search context, in particular in Wasmer and Weil (2004) who exhibited a financial multiplier, in a static context. In their numerical exercise, by setting $\alpha_C = \eta_C = 0.5$, the implied static financial multiplier was actually minimized, at a value of 1.74. If α_C and η_C differ, one obtains much larger financial multipliers. This is true in both directions: lowering α_C below η_C, and thus reducing the share of value added accruing to financial intermediaries; and raising α_C above η_C, thereby giving a larger shares of the surplus in bargaining to creditors. The dynamic multiplier Λ_C exhibited in the chapter in the case $s^C = 0$ was obtained in Petrosky-Nadeau and Wasmer (2013).

Nicoletti and Pierrard (2006) present a different modeling option but a similar focus. They allow for two types of firms, one of which must borrow on a search frictional financial market. They focus on the implications for cross-correlations between real quantities such as output and consumption and, while not emphasizing the feedback from credit to labor markets, they do discuss the existence of a financial multiplier. Shi (2015) contributes another important attempt to model and quantify the joint dynamics of financial and macroeconomic variables. The paper in particular assesses the role of financial shocks. An alternative route is in Petrosky-Nadeau (2014), which considers the case of external financing of period operating expenses, including recruiting costs, on imperfect financial markets. The imperfection takes the form of an agency problem between borrower and lender and, as in this chapter, financial frictions amplify the business cycle of labor market variables. See also Garin (2015) in which the financial frictions take the form of a collateral requirement.

Shocks in financial markets, and their consequences for the dynamic response of the economy, have been studied in the last few years in many papers. For instance, Jermann and Quadrini (2012) use a parsimonious two-shocks model (one on productivity innovation and one on the enforcement parameter of loans, that is the fraction of loans than can be recovered by lenders) to obtain large improvements in calibrated statistics; see also Monacelli et al. (2011b), who use a mechanism in which debt can be used as a strategic tool to reduce workers' wages and raise employment. This specific mechanism had been identified and discussed first by Bronars and Deere (1991), and Perotti and Spier (1993), and discussed in a search context in section IV in Wasmer and Weil (2004)

An early paper by Carlstrom and Fuerst (1997), which provided one of the first macroeconomic models with a financial accelerator in the DSGE framework, also offered a useful discussion of bankruptcy statistics. Altig et al. (2011) studied firm-specific shocks on embedded capital. Beaubrun-Diant and Tripier (2015) study a search economy with frictions in financial markets, and study the cyclical behavior of net interest margins of banks. Carrillo-Tudela et al. (2015) study a dynamic model with monopolistically competitive banks. They obtain a large increase in volatility due to the volatility of corporate interest rates.

The study of welfare costs of business cycles is an old classical question since Lucas (1987). A recent attempt to address it with financial frictions (à la Kiyotaki–Moore) is in Iliopulos et al. (2014). The authors argue that the nonlinearities lead the costs of recessions to exceed the gains from expansions.

Overall, this chapter joins Pissarides (2009) in arguing that part of the solution to the labor market volatility puzzle requires that hiring costs must be partly nonproportional to congestion in the labor market. The mechanism underlined here differs from the extensive literature on the role of financial market frictions for business cycles, as it is not based on collateral constraints, as in Kiyotaki and Moore (1997), nor on counter-cyclical agency costs as in Bernanke and Gertler (1989), but truly on the existence of acyclical entry costs.

6.6 Chapter appendix

6.6.1 Deriving a job creation condition

Start from the set of recursive equations and the free-entry conditions $E_{ct} = B_{ct} = 0$. The Bellman equations of the investment project, which faces a discount rate r, assuming that transitions from the credit to the labor market stages occur within a single period, are

$$E_{c,t} = 0 = -\kappa_I + p_t E_{vt} \tag{6.18}$$

$$E_{vt} = \beta^C \mathbb{E}_t \left[q_t E_{\pi t+1} + (1 - q_t) E_{vt+1} \right] \tag{6.19}$$

$$E_{\pi t} = x_t - w_t - \psi_t + \beta^C \mathbb{E}_t \left[\left(1 - s^L\right) E_{\pi t+1} + s^L E_{vt+1} \right]$$

The corresponding Bellman equations for the creditor are

$$B_{ct} = 0 = -\kappa_B + \check{p}_t B_{l,t} \tag{6.20}$$

$$B_{vt} = -\gamma + \beta^C \mathbb{E}_t \left[q_t B_{\pi t+1} + (1 - q_t) B_{vt+1} \right] \tag{6.21}$$

$$B_{\pi t} = \psi_t + \beta^C \mathbb{E}_t \left[\left(1 - s^L\right) B_{\pi t+1} + s^L B_{vt+1} \right] \tag{6.22}$$

Combine B_{vt} and E_{vt} to obtain $J_{vt} = E_{vt} + B_{vt} = K$ with

$$K = \frac{\kappa_I}{p(\phi^*)} + \frac{\kappa_B}{\phi^* p(\phi^*)} = -\gamma + q_t \beta^C \mathbb{E}_t J_{\pi t+1} + (1-q_t)\beta^C K$$

which can be rewritten as

$$\underbrace{K(\phi^*)(1+o_t)}_{\text{Cost of credit frictions}} \underbrace{+\frac{\gamma}{q(\theta_t)}}_{\text{Cost of labor frictions}} \underbrace{=\beta^C \mathbb{E}_t J_{\pi t+1}}_{\text{Expected profits}} \tag{6.23}$$

where $o_t \equiv \frac{(1-q_t)(r+s^C)}{(1+r)}$. Then

$$\Rightarrow \frac{\gamma + K(\phi)(1+o_t)}{q_t} = \beta^C \mathbb{E}_t \left[x_{t+1} - w_{t+1} + \left(1 - s^L\right) \frac{\gamma + K(\phi)\left(1 + o_{t+1}\right)}{q_{t+1}} + s^L \beta^C K(\phi) \right]$$

$$\Rightarrow \frac{\gamma + K(\phi)\left(1 + (1-q_t)\beta^C\right)}{q_t} = \beta^C \mathbb{E}_t \left[x_{t+1} - w_{t+1} + \left(1 - s^L\right) \frac{\gamma + K(\phi)\left(1 + (1-q_{t+1})\beta^C\right)}{q_{t+1}} + s^L \beta^C K(\phi) \right]$$

Define $x_t^{CL} = x_t - (1-\beta^C)K = x_t - k(\phi)$ and $\gamma_k = \gamma + K(\phi)(1-\beta^C) = \gamma + k(\phi)$. This can be simplified, and one obtains the following equation:

$$\frac{\gamma_k}{q_t} = \beta^C \mathbb{E}_t \left[x_{t+1}^{CL} - w_{t+1} + \left(1 - s^L\right) \frac{\gamma_k}{q_{t+1}} \right]$$

6.6.2 Financial repayment

This section provides the details in deriving the rental rate ψ_t. The sharing rule under Nash bargaining implied $B_{vt} = \alpha_C J_{vt} = \alpha_C K$ and $E_{vt} = (1-\alpha_C) J_{vt} = (1-\alpha_C)K$. Using the definitions of the asset values above, we have

$$\alpha_C \left\{ \beta^C \mathbb{E}_t \left[q_t E_{\pi t+1} + (1-q_t) E_{vt+1} \right] \right\} = (1-\alpha_C) \left\{ -\gamma + \beta^C \mathbb{E}_t \left[q_t B_{\pi t+1} + (1-q_t) B_{vt+1} \right] \right\}$$

$$\begin{aligned} \beta^C \mathbb{E}_{t-1} \psi_t = \alpha_C & \left\{ \beta^C \mathbb{E}_{t-1} \left[x_t - w_t \right] \right\} \\ & + (1-\alpha_C)\gamma / q_{t-1} + \alpha_C \left\{ \beta^C \mathbb{E}_{t-1} \left[\beta^C (1-s^L) \mathbb{E}_t E_{\pi t+1} \right] \right\} \\ & - (1-\alpha_C) \left\{ \beta^C \mathbb{E}_{t-1} \left[\beta^C (1-s^L) \mathbb{E}_t B_{\pi t+1} \right] \right\} \end{aligned}$$

Using that $\beta^C \mathbb{E}_t \left[q_t E_{\pi t+1}\right] = (1-\alpha_C)K\left[1-\beta^C(1-q_t)\right]$ and $\beta^C \mathbb{E}_t \left[q_t B_{\pi t+1}\right] = \alpha_C K\left[1-\beta^C(1-q_t)\right]$, we then have

$$\beta^C \mathbb{E}_{t-1}\psi_t = \alpha_C \left\{\beta^C \mathbb{E}_{t-1}\left[x_t - w_t\right]\right\} + (1-\alpha_C)\gamma/q_{t-1} + \alpha_C$$
$$\times \left\{\beta^C \mathbb{E}_{t-1}\left[\beta^C(1-s^C)\frac{(1-\alpha_C)K\left[1-\beta^C(1-q_t)\right]}{\beta^C q_t}\right]\right\}$$
$$-(1-\alpha_C)\left\{\beta^C \mathbb{E}_{t-1}\left[\beta^C(1-s^C)\frac{\alpha_C K\left[1-\beta^C(1-q_t)\right]+\gamma}{\beta^C q_t}\right]\right\}$$

which simplifies to

$$\beta^C \mathbb{E}_{t-1}\psi_t = \alpha_C \beta^C \mathbb{E}_{t-1}\left(x_t - w_t\right) + (1-\alpha_C)\gamma/q_{t-1}$$
$$-(1-\alpha_C)\beta^C(1-s^L)\mathbb{E}_{t-1}\left(\gamma/q_t\right)$$

6.6.3 Workers and wages

The value of employment and unemployment for workers are, respectively:

$$W_{nt} = w_t + \beta^C \mathbb{E}_t(1-s^L)W_{\pi,t+1} + \frac{s^C + (1-s^C)s^L}{1+r}\mathbb{E}_t W_{ut+1}$$
$$W_{ut} = z + \frac{1}{1+r}\mathbb{E}_t\left[f_t W_{\pi t+1} + (1-f_t)W_{ut+1}\right].$$

The sharing rule out of the Nash bargaining problem is

$$\alpha_L\left[J_{\pi t} - J_{vt}\right] = (1-\alpha_L)\left[W_{nt} - W_{ut}\right]$$

The total labor surplus, defined as $\Sigma_{lt}^T = W_{nt} - W_{ut} + J_{\pi t} - K$, can be rewritten, using $J_{\pi t} = x_t - w_t + \beta^C \mathbb{E}_t\left[\left(1-s^L\right)J_{\pi t+1} + s^L K\right]$, as

$$\Sigma_{lt}^T = x_t - K + \beta^C \mathbb{E}_t\left[\left(1-s^L\right)J_{\pi t+1} + s^L K\right]$$
$$+\beta^C(1-s^L)\mathbb{E}_t W_{\pi,t+1} + \frac{s^C + (1-s^C)s^L}{1+r}\mathbb{E}_t W_{ut+1} - W_{ut}$$

From the Bellman equation for the firms in stage π, we also have

$$J_{\pi t} - K = (1-\alpha_L)\Sigma_{lt}^T = x_t - w_t - K + \beta^C K + (1-\alpha_L)\beta^C(1-s^L)\mathbb{E}_t\Sigma_{lt+1}^T$$

Combining these two equations yields the wage rule in stage π:

$$x_t - w_t - K + \beta^C K + (1-\alpha_L)\beta^C(1-s^L)\mathbb{E}_t\Sigma_{lt+1}^T$$
$$= (1-\alpha_L)(x_t - z - K + K\beta^C + \beta^C\left(1-s^L\right)\mathbb{E}_t\Sigma_{lt+1}^T - \frac{f_t\alpha_L}{1+r}\mathbb{E}_t\Sigma_{lt+1}^T)$$

or

$$w_t = (x_t - K + K\beta^C)\alpha_L + (1-\alpha_L)(z + \frac{f_t\alpha_L}{1+r}\mathbb{E}_t\Sigma^T_{lt+1})$$

Finally, with

$$\frac{f_t\alpha_L}{1+r}\mathbb{E}_t\Sigma^T_{lt+1} = \frac{1}{1-\alpha_L}\frac{f_t\alpha_L}{1+r}\mathbb{E}_t\left(J^T_{lt+1} - K\right)$$
$$= \frac{1}{1-\alpha_L}\frac{\theta\alpha_L}{1+r}\left(\frac{K+\gamma}{\beta^C} - K\right)$$

with $\beta^C\mathbb{E}_tJ_{\pi t+1} = \frac{K+\gamma}{q_t} - \beta^C K(1-q_t)/q_t$, we have

$$w_t = \alpha_L\left(x_t - K(1-\beta^C)\right) + (1-\alpha_L)z + \frac{\alpha_L\theta_t}{1-s^C}\left(\gamma + (1-\beta^C)K\right)$$
$$w_t = \alpha_L x_t^{CL} + (1-\alpha_L)z + \left(\frac{\gamma_k}{1-s^C}\right)\alpha_L\theta_t$$

6.6.4 An extended setup

We extend our previous framework to include a representative household, along the lines developed in chapter 2. The household is composed of a continuum of members of unit mass who are either employment or unemployed. The employed earn per period wage W_t. The unemployed have utility from leisure $l > 0$, search for a job, and receive unemployment compensation (a transfer) $b > 0$. In the previous chapters, we had $z = l + b$. Household members pool resources, and the household chooses an aggregate level of consumption C_t, over which they have preferences $u(C)$ with the usual properties, and holdings of risk-free bonds A_t to maximize

$$H_t = \max_{C_t,A_t}[C_t + l\mathcal{U}_t] + \beta\mathbb{E}_t\left[H_{t+1}\right] \quad (6.24)$$

subject to $$W_t\mathcal{N}_t + b\mathcal{U}_t + A_{t-1}(1+r_{t-1}) + D_t^S + D_t^B = C_t + T_t + A_t \quad (6.25)$$

and subject to the laws of motion for employment and unemployment. The terms $D_t^S = X_t\mathcal{N}_t - W_t\mathcal{N}_t - \Psi_t\mathcal{N}_t - \kappa_I\mathcal{N}_{Ct}$ and $D_t^B = \Psi_t\mathcal{N}_t - \gamma\mathcal{V}_t - \kappa_{Bt}\mathcal{B}_{ct}$ in the budget constraint are period profits from firms and financial institutions, respectively, rebated lump sum at the end of the period. The household's budget constraint leads to the economy's aggregate resource constraint

$$Y_t = C_t + \gamma V_t + \kappa_{Bt}\mathcal{B}_{ct} + \kappa_I\mathcal{N}_{ct} \quad (6.26)$$

where now, credit market parameter κ_{Bt} is time varying. As a matter of fact, both labor productivity and the cost of search for financial institutions follow stationary AR(1) processes in logs. That is, we had $\log X_t = \rho_x \log X_{t-1} + \nu_{xt}$, where $0 < \rho_x < 1$ and ν_{xt} is white noise for labor productivity. In the financial market, the search costs are assumed to follow $\log\kappa_{Bt} = \left(1-\rho_{\kappa_B}\right)\log\overline{\kappa}_B + \rho_{\kappa_B}\log\kappa_{Bt-1} + \nu_{\kappa_{Bt}}$. The innovations ν_{xt} and $\nu_{\kappa_{Bt}}$ are assumed to be independent.

The marginal value of an additional unemployed, and employed worker, respectively, are obtained by differentiating the household's value function:

$$\frac{H_{Ut}}{\lambda_t} = Z_t + \beta \mathbb{E}_t \frac{\lambda_{t+1}}{\lambda_t} \left[f(\theta_t) \frac{H_{Nt+1}}{\lambda_{t+1}} + [1 - f(\theta_t)] \frac{H_{Ut+1}}{\lambda_{t+1}} \right] \tag{6.27}$$

$$\frac{H_{Nt}}{\lambda_t} = W_t + \beta \mathbb{E}_t \frac{\lambda_{t+1}}{\lambda_t} \left\{ \left(1 - s^C\right) \left(1 - s^L\right) \frac{H_{Nt+1}}{\lambda_{t+1}} \right.$$

$$\left. + \left[s^C + \left(1 - s^C\right) s^L \right] \frac{H_{Ut+1}}{\lambda_{t+1}} \right\} \tag{6.28}$$

An unemployed worker adds $Z_t = b + l/\lambda_t$ per period to the household value, where λ_t is the marginal utility of consumption C_t, and, if search is successful—with probability $f(\theta_t)$—adds an additional employed worker to the household. The latter are valued, in equation (6.28), for the wage earned every period, and with probability $\left(1 - s^C\right)\left(1 - s^L\right)$, in the subsequent period.

The-first order conditions for the household's problem in (6.24) yield the standard Euler equation relating the risk-free rate to expected aggregate consumption growth with

$$\frac{1}{1 + r_t} = \beta \tag{6.29}$$

The firm's side is unchanged and, under free entry into credit market, to the two equations using $\beta^C = \frac{1-s^C}{1+r}$:

$$J_{vt} = -\gamma + \mathbb{E}_t \beta^C \left[q_t J_{\pi t+1} + (1 - q_t) J_{vt+1} \right] \tag{6.30}$$

$$J_{\pi t} = X_t - W_t + \mathbb{E}_t \beta^C \left[(1 - s^L) J_{\pi t+1} + s^L J_{vt+1} \right] \tag{6.31}$$

The job creation condition thus generalizes that of previous section. The job creation condition for the model with search frictional credit and labor markets includes the stochastic discount factor, and a now time-dependent summary indicator of credit frictions, $K_t = \frac{\kappa_I}{p(\phi_t)} + \frac{\kappa_{Bt}}{\bar{p}(\phi_t)}$.

6.6.5 Elasticity of labor market tightness to productivity shocks

Financial frictions and a fixed wage

$$\frac{\gamma_k}{q(\theta_t^{CL})} = \beta^C \mathbb{E}_t \left[x_{t+1}^{CL} - \bar{w} + \left(1 - s^L\right) \frac{\gamma_k}{q(\theta_{t+1}^{CL})} \right]$$

around a stationary steady state, yields

$$\eta_L \frac{\gamma}{q(\theta^{CL})} \widehat{\theta}_t^{CL} = \beta^C \mathbb{E}_t \left[\widehat{x}_{t+1} + \left(1 - s^L\right) \eta_L \frac{\gamma_k}{q(\theta^{CL})} \mathbb{E}_t \widehat{\theta}_{t+1}^{CL} \right]$$

$$\eta_L \frac{\gamma_k}{q(\theta^{CL})} \left[1 - \left(1 - s^L\right) \beta^C \mathbb{E}_t L^{-1}\right] \widehat{\theta}_t^{CL} = \beta \mathbb{E}_t \widehat{x}_{t+1}$$

$$\widehat{\theta}_t^{CL} = \frac{q(\theta^{CL})}{\eta_L \gamma_k} \frac{\beta^C}{1 - (1 - s^L)\beta^C \mathbb{E}_t L^{-1}} \mathbb{E}_t \widehat{x}_{t+1}$$

$$\widehat{\theta}_t^{CL} = \frac{q(\theta^{CL})}{\eta_L \gamma_k} \beta^C \mathbb{E}_t \sum_{i=0}^{\infty} \left(\beta^{CL}\right)^i \rho_x^{1+i} \epsilon_t$$

$$\widehat{\theta}_t^{CL} = \frac{q(\theta^{CL})}{\eta_L \gamma_k} \beta^C \frac{\rho_x \epsilon_t}{1 - \beta^{CL} \rho_x}$$

Therefore, the elasticity of labor market tightness in the CL model is

$$\varsigma^{CL} = \frac{\partial \widehat{\theta}_t^{CL}}{\partial \epsilon_t} = \frac{q(\theta^{CL})}{\eta_L \gamma_k} \frac{\beta^C \rho_x}{1 - \beta^{CL} \rho_x}$$

To obtain equation (6.12), begin with

$$\widehat{\theta}_t^{CL} = \frac{1}{\eta_L} \frac{q(\theta^{CL})}{\gamma_k} \beta^C \sum_{i=0}^{\infty} \mathbb{E}_t \left(\left(1 - s^L\right) \beta^C\right)^i \widehat{x}_{t+1+i}$$

$$\widehat{\theta}_t^{CL} = \frac{1}{\eta_L} \left(\frac{\frac{1}{\beta^C} - \left(1 - s^L\right)}{x^{CL} - \bar{w}} \right) \beta^C \sum_{i=0}^{\infty} \mathbb{E}_t \left(\left(1 - s^L\right) \beta^C\right)^i \widehat{x}_{t+1+i}$$

$$\widehat{\theta}_t^{CL} = \frac{1}{\eta_L} \left(\frac{x}{x^{CL} - \bar{w}} \right) \left[1 - \beta^C \left(1 - s^L\right)\right] \sum_{i=0}^{\infty} \mathbb{E}_t \left(\left(1 - s^L\right) \beta^C\right)^i \widehat{x}_{t+1+i}$$

$$\widehat{\theta}_t^{CL} = \frac{1}{\eta_L} \left(\frac{x}{x - \bar{w} - k(\phi)} \right) \left(1 - \beta^{CL}\right) \sum_{i=0}^{\infty} \mathbb{E}_t \left(\beta^{CL}\right)^i \widehat{x}_{t+1+i}$$

making use of the CL model's steady-state job creation condition $\frac{\gamma_k}{q(\theta^{CL})} = \frac{x^{CL} - \bar{w}}{\frac{1}{\beta^C} - (1 - s^L)}$.

Financial multiplier: fixed wage

The general expression for the financial multiplier, assuming $s = s^L$, is:

$$\frac{\varsigma^{CL}}{\varsigma^L} = \frac{q(\theta^{CL})}{q(\theta^L)} \times \frac{\gamma}{\gamma_k} \times \left(1 - s^C\right) \frac{1 - \beta^L \rho_x}{1 - \beta^{CL} \rho_x}$$

and using the steady-state job creation conditions:

$$\begin{aligned} \frac{\varsigma^{CL}}{\varsigma^L} &= \frac{x - \bar{w}}{x - \bar{w} - k(\phi)} \times \left[\frac{1 - \left(1 - s^L\right) \beta \rho_x}{1 - (1 - s^L)\beta} \right] \times \left[\frac{1 - \left(1 - s^C\right)\left(1 - s^L\right)\beta}{1 - (1 - s^C)(1 - s^L)\beta \rho_x} \right] \\ &= \frac{x - \bar{w}}{x - \bar{w} - k(\phi)} \times \left[\frac{1 - \beta^L \rho_x}{1 - \beta^L} \right] \times \left[\frac{1 - \beta^{CL}}{1 - \beta^{CL} \rho_x} \right] \end{aligned}$$

The case in the main text when $s^C = 0$ is

$$\frac{\varsigma^{CL}}{\varsigma^{L}} = \frac{q(\theta^{CL})}{q(\theta^{L})}\frac{\gamma}{\gamma_k} = \frac{x-\bar{w}}{x-\bar{w}-k(\phi)}$$

In this case, $\frac{\partial\widehat{\theta}_t^{CL}}{\partial\epsilon_t}/\frac{\partial\widehat{\theta}_t^{L}}{\partial\epsilon_t} > 1$ requires that

$$\frac{\gamma}{q(\theta^L)} > \frac{\gamma_k}{q(\theta^{CL})}$$

This intuition for why this is true comes from the surplus diminishing effect of financial market frictions. To show this in a few steps, set $s^C = 0$ and $s = s^L$. Since $\frac{\gamma}{q(\theta^L)} = \frac{x-\bar{w}}{r+s^L}$ and $\frac{\gamma_k}{q(\theta^{CL})} = \frac{x^{CL}-\bar{w}}{r+s^L}$, and $x^{CL} = x - k(\phi)$, then the result is shown.

Financial frictions and a flexible wage

$$\frac{\gamma_k}{q(\theta_t^{CL})} = \beta^C\mathbb{E}_t\left[(1-\alpha_L)\left(x_{t+1}^{CL}-z\right) - \left(\frac{\gamma_k}{1-s^C}\right)\alpha_L\theta_{t+1} + \left(1-s^L\right)\frac{\gamma_k}{q(\theta_{t+1}^{CL})}\right]$$

around a stationary steady state, yields

$$\eta_L\frac{\gamma}{q(\theta^{CL})}\widehat{\theta}_t^{CL} = \beta^C\mathbb{E}_t\left[(1-\alpha_L)\widehat{x}_{t+1} - \left(\frac{\gamma_k}{1-s^C}\right)\alpha_L\theta^{CL}\widehat{\theta}_{t+1}^{CL} + \left(1-s^L\right)\eta_L\frac{\gamma_k}{q(\theta^{CL})}\widehat{\theta}_{t+1}^{CL}\right]$$

$$\eta_L\frac{\gamma}{q(\theta^{CL})}\widehat{\theta}_t^{CL} = \beta^C\mathbb{E}_t\left[(1-\alpha_L)\widehat{x}_{t+1}\widehat{\theta}_{t+1}^{CL} + \left[\left(1-s^L\right)\eta_L\frac{\gamma_k}{q(\theta^{CL})} - \left(\frac{\gamma_k}{1-s^C}\right)\alpha_L\theta^{CL}\right]\widehat{\theta}_{t+1}^{CL}\right]$$

$$\left[\eta_L\frac{\gamma_k}{q(\theta^{CL})} - \left[\left(1-s^L\right)\eta_L\frac{\gamma_k}{q(\theta^{CL})} - \left(\frac{\gamma_k}{1-s^C}\right)\alpha_L\theta^{CL}\right]\beta^C\mathbb{E}_tL^{-1}\right]\widehat{\theta}_t^{CL} = \beta\mathbb{E}_t\widehat{x}_{t+1}$$

$$\eta_L\frac{\gamma_k}{q(\theta^{CL})}\left[1-\left[\left(1-s^L\right) - \frac{\alpha_L}{\eta_L}\frac{f(\theta^{CL})}{1-s^C}\right]\beta^C\mathbb{E}_tL^{-1}\right]\widehat{\theta}_t^{CL} = \beta\mathbb{E}_t\widehat{x}_{t+1}$$

$$\widehat{\theta}_t^{CL} = \frac{q(\theta^{CL})}{\eta_L\gamma_k}\frac{\beta^C}{1-\left[\left(1-s^L\right)-\frac{\alpha_L}{\eta_L}\frac{f(\theta^{CL})}{1-s^C}\right]\beta^C\mathbb{E}_tL^{-1}}\mathbb{E}_t\widehat{x}_{t+1}$$

$$\widehat{\theta}_t^{CL} = \frac{q(\theta^{CL})}{\eta_L\gamma_k}\beta^C\mathbb{E}_t\sum_{i=0}^{\infty}\left(\left[\left(1-s^L\right) - \frac{\alpha_L}{\eta_L}\frac{f(\theta^{CL})}{1-s^C}\right]\beta^C\right)^i\rho_x^{1+i}\epsilon_t$$

$$\widehat{\theta}_t^{CL} = \frac{q(\theta^{CL})}{\eta_L\gamma_k}\frac{\beta^C\rho_x\epsilon_t}{1-\left[\left(1-s^L\right)-\frac{\alpha_L}{\eta_L}\frac{f(\theta^{CL})}{1-s^C}\right]\beta^C\rho_x}$$

7 Goods market frictions: LG and CLG models

Goods markets frictions, that is frictions in the exchange of goods between sellers and buyers or between producers and consumers, have been studied since the inception of search theory (e.g., Diamond, 1982). Goods market frictions have numerous empirical counterparts, mapping into different rates of capacity utilization, the existence of inventories, consumer shopping effort measured in time use surveys, or product turnover in consumption baskets. The introduction of goods market frictions leads to a new set of entry costs for the firm. Over and above the financial setup costs and the costs of the hiring labor, the firm must also face the opportunity cost of a period of endogenous length: it searches for a consumer during which it has to pay wages even though production cannot be sold. These three costs—in the labor, credit, and now in the goods markets—enter the job creation condition, and each plays a distinctly identified role in calibrated economies.

Chapter 7 is dedicated to the analysis of the canonical search model of goods market imperfections that we call the LG model. As in the opening chapters of the previous part, this chapter emphasizes the new economic concepts and insights of goods market frictions. We then extend it to incorporate financial frictions. Doing so, we obtain a model with frictions in all three markets that we call CLG and study its steady state, along with one important extension to endogenous effort.

The simplest model of goods market frictions is presented first. This chapter makes a set of simplifying assumptions on the structure of search in the goods market and its relation with income. These assumptions simplify the exposition of the main concepts and, in particular, imply a convenient recursive structure of the model. As a result, solutions in each market are derived sequentially with equilibrium tightness in the goods market determined first. This leads to transparent and closed form solutions characterizing a labor market equilibrium, extending the canonical search models of previous chapters.

The first sections of this chapter also assume that firms have perfect access to financial markets, as in the first part of the book. The sequence of events for a firm is as follows. First it recruits a worker according to the standard labor matching process. Second, once the worker is recruited, it is able to produce and advertise to sell its good, and begins to search actively for a consumer. However, the firm does not generate profits yet. There exists of a new stage in the life cycle of a firm, "search in the goods market," characterized by subscript g, that precedes the profit stage, still called stage π. In stage g, the firm makes no revenue and incurs losses. Third and last, it reaches the final stage in which it can sell to consumers and generate profits, stage π. The firm will obtain a price $\mathcal{P}$ per unit of good from the consumer, who continues to purchase the good over several periods as a long-term relationship. This assumption characterizes the existence of specificity in the match formed in the goods market. In the special case of the absence of search frictions in the goods market, the limiting case when stage g lasts an infinitely small amount of time, stages g and π are confounded. As in previous chapters, the details of the derivations and proofs are relegated to the chapter appendix, and generalizations to the online appendix.

7.1 Search in goods markets

7.1.1 Timing and notations

Time is continuous. Consumers have access to two types of goods: (i) one good is accessible with no frictions, indexed by 0, and can be thought as a set of inferior goods (food, basic utility, standard goods), with its price normalized to 1; (ii) another good, indexed by 1, is subject to search frictions. This second good can either be interpreted as services or consumer goods that enter a consumption basket for the first time, or as the flow consumption of a durable good such as car or housing services. The search good is produced by firms, while good 0 will be produced by consumers, as discussed in section 7.1.3.

A convenient intuition for the differences between the two goods is to think of the two main sources of heterogeneity across goods: spatial (similar goods are sold in different places), and horizontal (some differentiation across products). Both types of heterogeneity lead to higher search frictions. Good 0 is a good for which search is small, because it is sold in places known to the consumer and the degree of differentiation is low enough, or because the consumer has kept a record of its location and characteristics. Good 1 is a good for which either locations must be found or characteristics must be investigated. Once consumed, though, they are not subject to search frictions, until the consumption match dissolves. Hence, good 0 provides a constant flow of utility (e.g., the good is regularly consumed without the need to be searching for it). Instead, good 1 represents the permanent quest for new goods, due to both the arrival rates on the market of new consumption goods (e.g., a new restaurant in the neighborhood, a new brand for consumption goods) or replacement of old goods previously consumed and hit by a "consumer taste" shock.

This leads to the discussion of turnover in the goods market. The consumer of good 1 may change tastes and no longer desire the particular search good, or may lose its purchasing power and no longer be able to buy the search good. Such events lead to a separation in the consumer–seller relationship. The consumer–seller relationship ends with Poisson intensity s^G (see the discussion in chapter 1, subsection 1.1.2). This consumption–match termination shock s^G is the sum of a pure taste shock, arriving with intensity τ, and an income shock leading to the separation of the consumption relation. In the present part of the chapter this will arise with intensity s^L (when the worker separates from the firm). We therefore work with the compact notation

$$s^G = \tau + s^L$$

We denote, respectively, by $\mathcal{D}_M$ and $\mathcal{D}_U$, the number of consumers matched with good 1 or unmatched and searching in the goods market. We also denote by $\mathcal{N}_\pi$ and $\mathcal{N}_g$ the number of selling and searching firms (for consumers), respectively. The total number of employed workers is therefore equal to the total number of firms in each goods market stages g and π, that is

$$1 - \mathcal{U} = \mathcal{N}_\pi + \mathcal{N}_g$$

We also assume that each firm can serve only one consumer. This further implies

$$\mathcal{D}_M \equiv \mathcal{N}_\pi$$

This is therefore a *one-firm/one-worker/one-consumer* model.

7.1.2 Random matching in the goods market and goods market tightness

The usual assumptions in the labor market are maintained: workers and firms meet randomly, and the number of matches per unit of time is given by

$\mathcal{M}_L(\mathcal{U},\mathcal{V})$. In the goods market, we introduce the tightness of the goods market as the ratio of consumers searching to the number of goods looking for consumers:

$$\xi = \frac{\mathcal{D}_U}{\mathcal{N}_g} \tag{7.1}$$

As in standard search and matching models, we assume that firms and consumers match at a rate determined through an increasing, constant returns to scale matching function:

$$\mathcal{M}_G(\mathcal{D}_U,\mathcal{N}_g) \text{ with } \partial \log \mathcal{M}_G / \partial \log D_U = \eta_G(\xi) \quad \text{and } \partial \log \mathcal{M}_G / \partial \log \mathcal{N}_g = 1 - \eta_G(\xi) \tag{7.2}$$

where $\eta_G(\xi)$ is the elasticity of matching with respect to the mass of searching consumers. It follows that the transition rates for firms and for consumers are given respectively by

$$\frac{\mathcal{M}_G(\mathcal{D}_U,\mathcal{N}_g)}{\mathcal{N}_g} = \lambda(\xi) \qquad \text{with } \partial\lambda/\partial\xi > 0 \tag{7.3}$$

$$\frac{\mathcal{M}_G(\mathcal{D}_U,\mathcal{N}_g)}{\mathcal{D}_U} = \lambda(\xi)/\xi = \check{\lambda}(\xi) \qquad \text{with } \partial\check{\lambda}/\partial\xi < 0 \tag{7.4}$$

Consumers searching in the goods market, D_U, must be willing to exert search effort and be able to purchase search good 1. We assume here that only employed workers, who have access to a full salary, can purchase and consume. That is, we are assuming that all income available to the unemployed is spent on essential goods and that only the employed participate in the search goods market. The unemployed have no additional disposable income to spend on the search good. The assumption that only the employed consume simplifies the analysis. Alternatives are explored in the online appendix. It follows that unmatched and matched consumers of good 1 sum up to total employment:

$$\mathcal{D}_U + \mathcal{D}_M = 1 - \mathcal{U}$$

Stocks in this economy evolve according to the following dynamic stock-flow equations:

Firms:

$$\dot{\mathcal{N}}_\pi = \underbrace{\mathcal{M}_G(\mathcal{D}_U,\mathcal{N}_g)}_{\text{matches in G}} \quad \underbrace{-s^L\mathcal{N}_\pi}_{\text{loss of workers}} \quad \underbrace{-s^G\mathcal{N}_\pi}_{\text{loss of customers}} \tag{7.5}$$

$$\dot{\mathcal{N}}_g = \underbrace{\mathcal{M}_L(\mathcal{U},\mathcal{V})}_{\text{matches in L}} \quad \underbrace{+s^G\mathcal{N}_\pi}_{\text{loss of customers}} \quad \underbrace{-\mathcal{M}_G(\mathcal{D}_U,\mathcal{N}_g)}_{\text{matches in G}} \quad \underbrace{-s^L\mathcal{N}_g}_{\text{loss of workers}} \tag{7.6}$$

Consumers:

$$\dot{\mathcal{D}}_M = \underbrace{\mathcal{M}_G(\mathcal{D}_U,\mathcal{N}_g)}_{\text{matches in G}} \quad \underbrace{-s^L\mathcal{D}_M}_{\text{seller loses worker}} \quad \underbrace{-s^L\mathcal{D}_M}_{\text{matched consumer loses job}} \quad \underbrace{-\tau\mathcal{D}_M}_{\text{matched consumer changes tastes}} \tag{7.7}$$

$$\dot{\mathcal{D}}_U = \underbrace{-\mathcal{M}_G(\mathcal{D}_U,\mathcal{N}_g)}_{\text{matches in G}} \quad \underbrace{+\tau\mathcal{D}_M}_{\text{matched consumer changed tastes}} \quad \underbrace{+\mathcal{M}_L(\mathcal{U},\mathcal{V})}_{\text{matches L}} \quad \underbrace{-s^L\mathcal{D}_U}_{\text{unmatched consumer loses job}} \tag{7.8}$$

Unemployment:

$$\dot{\mathcal{U}} = -\mathcal{M}_L(\mathcal{U},\mathcal{V}) + s^L(1-\mathcal{U}) \tag{7.9}$$

7.1.3 The new concepts in a search in the goods market economy

A model with goods market imperfections has several important differences with a model with a perfect goods market. It is useful to review these differences and introduce the new concepts that come with goods market frictions before characterizing the equilibrium.

Unused production capacity

First, there are unused resources. Firms have the ability to produce, but not necessarily to sell unless they find a consumer. Production takes place only when the match with the consumer has been formed. Therefore, the firm does not use its capacity to produce in the stage where it has no consumer. Search frictions in the goods market introduce a new concept: the rate of capacity utilization. This can be denoted μ_{LG}, where LG indicates that it is specific to the LG model and defined as:

Rate of capacity utilization:

$$\mu^{LG} = \frac{\mathcal{N}_\pi}{\mathcal{N}_\pi + \mathcal{N}_g} \tag{7.10}$$

The rate of capacity utilization is the ratio of firms matched with a consumer, $\mathcal{N}_\pi$, to the total number of firms matched with a worker $\mathcal{N}_\pi + \mathcal{N}_g = \mathcal{N}$. This rate is a widely available statistic and will be used subsequently for calibrating a frictional economy. Increasing the degree of search frictions in the goods market, implying lower meeting rates λ for firms, leads to a lower rate of capacity utilization.

Transfers, Lucas trees and utility of consumers

The total resources available to consumers are always below the total value of production by the firms $\mu^{LG}\mathcal{N}\mathcal{P}x$. There are three sources of revenues dissipation: (i) search frictions in the labor market (the term $\gamma\mathcal{V}$); (ii) search frictions in the goods market (the term $\mu^{LG} \leq 1$); and (iii) if dividends of firms are returned to both the unemployed and the employed, some of the profits of the firms are therefore not returned to the consumers of good 1 (see the more detailed discussion in chapter appendix 7.7.1). It follows that, in the absence of additional sources of income for consumers, the economy would collapse to a home production economy with no frictional goods produced and sold. Both $\mathcal{P}$ and $\mathcal{V}$ would be equal to zero in equilibrium.

We therefore assume that consumers produce or receive additional resources for a nontrivial equilibrium to exist. These resources are expressed in terms of the Walrasian good 0. We assume that both the employed and the unemployed agents receive the fruits (in Walrasian good) of a Lucas tree growing in their individual garden. Each agent is endowed in each unit of time a quantity $\bar{y}$ of additional resources.

The utility function of consumers, $v(c^1, c^0, l)$, depends on the consumption of the search good, c^1, the Walrasian good, c^0, l. We discuss the implications of preferences in greater detail in chapter appendix 7.7.1.

7.2 The steady-state equilibrium in the LG model

7.2.1 Employment, consumption, and goods market tightness

The first step is to derive equilibrium goods market tightness. This is straightforward from combining the steady-state equations governing the evolution of (i) employment in matched firms and unmatched firms (equation (7.11)) and (ii) matched and unmatched consumers (equation (7.12)), along with the fact that total employment equals the amount of consumers in the search goods market (equation (7.13)):

$$\mathcal{N}_\pi + \mathcal{N}_g = \left[1 + \lambda/(s^L + s^G)\right] \mathcal{N}_g \tag{7.11}$$

$$\mathcal{D}_M + \mathcal{D}_U = \left[1 + \check{\lambda}/(s^L + s^G)\right] \mathcal{D}_U \tag{7.12}$$

$$\mathcal{N}_g + \mathcal{N}_\pi = \mathcal{D}_U + \mathcal{D}_M \tag{7.13}$$

A first result, from equation (7.11), is that the rate of capacity utilization μ^{LG} can be solved as a function of goods market tightness only:

Property 1 (rate of capacity utilization). *The rate of capacity utilization is, in the steady state, equal to*

$$\mu^{LG} = \frac{\lambda(\xi)}{s^G + s^L + \lambda(\xi)}$$

One can then calculate goods market tightness using the ratio of equations (7.11) and (7.12) on the one hand, along with the fact that $\mathcal{N}_g + \mathcal{N}_\pi = \mathcal{D}_U + \mathcal{D}_M$ from equation (7.13):

$$\frac{\mathcal{N}_g + \mathcal{N}_\pi}{\mathcal{D}_M + \mathcal{D}_U} = \frac{1 + \lambda/(s^L + s^G)}{1 + \check{\lambda}/(s^L + s^G)} \frac{\mathcal{N}_g}{\mathcal{D}_U} = 1 \tag{7.14}$$

Property 2 (steady-state goods market tightness). *Goods market tightness ξ in a steady state is equal to 1 when only employed workers have access to the frictional good:*

$$\mathcal{D}_U + \mathcal{D}_M = \mathcal{N} \quad \Rightarrow \quad \xi^* = 1 \tag{7.15}$$

The proof amounts to solving a fixed-point problem:

$$\xi = \frac{1 + \lambda(\xi)/(s^L + s^G)}{1 + \check{\lambda}(\xi)/(s^L + s^G)} \tag{7.16}$$

Using $\check{\lambda}(\xi) = \lambda(\xi)/\xi$, it is easy to see that $\xi = 1$ is one such fixed point. It can be shown that, under an Inada condition on the matching function, there is a second fixed point $\xi = 0$ corresponding to a degenerate case with no market. This would be a subsistence economy where everyone consumes the Walrasian good in quantity $\bar{y}$. There is no other fixed point for a standard matching function. When $\xi > 0$, one has $\xi + \lambda(\xi)/(s^L + s^G) = 1 + \lambda(\xi)/(s^L + s^G)$, which leads immediately to $\xi = 1$.

This result, when the ratio $\frac{\mathcal{N}_g+\mathcal{N}_\pi}{\mathcal{D}_M+\mathcal{D}_U}$ is equal to 1, arises from the apparently innocuous assumption that only employed workers search for the search in the goods market. It can be interpreted as a stochastic version of the old *Say's law* that demand equals supply. The firm produces one good, each consumer consumes one good, and each firm employs one employee-consumer. If instead each firm employed, say, two workers, this would lead to the creation of two consumers and thus goods market tightness would be equal to 2, in the steady state. If conversely, each firm produced 2 units of goods, each worker-consumer would be able to consume two units of goods (in another firm) and therefore goods market tightness would be equal to one half. Adapting this logic, if each firm could produce n_q units and employed n_w workers, the steady-state goods market tightness would be equal to n_w/n_q. Nonetheless, goods market tightness would still be a simple function of parameters.

7.2.2 The job creation equation

The property derived above implies that the transition probabilities in the goods market are solved. Indeed, we have that $\lambda(\xi^*) = \lambda(1)$ and $\check{\lambda}(\xi^*) = \lambda(\xi^*)/\xi^* = \lambda(1)$. The model is therefore block recursive, and the job creation curve is easy to derive from here. Let J_v, J_g, and J_π the respective steady-state asset values of a project in each stage (labor search, goods search, and profit). Given the notations introduced in the beginning of the chapter, we have

$$rJ_v = -\gamma + q\left(J_g - J_v\right) \tag{7.17}$$

$$rJ_g = -w_g + \lambda(\xi)\left(J_\pi - J_g\right) + s^L\left(J_v - J_g\right) \tag{7.18}$$

$$rJ_\pi = \mathcal{P}x \quad w_\pi + s^G\left(J_g - J_\pi\right) + s^L\left(J_v - J_\pi\right) \tag{7.19}$$

As discussed earlier, firms may lose their consumer for one of two reasons. First, the consumer receives a taste shock τ and abandons their product. Second, a worker may be hit by a job separation shock and no longer have the necessary income for the search good. Hence the capital loss $J_g - J_\pi$, from the profit stage to the goods market search stage, occurs at rate $s^G = \tau + s^L$.

The usual free-entry condition in the labor market drives the value of a vacancy J_v to 0, and the value of the goods market search stage to $J_g = \gamma/q(\theta)$. In addition, frictions in the goods market cause, the value of the revenue from production from the perspective of stage g, to be discounted by the factor

$$\mu_r^{LG} = \frac{\lambda}{r + s^G + s^L + \lambda} \tag{7.20}$$

This "discounted rate of capacity utilization" μ_r^{LG} takes into account that at the time of hiring, in stage g, the firm still has to find a consumer. The revenue generated by a worker accrues only after finding a consumer (at rate λ), and must be discounted for time, $r > 0$, and profit stage turnover risk, $s^G + s^L$. This term implies that $\mu_r^{LG} < \mu_{r=0}^{LG} = \mu^{LG}$. That is, firms discount future profits at a greater rate than the rate of capacity utilization. By analogy with chapter 5 on credit market frictions, let $x^{LG} = \mu_r^{LG} x$, and $\bar{w} = \mu_r^{LG} w_\pi + (1 - \mu_r^{LG}) w_g$ be the weighted average of wages, as anticipated by the firm in stage g. The free-entry equation can be written in a compact way as:

Job creation condition with frictions in the goods market:

$$\frac{\gamma}{q(\theta)} = \frac{\mathcal{P} x^{LG} - \bar{w}}{r + s^L} \tag{7.21}$$

where entry costs have to equalize future discounted profits that take into account that revenue will only be available when the firm has formed a relationship with a consumer (the discount factor $\mu_r^{LG} < 1$ in x^{LG}), and the good will be sold at a price $\mathcal{P}$. In order to further discuss the effects of goods market frictions on the job creation condition, we use an alternative formulation with stage-specific discounting terms:

$$Q_g = \frac{\lambda}{r + s^L + \lambda} \quad \text{and} \quad Q_\pi = \frac{s^G}{r + s^L + s^G}$$

Q_g reflects the market value of a contract delivering one dollar upon the realization of a Poisson event of parameter λ and ending with probability s^L. Q_π has a similar interpretation where instead the Poisson event is the goods market termination shock s^G. We then have the following alternative job creation condition:

$$\left(1 - Q_g Q_\pi\right) \frac{\gamma}{q(\theta)} + \frac{w_g}{r + s^L + \lambda} = Q_g \left(\frac{\mathcal{P} x - w_\pi}{r + s^G + s^L} \right) \tag{7.22}$$

This equation is similar to the job creation condition (1.13) of chapter 1 but with a few noticeable differences. On the profit side of the equation (the right-hand side), there is a discount factor Q_g that weights down the future expected profits from the perspective of stage g. Future profits are discounted more heavily as goods market frictions increase. At the limit, when it takes infinitely long to match with a consumer, that is when λ goes to zero, Q_g goes to zero. Likewise, a shorter duration of a match with the worker, or great s^L, reduces the probability of reaching the profit stage. This is reflected in a greater discounting, or lower Q_g. Q_g instead converges to 1 when frictions in the goods market disappear (e.g., when λ goes to infinity). Q_g may also converge to 1 when there is no opportunity cost time ($r = 0$), and risk from labor separation shocks ($s^L = 0$). On the cost side (left-hand side of equation (7.22)), the firm initially has to pay for the hiring costs γ/q, but recovers some of these costs when $Q_g Q_\pi > 0$. When the firm loses its consumer, it does not lose its worker and does not have to search in the labor market again. This has the value of the worker's replacement cost γ/q. The firm also pays a wage w_g to the worker even when it is not selling any goods making any profit, which adds up to the ex ante costs of production.

7.2.3 Price determination

Consumer–producer relationships are costly to create as they require several steps, with direct costs (search) and related opportunity costs. It is therefore natural to adopt a price determination rule that is the outcome of bargaining between the firm and the consumer. In what follows, on price and wage determination, we assume that bargaining takes place at the time of the meeting. In addition, we make a simplifying assumption that workers are paid the same wage w whether or not their employer is matched with a consumer. This implies that $w_g = w_\pi = w$, an assumption which greatly simplifies the analysis without being central to the main results.This equality of wages would arise in the presence of collective bargaining between workers and firms, or infrequent bargaining leading to wage rigidities. Additional alternative assumptions are discussed in the concluding section, and they do not qualitatively alter the main results.

A newly employed worker, not yet matched with a product in the goods market, has an asset value denoted by W_{D_U}. After a period of random search, the frictional good is found and consumed. The asset value in this stage is denoted by W_{D_M}. At any time the consumer may be hit by a labor turnover shock and move to unemployment with the asset value W_u. This arises with probability per unit of time s^L. Finally, a matched consumer may exit the consumption match while remaining employed, either following a taste shock τ, or the disruption of production due to labor turnover at the firm supplying the good at rate s^L. In both cases the consumer returns to the goods market search stage.

The Bellman equations of consumers, using the earlier result that $\check{\lambda}(1) = \lambda(1) = \lambda$, are

$$rW_{D_U} = v(0, \bar{y} + w, 0) + \lambda(W_{D_M} - W_{D_U}) + s^L(W_u - W_{D_U}) \tag{7.23}$$

$$rW_{D_M} = v(x, \bar{y} + w - \mathcal{P}x, 0) + s^L(W_u - W_{D_M}) + s^G(W_{D_U} - W_{D_M}) \tag{7.24}$$

$$rW_u = v(0, \bar{y}, z) + f(\theta)(W_{D_U} - W_u) \tag{7.25}$$

where the last equation is based on the fact that the unemployed have an additional z units of leisure. The surplus of the consumer in the goods market is the difference in the valuation of the consumption stage and the search stage $W_{D_M} - W_{D_U}$. Subtracting (7.23) from (7.24) we have

$$W_{D_M} - W_{D_U} = \frac{v(x, \bar{y} + w - \mathcal{P}x) - v(0, \bar{y} + w)}{r + s^L + s^G + \lambda} \tag{7.26}$$

The exposition of the main concepts of the LG model is straightforward under linear utility, while richer dynamics, explored in next chapter, require some concavity in utility v with respect to good 0. Assume that $v\left(x, c^0, l\right) = \Phi x + c^0 + l$, where the marginal utility of good 0 is 1 (hence it is a numeraire), and the marginal utility of good 1 is $\Phi > 1$. A nondegenerate equilibrium will require $\Phi > \mathcal{P}$. Under these preferences we obtain the consumer's surplus:

$$W_{D_M} - W_{D_U} = \frac{\Phi x - \mathcal{P}x}{r + s^L + s^G + \lambda}$$

The production of good 0 drops out of the consumption surplus due to the assumption of linearity. The surplus to a goods market match is the discounted, present value of flow net utility from consumption of the search good $(\Phi - \mathcal{P})x$. In a Walrasian market, for comparison, the price is the marginal utility of consumption of the good, and the consumer surplus is driven to zero at the equilibrium price.

In this search frictional goods market prices are bargained and set according to a Nash sharing rule. The price is the solution to

$$\mathcal{P} = \text{argmax}\left(W_{D_M} - W_{D_U}\right)^{\alpha_G}\left(J_\pi - J_g\right)^{1-\alpha_G} \tag{7.27}$$

where $\alpha_G \in (0,1)$ is the consumer's bargaining weight. The price must therefore satisfy the sharing rule

$$(1 - \alpha_G)\, W_{D_M} - W_{D_U} = \alpha_G \left(J_\pi - J_g\right)$$

The firm's surplus in the goods market match is, subtracting (7.18) from (7.19)

$$J_\pi - J_g = \frac{\mathcal{P}x - w_\pi + w_g}{r + s^L + s^G + \lambda} \tag{7.28}$$

If we make the earlier simplifying assumption that $w_g = w_\pi$ the wage cancels out of the surplus of the firm. Combining the definitions of the consumer and the firm goods market surplus with the Nash sharing rule leads to the bargained price:

$$\mathcal{P}x = (1 - \alpha_G)\Phi x \tag{7.29}$$

The price depends on the marginal utility for the good, Φ, and the relative bargaining power of the seller $(1 - \alpha_G)$. The property that the price is a function of consumer preferences and bargaining parameters is a general one. It also arises when the wage is allowed to vary across stages g and π.

7.2.4 Wage determination

We continue with the assumption of an identical wage w at idle firms (stage g) and selling firms (stage π). The wage is negotiated when the firm is in the goods market stage g. As we saw in the previous section, this assumption on wage implies that the wage does not affect the capital gain from a match in the goods market for either the consumer or the firm.

The bargained wage is the outcome of

$$w = \text{argmax}\left(J_g - J_v\right)^{1-\alpha_L}\left(W_{D_U} - W_u\right)^{\alpha_L}$$

leading to the labor match surplus sharing rule:

$$(1 - \alpha_L)\left(W_{D_U} - W_u\right) = \alpha_L\left(J_g - J_v\right)$$

Using the definition of the asset values described in sections 7.2.2 and 7.2.3, the wage can be expressed as a function of the firm's surplus with respect to the consumer:

$$w = (1 - \alpha_L)(rW_u - \bar{y}) + \left(\frac{\alpha_L - \alpha_G}{1 - \alpha_G}\right)\lambda\left(J_\pi - J_g\right)$$

Using the expression for the surplus in equation (7.28), and the compact notation $x^{LG} = \mu_r^{LG} x = x\lambda/(r + s^L + s^G + \lambda)$, the wage in the labor market can be linked to the price in the goods market:

$$w = (1 - \alpha_L)z + \alpha_L\gamma\theta + \left(\frac{\alpha_L - \alpha_G}{1 - \alpha_G}\right)\mathcal{P}x^{LG} \tag{7.30}$$

Replacing $\mathcal{P}$ by its equilibrium value, the wage equation simplifies further:

$$w = (1 - \alpha_L)z + \alpha_L\gamma\theta + (\alpha_L - \alpha_G)\Phi x^{LG} \tag{7.31}$$

The bargained wage in the LG model differs from the equilibrium wage in the baseline model of chapter 1 in one important aspect. The first two terms, $(1-\alpha_L)z$ and $\alpha_L\gamma\theta$, are identical. The intuition for the effect of goods market frictions on the wage can more easily be understood by rewriting the last term as $\left[(1-\alpha_G)\Phi x^{LG} - (1-\alpha_L)\Phi x^{LG}\right]$. The first element is a consumer surplus effect. The firm obtains a fraction $(1-\alpha_G)$ of the marginal utility of the search good, which affects the value of the labor match surplus that produces the good. A lower consumer bargaining weight increases the labor match surplus and the bargained wage. The second, negative term, is a worker threat point effect. The worker has more to lose from a breakdown in negotiations as the unemployed loses access to the search good which provides the utility flow Φx^{LG}. In the special case where the worker's bargaining weight in the labor market is equal to the consumer's bargaining weight in the goods market, $\alpha_L = \alpha_G$, the consumption surplus for the firm and the wage no longer depends on the price in the goods market or changes in the marginal revenue from production. We hereafter assume that $\alpha_G \leq \alpha_L$, so that the wage is always increasing in productivity and the marginal utility of the good.

There are two conditions under which we return to the baseline Pissarides wage, and that further illustrate the effect of goods market frictions on the wage. First, the firm must extract the entire surplus from trade with consumers in the goods market ($\alpha_G = 0$). Second, matching frictions in the goods market must vanish to ensure full capacity utilization. Indeed, $\mu_r^{LG} = 1$ when $\lambda \to \infty$, such that $x^{LG} = x$ and the wage becomes $w = (1-\alpha_L)z + \alpha_L(\gamma\theta + \Phi x)$.

In the general case, the model is closed with a condition on goods market tightness, a job creation condition with goods market frictions (JC), and a wage setting (WS) and a price setting (PS) equation:

Summary of the steady state equilibrium in the LG model with bargained price and wages (entry level):

$$\text{Labor market tightness: } \frac{\gamma}{q(\theta)} = \frac{x^{LG}\mathcal{P} - w}{r + s^L} \tag{7.32}$$

Goods market tightness: $\xi^* = 1$

with

$$\text{Wage setting: } w = (1-\alpha_L)z + \alpha_L\gamma\theta + (\alpha_L - \alpha_G)\,\Phi x^{LG}$$

$$\text{Price setting: } \mathcal{P} = (1-\alpha_G)\Phi$$

$$\text{Adjusted productivity: } x^{LG} = \mu_r^{LG} x = \frac{\lambda}{r + s^G + s^L + \lambda} x$$

Viability conditions ensure that the decentralized equilibrium is not degenerate. The full conditions are derived in appendix 7.7.4. To summarize these conditions, we need that wages fall into the interval $(x\mathcal{P}-\bar{y}, x\mathcal{P})$ where $\bar{y}$ is the transfer of Walrasian good (income). This means that workers can pay for the search good in numeraire and the firm can pay workers above the selling price. This condition is satisfied if the supply of Walrasian good $\bar{y}$ is large enough compared to a combination of parameters involving α_G as well as x, z, and θ. Finally to sustain the assumption that the unemployed workers cannot consume the inelastic supply of the search good x, it must be that $\bar{y} < x\mathcal{P} = (1-\alpha_G)\Phi x$.

Combining the wage and the job creation condition leads to an entry condition that is independent of α_G:

$$\frac{\gamma}{q(\theta)} = \frac{x^{LG}\mathcal{P} - w}{r+s^L} = \frac{\left(\Phi x^{LG} - z\right)(1-\alpha_L) - \alpha_L \gamma \theta}{r+s^L}$$

The intuition for this result is that a higher price, due to a lower value of α_G, is good for firms, but bad for consumers. Since the unemployed do not consume the search good, the worker's surplus is affected by α_G and is incorporated in wages. The compensation is one-to-one so that firms are indifferent about the exact value of α_G.

7.3 Efficiency and Hosios in the LG model

The social planner seeks to maximize the value of consumption of the search good and nonemployment utility, net of labor market search costs. Utility from consumption of the Walrasian good has no effect on the planner's choice, and drops out of the planner's social welfare function:

$$\Omega^{SP} = \int_0^\infty e^{-rt}\left[D_M \Phi x + z\mathcal{U} - \gamma \mathcal{V}\right] dt$$

The social planner chooses the optimal amount of vacancies taking the other stocks as state variables. The assumption that only the employed participate in the search goods market had given $1-\mathcal{U} = \mathcal{N}_g + \mathcal{N}_\pi = \mathcal{D}_U + \mathcal{D}_M$, and the implication that $\mathcal{D}_U = \mathcal{N}_g$ and $\mathcal{D}_M = \mathcal{N}_\pi$. This technological constraint on the planner leads to a simple associated Hamiltonian:

$$\begin{aligned}\max_{\mathcal{V},\mathcal{U},\mathcal{D}_U} \; H = {} & e^{-rt}\left[(1-\mathcal{U}-\mathcal{D}_u)\,\Phi x + z\mathcal{U} - \gamma \mathcal{V}\right] \\ & + \Psi_U\left[s^L(1-\mathcal{U}) - \mathcal{M}_L(\mathcal{U},\mathcal{V})\right] \\ & + \Psi_{D_u}\left[\mathcal{M}_L(\mathcal{U},\mathcal{V}) + s^G(1-\mathcal{U}-\mathcal{D}_u) - \mathcal{M}_G(\mathcal{D}_U,\mathcal{D}_U) - s^L\mathcal{D}_U\right]\end{aligned}$$

The first order conditions are

$$\frac{\partial H}{\partial \mathcal{V}} = 0 = -\gamma e^{-rt} + \left(\Psi_{D_U} - \Psi_U\right)(1-\eta_L)\, q \tag{7.33}$$

$$\mathring{\Psi}_U = -\frac{\partial H}{\partial \mathcal{U}} = (\Phi x - z)\, e^{-rt} + (\Psi_U - \Psi_{D_U})\eta_L f + s^L \Psi_U + s^G \Psi_{D_U} \tag{7.34}$$

$$\mathring{\Psi}_{D_U} = -\frac{\partial H}{\partial \mathcal{D}_U} = \Phi x . e^{-rt} + \Psi_{D_U}\left(\lambda + s^G + s^L\right) \tag{7.35}$$

The optimality condition for vacancies (7.33) states that the planner balances the cost of a new match in the labor market, the usual average search cost $e^{-rt}\gamma/q$, to the social benefit. Here the benefit has two components. First there is the value of an additional consumer searching in the goods market, Ψ_{D_U}. Second there is the change in marginal social value from one fewer unemployed worker $(-\Psi_U)$. After a few calculations in appendix, one can show that:

Social planner's and decentralized job creation conditions in the LG model:

Social planner: $$\frac{\gamma}{q(\theta^{opt})} = \frac{(\mu_r^{LG}\Phi x - z)(1-\eta_L) - \eta_L \gamma \theta^{opt}}{r + s^L} \tag{7.36}$$

Decentralized: $$\frac{\gamma}{q(\theta^{*})} = \frac{\left(\mu_r^{LG}\Phi x - z\right)(1-\alpha_L) - \alpha_L \gamma \theta^{*}}{r + s^L} \tag{7.37}$$

Comparing the social planner and decentralized job creation conditions, it becomes clear that one is back to a standard Hosios in the labor market when the following conditions on bargaining parameters hold:

Hosios efficiency conditions in the LG model:

$\theta^* = \theta^{opt}$ for any $\alpha_G \in (0,1)$ if and only if $\eta_L = \alpha_L$

Under this condition, the price of the search good can take any value between zero and to its marginal utility, Φ, as α_G covers its full range. As discussed in the previous subsection, the decentralized equilibrium is not affected by the value of the price, since wages reflect price changes. A higher price leads to a higher wage, so that both firms and workers are indifferent. This result leaves some degree of freedom to set the efficient level of labor market tightness since α_G can be thought of as a free parameter. However, this result arises due to a precise reason: the assumption that the unemployed do not consume the search good leads to the result that the wage comoves one-to-one with prices.

7.4 The CLG model

We now are in a position to integrate the three blocks into a full model where credit, labor, and goods market imperfections are interacting in a simple general equilibrium framework called the CLG model. The important result here is the block-recursiveness of the model. First, we solve for the credit market and obtain credit market tightness as a function of parameters. Second, we solve for the goods market and obtain goods market tightness in the steady state, equal to unity as a long-run equilibrium relation between demand and supply, determining profits and consumption. Third, we find the job creation curve as a function of the two previous market tightness which further delivers labor market tightness in equilibrium. Figure 7.1, summarizes the timing of the various transitions.

The lifetime of a project—still in continuous time—starts with identifying a creditor able to finance the next stages. In particular, the creditor will finance not only the posting of a vacancy, as in the CL model, but also the initial stage of the life of the firm, where it has to pay the worker but has not been able to sell its product yet. In this way, both the CL model and the L model itself (the benchmark model in chapter 1) are made more realistic, emphasizing that a view of job creation limited to the costs of posting vacancies is too restrictive. In the CLG model, entry costs before generating profits are the sum of three components: (i) cost of financial frictions; (ii) cost of recruiting labor; and (iii) opportunity costs of finding customers.

At each step, the existence of search frictions creates rents and those rents are conveniently split by Nash bargaining. In this very flexible method of splitting

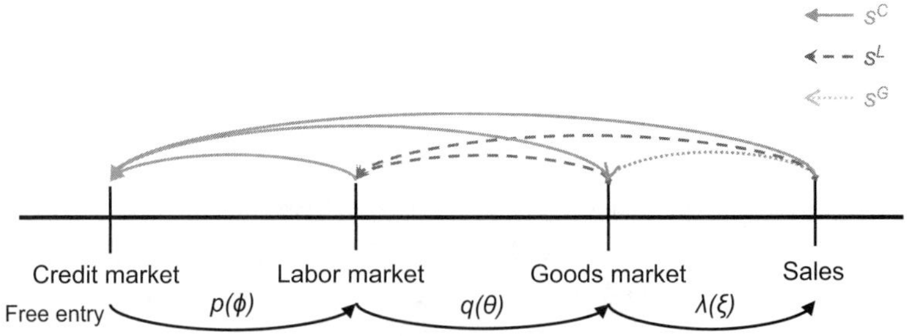

Figure 7.1
Timing and transitions in CLG model

rents, simply varying the bargaining parameter α_j, where $j = C, L, G$, between 0 and 1, one can reach all possible solutions ranging from the reservation value of the project ($\alpha_j = 1$) to the reservation value of its bargaining partner ($\alpha_j = 0$). Again, alternative rules for prices, wages and interest-rates are possible, and some are discussed along the way.

The dynamic equations and the steady-state values of the stocks can be found in the appendix. They are a combination of those in the CL and LG models. In particular, the number of job vacancies, that is, the amount of firms in the labor market search stage, $\mathcal{V}$, is also the number of creditors in stage v, $\mathcal{B}_v$. That is, $\mathcal{V} = \mathcal{N}_v = \mathcal{B}_v$. The stock-flow equations for a vacancy in the labor market are

$$d\mathcal{B}_v/dt = \phi p(\phi)\mathcal{B}_c - q(\theta)\mathcal{V} + s^L(\mathcal{B}_g + \mathcal{B}_\pi) \tag{7.38}$$
$$d\mathcal{V}/dt = p(\phi)\mathcal{N}_c - (q(\theta) + s^C)\mathcal{V} + s^L(\mathcal{N}_g + \mathcal{N}_\pi) \tag{7.39}$$

We proceed immediately with the Bellman equations of the entity made of the match between the creditor and the project. Let J_v, J_g, and J_π be the respective steady-state asset values of the project–creditor block, that we called a firm in chapter 5:

$$rJ_v = -\gamma + q(J_g - J_v) + s^C(J_c - J_v) \tag{7.40}$$
$$rJ_g = -w_g + \lambda(J_\pi - J_g) + s^C(J_c - J_g) + s^L(J_v - J_g) \tag{7.41}$$
$$rJ_\pi = x\mathcal{P} - w_\pi + s^C(J_c - J_\pi) + s^G(J_g - J_\pi) + s^L(J_v - J_\pi) \tag{7.42}$$

Note that we assume that the credit match termination shock can also arrive during the labor search stage. Firms may lose their consumer due to the taste shock τ but also due to the income shock in the consumer's own firm with rate $s^C + s^L$. Hence the capital loss $J_g - J_\pi$ occurs at rate $s^G = \tau + s^L + s^C$.

7.4.1 Job creation condition and equilibrium

Maintaining the assumption of free entry in the credit market, as in chapter 5, the value of a job opening, or the labor search stage, is equal to the average financial market search cost of both parties in forming a credit market match: $J_v = K(\phi) = \frac{\kappa_I}{p(\phi)} + \frac{\kappa_B}{\phi p(\phi)}$. In addition, free entry in the credit market implies that we still have $\phi^* = \frac{\kappa_B}{\kappa_I}\frac{1-\alpha_C}{\alpha_C}$. The assumptions on the goods markets imply that $\xi^* = 1$.

The equilibrium is a simple generalization of chapter 5 and the previous sections. We introduce turnover shocks arising from bankruptcies, denoted by s^C. The new discounted rate of capacity utilization, and the average wage are:

$$\mu_r^{CLG} = \frac{\lambda}{r + s^C + s^L + s^G + \lambda} \tag{7.43}$$
$$\bar{w} = \mu_r^{CLG} w_\pi + (1 - \mu_r^{CLG}) w_g \tag{7.44}$$

One can keep the notation for the annuity cost of search in financial markets: $k(\phi) = (r + s^C)K$. The new job creation condition and summary of the model are:

Summary of the equilibrium in the CLG model:

$$\text{Credit market tightness:} \quad \phi^* = \frac{\kappa_B}{\kappa_I} \frac{1 - \alpha_C}{\alpha_C} \tag{7.45}$$

$$\text{Labor market tightness:} \quad \frac{\gamma_k}{q(\phi^*)} = \frac{x^{CLG}\mathcal{P} - \bar{w}}{r + s^C + s^L} \tag{7.46}$$

$$\text{Goods market tightness:} \quad \xi^* = 1 \tag{7.47}$$

with

$$\text{Adjusted productivity:} \quad x^{CLG} = \mu_r^{CLG} x - k(\phi) = \frac{\lambda}{r + s^G + s^L + \lambda} x - k(\phi)$$

$$\text{Adjusted entry costs:} \quad \gamma_k = \gamma + k(\phi)$$

$$\text{Average wage:} \quad \bar{w} = \mu_r^{CLG} w_\pi + (1 - \mu_r^{CLG}) w_g$$

$$\text{Entry costs in the credit market:} \quad k(\phi) = (r + s^C)K(\phi) = (r + s^C)\left(\frac{\kappa_I}{p(\phi)} + \frac{\kappa_B}{\phi p(\phi)}\right)$$

Equation 7.46 states that entry costs are the sum of labor search costs and the annuitized value of financial costs $K(\phi)$, and that they are equal to the properly discounted streams of profits net of (again) the annuitized value of financial costs. Equation (7.46) is the most compact and the most comparable to the standard Pissarides model. It however has another form where the different entry costs are easier to decompose. We had such an expression in the CL model, in equation (5.18), and in equation (7.21) for the LG model. In the CLG model, this expression is now

$$\left(1 + \frac{r + s^C}{q}\right)K + \frac{\gamma}{q} + \frac{1}{1 - Q_\pi Q_g}\left(\frac{w_g - s^L K}{r + s^C + s^L + \lambda}\right)$$
$$= \frac{Q_g}{1 - Q_\pi Q_g}\left(\frac{x\mathcal{P} - w_\pi + s^L K}{r + s^T}\right) \tag{7.48}$$

where $Q_g = \lambda/(r + s^C + s^L + \lambda)$, $Q_\pi = s^G/(r + s^T)$, and $s^T = s^L + s^C + s^G$. On the left-hand side are the three different entry costs due to credit market frictions (the term $\left(1 + \frac{r+s^C}{q}\right)K$), to labor market frictions (γ/q), and to goods markets frictions comprised of the loss of revenue and the cost of labor while searching for consumers (the term $\frac{1}{1-Q_\pi Q_g}\left(\frac{w_g - s^L K}{r+s^C+s^L+\lambda}\right)$). The term $s^L K$ in the latter expression reflects that labor turnover leads to recovering K as the credit relationship is not undone, which alleviates the cost of having an employee in stage g.

7.4.2 Price, wage, and payments to creditors

The prices in all three markets, the repayment to the creditor ψ, the wage to the worker w, and the price for the good $\mathcal{P}$, are derived in the same manner as in the earlier respective subsections. In particular, given that $\check{\lambda} = \lambda$ when $\xi = 1$, the price equation remains a simple rule, as in the LG model, that is a function of the marginal utility of the search good, Φ (see the chapter and general appendices):

$$\mathcal{P} = (1 - \alpha_G)\Phi \tag{7.49}$$

Wages now incorporate the value of recoverable search costs in the financial markets, $K(\phi)$:

$$w = (1-\alpha_L)(rW_u - \bar{y}) + \alpha_L[\mathcal{P}x - k(\phi)] + \frac{\alpha_L - \alpha_G}{1-\alpha_G} x^{CLG}\mathcal{P} \tag{7.50}$$

The wage converges to the wage in chapter 5 in the CL model when goods market frictions disappear ($\lambda \to \infty$ and $\alpha_G = 0$), to the wage in the LG model when financial frictions disappear ($K \to 0$), and to the conventional Pissarides wage when both goods and financial frictions disappear. Finally, the repayment to the creditor, which solves the problem $\psi = \text{argmax}\,(B_v - B_c)^{\alpha_C}(E_v - E_c)^{1-\alpha_C}$, is now:

$$\frac{\psi}{r+s^T} = \alpha_C \frac{x\mathcal{P} - w_\pi}{r+s^T} + (1-\alpha_C)\left(\frac{1 - Q_g Q_\pi}{Q_g}\frac{\gamma}{q(\theta)} + \frac{w_g}{\lambda}\right)$$

7.4.3 Efficiency in the CLG model

The efficiency results exposed in section 7.3 can be generalized easily, as the dichotomy between the financial market block and the other two blocks (labor and goods) leads to a simple additional Hosios efficiency conditions.

The social planner now maximizes

$$\Omega^{SP} = \int_0^{\infty} e^{-rt}\left[D_m \Phi x + z\mathcal{U} - \gamma \mathcal{V} - \kappa_B \mathcal{B}_c - \kappa_I \mathcal{N}_c\right] dt$$

deciding on the masses of searchers on both sides of the credit market, $\mathcal{B}_c$ and $\mathcal{N}_c$. As shown in the appendix, optimality solves for the socially optimal level of credit market tightness, ϕ^{opt}:

$$\phi^{opt} = \frac{1-\eta_C}{\eta_C}\frac{\kappa_B}{\kappa_I} \tag{7.51}$$

This recovers the Hosios condition in credit markets already discussed in chapter 5. Still in the appendix, the derivation of the optimal level of labor market tightness yields:

Social planner's job creation condition in the CLG model:

$$\frac{\left[\Phi x \mu_r^{CLG} - k(\phi^{opt}) - z\right](1-\eta_L) - \gamma_k^{opt}\eta_L\theta^{opt}}{r + s^C + s^L} = \frac{\gamma_k^{opt}}{q(\theta^{opt})}$$

with $\gamma_k^{opt} = \gamma + k(\phi^{opt})$ and $k(\phi) = (r + s^C)K(\phi)$.

leading to the same Hosios condition on the labor market as in the LG model, that is, $\alpha_L = \eta_L$, $\alpha_C = \eta_C$, and once again, α_G is irrelevant to the result.

7.5 Extending the CLG model to endogenous effort

The steady state of the LG and CLG models implies that goods market tightness is equal to 1. This property leads to recursiveness of the solution of the three blocks and simplifies the exposition. However, a desirable feature for business cycle analysis is a rate of capacity utilization that varies with productivity and demand shocks. This can be achieved with a simple extension to an endogenous effort by consumers searching in the goods market. This provides one more margin of adjustment that will be important in the next chapter on the dynamic implications of goods market frictions.

Denote consumer's effort by e, at a utility cost $\sigma_G(e)$ with elasticity $\eta_{\sigma_G} > 1$, and an average effort in the population of unmatched consumers $\bar{e}$. The transition probabilities in the goods market are

$$\begin{aligned}
\text{Individual consumers: } & \left(\tfrac{e}{\bar{e}}\right) \frac{\mathcal{M}_G(\bar{e}\mathcal{D}_U,\mathcal{N}_g)}{\mathcal{D}_U} = \left(\tfrac{e}{\bar{e}}\right) \mathcal{M}_G\left(\bar{e}, 1/\xi\right) = \left(\tfrac{e}{\bar{e}}\right) \check{\lambda}\left(\xi, \bar{e}\right) \\
\text{Firms: } & \mathcal{M}_G(\bar{e}\mathcal{D}_U,\mathcal{N}_g)/\mathcal{N}_g = \mathcal{M}_G(\bar{e}\xi, 1) = \lambda(\xi, \bar{e}) \\
& = \xi \mathcal{M}_G(\bar{e}, 1/\xi) \\
\text{with } & \partial\lambda/\partial\xi > 0 \text{ and } \partial\lambda/\partial\bar{e} > 0
\end{aligned}$$

Stock-flow equations are unchanged, except that aggregate matching in the goods market is now $\mathcal{M}_G(\bar{e}\mathcal{D}_U,\mathcal{N}_g)$. The steady state implied by the equations leads to the same fixed point property, that is

$$\xi = \frac{s^T + \lambda(\xi, \bar{e})}{s^T + \lambda(\xi, \bar{e})/\xi}$$

which retains the convenient result that $\xi = 1$, and therefore that $\check{\lambda}(1, \bar{e}) = \lambda(1, \bar{e})$. The remainder of the model is easy to derive. The Bellman equation of unmatched consumers is modified to account for effort and its cost:

$$\begin{aligned}
rW_{D_U} &= w + \bar{y} - \sigma_G(e) + \left(\frac{e}{\bar{e}}\right) \check{\lambda}\left(\xi, \bar{e}\right) \left(W_{D_M} - W_{D_U}\right) \\
&\quad + \left(s^L + s^C\right) \left(W_U - W_{D_U}\right)
\end{aligned} \tag{7.52}$$

which leads to a first-order condition for consumer effort:

$$\bar{e}\sigma_G'(e) = \check{\lambda}(\xi, \bar{e}) \left(W_{D_M} - W_{D_U}\right)$$

which states that consumer search effort is increasing in the surplus in the goods market:

$$W_{D_M} - W_{D_U} = \frac{\Phi x - \mathcal{P}x + \sigma_G(e)}{r + s^T + \lambda(\xi, e)}$$

Combining the two equations, it is apparent that consumer effort positively depends on the utility for the good, and negatively on the price. The solution for the Nash-bargained price is now slightly modified and depends on effort:

$$\mathcal{P}x = (1 - \alpha_G) \left[\Phi x + \sigma_G(e)\right] \tag{7.53}$$

while, along similar lines, the wage is obtained as

$$\begin{aligned}
w &= (1 - \alpha_L) \left(z + \sigma_G(e)\right) + \alpha_L \left(\gamma + k(\phi)\right) \theta \\
&\quad + \left(\frac{\alpha_L - \alpha_G}{1 - \alpha_G}\right) \mu^{CLG} \mathcal{P}x - \alpha_L k(\phi)
\end{aligned} \tag{7.54}$$

Finally, the entry equation determining job creation is unchanged from equation (7.46), but prices and wages now follow (7.53) and (7.54). Replacing the price by its bargained value, and combining the consumer surplus with optimal effort leads, to a simple expression which determines search effort:

$$\left(\frac{\eta_{\sigma G}}{\mu_r^{CLG}} - \alpha_G\right)\sigma_G(\bar{e}) = \alpha_G \Phi x$$

Under standard assumptions consumer search effort depends positively on x, and also on the marginal utility from the good x. To see this, replace the rate of capacity utilization μ_r^{CLG} by its definition to obtain $\sigma(\bar{e})\left[\left(1+\frac{r+s^T}{\lambda(1,\bar{e})}\right)\eta_{\sigma G} - \alpha_G\right] = \alpha_G \Phi x$. Since the elasticity of λ to effort is less than 1, and the elasticity of the cost (iso-elastic) function is larger than 1, the left-hand side is increasing in effort. Therefore, consumer search effort is pro-cyclical.

7.6 Discussion of the literature and remaining issues

A recent strand of literature has revived the original ideas of the search literature where consumers needed to search in the goods market in order to consume (e.g., Diamond, 1971, 1982). Diamond (1982) assumed that two consumers were needed to consume indivisible units of good (the coconuts). Diamond (1971) instead assumed two sides in the market, consumers and sellers. Only consumers searched for different shops. Shops were located in different places. The striking result of Diamond (1971) was that prices would converge to the monopsony price even with infinitely small search costs. In this chapter, we adopt a similar logic and introduce consumers and sellers linked through a new matching function in the goods market. This follows Wasmer (2009), Petrosky-Nadeau and Wasmer (2011), Bai et al. (2011), and Michaillat and Saez (2014). An early attempt to integrate goods and labor frictions with money is in Shi (1998). Optimal fiscal and monetary policy is investigated with goods market frictions in Arseneau et al. (2015) with in particular a full discussion of the relative size of the Walrasian good and the frictional good in a dynamic setting.

The discussion on the cyclical properties of search margins and their pro-cyclicality has been done in Hall (2012) for advertising, and in Petrosky-Nadeau et al. (2016) for an empirical test of the pro-cyclicality of search effort by consumers. Their conclusions are in contrast with

Kaplan and Menzio (2016) whose result depends on consumer search effort rising in recessions.

The main assumption made here of a Walrasian good absorbing the excess liquidity when agents do not access the search good is a convenient one, not a necessarily realistic one. Goods 0 (frictionless) and 1 (frictional) resemble very much the night-and-day market in the search and money literature (Lagos and Wright, 2005; Nosal and Rocheteau, 2011). When the frictionless market opens in these models, any excess liquidity is absorbed so that agents start the next day being ex ante identical. This simplifies quite substantially the analysis and keeps the model tractable. Interesting applications to the money market can be found in Lehmann and Van der Linden (2010), to the housing market in Branch et al. (2014), and to inflation and unemployment in Berentsen et al. (2011). The latter incorporates various frictions as well as monetary policy and studies the long-run relation between monetary dimensions (inflation or interest rates) and unemployment. Bethune et al. (2015) study the relationship between the availability of unsecured credit to households and unemployment. In their model with a search frictional goods market consumers need credit for some trades. Relaxing limits on unsecured credit, in their environment, creates more demand in the goods market, and greater profit margins for firms who hire more labor.

Another important discussion is the interpretation given to $\bar{y}$, the fixed supply of the nonfrictional good, which relaxes the constraint on the consumption side and avoids the trivial equilibrium with no market production of the search good. Alternative assumptions exist that address the same issue of the consumer's resource constraint. For instance idle firms, which cannot yet sell and therefore decide not to produce the frictional good 1, may use their workers to produce $\bar{y}$ units of a Walrasian good. In this case, the total additional resources flowing to the economy would be $\mathcal{N}_g\bar{y}$. Another alternative is to suppose a public sector that can transform lump-sum taxes T into a public good as $G = T(1+m)$, where $m > 0$, and that this public good is a perfect substitute with the Walrasian good 0. If the public good is redistributed lump sum, the net gain in terms of aggregate resources is mT. A last possible assumption, more in the spirit of a static Keynesian model, is a monetary injection such as a helicopter drop of money that generates additional resources, M, redistributed lump sum to the consumers. These alternative assumptions can be developed to address the role of policy instruments on the efficiency of the allocations.

A calibration of the CLG model to three European economies (Germany, the UK, and Spain), and a decomposition of the three parts of the entry equation (7.48) has been done in Brzustowski et al. (2017). It shows that labor entry costs represent a relatively low share of total entry costs, around 15% of total entry costs. This, per se, is a good justification of the CLG approach. However, varying the labor market efficiency parameter has powerful effects on the rate of unemployment. Contrary to financial costs or goods market frictions, which strongly impact wages, labor market frictions leave wage curves unchanged and mostly affect labor demand. This in turn justifies the labor matching approach to the labor market: despite a small share in entry costs, hiring costs have a large effect on unemployment. This is not the case for entry costs in goods and credit markets.

Finally and most importantly, the model features aggregate demand externalities. When profits go down exogenously, fewer workers are employed in the steady state, and firms therefore face fewer consumers, amplifying the initial decline in employment. When these consumption multipliers are due to fiscal shocks as in next chapter, they are fiscal multipliers. In the steady-state context of this chapter, the consumption multiplier is estimated around 1.2 in Brzustowski et al. (2017). This type of demand externality has a long history in economics but has led to renewed interest from different traditions, as in Schaal and Taschereau-Dumouchel (2016) in a dynamic setup with monopolistically competitive firms, or in Kaplan and Menzio (2016) in a search framework, each of them dealing with multiple equilibria.

7.7 Chapter appendix

7.7.1 Documenting consumption flows in CLG

The circular flows of income in the economy

The firm receives a unit price $\mathcal{P}$ from the consumer in exchange of x units of good 1 produced. The good produced is assumed to be indivisible: it must be fully consumed by the consumer. In this chapter, x must therefore be interpreted as *quality of the good*, entering the utility function of the consumer. The consumer must, in addition, have the resources at the time of the meeting with the firm to pay for the price $\mathcal{P}$. No credit is allowed to customers.

At each point in time there is a mass $\mu^{LG}(1-\mathcal{U}) = \mu^{LG}\mathcal{N}$ of firms in stage π that is both producing and selling. In the aggregate, firms generate gross revenues $\mu^{LG}\mathcal{N}\mathcal{P}x$, and have total wage and search costs $\left[\mu^{LG}w_\pi + (1-\mu^{LG})w_g\right]\mathcal{N} + \gamma\mathcal{V}$. A fraction μ_G of firms pay the wage w_π, while the other firms pay the wage w_g. The difference between gross revenues and costs, the net revenues generated by firms in this economy, is rebated to unemployed workers as well as employed workers. Denote by $\mathcal{K}_U$ and $\mathcal{K}_W$ the dividends received by, respectively, the unemployed and employed. The total amount of resources accruing to employed and unemployed workers is equal to

$$\mathcal{K}_U + \mathcal{K}_W = \mu^{LG}\mathcal{N}\mathcal{P}x - \left[\mu^{LG}w_\pi + (1-\mu^{LG})w_g\right]\mathcal{N} - \gamma\mathcal{V}$$

The aggregate net income of consumers, in the absence of other transfers and additional resources, is therefore:

Aggregate net income of consumers:
$\mu^{LG}\mathcal{N}\mathcal{P}x - \gamma\mathcal{V} - \mathcal{K}_U$

These total resources available to consumers, it is important to note here, are always below the total revenue of the firms $\mu^{LG}\mathcal{N}\mathcal{P}x$. There are three sources of dissipation of revenues: (i) search frictions in the labor market (the term $\gamma\mathcal{V}$); (ii) search frictions in the goods market (the term $\mu^{LG} \leq 1$); and (iii) the fact that some of the profits of the firms are not returned to the consumers of good 1 (the term $-\mathcal{K}_U$ going to the unemployed). It follows that, in the absence of an additional source of income for consumers, the economy would collapse to a home production economy with no frictional goods produced and sold. Both $\mathcal{P}$ and $\mathcal{V}$ would be equal to zero in equilibrium.

Transfers and Lucas trees

Consumers must therefore produce or receive additional resources for a nontrivial equilibrium to exist. These resources are expressed in terms of the Walrasian good 0. We assume that both the employed and the unemployed agents receive the fruits (in Walrasian good) of a Lucas tree growing in their individual garden. Each agent is endowed in each unit of time a quantity $\bar{y}$ of additional resources. Hence, total disposable income of employed workers is now:

Aggregate disposable income of consumers:
$\left(\mu^{LG}\mathcal{P}x + \bar{y}\right)\mathcal{N} - \gamma\mathcal{V} - \mathcal{K}_U \lesseqgtr \mu^{LG}\mathcal{N}\mathcal{P}x$

As said earlier, in the absence of the Lucas tree, consumers' aggregate gross income is below the value of the sales of good 1, $\mathcal{N}_\pi\mathcal{P}x$. Consumers would be unable to purchase the search good. A nondegenerate equilibrium thus requires a positive and large enough value of $\bar{y}$ so that a nontrivial equilibrium exists. In fact, this endowment must be greater than the sum of labor search costs and the share of dividends accruing to the unemployed, $\gamma\mathcal{V} + \mathcal{K}_U$. This is a significant departure from Walrasian goods markets. We follow this assumption in the remainder of the chapter, and in the next chapters. Finally, note that if income were taxed, $\bar{y}$ would represent in a compact way the sum of a positive term, the Lucas fruit, and a negative term, the taxation of the income.

Utility, individual and aggregate consumption

The utility function of consumers depends on the consumption of both goods 1 and 0, and of leisure denoted by l. It is denoted by $v(c^1, c^0, l)$ where the first input is consumption of the search good, the second of the Walrasian good, and the third leisure. Denote by $c^0_{D_U}$ and $c^0_{D_M}$ the consumption of the Walrasian good by, respectively, the *employed unmatched* with a search good and the *employed matched* with a search good. We normalize leisure so that employed workers consume no leisure, and unemployed workers may consume up to a fixed quantity of leisure denoted by z. Unmatched consumers are employed and therefore have no leisure, and a flow utility $v(0, c^0_{D_U}, 0)$. Matched consumers have a flow utility $v(x, c^0_{D_M}, 0)$.

The viability of the search economy requires that consumers prefer the frictional good to the Walrasian good, otherwise they would not search for good 1. The equilibrium must therefore be such that

$$v(x, c^0_{D_M}) > v(0, c^0_{D_U})$$

The unemployed can transform part or all of their leisure endowment z into additional production of the Walrasian good. Denote by d this fraction transformed into Walrasian good, which might be smaller or larger than 1 (in the latter case the unemployed would enjoy negative leisure, that is exert more effort than the employed workers). They therefore supply $zd + \bar{y}$ units of good 0, and receive in turn a flow utility $v(0, \bar{y} + zd, z(1-d))$. Under the additional assumption that leisure and consumption of good 0 are additively separable in the utility function, the value of d is irrelevant hereafter in the utility of the unemployed. However, as shown below, this value matters to equalize the demand and supply of Walrasian good.

Since it is assumed there is no saving, or pooling of income across individuals, a consumer not matched with a search good spends his disposable income w on the Walrasian good. Thus $c^0_{D_U} = w + \bar{y}$. Matched consumers must sacrifice some consumption of the essential good in order to buy the search good. Thus the consumption of good 0 of a matched consumer is $c^0_{D_M} = c^0_{D_U} - \mathcal{P}x = \bar{y} + w - \mathcal{P}x$.

We denote by $C^1 = x\mathcal{D}_M$ the aggregate consumption of search good 1. The aggregate consumption of good 0, C^0, is the sum of individual consumptions of the unemployed, of the unmatched consumers and of the matched consumers $(\mathcal{U} + \mathcal{D}_U)\bar{y} + \mathcal{D}_U w + \mathcal{D}_M(\bar{y} + w - \mathcal{P}x)$. It must furthermore be equal to the supply of Walrasian good $dz\mathcal{U} + \bar{y}$. This leads to

$$C^0 = (\mathcal{U} + \mathcal{D}_U)\bar{y} + \mathcal{D}_U w + \mathcal{D}_M(\bar{y} + w - \mathcal{P}x) = dz\mathcal{U} + \bar{y}$$

Using $\mathcal{U} + \mathcal{D}_U + \mathcal{D}_M = 1$, this equality implies $\mathcal{D}_U w + \mathcal{D}_M(w - \mathcal{P}x) = zd\mathcal{U}$ or, equivalently,

$$\mathcal{N}w - \mathcal{D}_M\mathcal{P}x = zd\mathcal{U}$$

The labor revenue of workers, netted from their expenditures of good 1, are devoted to purchasing Walrasian good, which is produced from the transformation of leisure of the unemployed. This equation states that the revenue from firms net of expenses into the search good are spent into the supplementary Walrasian good provided by the transformation of leisure of the unemployed. Therefore, d adjusts to equalize demand and supply of Walrasian good. It is important to note that, once the fraction d of leisure is transformed into a Walrasian good to equalize demand and supply, its value disappears from the rest of the model. Only z will affect the equilibrium wages, and therefore labor market tightness. Hereafter, d does not need to be made explicit in the model when utility of agents is linear, but its value is such that the demand and supply of Walrasian good are always in equilibrium.

7.7.2 Stock-flow equations in the CLG model

In this part, we assume from the start the existence of credit shocks leading to the destruction of the firm in stages g and π. The stock-flow equations relevant for the CL model are obtained from setting $s^C = 0$. In this context, stocks evolve as follows.

The stock of firms in stage π receives the matches created in the goods market $\lambda\mathcal{N}_g$, and loses the firms in stage π losing their workers $s^L\mathcal{N}_\pi$, the consumers quitting the good $s^G\mathcal{N}_\pi$, and finally the firms destroyed by credit shocks $s^C\mathcal{D}_M$. The stock of firms in stage g receives the hirings $\mathcal{M}_L$ and the firms losing their clients $s^G\mathcal{N}_\pi$, loses the matches created in the goods market $\lambda\mathcal{N}_g$ and loses the firms in stage g losing their workers $s^L\mathcal{N}_g$ as well as those hit by a credit shock $s^C\mathcal{N}_g$. The stock of matched consumers increases with the matches created in the goods market $\check{\lambda}\mathcal{D}_U$, loses the matched consumers who lost their job $s^L\mathcal{D}_M$, loses the consumers whose firms lost their workers $s^L\mathcal{D}_M = \left(s^G - \tau\right)\mathcal{D}_M$, and loses the consumers who changed taste $\tau\mathcal{D}_M$. The stock of unmatched consumers loses the matches created in the goods market $\check{\lambda}\mathcal{D}_U$, gains the matches created in the labor market $\mathcal{M}_L$, gains the consumers whose firms lost their workers $s^L\mathcal{D}_M$, loses the unmatched consumers who lost their job $s^L\mathcal{D}_U$, and gains the consumers who changed taste $\tau\mathcal{D}_M$. Finally, the pool of unemployed workers loses the matches created in the labor market $\mathcal{M}_L$, and gains the job losses $s^L(1-\mathcal{U})$, which arise, from the firm side, from firms in stage π losing their workers $s^L\mathcal{N}_\pi$ and firms in stage g losing their workers $s^L\mathcal{N}_g$, or from matched consumers losing their job $s^L\mathcal{D}_M$ or from unmatched consumers losing their job $s^L\mathcal{D}_U$:

$$\frac{\partial\mathcal{N}_\pi}{\partial t} = \underbrace{\lambda\mathcal{N}_g}_{\text{matches G}} - \underbrace{s^L\mathcal{N}_\pi}_{\text{lost workers}} - \underbrace{s^G\mathcal{N}_\pi}_{\text{lost customers}} - \underbrace{s^C\mathcal{N}_\pi}_{\text{credit shock}} \tag{7.55}$$

$$\frac{\partial\mathcal{N}_g}{\partial t} = \underbrace{\mathcal{M}_L(\mathcal{U},\mathcal{V})}_{\text{matches L}} + \underbrace{s^G\mathcal{N}_\pi}_{\text{lost customers}} - \underbrace{\lambda\mathcal{N}_g}_{\text{matches G}} - \underbrace{s^L\mathcal{N}_g}_{\text{lost workers}} - \underbrace{s^C\mathcal{N}_g}_{\text{credit shock}} \tag{7.56}$$

$$\begin{aligned}\frac{\partial\mathcal{D}_M}{\partial t} = {} & \underbrace{\check{\lambda}\mathcal{D}_U}_{\text{matches G}} - \underbrace{s^L\mathcal{D}_M}_{\text{seller loses worker}} - \underbrace{s^C\mathcal{D}_M}_{\text{seller hit by a credit shock}} \\ & - \underbrace{s^L\mathcal{D}_M}_{\text{matched consumer loses job}} - \underbrace{\tau\mathcal{D}_M}_{\text{matched consumer changes tastes}}\end{aligned} \tag{7.57}$$

$$\begin{aligned}\frac{\partial\mathcal{D}_U}{\partial t} = {} & \underbrace{-\check{\lambda}\mathcal{D}_U}_{\text{matches G}} + \underbrace{\tau\mathcal{D}_M}_{\text{matched consumer changed tastes}} + \underbrace{\mathcal{M}_L(\mathcal{U},\mathcal{V})}_{\text{matches L}} \\ & + \underbrace{s^L\mathcal{D}_M}_{\text{seller loses worker}} + \underbrace{s^C\mathcal{D}_M}_{\text{seller hit by a credit shock}} \\ & - \underbrace{s^L\mathcal{D}_U}_{\text{unmatched consumer loses job}}\end{aligned} \tag{7.58}$$

$$\begin{aligned}\frac{\partial\mathcal{U}}{\partial t} &= -\mathcal{M}_L(\mathcal{U},\mathcal{V}) + \left(s^L + s^C\right)(1-\mathcal{U}) = -\mathcal{M}_L(\mathcal{U},\mathcal{V}) + (s^L + s^C)\left(\mathcal{N}_\pi + \mathcal{N}_g\right) \\ &= -\mathcal{M}_L(\mathcal{U},\mathcal{V}) + \left(s^L + s^C\right)(\mathcal{D}_M + \mathcal{D}_U)\end{aligned} \tag{7.59}$$

One can easily verify that $\partial \mathcal{N}_\pi/\partial t + \partial \mathcal{N}_g/\partial t + \partial \mathcal{U}/\partial t = 0$ and that $\partial \mathcal{D}_M/\partial t + \partial \mathcal{D}_U/\partial t + \partial \mathcal{U}/\partial t = 0$ at the same time. Hereafter, since it does not play an important role, we assume that the rate of taste changes τ is equal to zero.

7.7.3 Bellman equations in the LG model and free entry

Let J_v, J_g, and J_π be the respective steady-state asset values of a firm in each period (labor stage, goods stage, profit). We have

$$rJ_v = -\gamma + q(J_g - J_v) \tag{7.60}$$

$$rJ_g = -w_g + \lambda(J_\pi - J_g) + s^L(J_v - J_g) \tag{7.61}$$

$$rJ_\pi = x\mathcal{P} - w_\pi + s^L(J_v - J_\pi) + s^G(J_g - J_\pi) \tag{7.62}$$

Under free entry of both firms and creditors, we have

$$J_v = 0 \Rightarrow J_g = \gamma/q$$

$$J_g = \frac{-w_g + \lambda J_\pi}{r + s^L + \lambda} = \left(\frac{-w_g}{\lambda} + J_\pi\right) Q_g$$

$$J_\pi = \left(\frac{x\mathcal{P} - w_\pi}{s^G} + J_g\right) Q_\pi$$

with $Q_\lambda = \frac{\lambda}{r+s^L+\lambda}$ and $Q_G = \frac{s^G}{r+s^L+s^G}$. The last two equations combined deliver

$$J_\pi = \left(\frac{x\mathcal{P} - w_\pi}{s^G} + \left(\frac{-w_g}{\lambda} + J_\pi\right) Q_g\right) Q_\pi \Leftrightarrow J_\pi\left(1 - Q_g Q_\pi\right) = Q_\pi \frac{x\mathcal{P} - w}{s^G} + Q_\pi Q_g \left(\frac{-w_g}{\lambda}\right)$$

$$J_g = \left(\frac{-w_g}{\lambda} Q_g + \left(\frac{x\mathcal{P} - w_\pi}{r + s^L + s^G} + Q_\pi J_g\right) Q_g\right) \Leftrightarrow J_g = \frac{\frac{-w_g}{\lambda} Q_g + \left(\frac{x\mathcal{P} - w_\pi}{r+s^L+s^G}\right) Q_g}{1 - Q_g Q_\pi}$$

This equation says that the value of prospecting in the goods market is the negative of the expected value of the cost of paying the wage (first term), plus the expected value of the discounted profits minus—again—the future costs of being inactive and repaying wages with no profits in case consumers later on dislike the good produced.

The value of J_g is positive if

$$\frac{x\mathcal{P} - w_\pi}{r + s^L + s^G} > \frac{w_g}{\lambda}$$

7.7.4 The viability of the decentralized LG economy

Viability of the goods market: the circular income flows

Can workers afford the search good at the negotiating wage? Consider first the simple case $\alpha_L = \alpha_G$ and $\bar{y} = 0$. This implies

$$w > x\mathcal{P}$$

But, firms in stage π must make strictly profits: hence, $x\mathcal{P} > w$. Both cannot be simultaneously true. Formally, for the value of entry to be positive, one needs $J_g > 0$. One can show that, reintroducing the notations w_g and w_π to clearly see the timing of wage payments,

$$J_g > 0 \Leftrightarrow \frac{x\mathcal{P} - w_\pi}{r + s^L + s^G} > \frac{w_g}{\lambda} \Leftrightarrow x\mathcal{P} > w_\pi + \left(\frac{r + s^L + s^G}{\lambda}\right) w_g$$
$$= w\left(\frac{r + s^L + s^G + \lambda}{\lambda}\right)$$

where the second term in the inequality is how much the revenue must be above the current wage w_π to compensate for the initial losses in stage g. Hence, in the absence of the term $\bar{y}$, no circular flow of income is sustainable. For sustainability, the following condition must hold:

$$w + \bar{y} > x\mathcal{P} > w\left(1 + \frac{r + s^L + s^G}{\lambda}\right)$$

The first part of the inequality states that the purchasing power of the worker must be augmented by $\bar{y}$ in order for the customer to acquire the good. The second part of the inequality says that the revenue of the firm must be enough to pay workers the wage they demand. Then, this implies that

$$\bar{y} > (1 - \alpha_G)\Phi x - (1 - \alpha_L)z - \alpha_L \gamma\theta - (\alpha_L - \alpha_G)\frac{\lambda}{r + s^L + s^G + \lambda}\Phi x$$

$$\bar{y} > \left((1 - \alpha_G) + (\alpha_L - \alpha_G)\frac{\lambda}{r + s^L + s^G + \lambda}\right)\Phi x - (1 - \alpha_L)z - \alpha_L\gamma\theta \tag{7.63}$$

For instance, with $\alpha_L = \alpha_G$, this implies

$$\bar{y} > (1 - \alpha_G)(\Phi x - z) - \gamma\alpha_L\gamma\theta > \frac{r + s^L + s^G}{\lambda} w \tag{7.64}$$

Viability of the assumption that only employed workers consume
The unemployed have been assumed not to search for the Walrasian good. For this to be true, a condition is that

$$\bar{y} < x\mathcal{P} = (1 - \alpha_G)\Phi x \tag{7.65}$$

which is compatible with inequalities (7.63) or (7.64). However, there is one more issue. Firms may want to cut down prices in order to sell the unemployed. In such a world where the unemployed may consume, the only source of consumption separation s^G disappears since losing one's job leads to continued consumption. In that case, the surplus from consumption for the unemployed would be $W_{u1} - W_{u0}$ where

$$rW_{u0} = z + \bar{y} + \check{\lambda}(W_{u1} - W_{u0}) + f(\theta)(W_{D_U} - W_{u0}) \tag{7.66}$$
$$rW_{u1} = \Phi x + (z + \bar{y} - \mathcal{P}_u x) + f(\theta)(W_{D_M} - W_{u1}) + s^L(W_{u0} - W_{u1}) \tag{7.67}$$

A conjecture is that, under linear utility, the unemployed consuming face the same surplus of consumption as the employees; this would lead to a single price for all consumers. Another conjecture is that tightness in the goods market is presumably augmented by the presence of additional consumers. In that case, the new price would be larger than the price $\mathcal{P}$ in the benchmark economy. This would imply that inequality (7.65) is a sufficient condition for avoiding the unemployed to consume, as it prevents a new equilibrium to occur. These two conjectures are studied in next section and will be proven true.

Efficiency in LG

Start from the social planner's program:

$$\begin{aligned} H = \max_{\mathcal{V},\mathcal{U},\mathcal{D}_U} \quad & e^{-rt}\left[(1-\mathcal{U}-\mathcal{D}_U)\,\Phi x + z\mathcal{U} - \gamma\mathcal{V}\right] \\ & +\Psi_U\left[-M_L(\mathcal{U},\mathcal{V}) + s^L(1-\mathcal{U})\right] \\ & +\Psi_{D_U}\left[-M_G(\mathcal{D}_U,\mathcal{D}_U) + s^G(1-\mathcal{U}-\mathcal{D}_U) - s^L\mathcal{D}_U + M_L(\mathcal{U},\mathcal{V})\right] \end{aligned}$$

The first-order conditions already in the text can be simplified:

$$\begin{aligned} \frac{\partial H}{\partial \mathcal{V}} &= 0 = -\gamma e^{-rt} + (-\Psi_U + \Psi_{D_U})(1-\eta_L)q \\ \mathring{\Psi}_U = -\frac{\partial H}{\partial \mathcal{U}} &= (\Phi x - z).e^{-rt} + (\Psi_U - \Psi_{D_U})(\eta_L f) + s^L\Psi_U + s^G\Psi_{D_U} \\ \mathring{\Psi}_{D_U} = -\frac{\partial H}{\partial \mathcal{D}_U} &= (\Phi x).e^{-rt} + \Psi_{D_U}\left[\lambda + s^G + s^L\right] \end{aligned}$$

The last line proves that Ψ_{D_u} grows at exponential rate $-rt$; the same can therefore be proved for Ψ_U from the first line since it is a linear combination of an exponential of $-rt$ and of Ψ_{D_u}. Hence, the three equations become

$$\begin{aligned} \frac{\gamma}{(1-\eta_L)q}e^{-rt} &= -\Psi_U + \Psi_{D_u} \\ (r+s^L)\Psi_U + s^G\Psi_{D_u} &= (-\Phi x + z).e^{-rt} + (-\Psi_U + \Psi_{D_u})(\eta_L f) \\ \Psi_{D_u} &= \frac{(-\Phi x).e^{-rt}}{r+\lambda+s^G+s^L} \end{aligned}$$

Combining the first and third lines:

$$\Psi_U = -\frac{\gamma}{(1-\eta_L)q}e^{-rt} + \frac{(-\Phi x).e^{-rt}}{r+\lambda+s^G+s^L}$$

Combining the first and second lines:

$$(r+s^L)\Psi_U + s^G\Psi_{D_u} = (-\Phi x + z).e^{-rt} + \frac{\eta_L\gamma\theta}{(1-\eta_L)}e^{-rt}$$

Finally, replacing the multipliers on the left-hand side:

$$(r+s^L)\left(-\frac{\gamma}{(1-\eta_L)q}e^{-rt}+\frac{-\Phi x.e^{-rt}}{r+\lambda+s^G+s^L}\right)+s^G\left(\frac{-\Phi x.e^{-rt}}{r+\lambda+s^G+s^L}\right)$$
$$=(-\Phi x+z).e^{-rt}+\frac{\eta_L\gamma\theta}{(1-\eta_L)}e^{-rt}$$

Simplify:

$$\frac{(\Phi x-z)(1-\eta_L)-\eta_L\gamma\theta}{r+s^L}+\left(\frac{-\Phi x(1-\eta_L)}{r+\lambda+s^G+s^L}\right)+\frac{s^G}{r+s^L}\left(\frac{-\Phi x(1-\eta_L)}{r+\lambda+s^G+s^L}\right)=\frac{\gamma}{q}$$

or

$$\frac{(\Phi x-z)(1-\eta_L)-\eta_L\gamma\theta}{r+s^L}-\left(\frac{\Phi x(1-\eta_L)}{r+\lambda+s^G+s^L}\right)\frac{r+s^L+s^G}{r+s^L}=\frac{\gamma}{q}$$

or

$$\frac{(A\Phi x-z)(1-\eta_L)-\eta_L\gamma\theta}{r+s^L}=\frac{\gamma}{q}$$

where $A=\frac{\lambda}{r+\lambda+s^G+s^L}=\mu_r^{LG}$, that is, the entry equation in the text:

$$\frac{(\mu_r^{LG}\Phi x-z)(1-\eta_L)-\eta_L\gamma\theta}{r+s^L}=\frac{\gamma}{q}$$

7.7.5 Bellman equations of the CLG model and free entry

Let E_c, E_v, E_g, and E_π be the respective steady-state asset values of a project in each period (credit stage, labor stage, goods stage, profit). We have

$$rE_c = -\kappa_I + p(\phi)(E_v - E_c) \tag{7.68}$$
$$rE_v = -\gamma + \gamma + q(E_g - E_v) + s^C(E_c - E_v) \tag{7.69}$$
$$rE_g = -w + w + \lambda(E_\pi - E_g) + s^C(E_c - E_g) + s^L(E_v - E_g) \tag{7.70}$$
$$rE_\pi = x\mathcal{P} - w - \psi + s^C(E_c - E_\pi) + s^G(E_g - E_\pi) + s^L(E_v - E_\pi) \tag{7.71}$$

Let B_c, B_v, B_g, and B_π be the respective steady-state asset values of a creditor in each period (credit stage, labor stage, goods stage, profit). We have

$$rB_c = -\kappa_B + \phi p(\phi)(B_v - B_c) \tag{7.72}$$
$$rB_v = -\gamma + q(B_g - B_v) + s^C(B_c - B_v) \tag{7.73}$$
$$rB_g = -w + \lambda(B_\pi - B_g) + s^C(B_c - B_g) + s^L(B_v - B_g) \tag{7.74}$$
$$rB_\pi = \psi + s^C(B_c - B_\pi) + s^G(B_g - B_\pi) + s^L(B_v - B_\pi) \tag{7.75}$$

Summing up leads to the value of the firm J_v, J_g, and J_π as in the text. Further,

$$J_v = \left(-\frac{\gamma}{q} + J_g\right) Q_v$$

$$J_g = \left(-\frac{w_g}{\lambda} + J_\pi\right) Q_g$$

$$J_\pi = \left(\frac{x\mathcal{P} - w_\pi}{s^G} + J_g\right) Q_\pi + \frac{s^L}{r + s^T} K$$

where $Q_v = q/(r + s^C + q)$, $Q_g = \lambda/(r + s^C + s^L + \lambda)$, $Q_\pi = s^G/(r + s^L + s^C + s^G)$, and $s^T = s^L + s^C + s^G$
After simplification:

$$J_g = \frac{Q_g}{1 - Q_\pi Q_g} \left[\frac{s^L K - w_g}{\lambda} + \left(\frac{x\mathcal{P} - w_\pi + s^L K}{s^G}\right) Q_\pi\right] \tag{7.76}$$

$$J_\pi = \frac{Q_\pi}{1 - Q_\pi Q_g} \left[\frac{x\mathcal{P} - w_\pi + s^L K}{s^G} + \left(\frac{s^L K - w_g}{\lambda}\right) Q_g\right] \tag{7.77}$$

Combined with free entry $J_v = K$ immediately delivers:

$$\left(1 + \frac{r + s^C}{q}\right) K + \frac{\gamma}{q} + \frac{Q_g}{1 - Q_\pi Q_g} \left(\frac{w_g - s^L K}{\lambda}\right) = \frac{Q_g Q_\pi}{1 - Q_\pi Q_g} \left(\frac{x\mathcal{P} - w_\pi + s^L K}{s^G}\right) \tag{7.78}$$

The left-hand side is the sum of three terms, expressed in future value of the vacancy stage. This equation says that the value of prospecting in the goods market is the negative of the expected value of the cost of paying the wage (first term), plus the expected value of the discounted profits minus—again—the future costs of being inactive and repaying wages with no profits in case consumers later on dislike the good produced.

A set of additional calculations allow for a simplification of the equations; first, introduce the convenient "profit" discount factor δ

$$\delta = r + s^C + s^L$$

that is unaffected by s^G since the effect of s^G is otherwise included in the definition of the discounted factor $\mu_{CLG,r}$; also reintroduce the notation $k(\phi) = (r + s^C)K(\phi)$, the annuity value of financial costs, and finally "extended" flow-entry costs $\gamma_k = \gamma + k(\phi)$.

The derivation of the simple expression for the job creation condition includes several simple steps. First, the free-entry condition can be decomposed as

$$K + \frac{\gamma_k}{q} = \frac{Q_g Q_\pi}{1 - Q_\pi Q_g} \left(\frac{x\mathcal{P} - w_\pi + s^L K}{s^G}\right) - \frac{Q_g}{1 - Q_\pi Q_g} \left(\frac{w_g - s^L K}{\lambda}\right)$$

$$= \frac{Q_g Q_\pi}{1 - Q_\pi Q_g}\left(\frac{x\mathcal{P} - w_\pi}{s^G}\right) - \frac{Q_g}{1 - Q_\pi Q_g}\left(\frac{w_g}{\lambda}\right)$$
$$+ s^L K\left(\frac{Q_g Q_\pi}{1 - Q_\pi Q_g}\frac{1}{s^G} - \frac{Q_g}{1 - Q_\pi Q_g}\frac{1}{\lambda}\right)$$

Second, remark that

$$Q_\pi Q_g/(1 - Q_g Q_\pi) = \frac{\lambda s^G}{\delta(\delta + s^G + \lambda)}$$

and

$$\frac{Q_g}{1 - Q_g Q_\pi}\left(\frac{1}{\lambda} + \frac{Q_\pi}{s^G}\right) = \frac{1}{\delta}$$

It follows that the entry equation becomes

$$K + \frac{\gamma_k}{q} = \frac{\lambda}{\delta(\delta + s^G + \lambda)}(x\mathcal{P} - w_\pi) - \frac{s^G}{\delta(\delta + s^G + \lambda)}\left(w_g\right)\frac{1}{Q_\pi} + s^L K \frac{1}{\delta}$$
$$= \frac{\lambda}{\delta(\delta + s^G + \lambda)}(x\mathcal{P} - w_\pi) - \frac{\delta + s^G}{\delta(\delta + s^G + \lambda)}\left(w_g\right) + s^L K \frac{1}{\delta}$$

using $Q_\pi = s^G/(\delta + s^G)$.

Finally, with $\mu_r^{CLG} = \lambda/(\delta + s^G + \lambda)$, and $\gamma_k = \gamma + k(\phi)$, the equation becomes

$$K + \frac{\gamma_k}{q} = \frac{\mu_r^{CLG} x\mathcal{P} - \mu_r^{CLG} w_\pi - (1 - \mu_r^{CLG}) w_g + s^L K}{\delta}$$

Now subtract K on the left and on the right and get

$$\frac{\gamma_k}{q} = \frac{\mu_r^{CLG} x\mathcal{P} - \mu_r^{CLG} w_\pi - (1 - \mu_r^{CLG}) w_g - k}{\delta}$$

7.7.6 Price determination in CLG

Use first the sharing rule:

$$(1 - \alpha_G)(W_{D_M} - W_{D_U}) = \alpha_G(J_\pi - J_g)$$

Assuming $w_\pi = w_g = w$ in the value of J_π and J_g leads to

$$J_\pi - J_g = \frac{x\mathcal{P}}{r + s^C + s^L + s^G + \lambda}$$

For the worker, the same assumption leads to

$$W_{D_M} - W_{D_U} = \frac{(\Phi - \mathcal{P})x}{r + s^C + s^L + s^G + \check{\lambda}}$$

As a result of the sharing rule, in the general case where $\check{\lambda}$ and λ do not coincide, one has

$$(1 - \alpha_G)\frac{\Phi - \mathcal{P}}{r + s^C + s^L + s^G + \check{\lambda}} = \alpha_G \frac{\mathcal{P}}{r + s^C + s^L + s^G + \lambda}$$

The equation then simplifies to

$\mathcal{P} = \Phi(1 - \alpha_G)$

when ξ=1 $\Rightarrow \check{\lambda} = \lambda$.

7.7.7 Efficiency in CLG

From the social planner's program

$$\Omega^{SP} = \int_0^\infty e^{-rt}\left[D_m \Phi x + z\mathcal{U} - \gamma \mathcal{V} - \kappa_B \mathcal{B}_c - \kappa_I \mathcal{N}_c\right] dt$$

and the Hamiltonian

$$\begin{aligned}\max_{\mathcal{B}_c, \mathcal{N}_c, \mathcal{V}, \mathcal{U}, \mathcal{D}_U} \quad H = {} & e^{-rt}\left[(1 - \mathcal{U} - \mathcal{D}_U)\Phi x + z\mathcal{U} - \gamma \mathcal{V} - \kappa_B \mathcal{B}_c - \kappa_I \mathcal{N}_c\right] \\ & + \Psi_U \left[(s^C + s^L)(1 - \mathcal{U}) - M_L(\mathcal{U}, \mathcal{V})\right] \\ & + \Psi_V \left[s^L(1 - \mathcal{U}) + M_C(\mathcal{B}_c, \mathcal{N}_c) - M_L(\mathcal{U}, \mathcal{V}) - s^C \mathcal{V}\right] \\ & + \Psi_{D_U} \Big[-M_G(\mathcal{D}_U, \mathcal{D}_U) + s^G (1 - \mathcal{U} - \mathcal{D}_U) \\ & - (s^L + s^C)\mathcal{D}_U + M_L(\mathcal{U}, \mathcal{V})\Big]\end{aligned}$$

one obtains the following first-order conditions:

$$\begin{aligned}\frac{\partial H}{\partial \mathcal{N}_c} &= 0 = -\kappa_I e^{-rt} + \Psi_V \left[(1 - \eta_C) p(\phi)\right] \\ \frac{\partial H}{\partial \mathcal{B}_c} &= 0 = -\kappa_B e^{-rt} + \Psi_V \left(\eta_C \phi p(\phi)\right) \\ \mathring{\Psi}_{D_U} = -\frac{\partial H}{\partial \mathcal{D}_U} &= \Phi x e^{-rt} + \Psi_{D_U}\left(\lambda + s^G + s^L + s^C\right) \\ \mathring{\Psi}_V = -\frac{\partial H}{\partial \mathcal{V}} &= \gamma e^{-rt} + \Psi_U (1 - \eta_L) q + \Psi_V \left[(1 - \eta_L) q + s^C\right] - \Psi_{D_U}(1 - \eta_L) q \\ \mathring{\Psi}_U = -\frac{\partial H}{\partial \mathcal{U}} &= (\Phi x - z)\, e^{-rt} + \Psi_U\left(\eta_L f + s^C + s^L\right) + \Psi_V(+s^L + \eta_L f) \\ & \quad + \Psi_{D_U}\left(s^G - \eta_L f\right)\end{aligned}$$

The first two equations deliver the value of the multiplier in the text of this chapter: $\Psi_V = e^{-rt} K(\phi)$.. The third one gives the value of multiplier Ψ_{D_U} as

$$\Psi_{D_U} = \frac{-\Phi x e^{-rt}}{r + \lambda + s^G + s^L + s^C} = -\Phi x e^{-rt} \mu_r^{CLG} / \lambda$$

The next one implies that

$$\gamma + K\left[(1 - \eta_L) q + r + s^C\right] = e^{rt}\left(-\Phi x e^{-rt} \mu_r^{CLG}/\lambda - \Psi_U\right)(1 - \eta_L) q$$

or

$$\Psi_U e^{rt} = -\frac{\gamma}{(1 - \eta_L) q} - K\left[1 + \frac{r + s^C}{(1 - \eta_L) q}\right] - \Phi x \mu_r^{CLG}/\lambda$$

which proves that Ψ_U is proportional to e^{-rt} as all multipliers. This leads, from the last first-order condition, to

$$(\Phi x - z)\, e^{-rt} = -\Psi_U \left(\eta_L f + r + s^C + s^L\right) - e^{-rt} K(\phi)(s^L + \eta_L f)$$
$$+ \Phi x e^{-rt} \mu_r^{CLG}/\lambda \left(s^G - \eta_L f\right)$$

or, after replacement of Ψ_U:

$$(\Phi x - z) - \left\{\frac{\gamma}{(1-\eta_L)q} + K\left[1 + \frac{r+s^C}{(1-\eta_L)q}\right] + \Phi x \mu_r^{CLG}/\lambda\right\}\left(\eta_L f + r + s^C + s^L\right)$$
$$= -K(\phi)(s^L + \eta_L f) + \Phi x \mu_r^{CLG}/\lambda \left(s^G - \eta_L f\right) \quad (7.79)$$

The Pissarides case is obtained when $K = 0$ and $\lambda \to \infty$. When $K = 0$ one first obtains:

$$(\Phi x - z) - \left[\frac{\gamma}{(1-\eta_L)q} + \Phi \mu_r^{CLG}/\lambda\right]\left(\eta_L f + r + s^C + s^L\right) = \Phi x \mu_r^{CLG}/\lambda \left(s^G - \eta_L f\right)$$

which can be rearranged as

$$(\Phi x - z)\,(1-\eta_L) - (\eta_L \gamma \theta) - \frac{\gamma}{q}\left(r + s^C + s^L\right)$$
$$= (1-\eta_L)\left(\Phi x \mu_r^{CLG}/\lambda\right)\left(r + s^C + s^L + s^G\right)$$

or finally

$$\frac{\left(\Phi x \mu_r^{CLG} - z\right)(1-\eta_L) - \gamma \eta_L \theta}{r + s^C + s^L} = \frac{\gamma}{q}$$

and when further goods market frictions disappear, one gets

$$\frac{(\Phi x - z)\,(1-\eta_L) - \gamma \eta_L \theta}{r + s^C + s^L} = \frac{\gamma}{q}$$

In the general case, the main equation (7.79) can also be rearranged as

$$(\Phi x - z)\,(1-\eta_L) - \eta_L \gamma \theta - \frac{\gamma}{q}\left(r + s^C + s^L\right)$$
$$- \left\{K\left[(1-\eta_L) + \frac{r+s^C}{q}\right]\right\}\left(\eta_L f + r + s^C + s^L\right)$$
$$+ K(\phi)(s^L + \eta_L f)(1-\eta_L)$$
$$= +\Phi x \mu_r^{CLG}/\lambda \left(s^G - \eta_L f\right)(1-\eta_L)$$
$$+ \left[(1-\eta_L)\Phi x \mu_r^{CLG}/\lambda\right]\left(\eta_L f + r + s^C + s^L\right)$$

or

$$
\begin{aligned}
(\Phi x - z)(1-\eta_L) - \eta_L \gamma \theta - \frac{\gamma}{q}\left(r + s^C + s^L\right) \\
- \left\{ K\left[(1-\eta_L) + \frac{r+s^C}{q}\right]\right\}\left(\eta_L f + r + s^C + s^L\right) \\
+ K(\phi)(s^L + \eta_L f)(1-\eta_L) \\
= \left[(1-\eta_L)\Phi x \mu_r^{CLG}/\lambda\right]\left(r + s^C + s^L + s^G\right)
\end{aligned}
$$

and with $\gamma_k = \gamma + k(\phi)$, finally

$$
\frac{\left(\Phi x \mu_r^{CLG} - k - z\right)(1-\eta_L) - \gamma_k \eta_L \theta}{r + s^C + s^L} = \frac{\gamma_k}{q}
$$

8 The propagation of business cycles in CLG models

This chapter studies the dynamic extension of the CLG model. It presents how to write and solves the discrete time, stochastic version of the model of chapter 7. We show how to determine prices in a stochastic environment. We then use the model investigate the dynamic response to different types of shocks.

We first study the responses to technological shocks in the manner of chapters 2 and 6. Goods market frictions turn out to drastically change the dynamics of the labor market. In particular, if financial frictions studied in chapters 5 and 6 amplify shocks, goods market frictions introduced in chapter 7 add a lot to the persistence of the responses of endogenous variables. Goods market frictions truly propagate shocks, adding amplification and persistence to the responses of variables to innovations.

We present the simpler dynamic CLG model first, without endogenous search intensity in the goods market. We then introduce endogenous "shopping" effort by consumers, and advertisement intensity by firms to the model. These elements provide additional propagation. As in previous chapters on business cycles, an approximation of the equilibrium conditions is used to develop the intuition to the propagation mechanisms, before properly solving the model with the global solution method of chapter 2.

In the last section of this chapter, we exploit the fact that the model is well suited to introducing shocks that affect consumer demand. This requires relaxing the assumption of linearity on utility for Walrasian good 0. Utility over this good is now assumed to be concave. As a result, the goods market match surplus increases in consumer disposable income, and changes in disposable income affect the bargained price in the goods market. This creates a demand channel which affects the firm's demand for labor as the profit from hiring depends on the price bargained in the goods market. We then introducing demand shocks as follows. There is a government with the ability to affect a consumer's disposable income through the timing of taxes and transfers, financed though the accumulation of debt. An important implication is that Ricardian equivalence no longer holds. Innovations to government transfers are persistent, with some autocorrelation, such that the initial impact is an increase in demand for goods. Positive innovations are in effect a fiscal stimulus.

8.1 The discrete time CLG model

8.1.1 Search and matching in the goods markets

As in the previous chapters, consumers have a disposable income I_t, than can be spent on either an essential good (serving as a numeraire), c_0, or a preferred manufactured good, c_1. Consuming the latter first requires searching in the goods market. When a consumer is matched with a manufacturing firm, it purchases the production, x_t, at a unit price $\mathcal{P}_t$. The remaining income is spent on the essential good, c_0, which is supplied as a transfer of resource across individuals. Matched and unmatched consumers have mass $\mathcal{D}_{Mt}$ and $\mathcal{D}_{Ut}$, respectively, and, relative to the assumption in chapter 7, we assume that all individuals may participate in the goods market as incomes are pooled. That is, in this environment $\mathcal{D}_{Ut} + \mathcal{D}_{Mt} = 1$. This will introduce time-varying values of goods market tightness, thus leading to interesting and more complex dynamics.

Unmatched consumers $\mathcal{D}_{Ut}$ attempt to find suitable unmatched goods, $\mathcal{N}_{gt}$, while symmetrically, firms attempt to find unmatched consumers $\mathcal{D}_{Ut}$. The number of meetings $\mathcal{M}_G(\mathcal{D}_{Ut}, \mathcal{N}_{gt})$ is the direct equivalent of the assumption on goods market matching in the previous chapter. Transition rates are defined as in equations (7.3) and (7.4). We can define goods market tightness as

$$\xi_t = \frac{\mathcal{D}_{Ut}}{\mathcal{N}_{gt}}$$

Note that now this value will change over time, contrary to the previous chapter, and this will allow for richer dynamics. As a result, the finding rate for firms, λ_t, and for consumers, $\check{\lambda}_t$, in the goods market will fluctuate over time.

8.1.2 Timing of an investment project

The timing is the discrete time equivalent of the CLG model of the precious chapter; in the first stage, an investment project is initially in need of a financial partner. If matched with a creditor, the project enters the second stage where it searches in the labor market to hire a worker. In the third stage, now endowed with a worker, the firm attempts to sell the good produced on the goods market. A consumer arrives with probability λ_t, and all production can be sold in the fourth stage as matched consumers absorb the entire production. Assuming that production involves an infinitely small operating cost over and above the wage and that the good cannot be stored, the firm chooses not to produce in this stage. In the fourth and final stage, the firm is now matched with a consumer and its output x_t is sold at price $\mathcal{P}_t$. We assume that x_t is a random, stationary process. With revenue $\mathcal{P}_t x_t$, the firm pays the worker w_t and an amount ψ_t to the creditor, and enjoys the difference. The simplifying assumption that a worker is paid the same wage in the goods market and profit stage is adopted here for simplicity.

There are three types of separations. First, there is exogenous destruction of the labor match, which occurs each period with probability s^L. Second, the match between the investment project and its creditor may dissolve at the end of a time period, leading to the destruction of other, existing matches if they have been formed. Finally, consumers may separate from goods with probability s^G.

All profit opportunities are exhausted by new entrants such that the value of the entry stages are always driven to zero. In the case of the financial market, this implies that $J_{ct} = B_{ct} \equiv 0$ at all times, which is also the continuation value following the credit destruction shock s^C. We relegate to the chapter appendix the Bellman equations for the entry of projects and creditors. The Bellman equations of the value of a firm (matched creditor and project) in each stage can be obtained by summing the corresponding equations and are as follows:

$$J_{c,t} = 0 \Leftrightarrow \frac{\kappa_B}{\phi_t p_t} + \frac{\kappa_I}{p_t} = J_{vt} \tag{8.1}$$

$$J_{vt} = -\gamma + \beta^C \mathbb{E}_t \left[q_t J_{gt+1} + (1 - q_t) J_{vt+1} \right] \tag{8.2}$$

$$J_{gt} = -w_t + \beta^C \mathbb{E}_t \left\{ \left(1 - s^L\right) \left[\lambda_t J_{\pi t+1} + (1 - \lambda_t) J_{gt+1} \right] + s^L J_{vt+1} \right\} \tag{8.3}$$

$$\begin{aligned} J_{\pi t} = \mathcal{P}_t x_t - w_t + \beta^C \mathbb{E}_t \Big\{ \left(1 - s^L\right) \Big[\left(1 - s^G\right) J_{\pi t+1} + s^G J_{gt+1} \Big] \\ + s^L J_{vt+1} \Big\} \end{aligned} \tag{8.4}$$

where $\beta^C = \left(1 - s^C\right) / (1 + r)$. Equation (8.1) states that the value of a firm in the hiring stage is equal to the sum of capitalized search costs paid by each side in the previous financial market stage. This is driven to zero in the absence of credit market frictions. The formulation of the labor market stage in equation (8.2) describes the value of a job vacancy as a flow cost γ and an expected gain from hiring a worker, valued at J_g. The value of J_g in equation (8.3) takes into account the labor cost w_t, and, conditional on no credit destruction shock, the firm may or may not become profitable in the next period. This depends on meeting customers with probability λ_t, and whether the worker remains with the firm with probability $\left(1-s^L\right)$. If the worker leaves, the firm returns to the earlier stage v. Finally, in stage π, equation (8.4) shows that the match produces revenue $\mathcal{P}_t x_t$, pays a wage and other production costs, and may return to earlier stages depending on the occurrence of consumer change of taste, labor turnover, or credit market separation. The repayment ψ_t does not appear in the last equation as it is a transfer between the project and the creditor.

8.1.3 Disposable income and price determination

Total net profits in this economy are the sum of profit flows to projects and creditors. This corresponds to $\mathcal{P}_t x_t \mathcal{N}_{\pi t} - w_t \mathcal{N}_t - \gamma \mathcal{V}_t - \kappa_B \mathcal{B}_{ct}$, where $\mathcal{N}_t = \mathcal{N}_{\pi t} + \mathcal{N}_{gt}$ is the sum of the number of firms matched with a consumer, $\mathcal{N}_{\pi t}$, and of the number of firms in stage g, $\mathcal{N}_{gt}$ (that is, matched with a creditor and a worker but not with a consumer). The number of firms searching for workers in stage v, the labor market, is $\mathcal{V}_t$. The number of creditors screening projects in stage c is $\mathcal{B}_{c,t}$. The first term, $\mathcal{P}_t x_t \mathcal{N}_{\pi t}$, is revenue generated by firms in stage π. The second term represents wage payments in the economy. The remaining terms represent the creditor's outlays during the first stages due to search costs in labor and financial markets.

All profits net of search costs, made by firms and creditors, are pooled and distributed as lump sums to workers. This is a common assumption in macroeconomic business cycle models. The mass 1 of workers, the unemployed and employed, therefore receive all profits of firms and creditors each period as a transfer. The timing of the transmission of income from firm to consumer within a period corresponds to the simplest possible assumption.

We however assume that there is no co-insurance of fluctuations in consumption of the search good: unlucky consumers may not borrow the frictional good from their neighbor. In other words, there is a fluid market for the Walrasian good which may transfer wealth across individuals, but a rigid and frictional market for the other good, which creates a range of new and interesting issues.

Value functions for consumers

Individuals want to consume the search goods, but may not buy them before searching in the goods market. The generic utility of consuming both goods is denoted by $v(c_1, c_0)$. The asset values for a consumer of being unmatched and matched are, respectively:

$$W_{D_U t} = v(0, c_{0t}) + \frac{1}{1+r}\mathbb{E}_t\left[\check{\lambda}_t W_{D_M t+1} + \left(1-\check{\lambda}_t\right) W_{D_U t+1}\right] \tag{8.5}$$

$$W_{DMt} = v(c_{1t}, c_{0t}) + \beta^C \mathbb{E}_t \left(1 - s^L\right) \left[s^G W_{DUt+1} + \left(1 - s^G\right) W_{DMt+1}\right] + \frac{s^C + \left(1 - s^C\right) s^L}{1 + r} \mathbb{E}_t W_{DUt+1}. \quad (8.6)$$

Assuming the search good has greater marginal utility, matched consumers will always absorb x_t units of good 1 at the expense $\mathcal{P}_t x_t$ and then spend what is left, $I_t - \mathcal{P}_t x_t$, on the numeraire good $c_{0,t}$, where I_t is a consumer's disposable income. In other words, the utility in the first equation (unmatched consumer) is

$$v(0, I_t)$$

and the utility in the second equation (matched consumer) will be

$$v(x_t, I_t - \mathcal{P}_t x_t)$$

Finally, we will assume, for the moment, a linear utility:

$$v(c_{1t}, c_{0t}) = \Phi c_{1,t} + c_{0,t}$$

with $\Phi \geq 1$.

Determining the dynamics of the goods market surplus and price

The price $\mathcal{P}_t$ is bargained between a consumer and a firm. The total surplus to the consumption relationship is $\Sigma_{gt}^T = \left(J_{\pi t} - J_{gt}\right) + \left(W_{DMt} - W_{DUt}\right)$. The good's price is determined as $\mathcal{P}_t = \text{argmax} \left(J_{\pi t} - J_{gt}\right)^{1-\alpha_G} \left(W_{DMt} - W_{DUt}\right)^{\alpha_G}$, where $\alpha_G \in (0,1)$ is the share of the goods surplus, Σ_{gt}^T, going to the consumer. Under a linear utility for the search good, this results in the sharing rule

$$(1 - \alpha_G) \left(W_{DMt} - W_{DUt}\right) = \alpha_G \left(J_{\pi t} - J_{gt}\right) \quad (8.7)$$

leading to the simple negotiated price rule:

$$\mathcal{P}_t x_t = (1 - \alpha_G) \Phi x_t + \alpha_G (1 - \alpha_G) \left[\lambda_t \beta^C \left(1 - s^L\right) - \check{\lambda}_t \beta\right] \mathbb{E}_t \Sigma_{gt+1}^T \quad (8.8)$$

This rule emphasizes the forward-looking aspect of price determination: today's price is increasing in the expectation of tomorrow's surplus in the goods market. The latter effect on price depends on current goods-market congestion from the firm's side relative to the worker's side through the difference in their discounted meeting rates, $\lambda_t \beta^C \left(1 - s^L\right) - \check{\lambda}_t \beta$. This quantity reflects the effective relative demand faced by firms, given search frictions in the good market. The higher the demand, the better the bargaining position of the firm.

In addition, equation (8.8) states that the revenue accruing to the firm is increasing in marginal utility, Φ, from consuming good c_1. The worker will pay a higher price to consume the greater its utility for the good and the lower its bargaining power α_G.

8.1.4 Other markets

The equations in the credit market are identical to those of chapter 6. The matching rates of projects and creditors p_t and $\check{p}_t$, respectively, were already defined in chapter 5, and the equilibrium value of ϕ_t, denoted by ϕ^*, is obtained as in chapter 6:

$$\phi^* = \frac{\kappa_B}{\kappa_I}\frac{1-\alpha_C}{\alpha_C}\forall t \tag{8.9}$$

Finally, credit market frictions are summarized as $K(\phi^*) \equiv \frac{\kappa_B}{\phi^* p(\phi^*)} + \frac{\kappa_I}{p(\phi^*)}$.

In the labor market, in turn, a complication arises from the existence of two distinct phases in the life cycle of the firm, stages g and π, leading to two different labor surpluses and therefore to different ways of sharing that surplus. In the previous chapter, we assumed long-term contracts, so that the wage rule in stage g would be preserved in stage π, which we maintain in this chapter. The wage is the outcome to the Nash bargaining problem:

$$w_t = \text{argmax}\left(J_{gt} - J_{vt}\right)^{1-\alpha_L}\left(W_{gt} - W_{ut}\right)^{\alpha_L} \text{ if the firm is in stage } g \tag{8.10}$$

where W_g is the asset values of employment to a worker in stage g, and W_u is the value of unemployment. The resulting wage rule is:

Block-bargained wage in the discrete time CLG model:

$$w_t = (1-\alpha_L)z + \alpha_L\left[\left(\frac{\gamma_k}{1-s^C}\right)\theta_t + \mathbb{E}_t x_{t+1}^{CLG}\right] + \alpha_L\lambda_t\beta^{CL}\mathbb{E}_t\left[\Upsilon_{t+1}\right]$$

where $\gamma_k = \gamma + k(\phi)$, $k(\phi) = (1-\beta^C)K(\phi)$, $x^{CLG_0} = \mathcal{P}_t x_t - k(\phi)$, $x_t^{CLG} = \lambda_{t-1}\beta^{CL}\mathcal{P}_t x_t - k(\phi)$, and $\Upsilon_{t+1} = \beta^{CL}(1-s^G-\lambda_t)\left(J_{\pi t+2} - J_{gt+2}\right)$. The wage is the sum of the static wage in the absence of income of the firm, and a forward-looking term Υ_{t+1} reflecting future capital gains and future revenues.

An alternative wage rule is to assume that wages reflect the current level of productivity regardless of the status of the firm, and posit a wage rule that takes the functional form use in (Blanchard and Galí 2010)

$$w_t = \chi_w\left(\mathcal{P}_t x_t\right)^{\eta_w} \tag{8.11}$$

where η_w is the elasticity of wages to the marginal product of labor, $\mathcal{P}_t x_t$. This simple rule allows us to retain the main channel by which the elasticity of wages to productivity affects propagation through the elasticity parameter η_w. That is, for a given elasticity of wages, we can evaluate the propagation of shocks to the economy, and in particular the labor market, coming from frictional goods and credit markets.

8.2 Equilibrium dynamics of the CLG model

8.2.1 Equilibrium

The equilibrium is a set of policy and value functions for the consumers $\{W_{D_U t}, W_{D_M t}\}$ and firms $\{J_{ct}, J_{vt}, J_{gt}, J_{\pi t}\}$; a set of prices in goods, labor, and credit; and stocks and measures of tightness in the markets for goods, labor, and credit $\{\mathcal{B}_{ct}, \mathcal{N}_{ct}, \mathcal{V}_t, \mathcal{N}_{gt}, \mathcal{N}_{\pi,t}, \mathcal{D}_{Ut}, \mathcal{D}_{Mt}, \mathcal{U}_t\}$ and $\{\xi_t, \theta_t, \phi\}$ such that

1. Consumers' value follows functions (8.5) and (8.6).
2. The value for firms follows (8.1) to (8.4) with free entry in the financial market.
3. Prices in the goods, labor, and financial markets are determined by Nash bargaining given by conditions (8.7), (8.10) and (8.9).
4. Stock in the goods and labor markets follows the law of motions in the chapter appendix.

8.2.2 Job creation condition

Combining equations (8.1) and (8.2), and calling $o_t \equiv \frac{(1-q_t)}{q_t}(1-\beta^C)$, a quantitatively negligible term, the job creation condition is:

Job creation condition in the CLG model:

$$\underbrace{K(\phi^*)(1+o_t)}_{\text{Cost of credit frictions}} \underbrace{+\frac{\gamma}{q(\theta_t)}}_{\text{Cost of labor frictions}} \underbrace{=\beta^C \mathbb{E}_t J_{gt+1}}_{\text{Expected profits}} \tag{8.12}$$

which equates the average cost of creating a job—the left-hand side, equal to the financial costs properly discounted, K, and the expected costs of search on the labor market, $\gamma/q(\theta_t)$—to the discounted expected value of a worker to the firm in the goods market stage (the right-hand side).

A few words of comparison with the canonical labor search model are warranted here. First, the costs of financial intermediation enter the left-hand side of the equation and place a lower bound on the value of a "vacancy" to a firm, just as in the equivalent condition in chapter 6. Absent credit market frictions, the average cost of creation depends on the flow cost of a vacancy, γ, and congestion in the labor market. Second, the expected value on the right-hand side corresponds to the ability to produce and sell a good once a consumer has been located. Under frictionless goods markets, the right-hand side is simply the value of the profit stage. Thus, the current model nests the canonical search model when K tends to zero and the goods markets frictions are removed. The value of J_g, a function of the future profits of the firms, embeds the effect of goods market frictions through the transition probability to stage π and turnover in the goods market.

8.2.3 A log-linear relation

The relationship between labor market tightness and the expected value of a filled vacancy to a firm becomes very transparent when looking at a log-linear approximation of this job creation condition around the deterministic steady state:

Log-linearization (around the steady state) of the job creation condition in the CLG model:

$$\underbrace{\hat{\theta}_t}_{\text{Amplification from:}} = \underbrace{\frac{1}{\eta_L}}_{\text{Labor frictions}} \times \underbrace{\frac{J_g}{J_g - K}}_{\text{Credit frictions}} \times \underbrace{\mathbb{E}_t \hat{J}_{gt+1}}_{\text{Goods frictions}} \tag{8.13}$$

where η_L is the elasticity of the job-filling rate with respect to labor market tightness and "hatted" variables indicate proportional deviations from the steady state. Over and above the amplification of changes in J_g from frictions in the labor market, measured as the inverse of the elasticity of the labor matching function, credit market frictions create an amplifying factor of $\frac{J_g}{J_g - K}$. This financial accelerator is decreasing in the firm's surplus to hiring a worker, $J_g - K$. Note that frictions in the goods market will also affect the value of J_g and provide amplification through the known channel of reducing the firm's surplus, $J_g - K$. However the amplification from the goods market in the second term in the right-hand side $J_g/(J_g - K)$ only occurs when $K > 0$. Thus, the main additional and novel effects of goods market frictions on the dynamics of the labor market work through their impact on the dynamics of the expected value of a filled vacancy, $\mathbb{E}_t \widehat{J}_{gt+1}$.

Two features of the goods market fundamentally change the dynamics: (i) the likelihood of reaching the profit stage in the period after hiring the worker, λ_t, which will affect the value of $\mathbb{E}_t \widehat{J}_{gt+1}$, and (ii) the expected profit flow depends on the price of the good, $\mathcal{P}_t$. In order to see this more clearly, consider the value of a filled vacancy in a standard Mortensen–Pissarides matching model where the goods market is perfect: $J_{gt}^{MP} = J_{\pi t}^{MP} = x_t - w_t + \beta^C \mathbb{E}_t J_{\pi,t+1}^{MP}$. From the recursive nature of $J_{\pi t}^{MP}$, all that matters for the dynamics of labor market tightness under perfect goods markets is the expected path of the net profit flow, $x_t - w_t$.

8.3 Extension to endogenous search intensity in the goods market

We now postulate, as in chapter 7, section 7.5, that unmatched consumers $\mathcal{D}_{Ut}$ exert an average search effort, $\bar{e}_{Gt}$, to find unmatched goods, $\mathcal{N}_{gt}$, through a process summarized by a constant return-to-scale function. Symmetrically, firms exert an average advertising effort $\bar{e}_{A,t}$, to find unmatched consumers $\mathcal{D}_{Ut}$. Given these assumptions, the total number of matches is $\mathcal{M}_G(\bar{e}_{Gt}\mathcal{D}_{Ut}, \bar{e}_{A,t}\mathcal{N}_{gt})$. It follows that $\bar{e}_{Gt}\mathcal{D}_{Ut}$ can be thought of as the effective demand for new goods and $\bar{e}_{At}\mathcal{N}_{gt}$ is a measure of the effective supply of goods. Consumers influence their effective finding rate $e_{Gt}\check{\lambda}_t/\bar{e}_{Gt}$ through their search effort relative to other consumers, and firms affect their new customer finding rate $e_{At}\lambda_t/\bar{e}_{At}$ through their relative advertising effort.

The asset value of a firm searching for a consumer is now modified as follows, denoting by $\sigma_{A,t} = \sigma_{A,t}(e_{A,t})$ an advertising cost function with $\sigma_A'(e_A) > 0$, $\sigma_A''(e_A) \geq 0$, and $\sigma_{A\text{ß}}(0) = 0$, and with elasticity with respect to effort $\eta_{\sigma_A} > 0$:

$$J_{gt} = -w_t - \sigma_{A,t} + \beta^C \mathbb{E}_t \left\{ \left(1 - s^L\right) \left[\frac{e_{At}}{\bar{e}_{At}} \lambda_t J_{\pi t+1} + \left(1 - \frac{e_{At}}{\bar{e}_{At}} \lambda_t\right) J_{gt+1} \right] + s^L J_{vt+1} \right\} \tag{8.14}$$

Unmatched consumers search for a good at an effort cost $\sigma_G(e_G)$, with $\sigma_G'(e_G) > 0$, $\sigma_G''(e_G) \geq 0$, and $\sigma_G(0) = 0$, and with elasticity with respect to effort $\eta_{\sigma_G} > 0$. Consequently, we have

$$W_{D_U t} = v(0, c_{0t}) - \sigma_G(e_{Gt}) + \beta \mathbb{E}_t \left[\frac{e_{Gt}}{\bar{e}_{Gt}} \check{\lambda}_t W_{D_M t+1} + \left(1 - \frac{e_{Gt}}{\bar{e}_{Gt}} \check{\lambda}_t\right) W_{D_U t+1} \right] \tag{8.15}$$

$$W_{D_M t} = v(c_{1t}, c_{0t}) + \beta^C \mathbb{E}_t \left\{ \left(1 - s^L\right) \left[s^G W_{D_U t+1} + \left(1 - s^G\right) W_{D_M t+1} \right] \right\} + \frac{s^C + \left(1 - s^C\right) s^L}{1 + r} \mathbb{E}_t D_{U_U t+1} \tag{8.16}$$

The first-order condition for advertisement and consumer search effort are, respectively:

$$\sigma_A'(e_{At}) = \frac{\lambda_t}{\bar{e}_{At}}\left(1 - s^L\right)\beta^C \mathbb{E}_t\left(J_{\pi t+1} - J_{gt+1}\right) \tag{8.17}$$

$$\sigma_G'(e_{Gt}) = \frac{\check{\lambda}_t}{\bar{e}_{Gt}}\beta \mathbb{E}_t\left(D_{Mt+1} - D_{Ut+1}\right) \tag{8.18}$$

Optimal individual search effort is given by a condition equating the marginal cost of effort to the discounted, expected benefit yielded by that marginal unit of effort. Firms and consumers take all the right-hand side elements of the optimality condition (8.17) and (8.18) as given. As such, all firms choose the same amount of advertising effort and consumers choose the same amount of search effort in the goods market. We have the symmetrical equilibrium

$$e_{At} = \bar{e}_{At} \text{ and } e_{Gt} = \bar{e}_{Gt}$$

Equation (8.18) implies that consumer search effort is increasing in the expected capital gain from consuming the search good. Combining the first-order condition above and the asset-value equations for consumers, we have

$$\bar{e}_{Gt}\sigma_G'(\bar{e}_{Gt}) = \frac{\check{\lambda}_t}{1+r}\mathbb{E}_t \sum_{i=0} \left(\beta^{CLG}\right)^i \times \left[\left(\frac{\Phi}{\mathcal{P}_{t+1+i}} - 1\right) I_{t+1+i} + (1 - \eta_{\sigma G})\sigma\left(\bar{e}_{Gt+1+i}\right)\right] \tag{8.19}$$

where $\beta^{CLG} \equiv (1 - s^G)\left(1 - s^L\right)\left(1 - s^C\right)/(1+r)$ is a generalized discount factor. This expression reveals that the level of effort will depend on expected disposable income and the dynamics of the price $\mathcal{P}$. A drop in the bargained price raises the incentive to exert search effort in the goods market, as does an expected increase in future income.

Finally, in this setup, bargaining over price has an interesting implication on search efforts: combining the optimality conditions for the intensive search margins (8.18) and (8.17), we have

$$\frac{\bar{e}_{A,t}\sigma_A'(e_{At})}{\bar{e}_{Gt}\sigma_G'(e_{Gt})} = \left(\frac{1 - \alpha_G}{\alpha_G}\right)\left(1 - s^L\right)\left(1 - s^C\right)\xi_t$$

Since the effort of one side increases the returns to effort of the other side, we have a strategic complementarity arising from bilateral search effort. This can potentially increase the amplification of productivity shocks.

8.4 Quantitative implications I: the propagation of productivity shocks

8.4.1 Calibration strategy

The basic unit of time is a month. The process for productivity is assumed to be an AR(1) in logs with persistence of $\rho_x = 0.95^{1/3}$, and conditional volatility, σ_x, of 0.00625. The matching functions in the labor, goods, and credit markets take the functional form proposed in den Haan et al. (2000). All parameter values are reported in table 8.1, and the strategies for calibrating the labor and credit market follow those described in chapters 2 and 6. We detail in this

Table 8.1
A calibration of goods, labor, and credit markets: Parameter values

	Parameter	Value		Reference or Target:
Technology:				
persistence parameter	ρ_x	$0.95^{1/3}$	→	BLS labor productivity
standard deviation	σ_x	0.00625	→	BLS labor productivity
Labor market:				
job separation rate	s^L	0.032	→	JOLTS
matching curvature	ν_L	1.25	→	den Haan et al. (2000)
vacancy cost	γ	0.10	→	Unemployment rate
worker bargaining weight	α_L	0.15	→	Wage elasticity
nonemployment	z	0.71	→	Chapter 2
Credit market:				
separation rate	s^C	0.01/3	→	Bernanke et al. (1996)
creditor bargaining weight	α_C	0.12	→	Spread on returns
search costs	κ_B	0.1	→	Financial sector's share of GDP
search costs	κ_I	0.1	→	Volatility of unemployment
matching curvature	ν_C	1.35	→	Credit market transition rate
risk-free rate	r	0.01/3	→	3-month US T-bill
Goods market:				
goods exit rate	s^G	0.005	→	Broda and Weinstein (2010)
matching curvature	ν_G	1.40	→	Goods market transition rate
cost function level parameter	$\chi_{\sigma G}$	0.44	→	American Time Use Survey
cost function elasticity	$\eta_{\sigma G}$	2	→	Quadratic cost
consumer bargaining weight	α_G	0.30	→	Share of expenditure on essential good
marginal utility of c_1	Φ	1.15	→	Price markup

section the calibration of the goods market, and refer to the previous chapters for the calibration of the labor and credit markets.

Goods market parameters: s^G, ν_G, $\chi_{\sigma G}$, $\eta_{\sigma G}$, α_G, Φ.

The strategy for calibrating goods market parameters begins with evidence in Broda and Weinstein (2010) of a four-year product exit rate of 0.46, and a median one-year exit rate of 0.24. These statistics represent the turnover in consumption goods from the consumer's perspective. The model's equivalent rate $s^C + (1 - s^C)\left[(1 - s^L)s^G + s^L\right]$, which reflects consumers' transitions from matched to unmatched states, implies a monthly goods separation rate $s^G = 0.005$. Broda and Weinstein (2010) also report a rate of product entry of 0.25 on an annualized basis. This implies an average transition rate for consumers in the goods market of $\check{\lambda} = 0.20$, targeted with the curvature parameter in the goods market matching function $e_G \mathcal{D}_U \mathcal{N}_g / \left((e_G \mathcal{D}_U)^{\nu_G} + \mathcal{N}_g^{\nu_G}\right)^{1/\nu_G}$. At a steady state the annual entry rate of 0.25 implies a monthly consumer finding rate in the goods market of $\tilde{\lambda} = 0.25 \mathcal{C}_1 \tau / \left[\mathcal{C}_0 \left(1 - (1 - \tau)^{12}\right)\right] = 0.20$ given an average share of matched consumers of $\mathcal{C}_1 = 0.90$ that results from our calibration. It is verified in simulations that the average product exit rate is consistent with the empirical evidence reported above. This results in $\nu_G = 1.40$.

The search costs in the goods market are calibrated using the Bureau of Labor Statistics' time-use survey. This survey reports that households spend on average half an hour a day purchasing goods and services (0.4 hour for men, 0.6 hour for women). Of course, this is not necessarily time spent searching and comparing goods before making a choice. Nor does it include travel related to these activities. Assuming an individual works on average seven hours a day, the cost of time searching in the goods market corresponds to approximately 7% of wage income. That is, the target is an average value for $\sigma_G(\bar{e}_G)/w \simeq 0.07$. Assuming a cost function $\sigma_G(e_G) = \left(\chi_{\sigma G}/\eta_{\sigma G}\right) e_G^{\eta_{\sigma G}}$, we obtain $\chi_{\sigma G} = 0.44$. The baseline parameterization specifies the costs as quadratic with $\eta_{\sigma G} = 2$, which is what we assume for the curvature of the advertising cost function, $\eta_{\sigma_A} = 2$. The level parameter of the latter cost function is calibration to a share of advertising expenditure to GDP estimated in Hall (2012). The share of the goods market surplus accruing to the consumer, α_G, is determined by targeting an expenditure share on the essential good in the data. Data from the Household Consumption Expenditure Survey reveal that the average annual expenditure on food consumed at home, plus utilities, over the period 1984 to 2009 amounts to 10% to 15% of total annual expenditures. The share in the model is defined as the ratio of consumption expenditures $\mathcal{C}_0 / \left[\mathcal{P}\mathcal{C}_1 + \mathcal{C}_0\right]$, where the expenditures are weighted by the fraction of unmatched and matched consumers. This results in $\alpha_G = 0.30$. The marginal utility Φ is set to 1.15 for an average markup over marginal cost of

10%, in the lower range of values reported in Basu and Fernald (1997) and Nekarda and Ramey (2011).

8.4.2 Business cycle moments and impulse responses

The business cycle moments of the CLG model are reported in table 8.2. The same table also reports the business cycle moments after the credit market frictions are removed. The first takeaway from the table of results is the substitutability of credit and goods market frictions in generating amplification. In the version of the model without credit market frictions, the LG model, the standard deviation of unemployment is 0.08. In the version of the model without goods market frictions, the CL model, the standard deviation of unemployment is 0.07. In this sense both goods and credit market frictions amplify shocks. The second takeaway is that goods market frictions are unique in endogenously generating persistence. This can be seen in the row reporting the autocorrelation of the growth rates of endogenous variables. The autocorrelation of the growth rate of labor market tightness in the CLG model is 0.25. In the LG model the autocorrelation is 0.22 whereas in the CL model, it is −0.09.

These distinctive features of goods market frictions are clearly illustrated with the impulse responses to a positive productivity shock in the different variants of the model. This is reported in figure 8.1. The solid line reports the impulse response of the CLG model. It is the largest response, with the highest peak, and the peak occurs the latest, in this case after five quarters. Consider next the responses in the LG and CL models, the circled and diamond lines, respectively. They have a similar amplitude, another way of observing their equivalent amplifying properties. However, the peak response in the CL model occurs at the same time as the shock whereas in the LG model it takes a few quarters for labor market tightness to reach its peak.

Table 8.2
Labor market moments: Model with credit, goods, and labor market frictions

	$\mathcal{U}$	$\mathcal{V}$	θ		$\mathcal{U}$	$\mathcal{V}$	θ
	Panel A: Credit, Goods, and Labor Frictions				Panel B: Removing Credit Frictions		
Standard deviation	0.127	0.153	0.264		0.08	0.102	0.165
Autocorrelation	0.332	0.150	0.245		0.332	0.123	0.224
Correlation matrix		−0.782	−0.883	$\mathcal{U}$		−0.791	−0.893
			0.947	$\mathcal{V}$			0.953

In Panel A, we take the quarterly averages of monthly $\mathcal{U}, \mathcal{V}$, and x to convert to quarterly series, and all variables are in HP-filtered proportional deviations from the mean with a smoothing parameter of 1,600. We then report cross-simulation averages.

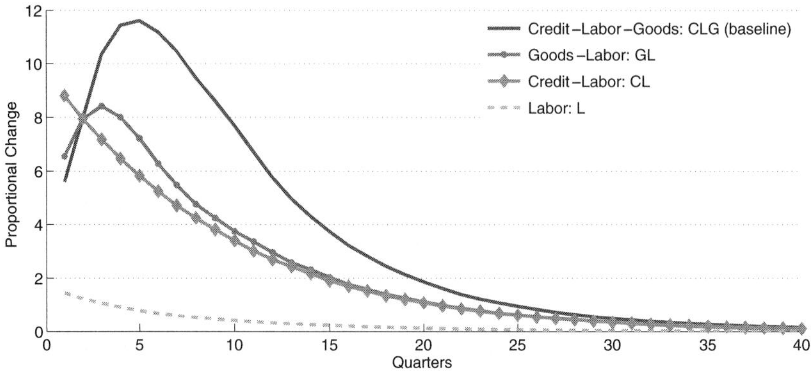

Figure 8.1

Comparing frictions: impulse responses to a positive technology shock across the Credit-Labor-Goods frictions mode and its variants Goods-Labor, Credit-Labor, and Labor market frictions alone.

8.5 Quantitative implications II: the propagation of demand shocks

By symmetry with chapter 6, where we introduced financial shocks, we now introduce and study a few results on demand shocks. In this section, a demand shock is either a utility shock affecting preferences, or a fiscal shock affecting disposable income. We explore the effects, of observable fiscal shocks. Before proceeding any further, it is necessary to clarify the relation between utility, income, and consumption.

8.5.1 The relation between utility, income, and consumption

Under linear utility, the consumer surplus in the goods market is independent of income. Indeed, total income $\bar{y} + w$ disappears from all consumption surplus equations since additional income in each state (matched or not with a good) adds up linearly to the value of consumption in each state. This results in a bargained price independent of income. The implication for firms and their decisions is that total revenue is independent of consumer income as well. We therefore introduce concave utility with respect to a Walrasian good (good 0). Assume now that utility is

$$v = v_1(x) + v_0(I - \mathcal{P}x) + l$$

where I is disposable income expressed in units of good 0, and where v_0 is increasing and concave, $v_0' > 0$ and $v_0" \leq 0$. It follows that the consumption surplus is now

$$W_{D_M} - W_{D_U} = \frac{v_1(x) + v_0(I - \mathcal{P}x) - v_0(I)}{r + s^L + s^G + \lambda}$$

The consumer's match surplus now depends on disposable income. It is no longer linearly decreasing in prices. This has several consequences. First, the outcome of price negotiation won't lead to a price being a simple function of parameters. Instead it will include cyclical terms from the equilibrium in the goods market. Second, given that v_0 is increasing concave, a marginal increase in income lowers the marginal utility of good 0. It follows that with higher income, consumers face lower sacrifices (in terms of good 0) from consuming good 1. Price per unit of good $\mathcal{P}$ will therefore be positively associated with income. This can be summarized as follows:

Proposition: demand effects for the search good

1. *Under linear utility, there is no demand effect of higher income.*
2. *Under a concave utility for good 0, higher income will generate higher demand, higher prices and thus in turn, higher entry of firms.*

With a general utility function, the price equation derived from the generalized bargaining rule must satisfy the sharing rule:

$$(1 - \alpha_G)(D_{Mt} - D_{Ut}) = \alpha_G \left(J_{\pi t} - J_{gt}\right) v'_{0t}$$

where v'_{0t} is the marginal utility of good 0. The CLG model is easily extended by using the effective (stochastic) bargaining power

$$\tilde{\alpha}_{Gt} = \frac{\alpha_G}{\alpha_G / v'_{0t} + 1 - \alpha_G}$$

as the equilibrium is unchanged with the exception of the price equation.

This opens the door for redistribution or fiscal policies. These policies can work by affecting the level of disposable income. They will therefore impact the goods market and economy in general.

8.5.2 Fiscal innovations

Denote by G_t the real amount of government spending, expressed in units of a Walrasian good and affecting the disposable income of consumers. We will assume throughout that fiscal policies exhibit some persistence known to economic agents. That is, government spending follows the stochastic process

$$G_t = \rho_G G_{t-1} + \sigma_G \epsilon_t^G$$

where $\rho_G \in (0, 1)$ is the first-order autocorrelation of the policy and ϵ_t^G is drawn from a standard normal distribution.

Further, we assume that the intertemporal budget constraint is satisfied through a constant taxation of the additional spending arising from the shocks. Agents repay a constant share of the total present discounted value of the cost of a stimulus program. Denote by $r_G = 1/\beta_G - 1$ the interest rate faced by the government. If the current debt at time t_0 is D_{t_0}, given our previous assumption on financing of government expenditure, we have that the stream of government revenue calculated at time t_0, denoted by $T_t - G_t = -\tau_t$, must be calculated as a constant value $-\tau(D_{t_0})$ for all future periods that solves

$$D_{t_0} = \sum_{i=0}^{\infty} \left\{ \left(\frac{1}{1+r_G} \right)^i \left[-\tau(D_{t_0}) \right] \right\} = \left[-\tau(D_{t_0}) \right] \sum_{i=0}^{\infty} (\beta_G)^i = \frac{-\tau(D_{t_0})}{1-\beta_G}$$

That is, the government levies taxes such that current debt is entirely reimbursed in the limit with equal payments. For the debt to decay at the rate $1/(1+r_G)$, the government needs to tax households at rate

$$T_t = \frac{r_G}{1+r_G} D_t$$

8.5.3 Fiscal multipliers

Denote by Y_t the per-period output of the economy, and by Y_{t_0-1} the value of output in the instant before the fiscal stimulus. Denote by ΔY_t the deviation from Y_{t_0-1} due to the fiscal policy shock, and by $\Delta^{cum} Y_t$ its cumulated value. We can define a GDP multiplier at time horizon t as the quantity $M_D(t)$, where D stands for debt-financed government spending:

$$M_D(t) = \frac{\sum_{k=0}^{t} \Delta^{cum} Y_{t_0+k}}{\sum_{k=0}^{t} G_{t_0+k}} \tag{8.20}$$

From this convenient expression we have the short-run and the long-run multipliers quite readily as

$$\text{Short-run fiscal multiplier:} \quad M_D(0) = \frac{Y_{t_0} - Y_{t_0-1}}{G_{t_0}}$$

$$\text{Long-run fiscal multiplier:} \quad M_D(\infty) = \frac{\sum_{k=0}^{\infty} \Delta^{cum} Y_{t_0+k}}{\sum_{k=0}^{\infty} G_{t_0+k}}$$

Further, the short-run multiplier itself, in a rational expectations setup, depends on the future sequence of spending and how this spending is anticipated by agents. Hence, an interesting special case is a one-shot fiscal impulse on the economy, that is, when $\rho_G = 0$. This isolates the direct effect of government spending from the dynamic effects of spending, and changes in taxes, at different time horizons on the fiscal multiplier function (8.20).

8.5.4 Calibration parameters

We assume that persistence parameter $\rho_G = 0.75^{(1/3)}$, and a standard deviation to the government spending innovations of $\sigma_G = 0.05$. The dynamic response of the economy under log utility for the Walrasian good is represented in figure 8.2. The darker curve is a fiscal expansion, the lighter grey curve is

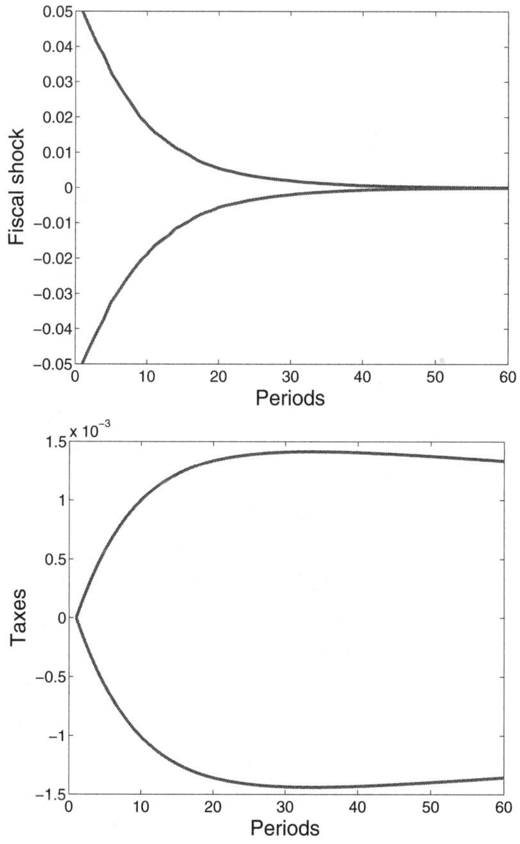

Figure 8.2

Impulse responses to a positive (top curve) or negative (bottom curve) fiscal shock: spending and taxes

a fiscal consolidation, and both imply a perfectly symmetrical sequence of changes. The right panel is taxation as a proportion of the current debt. Since repayment is over an infinite horizon, repayment is much lower than the fiscal impulse for the first part of the sample.

The main channel of transmission of the fiscal expansion is through prices. Due to higher income, the marginal utility of good 0 goes down. The price of good 1 goes up, as the sacrifice of buying good 1 is lower in terms of good 0. Hence, the surplus from consumption goes up. GDP goes up as expected, while unemployment goes down. The number of profitable firms also increases, peaks, and slowly returns to the steady state.

Finally, we can calculate the dynamic fiscal multiplier as the cumulated impact on GDP over the cumulated spending. The multiplier is calculated as the ratio of the cumulated deviation of GDP since impact to the cumulated fiscal expansion. The multiplier is expressed in nominal terms (where GDP is calculated at current prices). It is larger than 1, as reported in figure 8.3, it is evolving between 1.445 on impact, due to the price effect, to 1.485 in the longer run as the entry of more firms propagates the fiscal shock. In the short run, as production does not react to the impulse, the fiscal shock produces inflation in the price of good 1. As time goes on, the price returns to the steady state. A fiscal consolidation, in turn, produces deflation. The fiscal multiplier is larger a fiscal consolidation which corresponds to the intuition on the asymmetries in the cycle seen in chapter 2.

The multiplier is however larger than 1 mostly because prices of the search good 1 increase relative to the Walrasian good. Hence, we also calculate a real multiplier, where the production of the search good is expressed at the initial price of the good at the start of the fiscal expansion, while the other components of GDP are left unchanged. This real multiplier is still above 1, but only marginally so. This is, however, not a result we see as general. In particular, higher values of real multipliers are easily obtained with more concave utility functions and less elastic costs of effort of consumption and advertisement. Extensions of this setup with heterogenous agents would also lead to higher multipliers if the marginal agents affected by policy are facing higher marginal utility of consumption.

8.6 Discussion of the literature and remaining issues

The cyclical behavior of advertisement spending has been studied in Hall (2012). Aguiar et al. (2013), Paciello et al. (2014), and Petrosky-Nadeau et al. (2016) all find evidence of a pro-cyclical movement of consumer search effort.

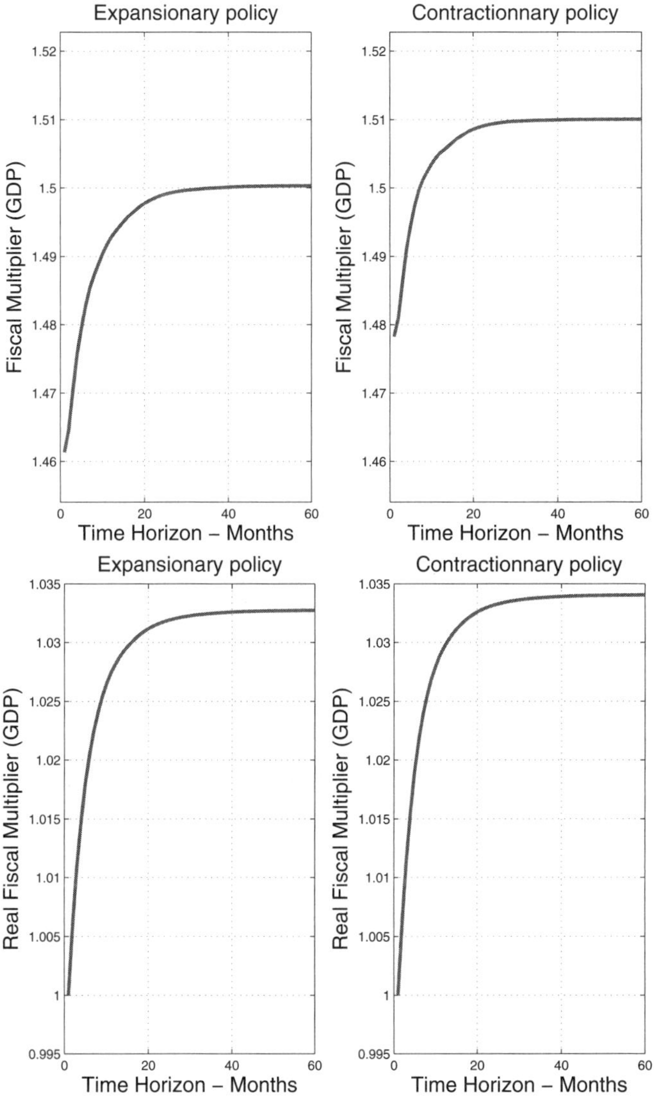

Figure 8.3

Impulse responses to a positive or negative fiscal shock: multiplier and real multiplier, benchmark case

This effort level positively depends on income, and negatively on working hours. The latter effect is used in Kaplan and Menzio (2016) to justify a theory of countercyclical search effort in the goods market, while our model, in line with the other papers in the literature (den Haan, 2013, Gourio and Rudanko, 2014) emphasizes the pro-cyclicality of search effort in that market. Gourio and Rudanko (2014), for instance, find support for firms responding to product market frictions in firm-level data on advertising expenses. The dynamics of the CLG economy were studied and quantified in Petrosky-Nadeau and Wasmer (2015). The particular ability of the model to generate humped-shaped responses to shocks was emphasized in that paper.

Bai et al. (2011) have introduced demand shocks in a model with a (directed) search frictional product market. They have shown that demand-induced changes in capacity utilization, depending on the matching with customers, can cause movements in measured total factor productivity. As a result, what can be thought of having been a technology shock to the econometrician could, in fact, be interpreted as a demand shock. In a related work, Huo and Ríos-Rull (2013) have shown that negative shocks to household wealth can lead to demand-driven recessions that explain part of the recent experience of southern European countries.

The results in this chapter are unchanged when we use Nash bargaining to determine wages. The alternative form for wages from Blanchard and Galí (2010) is convenient. In this setup, wages are isoelastic in productivity, which can sometimes be useful for calibration and robustness exercises. Finally, the model of this chapter had both consumer effort and advertising costs in the goods market Petrosky-Nadeau and Wasmer (2015) show the respective role of each margin. It turns out that the model is not very sensitive to the exact specification of the intensive search margins. The most important features in the dynamics of the goods price and the goods market meeting rates are preserved when search effort is exogenously fixed at a constant.

Alternative models of the goods market and its imperfections are those in the New Keynesian approach, with monopolistically competitive firms. Some, but not all models, capture deviations from perfect competition by the degree of substitutability between various differentiated goods, which is harder to calibrate. In contrast, our approach of frictions in the goods market relies on the rate of capacity utilization, a widely used and comparable statistic across countries, and turnover of consumption flows at the goods level and their cyclical properties. These are studied increasingly studied following the pioneering papers of Aguiar et al. (2013) and Broda and Weinstein (2010). However, the New Keynesian literature has brought many insights, in particular on the optimal monetary policy as in the pathbreaking contributions summarized in Galí (2008) and Clarida et al. (1999), which the new framework has yet to fully explore.

The effect of the fiscal shock is greater when the unemployment rate is high, a feature also present in the work of Michaillat (2014) and Rendahl (2016). The state dependance of the effect of shocks, and policy interventions, opens the door to a fruitful avenue of new research. Indeed, theories are needed to rationalize findings in US data, such as Auerbach and Gorodnichenko (2012), that fiscal multipliers are greater in recessions than in expansions (see also Fazzari et al. (2015)). Owyang et al. (2013) find similar evidence for Canada.

8.7 Concluding words

To conclude this chapter and the overall book, our claim is that the three-market frictional model is a promising approach. It is simple and transparent enough to be summarized by a single equation where all terms identify a well-defined frictional block. It is built sequentially so as to be easily extended in a DSGE framework. It turns out that credit and goods market imperfections are substitutable in raising volatility. Goods market frictions are however *unique* in generating persistence. Contrary to the models of previous chapters, the impulse response of labor market tightness to a productivity shock is humped shaped, reaching a peak after several periods, just as is the case in US data. Very few business cycle models are able to deliver humped-shaped impulse responses to productivity shocks, and generate a positive autocorrelation of growth rates. However, more work will be needed to incorporate proper fiscal and monetary policies in this framework, along the lines of the influential work of Smets and Wouters (2003) and Smets and Wouters (2007), a more systematic task postponed to future research.

8.8 Chapter appendix

8.8.1 Appendix for dynamics of CLG

This appendix introduces the main equations for the discrete time setup. The asset values of the project in the three stages described above are denoted by $E_{j,t}$ with $j = c, v, g$, or π, standing, respectively, for the credit, labor, and goods markets, and the market in which the project is operating. We treat here directly the general case with effort by firms and by consumers. To recover the first three sections of the chapter, it is sufficient to assume that consumer effort e_G and advertising effort e_A are inelastic and equal to 1 and that their cost is a constant equal to zero as a normalization. We use the convenient notation $\beta^C = (1 - s^C)/(1 + r)$ for the generalized discount factor given additional destructions from the credit market, as in chapter 5.

We also assume free entry on the financial market, that is $E_{ct} \equiv 0$ for all t. The Bellman equations of the investment project, which faces a discount rate r, assuming that transitions from the credit to the labor market stages occur within a single period, are

$$E_{ct} = 0 = -\kappa_I + p_t E_{vt} \tag{8.21}$$
$$E_{vt} = \beta^C \mathbb{E}_t \left[q_t E_{gt+1} + (1-q_t) E_{vt+1} \right] \tag{8.22}$$
$$E_{gt} = \beta^C \mathbb{E}_t \left[\left(1 - s^L\right) \left[\frac{e_{At}}{\bar{e}_{At}} \lambda_t E_{\pi t+1} + (1 - \lambda_t \frac{e_{At}}{\bar{e}_{At}}) E_{gt+1} \right] + s^L E_{vt+1} \right] \tag{8.23}$$
$$\begin{aligned} E_{\pi t} &= \mathcal{P}_t x_t - w_t - \psi_t \\ &\quad + \beta^C \mathbb{E}_t \left[\left(1 - s^L\right) \left[(1 - s^G) E_{\pi t+1} + s^G E_{gt+1} \right] + s^L E_{vt+1} \right] \end{aligned} \tag{8.24}$$

The corresponding Bellman equations for the creditor are

$$B_{ct} = 0 = -\kappa_B + \breve{p}_t B_{vt} \tag{8.25}$$
$$B_{vt} = -\gamma + \beta^C \mathbb{E}_t \left[q_t B_{gt+1} + (1-q_t) B_{vt+1} \right] \tag{8.26}$$
$$B_{gt} = -w_t + \beta^C \mathbb{E}_t \left[\left(1 - s^L\right) \left[\frac{e_{At}}{\bar{e}_{At}} \lambda_t B_{\pi t+1} + (1 - \lambda_t \frac{e_{At}}{\bar{e}_{At}}) B_{gt+1} \right] + s^L B_{vt+1} \right] \tag{8.27}$$
$$B_{\pi t} = \psi_t + \beta^C \mathbb{E}_t \left[\left(1 - s^L\right) \left[(1-\tau) B_{\pi t+1} + \tau B_{gt+1} \right] + s^L B_{vt+1} \right] \tag{8.28}$$

where $\mathbb{E}_t$ is an expectations operator over productivity. In the second line, the hiring cost γ does not show up because it is financed by the creditor.

These equations reflect entry conditions: expected entry costs paid by projects or by creditors on financial markets, over and above the costs of hiring labor, have to be equal to the properly discounted value of payoffs received by the different sides of the market. Summing up the value functions, one obtains

$$J_{ct} = 0 \Leftrightarrow \frac{\kappa_B}{\phi_t p_t} + \frac{\kappa_I}{p_t} = J_{vt} \tag{8.29}$$
$$J_{vt} = -\gamma + \beta^C \mathbb{E}_t \left[q_t J_{gt+1} + (1-q_t) J_{vt+1} \right] \tag{8.30}$$
$$\begin{aligned} J_{gt} &= -w_t^g - \sigma_{At} + \beta^C \mathbb{E}_t \\ &\quad \left\{ \left(1 - s^L\right) \left[\frac{e_{At}}{\bar{e}_{At}} \lambda_t J_{\pi t+1} + (1 - \frac{e_{At}}{\bar{e}_{At}} \lambda_t) J_{gt+1} \right] + s^L J_{vt+1} \right\} \end{aligned} \tag{8.31}$$
$$\begin{aligned} J_{\pi t} &= \mathcal{P}_t x_t - w_t^\pi + \beta^C \mathbb{E}_t \\ &\quad \left\{ \left(1 - s^L\right) \left[(1 - s^G) J_{\pi t+1} + s^G J_{gt+1} \right] + s^L J_{vt+1} \right\} \end{aligned} \tag{8.32}$$

The first and second equations can be combined to deliver

$$\frac{\gamma + K(q_t - \beta^C(1-q_t))}{q_t} = \beta^C \mathbb{E}_t J_{gt+1}$$

or with notation $o_t = \frac{1-q_t}{q_t}(1-\beta^C)$,

$$\frac{\gamma}{q_t} + (1+o_t)K = \beta^C \mathbb{E}_t J_{gt+1}$$

8.8.2 Price and wage determination

Utility

We begin by assuming a quasilinear form for consumer utility:

$$U(c_{1,t}, c_{0,t}) = v(c_{1,t}) + c_{0,t}$$

Given these preferences, we can determine the negotiated price for the good c_1 as the outcome of Nash bargaining over the consumption surplus. $\Sigma_g^T = (J_{\pi t} - J_{gt}) + (D_{Mt} - D_{Ut})$. $\alpha_G \in (0,1)$ will be the consumer's bargaining weight. As a first step, we derive expressions for the surplus to the consumption relationship for each side of the market. We have a budget constraint per period (since we assume no savings):

$$\mathcal{P}_t c_{1t} + c_{0t} = I_t$$

Consumer surplus

When matched, the consumer consumes what is available, that is

$$c_{1t} = x_t.$$

Recall the Bellman equations for unmatched and matched consumers, and using for the second line the symmetric equilibrium in efforts with notation $\sigma_{Gt} = \sigma_{Gt}(\bar{e}_{gt})$, we have

$$\begin{aligned} D_{Ut} &= c_{0,t} - \sigma_G(e_{git}) + \beta \mathbb{E}_t \left[\frac{e_{Git}\check{\lambda}_t}{\bar{e}_{Gt}} D_{Mt+1} + \left(1 - \frac{e_{Git}\check{\lambda}_t}{\bar{e}_{Gt}}\right) D_{Ut+1} \right] \\ &= I_t - \sigma_G(\bar{e}_{gt}) + \beta \mathbb{E}_t \left[\check{\lambda}_t \left(D_{Mt+1} - D_{Mt+1}\right) + D_{Ut+1} \right] \\ D_{Mt} &= v(c_{1,t}) + I_t - \mathcal{P}_t c_{1,t} \\ &\quad + \beta^C \left(J_{\pi t+1} - J_{gt+1}\right) + \frac{s^C}{1+r} \mathbb{E}_t D_{Ut+1} \\ &= v(x_t) + I_t - \mathcal{P}_t x_t + \beta^C \left(1 - s^L\right) \mathbb{E}_t \left[D_{Mt+1} - s^G \left(D_{Mt+1} - D_{Mt+1}\right) \right] \\ &\quad + \frac{s^C + (1 - s^C) s^L}{1+r} \mathbb{E}_t D_{Ut+1} \end{aligned}$$

Then the surplus to a match for a consumer is

$$\begin{aligned} D_{Mt} - D_{Ut} = {} & v(x_t) - \mathcal{P}_t x_t + \sigma(\bar{e}_{Gt}) + \\ & + \left[\beta^C \left(1 - s^L\right)(1 - s^G) - \beta \check{\lambda} \right] \mathbb{E}_t \left[D_{Mt+1} - D_{Ut+1} \right] \end{aligned} \tag{8.33}$$

Firm surplus

Similarly, turning to the surplus of a consumption match for a firm, we have, in a symmetric equilibrium on advertising effort

$$J_{\pi t} - J_{gt} = \mathcal{P}_t x_t - w_{\pi_t} + w_{gt} - \sigma_{At} + \left[\beta^C \left(1 - s^L\right)(1 - s^G - \lambda) \right] \mathbb{E}_t \left(J_{\pi t+1} - J_{gt+1}\right)$$

Goods surplus

Summing up the consumption surplus of the firm and of the worker, one obtains

$$\begin{aligned}\Sigma_{gt}^{T} &= v(x_t) - w_{\pi_t} + w_{gt} + \sigma_{Gt} + \sigma_{At} + \\ &+ \left[\beta^{C}\left(1-s^{L}\right)(1-s^{G})\right]\mathbb{E}_t S_{gt+1}^{T} \\ &- \left[\lambda_t \beta^{C}\left(1-s^{L}\right)(1-\alpha_G) + \alpha_G \beta \check{\lambda}_t\right]\mathbb{E}_t S_{gt+1}^{T}\end{aligned}$$

Sharing rule of consumption surplus

From now on, we assume a linear v, with slope Φ. The sharing rule implies constant shares:

$$\mathcal{P}_t = \underset{\mathcal{P}_t}{\operatorname{argmax}} \left(J_{\pi t} - J_{gt}\right)^{1-\alpha_G}\left(D_{Mt} - D_{Ut}\right)^{\alpha_G}$$

$$\Rightarrow (1-\alpha_G)\left(D_{Mt} - D_{Ut}\right) = \alpha_G\left(J_{\pi t} - J_{gt}\right)$$

since $\partial(J_{\pi t} - J_{gt})/\partial \mathcal{P}_t = x_t$ and $\partial(D_{Mt} - D_{Ut})/\partial \mathcal{P}_t = -x_t$. This implies that

$$\begin{aligned}(1-\alpha_G)&\left\{v(x_t) - \mathcal{P}_t x_t + \sigma_{Gt} + \left[\beta^{C}\left(1-s^{L}\right)(1-s^{G}) - \beta\check{\lambda}\right]\alpha_G \mathbb{E}_t S_{gt+1}^{T}\right\} = \\ &\alpha_G\left\{v(x_t) - \mathcal{P}_t x_t + \sigma_{Gt} + \left[\beta^{C}\left(1-s^{L}\right)(1-s^{G}) - \beta\check{\lambda}\right]\alpha_G \mathbb{E}_t S_{gt+1}^{T}\right\}\end{aligned}$$

or

$$\begin{aligned}(1-\alpha_G)&\left\{v(x_t) - \mathcal{P}_t x_t + \sigma_{Gt} + \left[\beta^{C}\left(1-s^{L}\right)(1-s^{G}) - \beta\check{\lambda}\right]\alpha_G \mathbb{E}_t S_{gt+1}^{T}\right\} \\ &= \alpha_G\left\{\mathcal{P}_t x_t - w_{\pi_t} + w_{gt} - \sigma_{At} + \left[\beta^{C}\left(1-s^{L}\right)(1-s^{G})(1-s^{G}-\lambda\right]\right. \\ &\left.\times (1-\alpha_G)\mathbb{E}_t S_{gt+1}^{T}\right\}\end{aligned}$$

After simplification, one obtains

$$\begin{aligned}\mathcal{P}_t x_t = \alpha_G\left(w_{\pi_t} - w_{gt} + \sigma_{At}\right) + (1-\alpha_G)\left(v(x_t) + \sigma_{Gt}\right) \\ + \alpha_G(1-\alpha_G)\left(\left[\beta^{C}\left(1-s^{L}\right)\lambda - \beta\check{\lambda}\right]\right)\mathbb{E}_t S_{gt+1}^{T}\end{aligned}$$

Wage bargaining

Let us start with some definitions and simple math. We have W_{Ut}, the value to a worker of being in the unemployment state, and W_{gt} and $W_{\pi t}$ are the values of being employed at firms in stages g and π, respectively. These values are

$$\begin{aligned}W_{gt} &= w_t^{g} + \beta^{C}\left(1-s^{L}\right)\mathbb{E}_t\left[(1-\lambda_t)W_{gt+1} + \lambda_t W_{\pi t+1}\right] \\ &+ \frac{s^{C} + (1-s^{C})s^{L}}{1+r}\mathbb{E}_t W_{ut+1} \\ W_{\pi t} &= w_t^{\pi} + \beta^{C}\left(1-s^{L}\right)\mathbb{E}_t\left[(1-s^{G})W_{\pi t+1} + s^{G} W_{gt+1}\right] \\ &+ \frac{s^{C} + (1-s^{C})s^{L}}{1+r}\mathbb{E}_t W_{ut+1} \\ W_{ut} &= z + \frac{1}{1+r}\mathbb{E}_t\left[f_t W_{gt+1} + (1-f_t)W_{ut+1}\right]\end{aligned}$$

We will use these to determine the worker's surplus. Introducing the outside option of the worker, we have

$$
\begin{aligned}
W_{gt} &= w_t^g + \beta^C\left(1-s^L\right)\mathbb{E}_t\left[(1-\lambda_t)\left(W_{gt+1}-W_{ut+1}\right)+\lambda_t\left(W_{\pi t+1}-W_{ut+1}\right)\right] \\
&\quad + \frac{s^C+(1-s^C)s^L}{1+r}\mathbb{E}_t W_{ut+1} + \beta^C(1-s^L)\mathbb{E}_t W_{ut+1} \\
&= w_t^g + \beta^C\left(1-s^L\right)\mathbb{E}_t\left[(1-\lambda_t)\left(W_{gt+1}-W_{ut+1}\right)+\lambda_t\left(W_{\pi t+1}-W_{ut+1}\right)\right] \\
&\quad + \beta\mathbb{E}_t W_{ut+1} \\
W_{\pi t} &= w_t^\pi + \beta^C\left(1-s^L\right)\mathbb{E}_t\left[(1-s^G)\left(W_{\pi t+1}-W_{ut+1}\right)+s^G\left(W_{gt+1}-W_{ut+1}\right)\right] \\
&\quad + \frac{s^C+(1-s^C)s^L}{1+r}\mathbb{E}_t W_{ut+1} + \beta^C(1-s^L)\mathbb{E}_t W_{ut+1} \\
&= w_t^\pi + \beta^C\left(1-s^L\right)\mathbb{E}_t\left[(1-s^G)\left(W_{\pi t+1}-W_{ut+1}\right)+s^G\left(W_{gt+1}-W_{ut+1}\right)\right] \\
&\quad + \beta\mathbb{E}_t W_{ut+1} \\
W_{ut} &= z + \beta\mathbb{E}_t f_t\left(W_{gt+1}-W_{ut+1}\right) + \beta W_{ut+1}.
\end{aligned}
$$

and from there, by difference:

$$
\begin{aligned}
W_{gt}-W_{ut} &= w_t^g - z + \mathbb{E}_t\left\{\left[\beta^C\left(1-s^L\right)(1-\lambda_t)-\beta f_t\right]\right. \\
&\qquad \left.\left(W_{gt+1}-W_{ut+1}\right)+\beta^C\lambda_t\left(W_{\pi t+1}-W_{ut+1}\right)\right\} \\
W_{\pi t}-W_{ut} &= w_t^\pi - z + \mathbb{E}_t\left[\left\{\beta^C\left(1-s^L\right)(1-\lambda_t)\right\}\left(W_{\pi t+1}-W_{ut+1}\right)\right. \\
&\qquad \left.+\left(\beta^C(1-s^L)s^G-\beta f_t\right)\left(W_{gt+1}-W_{ut+1}\right)\right]
\end{aligned}
$$

Using the notation $\gamma_k = \gamma + (1-\beta^C)k$, the firm's value equations in a symmetric equilibrium are, introducing the outside option of the firm:

$$
\begin{aligned}
J_{gt} &= -w_t^g - \sigma_{At} + \left(1-s^L\right)\beta^C\mathbb{E}_t\left[\lambda_t\left(J_{\pi t+1}-J_{vt+1}\right)+(1-\lambda_t)(J_{gt+1}-J_{vt+1})\right] \\
&\quad + \beta^C s^L\mathbb{E}_t J_{vt+1} + \left(1-s^L\right)\beta^C\mathbb{E}_t J_{vt+1} \\
&= -w_t^g - \sigma_{At} + \left(1-s^L\right)\beta^C\mathbb{E}_t\left[\lambda_t\left(J_{\pi t+1}-J_{vt+1}\right)+(1-\lambda_t)(J_{gt+1}-J_{vt+1})\right] \\
&\quad + \beta^C\mathbb{E}_t J_{vt+1} \\
J_{\pi t} &= \mathcal{P}_t x_t - w_t^\pi + \left(1-s^L\right)\beta^C\mathbb{E}_t\left[(1-s^G)\left(J_{\pi t+1}-J_{vt+1}\right)+s^G\left(J_{gt+1}-J_{vt+1}\right)\right] \\
&\quad + s^L\beta^C\mathbb{E}_t J_{vt+1} + \left(1-s^L\right)\beta^C\mathbb{E}_t J_{vt+1} \\
&= \mathcal{P}_t x_t - w_t^\pi + \left(1-s^L\right)\beta^C\mathbb{E}_t\left[(1-s^G)\left(J_{\pi t+1}-J_{vt+1}\right)+s^G\left(J_{gt+1}-J_{vt+1}\right)\right] \\
&\quad + \beta^C\mathbb{E}_t J_{vt+1}
\end{aligned}
$$

$$\gamma_k/q = \beta^C \mathbb{E}_t \left(J_{gt+1} - J_{vt+1}\right) \tag{8.34}$$

Assume that the wage rule is decided in stage g and remains constant. This implies that $w_t^g = w_t^\pi$ at a given x^t. The wage rule is therefore the solution to

$$w_t = \text{argmax} \left(J_{gt} - J_{vt}\right)^{1-\alpha_L} \left(W_{gt} - W_{ut}\right)^{\alpha_L} \text{ for both stages in stage } g \tag{8.35}$$

where $\alpha_L \in (0,1)$ is the worker's bargaining weight. The sharing rule implies

$$\alpha_L \left(J_{gt} - J_{vt}\right) = (1-\alpha_L)\left[W_{gt} - W_{ut}\right]$$

This leads to

$$\alpha_L \Big\{-w_t - K - \sigma_{At} + \left(1 - s^L\right)\beta^C \mathbb{E}_t \left[\lambda_t \left(J_{\pi t+1} - J_{vt+1}\right)\right.$$
$$\left. + (1-\lambda_t)(J_{gt+1} - J_{vt+1})\right] + \beta^C \mathbb{E}_t K\Big\} =$$
$$(1-\alpha_L)\Big\{w_t - z + \mathbb{E}_t \Big\{\Big[\beta^C\left(1 - s^L\right)(1-\lambda_t) - \beta f_t\Big]\left(W_{gt+1} - W_{ut+1}\right)$$
$$+ \beta^C \lambda_t \left(W_{\pi t+1} - W_{ut+1}\right)\Big\}\Big\}$$

Using the bargaining equation in stage g at t+1, one simplifies to

$$w_t = \alpha_L \Big\{-k(\phi) - \sigma_{At} + \left(1 - s^L\right)\beta^C \mathbb{E}_t \left[\lambda_t \left(J_{\pi t+1} - J_{vt+1}\right)\right]\Big\}$$
$$+ (1-\alpha_L)\left\{z + \mathbb{E}_t\left[\beta f_t \left(W_{gt+1} - W_{ut+1}\right) - \lambda_t \left(W_{\pi t+1} - W_{ut+1}\right)\right]\right\}$$

Replacing $(1-\alpha_L)\beta f_t \left(W_{gt+1} - W_{ut+1}\right)$ by $\frac{\alpha_L \beta^C f_t}{1-s^C}\left(J_{gt+1} - J_{vt+1}\right) = \alpha_L \frac{\gamma_k \theta}{1-s^C}$, the latter replacement coming from equation (8.34), one further has

$$w_t = \alpha_L \Big\{-k(\phi) - \sigma_{At} + \left(1 - s^L\right)\beta^C \mathbb{E}_t \left[\lambda_t \left(J_{\pi t+1} - J_{vt+1}\right)\right] + \gamma_k \theta/(1 - s^C)\Big\}$$
$$+ (1-\alpha_L)\Big\{z + \beta^C \left(1 - s^L\right)\mathbb{E}_t \left[-\lambda_t \left(W_{\pi t+1} - W_{ut+1}\right)\right]\Big\}$$

Denote by ω_0 the (Pissarides-equivalent) wage with

$$\omega_0 = \alpha_L \Big[-k(\phi) - \sigma_{At} + \gamma_k \theta/(1 - s^C)\Big] + (1-\alpha_L) z$$

Then the wage w_t is the sum of ω_0 and of forward-looking terms proportional to A_{t+1} where

$$A_{t+1} = \left(1 - s^L\right)\beta^C \lambda_t \mathbb{E}_t \left[\alpha_L \left(J_{\pi t+1} - J_{vt+1}\right) - (1-\alpha_L)\left(W_{\pi t+1} - W_{ut+1}\right)\right]$$

Note however that A_{t+1} can be simplified too. Notice first that

$$W_{\pi t+1} = W_{gt+1}$$

Note also that, using $J_{\pi t+1} - J_{vt+1} = \left(J_{\pi t+1} - J_{gt+1}\right) + \left(J_{gt+1} - J_{vt+1}\right)$, the last part cancels out with the surplus of the worker in t+1, so that

$$\begin{aligned} A_{t+1} &= \left(1 - s^L\right) \beta^C \lambda_t \alpha_L \mathbb{E}_t \left(J_{\pi t+1} - J_{gt+1}\right) \\ &= \left(1 - s^L\right) \beta^C \lambda_t \alpha_L \left[\mathbb{E}\mathcal{P}x_{t+1} + \left(1 - s^L\right) \beta^C (1 - s^G - \lambda_t) \left(J_{\pi t+2} - J_{gt+2}\right)\right] \end{aligned}$$

In other words, the wage is the sum of the static wage and a term reflecting the future revenues discounted at rate $\left(1 - s^L\right) \beta^C \lambda_t$ and their continuation value.

Bibliography

Abeille-Becker, C. and Clerc, P. (2013). The cyclical behavior of the unemployment, job finding and separation rates,. *Revue Economique*, 64(3):519–526.

Acemoglu, D. and Hawkins, W. B. (2014). Search with multi-worker firms. *Theoretical Economics*, 9(3):583–628.

Acemoglu, D. and Shimer, R. (1999a). Efficient Unemployment Insurance. *Journal of Political Economy*, 107(5):893–928.

Acemoglu, D. and Shimer, R. (1999b). Holdups and efficiency with search frictions. *International Economic Review*, 40(4):827–849.

Acemoglu, D. and Shimer, R. (2000). Productivity gains from unemployment insurance. *European Economic Review*, 44(7):1195–1224.

Aguiar, M., Hurst, E., and Karabarbounis, L. (2013). Time use during the great recession. *The American Economic Review*, 103(5):1664–1696.

Albrecht, J., Decreuse, B., and Vroman, S. (2015). Directed search with phantom vacancies. Mimeo, Georgetown University.

Altig, D., Christiano, L., Eichenbaum, M., and Linde, J. (2011). Firm-specific capital, nominal rigidities and the business cycle. *Review of Economic Dynamics*, 14(2):225–247.

Amaral, P. S. and Tasci, M. (2016). The cyclical behavior of equilibrium unemployment and vacancies across oecd countries. *European Economic Review*, 84:184–201.

Andolfatto, D. (1996). Business cycles and labor-market search. *The american economic review*, 86(1):112–132.

Andolfatto, D. (1997). Evidence and theory on the cyclical asymmetry in unemployment rate fluctuations. *Canadian Journal of Economics*, 30(3):709–21.

Arseneau, D. M., Chahrour, R., Chugh, S. K., and Shapiro, A. F. (2015). Optimal fiscal and monetary policy in customer markets. *Journal of Money, Credit and Banking, Blackwell Publishing*, 47(4):617–672.

Arseneau, D. M. and Chugh, S. K. (2012). Tax smoothing in frictional labor markets. *Journal of Political Economy, University of Chicago Press*, 120(5):926 – 985.

Aruoba, B. S., Rocheteau, G., and Waller, C. (2007). Bargaining and the value of money. *Journal of Monetary Economics*, 54(8):2636–2655.

Auerbach, A. J. and Gorodnichenko, Y. (2012). Fiscal Multipliers in Recession and Expansion. In *Fiscal Policy after the Financial Crisis*, NBER Chapters, pages 63–98. National Bureau of Economic Research, Inc.

Bai, Y., Rios-Rull, V., and Storesletten, K. (2011). Demand shocks that look like productivity shocks. Mimeo University of Minnesota.

Barnichon, R. (2010). Building a composite help-wanted index. *Economics Letters*, 109(3): 175–178.

Basu, S. and Fernald, J. G. (1997). Returns to scale in u.s. production: Estimates and implications. *Journal of Political Economy*, 105(2):249–83.

Bauducco, S. and Janiak, A. (2015). Can a non-binding minimum wage reduce wages and employment? Documentos de Trabajo 308, Centro de Economía Aplicada, Universidad de Chile.

Beaubrun-Diant, K. E. and Tripier, F. (2015). Search frictions, credit market liquidity and net interest margin cyclicality. *Economica*, 82:79–102.

Bentolila, S., Jansen, M., Jiménez, G., and Ruano, S. (2013). When Credit Dries Up: Job Losses in the Great Recession. CEPR Discussion Papers 9776, C.E.P.R. Discussion Papers.

Berentsen, A., Menzio, G., and Wright, R. (2011). Inflation and unemployment in the long run. *American Economic Review*, 101(1):371–98.

Berger, A. N. and Udell, G. F. (1995). Relationship Lending and Lines of Credit in Small Firm Finance. *The Journal of Business*, 68(3):351–81.

Bernanke, B. and Gertler, M. (1989). Agency costs, net worth, and business fluctuations. *American Economic Review*, 79(1):14–31.

Bernanke, B., Gertler, M., and Gilchrist, S. (1996). The financial accelerator and the flight to quality. *The Review of Economics and Statistics*, 78(1):1–15.

Bernanke, B. S. and Gertler, M. (1995). Inside the black box: The credit channel of monetary policy transmission. *Journal of Economic Perspectives*, 9(4):27–48.

Bethune, Z., Rocheteau, G., and Rupert, P. (2015). Aggregate unemployment and household unsecured debt. *Review of Economic Dynamics*, 18(1):77–100.

Binmore, K., Rubinstein, A., and Wolinsky, A. (1986). The nash bargaining solution in economic modelling. *The RAND Journal of Economics*, pages 176–188.

Blanchard, O. and Galí, J. (2010). Labor markets and monetary policy: A new keynesian model with unemployment. *American Economic Journal: Macroeconomics*, 2(2):1–30.

Blanchflower, D. G. and Oswald, A. J. (1998). What Makes an Entrepreneur? *Journal of Labor Economics*, 16(1):26–60.

Boeri, T., Garibaldi, P., and Moen, E. R. (2015). Financial Frictions, Financial Shocks and Unemployment Volatility. CEPR Discussion Papers 10648, C.E.P.R. Discussion Papers.

Branch, W. A., Petrosky-Nadeau, N., and Rocheteau, G. (2014). Financial frictions, the housing market, and unemployment. Working Paper Series 2014-26, Federal Reserve Bank of San Francisco.

Broda, C. and Weinstein, D. E. (2010). Product creation and destruction: Evidence and price implications. *American Economic Review*, 100(3):691–723.

Bronars, Stephen, G. and Deere, Donald, R. (1991). The threat of unionization, the use of debt, and the preservation of shareholder wealth. *The Quarterly Journal of Economics V*, 106(1): 231–254.

Brugemann, B. (2014). Privately Efficient Wage Rigidity Under Diminishing Returns. VU University Amsterdam and Tinbergen Institute.

Brügemann, B., Gautier, P., and Menzio, G. (2015). Intra firm bargaining and shapley values. Technical report, National Bureau of Economic Research.

Brzustowski, T., Petrosky-Nadeau, N., and Wasmer, E. (2017). Disentangling goods, labor, and credit market frictions in three european economies. *Labour Economics*, forthcoming.

Burda, M. and Wyplosz, C. (1994). Gross worker and job flows in europe. *European Economic Review*, 38(6):1287–1315.

Burda, M. C. (1992). A note on firing costs and severance benefits in equilibrium unemployment. *The Scandinavian Journal of Economics*, 94(3):pp. 479–489.

Burda, M. C. and Profit, S. (1996). Matching across space: Evidence on mobility in the czech republic. *Labour Economics*, 3(3):255 – 278.

Burdett, K. and Mortensen, D. T. (1998). Wage differentials, employer size, and unemployment. *International Economic Review*, 39(2):pp. 257–273.

Cahuc, P. and Challe, E. (2012). Produce of speculate? asset bubbles, occupational choices and efficiency. *International Economic Review*, 53:1005–1035.

Cahuc, P., Marque, F., and Wasmer, E. (2008). A theory of wages and labor demand with intra-firm bargaining and matching frictions. *International Economic Review*, 49(3):943–972.

Cahuc, P. and Wasmer, E. (2001). Does intrafirm bargaining matter in the large firm's matching model? *Macroeconomic Dynamics*, 5(05):742–747.

Carbonnier, C. (2014). Payroll taxation and the structure of quali cations and wages in a segmented frictional labor market with intra-rm bargaining. Technical report, THEMA (THéorie Economique, Modélisation et Applications), Université de Cergy-Pontoise.

Carlstrom, C. T. and Fuerst, T. S. (1997). Agency costs, net worth, and business fluctuations: A computable general equilibrium analysis. *American Economic Review*, 87(5):893–910.

Carrillo-Tudela, C., Graber, M., and Wälde, K. (2015). Unemployment and vacancy dynamics with imperfect financial markets.

Carrillo-Tudela, C., Menzio, G., and Smith, E. (2011). Job search with bidder memories. *International Economic Review*, 52(3):639–655.

Cheron, A. and Decreuse, B. (2017). Matching with phantoms. *Review of Economic Studies*, forthcoming.

Chodorow-Reich, G. and Karabarbounis, L. (2015). The cyclicality of the opportunity cost of employment. Working Paper 126541, Harvard University OpenScholar.

Cipollone, A. and Giordani, P. (2015). Market frictions in entrepreneurial innovation: Theory and evidence. Technical report, Dipartimento di Economia e Finanza, LUISS Guido Carli.

Cipollone, A. and Giordani, P. (2016). When entrepreneurs meet financiers: Evidence from the business angel market. *MPRA Paper, University Library of Munich, Germany*.

Clarida, R., Gali, J., and Gertler, M. (1999). The science of monetary policy: A new keynesian perspective. *Journal of Economic Literature*, 37(4):1661–1707.

Clerc, P. (2015). Alternating offers with asymmetric information and the unemployment volatility puzzle. mimeo, Banque de France.

Cogley, T. and Nason, J. M. (1995). Effects of the hodrick-prescott filter on trend and difference stationary time series implications for business cycle research. *Journal of Economic Dynamics and Control*, 19(1–2):253 – 278.

Cole, H. L. and Rogerson, R. (1999). Can the mortensen-pissarides matching model match the business-cycle facts? *International Economic Review*, 40(4):933–959.

Coles, M. and Petrongolo, B. (2009). A test between stock-flow matching and the random matching function approach. *International Economic Review*, 49(4):1113–1141.

Coles, M. G. and Muthoo, A. (1998). Strategic bargaining and competitive bidding in a dynamic market equilibrium. *Review of Economic Studies*, 65:235– 260.

Coles, M. G. and Smith, E. (1998). Marketplaces and matching. *International Economic Review*, 39(239-255).

Cooper, R., Haltiwanger, J., and Willis, J. L. (2007). Search frictions: Matching aggregate and establishment observations. *Journal of Monetary Economics*, 54(Supplemental):56–78.

Costain, J. S. and Reiter, M. (2008). Business cycles, unemployment insurance, and the calibration of matching models. *Journal of Economic Dynamics and Control*, 32(4):1120 – 1155.

de Fontenay, C. C. and Gans, J. S. (2003). Organizational Design and Technology Choice under Intrafirm Bargaining: Comment. *American Economic Review*, 93(1):448–455.

de Fontenay, C. C. and Gans, J. S. (2004). Intrafirm bargaining with heterogeneous replacement workers. MBS working papers; 2004, 34.

Delacroix, A. and Wasmer, E. (2009). Layoff Costs and Efficiency with Asymmetric Information. IZA Discussion Papers 4524, Institute for the Study of Labor (IZA).

den Haan, W. (2013). Inventories and the role of goods-market frictions for business cycles. mimeo London School of Economics.

den Haan, W. J., Ramey, G., and Watson, J. (2000). Job destruction and propagation of shocks. *American Economic Review*, 90(3):482–498.

den Haan, W. J., Ramey, G., and Watson, J. (2003). Liquidity flows and fragility of business enterprises. *Journal of Monetary Economics*, 50(6):1215–1241.

Diamond, P. A. (1971). A model of price adjustment. *Journal of Economic Theory*, 3(2): 156–168.

Diamond, P. A. (1982). Aggregate demand management in search equilibrium. *Journal of Political Economy*, 90(5):pp. 881–894.

Diamond, P. A. and Maskin, E. (1979). An Equilibrium Analysis of Search and Breach of Contract, I: Steady States. *Bell Journal of Economics*, 10(1):282–316.

Duffie, D., Gârleanu, N., and Pedersen, L. H. (2005). Over-the-counter markets. *Econometrica*, 73(6):pp. 1815–1847.

Ebell, M. and Haefke, C. (2006). Product Market Regulation and Endogenous Union Formation. IZA Discussion Papers 2222, Institute for the Study of Labor (IZA).

Ebell, M. and Haefke, C. (2009). Product Market Deregulation and the U.S. Employment Miracle. *Review of Economic Dynamics*, 12(3):479–504.

Ebrahimy, E. and Shimer, R. (2010). Stock-flow matching. *Journal of Economic Theory*, 145(4):1325–1353.

Elsby, M. W. and Michaels, R. (2013). Marginal jobs, heterogeneous firms, and unemployment flows. *American Economic Journal: Macroeconomics*, 5(1):1–48.

Engelhardt, B. and Rupert, P. (2009). Competitive search versus random matching with bargaining: A test of direction and efficiency. Mimeo, UC Santa Barbara.

Faberman, J. and Menzio, G. (2010). Evidence on the relationship between recruiting and the starting wage. mimeo, University of Pennsylvannia.

Fazzari, S. M., Morley, J., and Panovska, I. (2015). State-dependent effects of fiscal policy. *Studies in Nonlinear Dynamics and Econometrics*, 19(3):285–315.

Felbermayr, G. J., Larch, M., and Lechthaler, W. (2012). The shimer-puzzle of international trade: A quantitative analysis. Ifo Working Paper Series Ifo Working Paper No. 134, Ifo Institute for Economic Research at the University of Munich.

Fenn, G. W., Liang, N., and Prowse, S. (1995). The economics of the private equity market. Staff Studies 168, Board of Governors of the Federal Reserve System (U.S.).

Fujita, S. and Ramey, G. (2007). Job matching and propagation. *Journal of Economic Dynamics and Control*, 31(11):3671–3698.

Fujita, S. and Ramey, G. (2009). The Cyclicality Of Separation And Job Finding Rates. *International Economic Review*, 50(2):415–430.

Galí, J. (2008). *J Gali Monetary Policy, Inflation, and the Business Cycle: An Introduction to the New Keynesian Framework*. Princeton University Press.

Galí, J. and van Rens, T. (2014). The vanishing procyclicality of labor productivity. CREI working paper.

Garibaldi, P. and Wasmer, E. (2005). Equilibrium search unemployment, endogenous participation, and labor market flows. *Journal of the European Economic Association, MIT Press*, 3(4): 851–882.

Garin, J. (2015). Borrowing constraints, collateral fluctuations, and the labor market. *Journal of Economic Dynamics and Control*, 57:112–130.

Gertler, M. and Trigari, A. (2009). Unemployment fluctuations with staggered nash wage bargaining. *Journal of Political Economy*, 117(1):38–86.

Gilchrist, S. and Zakrajšek, E. (2012). Credit spreads and business cycle fluctuations. *American Economic Review*, 102(4):1692–1720.

Gourio, F. and Rudanko, L. (2014). Customer capital. *Review of Economic Studies*, 81(3):1102–1136.

Guerrieri, V. (2008). Inefficient unemployment dynamics under asymmetric information. *Journal of Political Economy*, 116(4):pp. 667–708.

Guerrieri, V., Shimer, R., and Wright, R. (2010). Adverse Selection in Competitive Search Equilibrium. *Econometrica*, 78(6):1823–1862.

Haefke, C., Sonntag, M., and van Rens, T. (2013). Wage rigidity and job creation. *Journal of Monetary Economics*, 60(8):887–899.

Hagedorn, M. and Manovskii, I. (2008). The cyclical behavior of equilibrium unemployment and vacancies revisited. *American Economic Review*, 98(4):1692–1706.

Hairault, J.-O., Langot, F., and Osotimehin, S. (2010). Matching frictions, unemployment dynamics and the cost of business cycles. *Review of Economic Dynamics*, 13(4):759 – 779.

Hall, R. E. (2005). Employment fluctuations with equilibrium wage stickiness. *American Economic Review*, 95(1):50–65.

Hall, R. E. (2012). The cyclical response of advertising refutes counter-cyclical profit margins in favor of product-market frictions. NBER Working Papers 18370, National Bureau of Economic Research, Inc.

Hall, R. E. (2017). High discounts and high unemployment. *American Economic Review*, 107(2):305–30.

Hall, R. E. and Krueger, A. B. (2012). Evidence on the incidence of wage posting, wage bargaining, and on-the-job search. *American Economic Journal: Macroeconomics*, 4(4):56–67.

Hall, R. E. and Milgrom, P. R. (2008). The limited influence of unemployment on the wage bargain. *American Economic Review*, 98(4):1653–74.

Hall, R. E. and Schulhofer-Wohl, S. (2016). Measuring job-finding rates and matching efficiency with heterogeneous jobseekers. mimeo, Stanford University.

Hawkins, W. B. (2011). Do large-firm bargaining models amplify and propagate aggregate productivity shocks? Mimeo, University of Rochester.

Helpman, E. and Itskhoki, O. (2010). Labour market rigidities, trade and unemployment. *Review of Economic Studies*, 77(3):1100–1137.

Hertweck, M. S. (2013). Strategic wage bargaining, labor market volatility, and persistence. *The B.E. Journal of Macroeconomics*, 13(1):27.

Hodrick, R. J. and Prescott, E. C. (1997). Postwar us business cycles: An empirical investigation. *Journal of Money, Credit and Banking*, 29(1):1–16.

Hornstein, A. and Kudlyak, M. (2016). Estimating matching efficiency with variable search effort. Working Paper 2016-24, Federal Reserve Bank of San Francisco.

Hosios, A. J. (1990). On the efficiency of matching and related models of search and unemployment. *The Review of Economic Studies*, 57(2):279–298.

Huo, Z. and Ríos-Rull, J.-V. (2013). Paradox of thrift recessions. Working Paper 19443, National Bureau of Economic Research.

Iliopulos, E., Langot, F., and Sopraseuth, T. (2014). Welfare Cost of Fluctuations: when Labor Market Search Interacts with Financial Frictions. Documents de travail du Centre d'Economie de la Sorbonne 14042, Université Panthéon-Sorbonne (Paris 1), Centre d'Economie de la Sorbonne.

Jaffee, D. and Stiglitz, J. (1990). Credit rationing. In Friedman, B. M. and Hahn, F. H., editors, *Handbook of Monetary Economics*, volume 2 of *Handbook of Monetary Economics*, chapter 16, pages 837–888. Elsevier, Amsterdam.

Janiak, A. (2013). Structural unemployment and the costs of firm entry and exit. *Labour Economics*, 23:1–19.

Janiak, A. and Wasmer, E. (2014). Employment protection and capital-labor ratios. IZA Discussion Papers 8362, Institute for the Study of Labor (IZA), http://ideas.repec.org/p/iza/izadps/dp8362.html.

Jermann, U. and Quadrini, V. (2012). Macroeconomic Effects of Financial Shocks. *American Economic Review*, 102(1):238–71.

Jung, P. and Kuester, K. (2011). The (un)importance of unemployment fluctuations for the welfare cost of business cycles. *Journal of Economic Dynamics and Control*, 35(10):1744–1768.

Kaas, L. and Kircher, P. (2015). Efficient firm dynamics in a frictional labor market. *The American Economic Review*, 105(10):3030–3060.

Kalai, E. (1977). Proportional solutions to bargaining situations: Interpersonal utility comparisons. *Econometrica*, 45(7):pp. 1623–1630.

Kalai, E. and Smorodinsky, M. (1975). Other solutions to nash's bargaining problem. *Econometrica*, 43(3):pp. 513–518.

Kaplan, G. and Menzio, G. (2016). Shopping Externalities and Self-Fulfilling Unemployment Fluctuations. *Journal of Political Economy*, 124(3):771–825.

Kennan, J. (2010). Private information, wage bargaining and employment fluctuations. *The Review of Economic Studies*, 77(2):633–664.

Kim, J. (2015). *Wage Negotiations in Multi-worker Firms and Stochastic Bargaining Powers of Existing Workers*. PhD thesis, University of Minnesota.

Kiyotaki, N. and Moore, J. (1997). Credit cycles. *Journal of Political Economy*, 105(2):211–48.

Kiyotaki, N. and Wright, R. (1989). On money as a medium of exchange. *Journal of Political Economy*, 97(4):pp. 927–954.

Kocherlakota, N. (2011). Bubbles and unemployment. President's speech, Federal Reserve Bank of Minneapolis.

Krause, M. U. and Lubik, T. A. (2007). The (ir)relevance of real wage rigidity in the New Keynesian model with search frictions. *Journal of Monetary Economics*, 54(3):706–727.

Krause, M. U. and Lubik, T. A. (2013). Does Intra-Firm Bargaining Matter for Business Cycle Dynamics? *Economic Quarterly*, (3Q):229–250.

Krusell, P., Mukoyama, T., Rogerson, R., and Sahin, A. (2011). A three state model of worker flows in general equilibrium. *Journal of Economic Theory*, 146(3):1107–1133.

Kurmann, A. (2014). Holdups and overinvestment in capital markets. *Journal of Economic Theory*, 151:88–113.

Lagos, R. and Rocheteau, G. (2009). Liquidity in asset markets with search frictions. *Econometrica*, 77(2):pp. 403–426.

Lagos, R. and Wright, R. (2005). A unified framework for monetary theory and policy analysis. *Journal of Political Economy*, 113(3):pp. 463–484.

Lale, E. (2016). Labor-market frictions, incomplete insurance and severance payments. mimeo, University of Bristol.

Langot, F. (1995). Unemployment and business cycle: A general equilibrium matching model. In Henin, P.-Y., editor, *Advances in Business Cycle Research*, pages 287–325. Springer, Berlin.

Launov, A. and Walde, K. (2013). Estimating incentive and welfare effects of non-stationary unemployment benefits. *International Economic Review*, 54(4):1159–1198.

Lehmann, E. and Van der Linden, B. (2010). Search frictions on product and labor markets: Money in the matching function. *Macroeconomic Dynamics*, 14(1):56–92.

l'Haridon, O., Malherbet, F., and Pérez-Duarte, S. (2013). Does bargaining matter in the small firms matching model? *Labour Economics*, 21:42 – 58.

Ljungqvist, L. and Sargent, T. J. (2015). The Fundamental Surplus in Matching Models. CEPR Discussion Papers 10489, C.E.P.R. Discussion Papers.

Ljunqvist, L. (2002). How do lay-off costs affect employment? *The Economic Journal*, 112(482):829–853.

Lucas, R. E. (1987). *Models of Business Cycles*. Oxford: Basil Blackwell.

Lucas, R. E. (2003). Macroeconomic priorities. *American Economic Review*, 93(1):1–14.

MacLeod, W. B. and Malcomson, J. M. (1993). Investments, holdup, and the form of market contracts. *American Economic Review*, 83(4):811–37.

Malcomson, J. M. (1999). Individual employment contracts. In Ashenfelter, O. and Card, D., editors, *Handbook of Labor Economics*, volume 3 of *Handbook of Labor Economics*, chapter 35, pages 2291–2372. Elsevier, Amsterdam.

Marimon, R. and Zilibotti, F. (1999). Unemployment vs. mismatch of talents: Reconsidering unemployment benefits. *The Economic Journal*, 109(455):266–291.

Marinescu, I. and Wolthoff, R. (2015). Opening the black box of the matching function: The power of words. mimeo, University of Toronto.

Menzio, G. and Moen, E. R. (2010). Worker replacement. *Journal of Monetary Economics*, 57(6)(623-636).

Menzio, G. and Shi, S. (2011). Efficient search on the job and the business cycle. *Journal of Political Economy*, 119(3):468 – 510.

Merz, M. (1995). Search in the labor market and the real business cycle. *Journal of Monetary Economics*, 36(2):269–300.

Merz, M. and Yashiv, E. (2007). Labor and the market value of the firm. *American Economic Review*, 97(4):1419–1431.

Michaillat, P. (2014). A theory of countercyclical government multiplier. *American Economic Journal: Macroeconomics*, 6(1):190–217.

Michaillat, P. and Saez, E. (2014). An Economical Business-Cycle Model. NBER Working Papers 19777, National Bureau of Economic Research, Inc.

Michelacci, C. and Quadrini, V. (2009). Financial markets and wages. *Review of Economic Studies*, 76(2):795–827.

Moen, E. R. (1997). Competitive search equilibrium. *Journal of Political Economy*, 105(2):385–411.

Moen, E. R. and Rosén, Å. (2011). Incentives in competitive search equilibrium. *The Review of Economic Studies*, 4(6):733–761.

Monacelli, T., Quadrini, V., and Trigari, A. (2011a). Financial Markets and Unemployment. NBER Working Papers 17389, National Bureau of Economic Research, Inc.

Monacelli, T., Quadrini, V., and Trigari, A. (2011b). Financial markets and unemployment. Technical report, National Bureau of Economic Research.

Mortensen, D. and Nagypal, E. (2007). More on unemployment and vacancy fluctuations. *Review of Economic Dynamics*, 10(3):327–347.

Mortensen, D. T. (1982a). The matching process as a noncooperative bargaining game. In *The Economics of Information and Uncertainty*, NBER Chapters, pages 233–258. National Bureau of Economic Research, Inc.

Mortensen, D. T. (1982b). Property Rights and Efficiency in Mating, Racing, and Related Games. *American Economic Review*, 72(5):968–79.

Mortensen, D. T. (1986). Job search and labor market analysis. In Ashenfelter, O. and Layard, R., editors, *Handbook of Labor Economics*, volume 2 of *Handbook of Labor Economics*, chapter 15, pages 849–919. Elsevier, Amsterdam.

Mortensen, D. T. (1999). Equilibrium unemployment dynamics. *International Economic Review*, 40(4):889–914.

Mortensen, D. T. (2009). Wage dispersion in the search and matching model with intra-firm bargaining. Working Paper 15033, National Bureau of Economic Research, http://www.nber.org/papers/w15033.

Mortensen, D. T. and Pissarides, C. A. (1994). Job creation and job destruction in the theory of unemployment. *The Review of Economic Studies*, 61(3):397–415.

Mortensen, D. T. and Pissarides, C. A. (1999a). New developments in models of search in the labor market. In Ashenfelter, O. and Card, D., editors, *Handbook of Labor Economics*, volume 3 of *Handbook of Labor Economics*, chapter 39, pages 2567–2627. Elsevier.

Mortensen, D. T. and Pissarides, C. A. (1999b). Unemployment responses to 'skill-biased' technology shocks: the role of labour market policy. *The Economic Journal*, 109(455):242–265.

Mortensen, D. T. and Pissarides, C. A. (2011). *Job Matching, Wage Dispersion, and Unemployment*. Oxford University Press Oxford.

Mulligan, C. B. (2012). Do welfare policies matter for labor market aggregates? quantifying safety net work incentives since 2007. Working Paper 18088, National Bureau of Economic Research.

Myerson, R. B. (1984). Two-person bargaining problems with incomplete information. *Econometrica*, 52(2):461–487.

Neftci, S. N. (1984). Are Economic Time Series Asymmetric over the Business Cycle? *Journal of Political Economy*, 92(2):307–28.

Nekarda, C. J. and Ramey, V. A. (2011). Industry evidence on the effects of government spending. *American Economic Journal: Macroeconomics*, 3(1):36–59.

Nicoletti, G. and Pierrard, O. (2006). Capital market frictions and the business cycle. Discussion Papers (ECON - Département des Sciences Economiques) 2006053, Université catholique de Louvain, Département des Sciences Economiques, http://ideas.repec.org/p/ctl/louvec/2006053.html.

Nosal, E. and Rocheteau, G. (2011). *Money, Payments, and Liquidity*, volume 1 of *MIT Press Books*. The MIT Press, Cambridge, United States of America.

Osborne, M. and Rubinstein, A. (1990). *Bargaining and Markets*. Academic Press, San Diego.

Owyang, M. T., Ramey, V. A., and Zubairy, S. (2013). Are government spending multipliers greater during periods of slack? evidence from twentieth-century historical data. *American Economic Review*, 103(3):129–34.

Paciello, L., Pozzi, A., and Trachter, N. (2014). Price dynamics with customer markets. Working Paper No. 14-17, FRB Richmond.

Perotti, Enrico, C. and Spier, Kathryn, E. (1993). Capital structure as a bargaining tool: The role of leverage in contract renegotiation. *The American Economic Review*, 83(5):1131–1141.

Petersen, M. A. and Rajan, R. G. (1994). The benefits of lending relationships: Evidence from small business data. *The Journal of Finance*, 49(1):pp. 3–37.

Petrongolo, B. and Pissarides, C. A. (2001). Looking into the black box: A survey of the matching function. *Journal of Economic Literature*, 39(2):390–431.

Petrosky-Nadeau, N. (2013). Tfp during a credit crunch. *Journal of Economic Theory*, 148(3): 1150–1178.

Petrosky-Nadeau, N. (2014). Credit, Vacancies and Unemployment Fluctuations. *Review of Economic Dynamics*, 17(2):191–205.

Petrosky-Nadeau, N., Tengelsen, B., and Wasmer, E. (2015). Credit and labor market frictions over the business cycle.

Petrosky-Nadeau, N. and Wasmer, E. (2011). Macroeconomic Dynamics in a Model of Goods, Labor and Credit Market Frictions. IZA Discussion Papers 5763, Institute for the Study of Labor (IZA).

Petrosky-Nadeau, N. and Wasmer, E. (2013). The cyclical volatility of labor markets under frictional financial markets. *American Economic Journal: Macroeconomics*, 5(1):193–221.

Petrosky-Nadeau, N. and Wasmer, E. (2015). Macroeconomic dynamics in a model of goods, labor, and credit market frictions. *Journal of Monetary Economics*, 72(C):97–113.

Petrosky-Nadeau, N., Wasmer, E., and Zeng, S. (2016). Shopping time. *Economics Letters*, 143:52–60.

Petrosky-Nadeau, N. and Zhang, L. (2013). Unemployment crises. Working Paper 19207, National Bureau of Economic Research.

Petrosky-Nadeau, N. and Zhang, L. (forthcoming). Solving the dmp model accurately. *Quantitative Economics*.

Pissarides, C. A. (1979). Job Matchings with State Employment Agencies and Random Search. *Economic Journal*, 89(356):818–33.

Pissarides, C. A. (1984). Search Intensity, Job Advertising, and Efficiency. *Journal of Labor Economics*, 2(1):128–43.

Pissarides, C. A. (1985). Short-run equilibrium dynamics of unemployment vacancies, and real wages. *American Economic Review*, 75(4):676–90.

Pissarides, C. A. (1990). *Equilibrium Unemployment Theory*. Oxford: Basil Blackwell, 1st edition.

Pissarides, C. A. (1998). The impact of employment tax cuts on unemployment and wages; the role of unemployment benefits and tax structure. *European Economic Review*, 42(1):155–183.

Pissarides, C. A. (2000). *Equilibrium unemployment theory*. The MIT press, United States of America, 2nd edition.

Pissarides, C. A. (2009). The unemployment volatility puzzle: Is wage stickiness the answer? *Econometrica*, 77(5):1339–1369.

Postel-Vinay, F. and Robin, J.-M. (2002). Equilibrium wage dispersion with worker and employer heterogeneity. *Econometrica*, 70(6):pp. 2295–2350.

Pries, M. and Rogerson, R. (2005). Hiring policies, labor market institutions, and labor market flows. *Journal of Political Economy*, 113(4):811–839.

Pries, M. and Rogerson, R. (2009). Search frictions and labor market participation. *European Economic Review*, 53(5):568–587.

Rendahl, P. (2016). Fiscal policy in an unemployment crisis. *The Review of Economic Studies*, 83(3):1189–1224.

Rotemberg, J. J. (2000). Wages and labor demand in an individualistic bargaining model with unemployment. Mimeo Harvard Business School.

Rudanko, L. (2009). Labor market dynamics under long-term wage contracting. *Journal of Monetary Economics*, 56(2):170 – 183.

Sahin, A., Song, J., Topa, G., and Violante, G. L. (2014). Mismatch unemployment. *American Economic Review*, 104(11):3529–64.

Schaal, E. and Taschereau-Dumouchel, M. (2016). Aggregate demand and the dynamics of unemployment. Mimeo, New York University.

Shi, S. (1996). Credit and money in a search model with divisible commodities. *Review of Economic Studies*, 63(4):627–652.

Shi, S. (1998). Search for a monetary propagation mechanism. *Journal of Economic Theory*, 81(2):314–352.

Shi, S. (2015). Liquidity, assets and business cycles. *Journal of Monetary Economics*, 70(0):116–132.

Shi, S. and Wen, Q. (1999). Labor market search and the dynamic effects of taxes and subsidies. *Journal of Monetary Economics*, 43(2):457 – 495.

Shimer, R. (2005). The cyclical behavior of equilibrium unemployment and vacancies. *American Economic Review*, 95(1):25–49.

Shimer, R. (2006). On-the-job search and strategic bargaining. *European Economic Review*, 50(4):811–830.

Silva, J. I. and Toledo, M. (2009). Labor turnover costs and the cyclical behavior of vacancies and unemployment. *Macroeconomic Dynamics*, 13:76–96.

Smets, F. and Wouters, R. (2003). An estimated dynamic stochastic general equilibrium model of the euro area. *Journal of the European Economic Association, Blackwell Publishing Ltd*, 1(5):1123–1175.

Smets, F. and Wouters, R. (2007). Shocks and frictions in us business cycles: A bayesian dsge approach. *The American Economic Review*, 97(3):586–606.

Smith, E. (1999). Search, concave production, and optimal firm size. *Review of Economic Dynamics*, 2(2):456–471.

Solow, R. M. (1979). Another possible source of wage stickiness. *Journal of Macroeconomics*, 1(1):79–82.

Stole, L. A. and Zwiebel, J. (1996a). Intra-firm Bargaining under Non-binding Contracts. *Review of Economic Studies*, 63(3):375–410.

Stole, L. A. and Zwiebel, J. (1996b). Organizational design and technology choice under intrafirm bargaining. *The American Economic Review*, 86(1):195–222.

Taylor, C. R. (1995). The long side of the market and the short end of the stick: Bargaining power and price formation in buyers, sellers, and balanced markets. *Quarterly Journal of Economics*, 110(3):837–855.

Tripier, F. (2011). The efficiency of training and hiring with intrafirm bargaining. *Labour Economics*, 18(4):527–538.

Vuillemey, G. and Wasmer, E. (2016). Frictional unemployment with stochastic bubbles. paper presented at the Annual Search and Matching Conference, Amsterdam.

Wasmer, E. (2006). General versus specific skills in labor markets with search frictions and firing costs. *American Economic Review*, 96(3):811–831.

Wasmer, E. (2009). A steady-state model of a non-walrasian economy with three imperfect markets. Discussion Paper 2011-5758, IZA.

Wasmer, E. and Weil, P. (2000). The macroeconomics of labor and credit market imperfections. IZA Discussion Papers 179, Institute for the Study of Labor (IZA).

Wasmer, E. and Weil, P. (2004). The macroeconomics of labor and credit market imperfections. *American Economic Review*, 94(4):944–963.

Wolinsky, A. (2000). A theory of the firm with non-binding employment contracts. *Econometrica*, 68(4):875–910.

Yashiv, E. (2000). The determinants of equilibrium unemployment. *American Economic Review*, 90(5):1297–1322.

Yashiv, E. (2006). Evaluating the performance of the search and matching model. *European Economic Review*, 50(4):909–936.

Index